THE MENSTRUAL CYCLE

The menstrual cycle is a 'hot topic' in gender politics, from nineteenth-century ideas that studying during menstruation would ruin women's health to twentieth-century notions that women are unfit for responsible careers because of their 'raging hormones'. As a result, the relationship between the menstrual cycle and women's cognitive and emotional state has fascinated scientists for over a century. While biomedical researchers have been preoccupied by the nature and biological causes of 'premenstrual syndrome', feminist scholars and scientists have challenged the conception that cycles of oestrogen and progesterone are necessarily problematic for all women.

In this book, Anne Walker critically examines the theories and studies which have considered the relationship between menstruation, the menstrual cycle and women's psychological state, and sets them in their historical and socio-cultural context. She traces the development of modern scientific preoccupations with 'premenstrual syndrome' and the 'menstrual cycle' (rather than menstruation itself or the menstrual problems for which many women seek help), and asks what part psychology has to play as a discipline in the development of this research. Her conclusion is that menstrual cycle research is entering a new phase of development, with a shift towards biopsychosocial models in medical research and therapy and a growing concern with women's experiences and the meaning of menstruation in the social sciences, reflecting a change in the way that psychology and sociology conceptualise the body.

This contemporary and comprehensive text is an invaluable resource for all serious students of psychology, gender and women's health. It offers hope for a future in which psychology can bring new perspectives and new understandings to women's experience and can reconceptualise the relationship between the menstrual cycle, women's feelings and women's lives.

Anne E. Walker is Lecturer in Health Psychology at the University of Leeds. She is joint editor of the *Journal of Reproductive and Infant Psychology* and has co-edited (with Catherine Niven) a series of three books on *The Psychology of Reproduction: 1: Reproductive Potential and Fertility Control* (1996); *2: Conception, Pregnancy and Birth* (1996) and *3: Current Issues in Infancy and Early Parenthood* (1997).

WOMEN AND PSYCHOLOGY
Series Editor: Jane Ussher, *Department of Psychology*
University College London

This series brings together current theory and research on women and psychology. Drawing on scholarship from a number of different areas of pschology, it bridges the gap between abstract research and the reality of women's lives by integrating theory and practice, research and policy.

Each book addresses a 'cutting edge' issue of research, covering such topics as postnatal depression, eating disorders, theories and methodologies.

The series provides accessible and concise accounts of key issues in the study of women and psychology, and clearly demonstrates the centrality of psychology to debates within women's studies or feminism.

Other titles in this series:

THIN WOMAN
Helen Malson

POSTNATAL DEPRESSION
Paula Nicolson

RETHINKING ABORTION
Mary Boyle

THE MENSTRUAL CYCLE

Anne E. Walker

London and New York

First published 1997
by Routledge
11 New Fetter Lane, London EC4P 4EE

Simultaneously published in the USA and Canada
by Routledge
29 West 35th Street, New York, NY 10001

Typeset in Baskerville by Routledge
Printed and bound in Great Britain by TJ International Ltd,
Padstow, Cornwall

British Library Cataloguing in Publication Data
A catalogue record for this book is available from the British Library

Library of Congress Cataloguing in Publication Data
A catalogue record for this book has been requested

ISBN 0–415–16330–7 (hbk)
ISBN 0–415–16331–5 (pbk)

CONTENTS

ILLUSTRATIONS

FIGURES

TABLES

PREFACE

My research interest in the menstrual cycle began in 1983. At the time, I was a psychology student, and looking for inspiration for my honours thesis. I had settled on the broad area of stress, and it was while browsing the library shelves for books on that subject that I came across Katharina Dalton's book *The Premenstrual Syndrome and Progesterone Therapy* (Dalton, 1977). As with many women before and since, the experiences described in the book made sense to me. I recognised the moodiness, irritability and tension – the apparently irrational anger and depression.[1] Not only did these descriptions seem to fit emotions which I had experienced, but her explanation of them fitted well into my understanding of human experience at that time – an understanding based on a largely scientific education and undergraduate career. The possibility that there might be a link between apparently inexplicable emotions and the biological fluctuations of the menstrual cycle had great appeal, so I went back to my thesis supervisor and planned a project on the menstrual cycle instead of stress. Like many undergraduate projects, mine did not answer the questions I was really interested in, and left me wanting to do more menstrual cycle research. This I did through a PhD concerned with the relationship between ovarian hormones and premenstrual experiences.[2] After three years of collecting thousands of daily diaries and hundreds of urine samples for hormone assay, I found that women's experiences are far more variable than my reading of Dalton's book implied, and not related in a simple way to any of the hormone measures I assessed.[3] My personal journey for a straightforward hormonal explanation for premenstrual experiences had ultimately been a fruitless one.

It was the next phase of my career which sparked the questions this book addresses. I returned to psychology and started going to psychology conferences, becoming aware both of feminist perspectives on PMS and the absence of women's voices in menstrual cycle research. I noticed the general lack of interest of mainstream psychology in anything to do with women's reproductive bodies or menstruation in particular. For instance, there was no mention of menstruation in the mainstream introductory psychology texts I was using at the time. I began to wonder whether I was in the wrong discipline. Was there in fact a distinct psychological perspective on the menstrual cycle?[4] Could there be a psychology⁵ of the menstrual cycle – and should there be? It is these questions which are explored in this book.

I begin my exploration of these questions by putting menstrual cycle research into the context of discourses about menstruation, and giving some historical perspective before considering the methods used by menstrual cycle researchers. In the next section of the book, I describe the findings of menstrual cycle research. Finally, I complete my investigation by considering the dominant feature of twentieth-century menstrual cycle research – premenstrual syndrome. This discussion leads me to the conclusion that there are several psychologies of the menstrual cycle. These have made major contributions to menstrual cycle research, although currently none can be described as autonomous from biomedical approaches. I believe that an autonomous psychology of the menstrual cycle is both possible and necessary, to link the insights of biomedical research and feminist deconstruction into new theoretical accounts of menstruation. Such a discipline is embryonic, and dependent in part on changes in psychology itself, but nonetheless offers hope for a better understanding of women's experiences.

ACKNOWLEDGEMENTS

Most of this book is a literature review, and therefore I am indebted to all the researchers and writers who have contributed to this literature. I appreciate too the voluntary contribution of the many women who have participated in menstrual cycle research, completing daily diaries and questionnaires, participating in experiments or clinical trials and talking to researchers about their experiences. I am particularly grateful to the women who have taken part in my own studies over the years, especially to those who were willing to talk to me, both in clinics and elsewhere, about their premenstrual experiences. Thanks are also due to the people who have supported me during the writing of this book – family, friends and colleagues – and to Jane Ussher, Nicola Horton, Vivien Ward and an anonymous reviewer for their advice and comments. I am grateful to the Haworth Press for permission to reproduce the material included in Table 4.1.

1

MENSTRUATION

Menstruation is the only tangible evidence that most women have of the continuous cycle of fertility going on within the reproductive system. For most of human history, menstruation has been the only evidence anyone has had of women's reproductive potential. As a result, scientists, physicians and writers have focused on menstruation as the source of femininity – the essential difference between men and women. In this century, scientists have developed a variety of means to investigate the various endocrine events of the menstrual cycle. Levels of hormones can be measured in blood, urine or saliva. The ovaries, uterus and fallopian tubes can be examined by ultrasonography or laparoscopy. As a result of these intensive investigations, we now see menstruation as only one event within a 'cycle' – the menstrual cycle. Scientific accounts no longer describe menstruation as the most significant event within the cycle. Instead ovulation is the lynchpin – the 'purpose' of the rhythm. The shift in scientific attention from menstruation to the menstrual cycle began in the nineteenth century with the discovery of ovulation, but had its greatest boost in the early twentieth century with the discovery of the 'ovarian hormones'[1] – oestrogen and progesterone. At this time, too, the menstrual cycle rather than menstruation itself came to be seen as the most significant determinant of female emotional and intellectual experience. So, in the late twentieth century, it is possible to consider the psychology of the menstrual cycle – a subject which would have made little sense a hundred years ago. This book is about twentieth-century attempts to understand the relationship between the menstrual cycle and women's minds. The assumption that there is such a relationship, however, comes from the earlier assumptions of the links between menstruation and the nature of womankind. These ideas are too recent and have too long a history to have disappeared from our cultural imagination. Ideas about menstruation and the moon, or the metaphor of menstruation as 'seed' or 'heat', for example, still influence at some level both the questions which scientists ask about the menstrual cycle and the meaning which the menstrual cycle has for many women. A study of the psychology of the menstrual cycle, while possible in the twentieth century, is still incomplete without some consideration of what menstruation means. The purpose of this chapter, then, is to consider what

1

menstruation means, both in women's writing about it and in scientific and mythological accounts. What is menstruation and what sort of stories are told about it?[2]

WHAT IS MENSTRUATION?

Experiencing menstruation

Approximately half the world's human population experience menstruation. The mythical average Western woman who has regular periods between the ages of 13 and 50, interrupted by two pregnancies, will menstruate more than four hundred times. Between one-seventh and one-fifth of a woman's adult life could be spent menstruating (Greer, 1971). Menstruation is not a rare or even unusual experience. However, in our culture and many others it is a private and largely hidden one. As a result we know little about women's experiences of menstruation, what it feels like to menstruate or to be a menstruating woman, either now or in previous times. In the nineteenth century, for example, menstruation was rarely mentioned in women's diaries or correspondence, which are the main documentary source about women's lives (Jalland and Hooper, 1986; Blodgett, 1988). It seems that there is either nothing to say about menstruation – or an absence of words in which to say it.[3] The absence of menstruation from women's diaries, etc., can be seen as one aspect of female repression through language. Menstruation was literally unmentionable because there were no words in the man-made language which could be used to describe the experience politely. As Blodgett (1988) notes, any references which were made may have been removed by fastidious editors before publication, suggesting that even if words exist they are not suitable for public expression. This silence remains a feature of modern life. Sophie Laws (1990) identified a 'menstrual etiquette' in her research on men's views of menstruation, forbidding mention of menstruation in male company. Similarly, Kathryn Lovering (1995) has found that adolescents have nothing to say about menstruation itself. The only discourses which they can use to describe their experiences are medical ones, which describe pain, distress and mess. Unless these girls have period pain, or difficulties obtaining sanitary towels, they have nothing to say. Emily Martin (1989) too, in her interviews with women, found that medical descriptions of menstruation dominated in women's accounts with virtually no references being made to the phenomenology of menstruation. There are simply no words to describe how menstruation feels unless it is painful, traumatic or messy. This is all that we can say about menstruation – and not surprisingly, accounts of it in literature are dominated by this discourse. For example, the heroine of Erica Jong's novel *Fear of Flying* mentions her period because she has no tampons. The terms she uses emphasise blood 'gushing' and being taken by surprise. This kind of menstrual experience can be described, but it is relatively rare. The majority of periods pass unremarked and even unnoticed, without pain, gushing blood or fear of public embarrassment. It seems that there are no discourses or even words available which can be used to describe these ordinary and unexceptional experiences.

When menstruation is mentioned, it is rarely spoken of directly but more often euphemistically. Victorian women used phrases such as 'turns', 'monthlies', 'poorliness', 'the curse' or 'being unwell' (Perkin, 1993). Some diarists used an idiosyncratic code to record menstruation or wrote parts of the diary in a foreign language (see Blodgett, 1988; Rosenblatt, 1983). Women in the twentieth century also use a wide variety of euphemisms (see Joffe, 1948; Ernster, 1975). Sharon Golub (1992) lists 53 common North American expressions. Like the earlier names for menstruation, many of these refer to pain or discomfort (e.g. 'unwell', 'the curse', 'wrong time of the month') or emphasise the regularity of menstruation, sometimes describing it as a visitor (e.g. 'period', 'monthlies', 'that time of the month', 'Aunt Tilly is here', 'I've got my friend'). A second category refers to menstruation as a sign of sexual non-availability (e.g. 'the red flag is up'), non-pregnancy (e.g. 'safe again', 'celebrating') or a symbol of femininity (e.g. 'woman's friend', 'Mother Nature's gift'). Others refer to the colour of menstruation (e.g. 'the reds') or menstrual accoutrements (e.g. 'riding the cotton pony', 'on the rag', 'white cylinder week'). Studies of men suggest that they also refer to menstruation euphemistically, although the range of terms found in male discourse is narrower, referring usually to menstrual paraphernalia (e.g. 'jammy rags') or presumed sexual non-availability (Ernster, 1975; Laws, 1990). Sophie Laws notes that these phrases can also be used differently by men, as terms of abuse towards other men, as well as menstrual euphemisms (Laws, 1990).

The silence about menstrual experiences in literature has, until recently, been broken only by accounts of a woman's first period. These accounts often recollect feelings of horror and confusion, or fear about apparently inexplicable bleeding. Hence, they fit the dominant patriarchal discourse of menstruation as unexpected, painful, gushing blood. This is what we are allowed to say about menstruation. So, for example, Simone de Beauvoir describes her first period like this:

> We were staying with friends during the stifling heat of mid-July; I awoke horror-stricken one morning: I had spoiled my nightdress. I washed it, and got dressed: again I soiled my underclothes. I had forgotten Madeleine's vague prophecies, and I wondered what shameful malady I was suffering from.

> (de Beauvoir, 1963:101)

Fear was also the chief recollection of Kathleen Dayus writing of her impoverished working-class life in Birmingham before the First World War. 'When I saw my first period I was scared to death. I ran all the way home from school thinking I was going to bleed to death' (Dayus, 1985:95). In Germaine Greer's account it is the need for secrecy and the suspense of waiting for the first period to come which make it memorable, rather than the blood itself. She writes: 'For six months while I was waiting for my first menstruation I toted a paper bag with diapers and pins in my school satchel. When it finally came, I suffered agonies lest anyone should guess or smell it or anything' (Greer, 1971: 50). Interview studies suggest that first menstruation (menarche) is not memorable for all women. It is more likely to be memorable if it happens at school, or causes embarrassment, otherwise it may be unremarkable (Lovering, 1991, 1995; Kissling, 1996). They also suggest that menarche can be framed within a discourse of 'growing up' – as a step on the way to adulthood. So, for example, Gina, one of the participants in Emily Martin's study, says: 'The first time I had my period I was so happy that I remember singing in the bathroom, "You are a big girl now"' (Martin, 1989: 102).

The experience of menstruation after the first occasion is written and spoken about much less. Ordinary, repeated menstruation is much less likely to be unexpected or messy, and, after adolescence, less likely to be painful. There is nothing left to say. As the women interviewed by Nancy Friday said, 'What's there to discuss? It's like fingernails, hair – they grow. It's just a fact of life. What's there to feel?' (Friday, 1979:149). One of the rare accounts is found in Anne Frank's diary. For her, menstruation is a bittersweet event.

> Each time I have a period . . . I have the feeling that in spite of all the pain, unpleasantness and nastiness, I have a sweet secret . . . that is why, although it is nothing but a nuisance to me in a way, I shall always long for the time that I shall feel that secret within me again.
>
> (Frank, 1953:115)

Anne Frank's words suggest the possibility of alternative discourses which could be used to describe menstruation. Hints of other ways of talking about it also emerged in the 1970s, as the feminist revival brought an increased 'menstrual consciousness' among many women, and a forum in which experiences could be described, at least for those women active in consciousness-raising and broadly feminist activities. The descriptions of the menstrual experience given by women writing and researching in this tradition suggest that there is something to feel, and something to talk about, at least for some women. The feelings that they describe range from physical experiences of pain and discomfort to more abstract feelings of purification and sisterhood. For example, one of the women in Paula Weideger's study in the 1970s describes menstruation as 'a pain in the vagina', while others say: 'It makes me very much aware of the fact that I am a woman . . . It's also a link to other women. I actually enjoy having my period. I feel like I've been cleaned out inside.' Another says,

> the menstrual cycle has become such a part of my life by now, I don't want to change it. It is a part of being a woman, which I am proud to be. I really like it. It's difficult to explain, but it's the same way I like the changing of the seasons. I guess the monthly cycles are 'earthy' and symbolic to me.
>
> (Weideger, 1976: 4–5)

4

Imogen Sutton also writes of the feeling of identification with other women which menstruation gives her:

I was newly inaugurated into the business of blood each month; blood every month – did it really happen to all women? I would stare out of the window of the bus and gaze at the women around me. 'So she is probably bleeding now . . . and her, and her.' It made me identify with other women in a way I had never done before.

(Sutton, 1989: 1)

In the same vein, Lara Owen writes of the power of menstruation – its reminder to her that we are a part of nature and its ability to connect women across the centuries:

Periods . . . are a wild and basic, raw and instinctual, bloody and eternal aspect of the female – and no amount of 'civilization' will change that. My period is a monthly occurrence in my life that I have in common with all women who have ever lived. Women living in caves twenty thousand years ago, priestesses in palaces in ancient Egypt, seers in temples in Sumeria, all bled with the moon. The first woman who made fire might well have had her period at the time . . . If menstruation is a highly creative time for women psychically and spiritually, who knows what gifts humankind has been brought by women during their menses.

(Owen, 1993: 66)

These descriptions refer to menstruation in an abstract and even poetic way – emphasising its symbolism and 'power'. In this way they are similar to the religious and mythological accounts of menstruation (see below). We discover little of the pragmatic emotional and practical reality of menstruation from them. Is the menstrual experience always the same? Dena Taylor's book *Red Flower: Rethinking Menstruation* (1988) is full of women's own accounts of menstruation, positive and negative, in prose and poetry, including extracts from a menstrual diary kept by Miriam Sagan. These suggest that the feelings aroused by menstruation may vary from one month to the next, and also remind us of the often ambivalent link between menstruation and pregnancy:

April 8: Began to bleed standing in the Museum of Science . . . Felt a surge of interest in the exhibit on reproduction, the cross section of ovaries. 'That's me!' I wanted to say. Then, felt sudden exhaustion on the subway coming home. Bleeding, bleeding. Exhaustion under my eyes, cramps. Yet energy flowing beneath the fatigue. Felt exhilarated, ultra-sensitive.

May 8: Menstruating: two days late, was already having pregnancy fantasies. Imagined sitting in the waiting room of an abortion clinic. Almost more of a wish than a fear. Every period the loss of a potential child; loss, sadness, even though there is no room in my life for a child now.

August 1: Feel very low. Depressed, suicidal. Menstruating. Physically shakey, spacey. No energy. No mail. No phone call.

(Sagan, cited in Taylor, 1988: 65–66)

Erica Jong's description of her heroine's desperate search for tampons is a reminder of the practical aspect of menstruation, and the emphasis on secrecy and absence of 'mess' in our Western culture. This aspect of the menstrual experience is less often described in literature but is inferred in the adverts and information provided by the menstrual products industry (Berg and Block Coutts, 1994; Treneman, 1988). Women experiencing menorrhagia (very heavy menstruation) often describe a feeling of loss of control and concern about leakage and mess, which can severely restrict their activities and self-confidence (Marshall and Bundred, 1994; Hodges, 1996). These concerns and fears fit well into the dominant menstrual discourse – they can be talked about, even to a clinician. Similarly, anxiety about the unpredictability of menstruation can be expressed. As Owen puts it: 'Menstruation is predictably unpredictable. You never know exactly when it's going to come, and sometimes it completely surprises you' (Owen 1993: 66). Menstruation which fits the messy, bloody, painful, potentially embarrassing description is perceived as problematic and a medical solution can be sought.[4] So, for example, some women welcome the oral contraceptive pill because it controls this unpredictability. Nancy Friday says: 'What I myself liked about the pill was that you always knew when you would menstruate, the flow was less and so were the cramps' (Friday 1979: 152). Others seek more direct help from a physician, although for most this is a disillusioning experience (Scambler and Scambler, 1993; see chapter six). Not surprisingly, a high proportion of women who experience menstrual pain, heavy menstrual loss or unpredictability also express antipathy towards menstruation. As one said, 'I don't bloody like them. I think it's because I have so much trouble with them – all the backaches and the stomach aches and the heavy bleeding. I've had so many problems with it ever since I started' (Scambler and Scambler, 1993: 32).

These anecdotal descriptions in women's writing and interviews with women suggest that menstruation can be anything from a messy and painful discharge to a mystical or near-religious experience. The sensation of menstruation (its look, feel and smell) and its emotional interpretation vary from woman to woman and period to period. The dominant menstrual discourse is one of pain, mess and unpredictability and it is this which is most often remarked upon and talked about. It may not be this which is the most common experience, however. We have very little phenomenological information about 'unremarkable' periods. Perhaps statistical information from general population studies will cast some light on this.

Menstrual statistics

The development of natural history and science in the eighteenth century and the 'science of woman' (Moscucci, 1993) in the nineteenth century led to an interest in cataloguing and describing menstruation and its associated customs and practices. The early studies of this kind were anthropological in nature, the best known being *Das Weib*.[5] This weighty work attempted to describe all aspects of women's life in 'primitive' (sic) cultures, in a nineteenth-century anthropological tradition. In modern times, these works can be criticised for racism and *Das Weib* in particular for its objectification of woman as a separate species from man (Weideger, 1985; Moscucci, 1993). However, much of our knowledge of the practices and customs associated with menstruation in non-Western cultures is derived from these works – and often quoted uncritically by modern researchers.[6] These studies were principally concerned with customs and practices rather than with the apparently more mundane questions: How often do women menstruate? Is the frequency of menstruation constant over a lifetime? How many days do women menstruate for? Is the amount of menstrual fluid lost equal, or of the same 'quality', on all menstruating days? and so on. Comments were made, however, on the ages at which menstruation began and ended. This aspect of menstruation has long fascinated recorders of human experience, so that age at menarche in particular can be traced back over many centuries (see Shorter, 1983).

In Western cultures, girls usually experience their first menstruation between the ages of 10 and 16, with 13 being the average age (Asso, 1983; Coleman and Hendry, 1990). Throughout this century, the age at which menarche occurs in Western industrialised countries has been gradually reducing – at the rate of approximately one month per decade. The reason for this so-called 'secular trend' is unknown, but it is usually attributed to improvements in general health or diet (Coleman and Hendry, 1990). Menarche is one of the later events of puberty for girls, and although it came as a shock to many young women of previous generations, it is now more likely to be an anticipated event.[7] Many textbook descriptions imply that once the first period has occurred, menstruation occurs regularly every 28 days (the menstrual cycle), unless interrupted by pregnancy, until the menopause at around age 50.[8] A number of extensive longitudinal studies in which women record the dates of menstruation as it happens have shown this to be relatively rare, however (Treloar *et al.*, 1967; Vollman, 1977; Voda *et al.*, 1991). The time between periods can vary between 10 and 60 days (Vollman, 1977). Menstrual cycles vary in length both among women and from one cycle to the next, with only around one in eight cycles being exactly 28 days in length. Vollman (1977) found that cycle length also changes with age, with an average length of 35 days in the early teenage years reducing to a minimum of 27 days in the early forties and then increasing to 52 days in the mid-fifties. In the first year after menarche, over 40 per cent of girls in Finland report irregular cycles, compared to only 9 per cent of their mothers

(Widholm and Kantero, 1971). So, menstruation is not as predictable as folklore and medical texts would have us believe. Neither is menstruation always preceded by the release of an egg from the ovary (ovulation). Glen Metcalf and her colleagues collected weekly urine samples for three months from 209 women in New Zealand, and found that in the first year after menarche only 23 per cent of the women's periods were preceded by ovulation, rising to 83 per cent among women who had been menstruating for nine years or more (Metcalf *et al.*, 1983; Metcalf, 1983). Menstrual cycles are a variable experience.

Menstruation is not the only type of blood loss from the vagina. Many women will experience bleeding after childbirth, or when they have an infection or other disorder of the womb or vagina. Some women experience 'break-through bleeding' while taking the pill, or slight bleeding at ovulation. Menstruation itself is also a variable experience and can be difficult to define. The most detailed study of normal menstrual bleeding was commissioned by the World Health Organisation in the late 1970s (WHO, 1981; Snowden and Christian, 1983). The survey involved 5,322 women in ten countries around the world (Egypt, India, Indonesia, Jamaica, Korea, Mexico, Pakistan, Philippines, United Kingdom and Yugoslavia), with around fifty women in each country keeping a daily diary of menstrual bleeding. Across all of these countries, a menstrual bleed of 4 or 5 days was most commonly reported, and the majority of women described their menstrual loss as 'moderate'. However, there were large variations among women. For instance, more of the women in Egypt, India and Mexico reported short periods (1 to 3 days) than women in other countries, while British, Indonesian and Pakistani women were more likely to report periods of 6 or more days than women in other countries. It is difficult to know whether these findings reflect a real difference in the number of menstruating days or a difference in the definition of menstruation in the different countries. Snowden and Christian (1983) also report different 'shapes' of menstrual bleeding. Some women reported heavy menstrual loss on the first days of their period, becoming lighter towards the end (about 45 per cent), while other women reported a few days of light loss (spotting or staining), followed by two or three days of heavy menstruation and a gradual tail-off (around 30 per cent). Still other women reported an equal menstrual loss on each day of their period. The duration, volume and shape of menstruation was found to vary with the type of contraception used. IUD (intra-uterine device) users were more likely to experience a gradual onset of menstruation and more loss overall, while pill users were more likely to report an equal menstrual loss on each day of the period, and a lighter bleed overall than other women. There may be some ambiguity about the start and end of menstruation – especially for those women who experience the gradual onset pattern. Hence, the possibility arises that differences in the way menstruation is defined may influence the reporting of menstrual onset, even in diary studies, and result in apparent differences in menstrual length between different countries (McNeill, 1992).[9] There is some evidence that menstruation lasts longer in the winter and spring than in the summer (Datta, 1960), so it is also possible that climatic changes contribute to this finding.

Therefore, not only is the menstrual cycle variable among women, but so also is menstruation itself. While having periods may connect us with other women, as Imogen Sutton (above) suggests, and there may be similarities between our own menstrual experiences and those of other women, there are also differences. Each woman has her own idiosyncratic menstrual pattern, falling somewhere within normal ranges of cycle length, volume of fluid lost and days of menstruation. Erin McNeill (1992) notes that women are often implicitly criticised in menstrual research for reporting 'regular' cycles and 'moderate' periods, when in fact these are both variable experiences. Following Treloar (1967), she suggests that terms like 'regular', 'twenty-eight days' and 'moderate' are used by women as a shorthand to mean 'normal for me'. There may be other reasons for this too. Perhaps menstruation is too commonplace an experience to merit special attention (as Nancy Friday suggests, above), so that most women don't routinely chart its occurrence, noticing it only when it changes in some way. Alternatively, perhaps the silence surrounding menstruation is so great that we avoid consciously acknowledging it even to ourselves and are not aware of our own variability. Terms like 'regular' may be used (or more likely ticked on a questionnaire) to mean that we have no reason to think that we are different from anyone else and are not concerned about our periods, or because none of the other ways of describing them fit the experience either.

Some menstrual experiences do fall outside the normal range, and increasingly these are defined as disorders requiring medical attention (Scambler and Scambler, 1993). The most common of these are menorrhagia (excessive menstrual blood loss) and amenorrhea (absence of periods). Apart from these, many women experience pain associated with menstruation. Dysmenorrhea, or severe period pain, results from strong contractions of the uterine wall and is associated with high levels of prostaglandin in the endometrium. Women who experience severe period pain may have up to seventeen times more of the prostaglandin PG2a in the uterus than women who don't (Chan *et al.*, 1979). This type of smooth muscle contraction can be exacerbated by psychosocial factors, such as stress (Nicassio, 1980), so dysmenorrhea can vary from month to month for psychosocial or physiological reasons. This makes it difficult to assess the number of women experiencing severe pain. We do know, though, that dysmenorrhea is most frequent during adolescence. For example, Widholm and Kantero (1971) studied the menstrual experiences of 5,485 adolescent women (aged 10–20 years) and their mothers in Finland. They found that 8 per cent of the mothers reported severe menstrual pain with every period compared to 26 per cent of the regularly menstruating adolescents. Just as menstruation is not the only form of blood loss from the vagina, dysmenorrhea is not the only form of pain associated with periods. A substantial number of women report breast pain either before or during menstruation, and descriptions of backache and headaches or migraine are not uncommon.

Epidemiological studies of menstruation suggest that menstruation is a variable experience across the whole population, but possibly less variable for individual women. We may all have our own usual pattern of menstrual cycle length, days and 'shape' of bleeding – a pattern which changes with age, and possibly with other factors such as having children or changing diet or exercise or being ill. Very few of these experiences fit the textbook 28-day cycle, and it seems too that the majority do not fit the painful and bloody unpredictability of the dominant menstrual discourse. Periods which do fit this picture are likely to prompt a woman to seek medical help. The majority of periods, though, are ordinary, unremarkable and undramatic. It is not this unspoken routine which has made menstruation, and later the menstrual cycle, interesting throughout the centuries, but an extreme and perhaps imaginary experience.

STORIES ABOUT MENSTRUATION

Women have been menstruating, as far as we know, for as long as there have been women. We are not the only menstruating species: several types of primate also have menstrual cycles (see Profet, 1993; Strassman, 1996), although most other mammals experience oestrus cycles, which, we now know, differ physiologically from menstrual cycles. The first appearance of a bloody discharge in young girls and its repetition at intervals thereafter has, not surprisingly, intrigued most civilisations and cultures. Why do women menstruate? What purpose does it have? What significance does this blood have? Explanations for menstruation can be found not only in medical and scientific writing but also in anthropological accounts, folklore and mythology. There are many of these accounts and for the purpose of this chapter, I have grouped them into broad categories. Some of these ideas are more common in some cultures than others, and some have been more popular than others at particular points in history. Echoes of all of them can be found in the descriptions given by women of their own menstruation, quoted earlier in this chapter, and some of them have profound implications for gender politics, as will be shown in the next chapter. Running through all of these accounts is the assumption that menstruation is somehow related to reproduction or fertility, although how this relationship is manifest is not a concern for most of the explanations. Much more important is the regular appearance of blood in the absence of injury. The descriptions given are relatively brief because of the focus of this book.[10]

Menstruation as blood loss

The most consistent metaphor in accounts of menstruation is that of blood loss. Most women would recognise that menstrual fluid is not the same as circulating blood. It has a different consistency, appearance and smell, for instance. It also behaves differently, not clotting in the same way as circulating blood does, and not flowing in the way blood from a cut finger flows either. Menstrual fluid does

10

contain some blood, but it also contains the broken-down uterine lining, mucus from the vagina and other fluids. It is not blood, but the perception of it as blood has given it a powerful symbolic significance, both in mythology and in medicine.

In some psychoanalytic theories, it is the bloody nature of menstruation which makes it taboo. The unconscious association between blood and death makes menstruation a powerful symbol and source of fear (Chadwick, 1933; Daly, 1935; Bettelheim, 1955; see Lupton, 1993, for a review). Anthropological accounts, too, focus on the perception of menstruation as blood in their interpretations of the cultural practices surrounding it, as shown in the titles of books such as *Blood Magic* (Buckley and Gottlieb, 1988) or *Blood Relations* (Knight, 1991). For many writers, it is the bloodiness of menstruation which links it with 'nature' rather than 'culture'. Nature is seen to be uncivilised, governed by biological impulses and 'red in tooth and claw'. Humans can overcome this through intellectualisation. However, it is harder for women to separate themselves from their biological selves in the same way that men can because of their repeated blood loss. This idea is found both in nineteenth-century accounts of women's character (see Bland, 1995) and in some contemporary feminist accounts (e.g. Owen, 1993), with differing perceived implications. In medicine the significance of menstrual blood loss is attributed to the risk of anaemia. So, for example, menorrhagia is defined in terms of the amount of blood lost because this may leave a woman at risk of anaemia, not in terms of the total amount of fluid lost during a period, or the number of days on which menstruation occurs (Hallberg *et al.*, 1966). Hence, a period which a woman perceives to be 'heavy' may not be defined by her doctor as menorrhagic because the amount of blood within it is not enough to put her at risk of anaemia (Hallberg *et al.*, 1966; Fraser *et al.*, 1984; Warner 1994; Hodges 1996). However, the language used by women seeking help for menorrhagia suggests that they are concerned about the degree of inconvenience and 'menstrual handicap' caused by having to manage the amount of fluid lost, rather than about the risk of anaemia (Hodges, 1996). So, while the blood in menstruation may be of key significance in mythology, psychoanalysis and medicine, for a menstruating woman the quantity of fluid may be just as important.

Blood is a powerful and meaningful symbol for humans. Bleeding is often a frightening experience, with a proportion of people being actively blood phobic (Costello, 1982; Öst *et al.*, 1989). The absence of reports of an equivalent 'menstruation phobia' in the literature, despite many accounts of blood phobia among women, adds to the suggestion that menstruation is not always perceived as blood.[11] Until recently, most of the writers about menstruation have been men, so perhaps it is not surprising that the focus has been on blood – the only part of menstrual fluid which men will have experienced. A focus on blood may increase the power and fearfulness of menstruation in some men's eyes, as it did for Sigmund Freud. For others, though, a perceived equivalence between menstrual fluid and blood may reduce the mystery of menstruation and make it

11

less frightening. One of the men in Sophie Laws' study of menstrual etiquette describes this. He says:

> Well when I was younger and they said that there was a lining on the womb, and that all this lining and a lot of blood came out as well, and I used to imagine all sorts of horrible things coming out. . . . Until I was going out with this present girlfriend I still imagined what I'd thought when I had the biology lessons, but since I've been going out with my present girlfriend, I've just thought of it as just blood, just the same, because we've had sex when she's been on a period, and there has been, you know , some blood . . . and it's just the same, it's not different, so now, it doesn't bother me at all. I must admit at first I was a bit worried, in case there was . . . God knows what coming out.
>
> (Laws, 1990:113)

In either case, arguably the association of menstruation with blood makes it a controllable experience. Either it is so powerful and mysterious that it is taboo and must be controlled by silence and limitations on activity, or it is so ordinary and nonsignificant that it is not worth mentioning and ignored.

Menstruation, rhythm and time

The idea that menstruation is a regular and time-related event is almost as prevalent as its association with blood in both scientific and non-scientific accounts. As noted earlier, longitudinal studies suggest that the number of days between periods varies both between women and between cycles, with only about one in eight cycles being of twenty-eight days. Menstruation is a repeated experience, but in reality not always the clockwork-like phenomenon that it is often suggested to be. Several writers have argued that repeated menstrual cycles are a more significant feature of modern life than they would have been for women without access to (or freedom to use) contraception. For example, Short (1984) has described the menstrual pattern of modern !Kung women, whose experience may be similar to that of Palaeolithic women.[12] They typically experience a later menarche and earlier menopause than industrialised women, coupled with prolonged breast-feeding between pregnancies. These factors make menstruation a relatively rare event, and suggest that for most women it would not have been regular enough to be a reliable measure of time. Knight (1991) argues that women living in largely female groups would experience menstrual synchrony;[13] hence menstruation would be a collective rather than an individual experience. If all of the women in a group menstruated at the same time, even if some were pregnant or breast-feeding, the menstrual rhythm among the others would continue. As a woman stopped lactating, her menstrual cycles would return in the same rhythm as those of the women around her. As long as all the women were not pregnant or feeding babies, the underlying cycle would continue and could be an accurate marker of time. As with the perception of menstruation as blood, the view of menstruation as a time-related event of strict periodicity has a basis in reality, but is an exaggeration of (modern) women's experience. It may, too, serve the political purpose of making menstruation controllable. Either it is so magical and mysterious, amazingly happening every month, that it is taboo, or it is predictable and can be controlled, by men or by women.

The phrases used to describe menstruation often refer to its temporality: for example, 'period' and 'the monthlies' in English and *das Regule* in German. The name *menses* is from the Latin for month. In Gaelic, the words for menstruation and calendar are the same (*miosach* and *miosachan*). Some anthropologists and historians have suggested that menstrual cycles were used as a way of measuring time in early history. Marshack (1972) describes bone slates or 'batons' dating from Palaeolithic times (around 35,000 BC). These are small and light enough to be carried around, and are marked by notches which may have indicated the passing of days. Female figurines have also been found with similar notches, which Boulding (1976) suggests were used to count the days of the menstrual cycle. Further evidence comes from a large Palaeolithic female figure, found at Laussel in the Dordogne area of France and dating from around 20–25,000 years BC. In one hand she holds a horn (or broken crescent) on which are thirteen incisions, while her other hand is placed on her abdomen. A number of writers have suggested that this represents the thirteen menstrual cycles which could occur in a year and links them with fertility (Fisher, 1979; Stonehouse, 1994).

The idea of menstruation as a time-related event is also found in assertions of a link between women's cycles and the changing phases of the moon. The association of the moon with femininity and menstruation is a long one, and has been well documented (e.g. Harding, 1989; Shuttle and Redgrove, [1978] 1986). Briffault ([1927] 1952) recounts numerous instances of the same word being used to describe both menstruation and the moon. For example, he says that French peasants describe menstruation as *le moment de la lune*; in the (then) Congo, menstruation is called *ngonde*, which means moon, and so on. Stories which link the moon with menstruation fall into two categories, those which associate some aspect of the moon (or moon god/goddess) with the origins of menstruation, and those which link the menstrual cycle with the phases of the moon. For example, Ploss *et al.* (1935) describe a Sinaugolo myth from the Rigo area of New Guinea: 'The moon lived on earth as a tiny youth covered with silvery hair, cohabited with a woman, was slain by her husband and has punished women ever since' (Ploss *et al.* 1935: 651). The association of the moon with menstruation is also found in accounts of numerous myths and rituals (see Shuttle and Redgrove, 1986; Harding, 1989; Knight, 1991).

As well as being seen as the originator of menstruation, the phases of the moon are often linked to the timing of menstruation (see Harding, 1989; B. Walker, 1983; Shuttle and Redgrove, 1986). The stereotypical menstrual cycle is remarkably similar in length to the lunar cycle of 29.5 days. Evidence that fertility in non-human primates and other species is influenced by day length (or

13

night length) also suggests that associations between moonlight and ovulation may have as much to do with biology as mythology (Gwinner, 1981). Although our current systems of marking time are not based around the moon, there is evidence for the earlier use of a lunar calendar in many rituals, nursery rhymes and fairy tales. Barbara Walker (1983) argues that a lunar-based calendar was used before the Julian calendar was introduced by the Christian Church. In the lunar calendar there would be 13 lunar months of 28 days – giving a year of 364 days. Hence the phrase 'a year and a day' in many nursery tales to refer to the 'new' Christian year of 365 days. She then argues that lunar calendars are typical of matriarchal and goddess-worshipping cultures, in which the moon and menstruation are often linked. Hence, the lunar calendar may originally have been a menstrual calendar, or may have been a menstrual calendar in practice. Such links are difficult to establish in modern times. Although repeated individual experiences of menstruation are more a feature of modern life than they may have been in ancient cultures, the influence of artificial light has obscured possible effects of natural light. Nonetheless, the link between the moon and menstruation is still made, with modern research continuing to investigate the effect of day length and moon phase on the occurrence of menstruation and ovulation (Cutler *et al.*, 1987; Jacobsen *et al.*, 1988; Graham *et al.*, 1992).

The notion of menstruation as a regular and predictable event was reinforced by the discovery of ovulation and fluctuating levels of ovarian hormones in the late nineteenth and early twentieth centuries (see below). Modern scientific textbooks emphasise the cyclicity of menstruation, considering it to be only one part of a larger rhythm which is focused on conception (Martin, 1989). Hormonally, menstrual cycles are remarkably variable – ovulation does not always occur, and circulating levels of oestrogen and progesterone can differ greatly from one cycle to the next. This can make the identification of hormonal dysfunctions very difficult. However, this is not the story of menstrual cycles which is found in the textbooks, and it is not the story which most psychologists and clinicians have access to in their design and interpretation of studies concerned with menstrual cycles and well-being. Hence, the metaphor of a menstrual rhythm has had a powerful influence on descriptions of women's psychology, as will be seen in chapter two.

The power of this story lies in the implication that menstruation, and menstrual processes can be contained and controlled. This is a possibility which figures significantly in modern self-help guides for PMS, for example, which advise women to limit the impact on their lives of negative premenstrual mood changes by being conscious of where they are in their cycles and by planning crucial events (e.g. taking a child to the dentist) around them (e.g. Dalton, 1969). From a different perspective, writers such as Shuttle and Redgrove (1986) and Owen (1993) advocate an increased menstrual consciousness, allowing women to be 'in tune' with their cyclicity. While these writers are concerned with controlling feelings which may be associated with menstruation, other researchers are concerned with controlling menstruation itself through an understanding of its cyclicity. So, research into the mechanisms which cause menstrual synchrony, for instance, can be justified not only on the grounds of 'purely' academic interest but also because an understanding of the mechanisms may result in better forms of contraception or infertility treatment. Hence the research is concerned not only with the way menstrual cycles work, but also with how the process can be controlled. An awareness by women of their own ability to control menstrual rhythms, sexuality and fertility is seen by Chris Knight (1991) as one of the cornerstones of the development of civilisation 40,000 years ago.

Menstruation and fertility

All of the stories about menstruation link it in some way with reproduction or fertility. Interpretations of European Palaeolithic cave paintings and figures suggest that women were thought to be parthenogenetic,[14] and that an association was made between menstruation and fertility (Stonehouse, 1994). As ideas about how humans reproduce have evolved, however, the role of menstruation within them has changed, from the concept of menstruation as 'seed', a vital component of a foetus, to the analogy of menstruation with 'heat' or oestrus, a time of fertility, to modern ideas of menstruation as a waste product having no active role in the reproductive process.

Menstruation as seed

The idea of menstruation as female 'seed' suggests that it has a direct role in the creation of human life and is not just a symbol of fertility. Barbara Walker (1983) writes that, in Hindu legend, the menstrual blood of the Great Mother formed a clot or crust from which she gave birth to the cosmos, while the great goddess Ninhursag in South American Indian mythology made humankind out of clay mixed with her menstrual blood. The concept of menstrual fluid coagulating to form a baby has a long history, and dominated medical thinking until the eighteenth century.

The earliest written ideas of menstruation as seed occur in the Hippocratic texts. According to these writers, human reproduction is based on pangenesis, and requires two seeds (Laqueur, 1990; Cadden, 1993). In this theory, both parents are thought to contribute 'seed', which is drawn from all parts of the body and stored in the testes/ovaries (pangenesis).[15] This seed takes the form of semen in the male parent and menstrual fluid in the woman. These combine to form the baby. Hence, menstrual fluid is the crucial female contribution to a baby, rather than a source of nourishment for a developing foetus.

The most influential exponents of the idea of menstruation as seed were Aristotle (384–322 BC) and his followers. His works, and the works attributed to him, were the major influence on thinking about reproduction until at least the Renaissance. Even up to the 1930s, the most widely used lay guide to midwifery and 'sex education' was entitled 'Aristotle's Masterpiece' (see Blackman, 1977).

This work is not directly attributable to Aristotle but owes much to Aristotelian ideas. It appears in many printed versions published and distributed privately, and probably handed down from mother to daughter – a slightly 'disreputable' book, but one of the few available sources of information about sexuality, conception and childbirth. The ideas about menstruation contained within it probably influenced both physicians and women themselves.

Aristotle also thought of menstruation as female seed, or the vehicle for female seed, but inferred different functions for the male and female seed in reproduction. In Hippocratic descriptions semen and menstruation each contain both male and female forms of the parental characteristics. This led Aristotle to ask why women can't make babies by themselves. He solved the difficulty by suggesting that male and female seed are different. The male seed, in its semen vehicle, provides the essence or soul of the child, its fundamental humanity. The female provides the matter, or material from which the child is formed, in her menstrual fluid. Women are not capable, by this account, of making semen because females are cooler than males and can only change excess food into blood. Men, with their extra heat, can convert blood into semen. However, menstrual fluid is still seen as an essential component in reproduction, providing the 'clay' from which the child is formed (Laqueur, 1990; Cadden, 1993).

These ideas have little resonance today – they may even seem ridiculous to modern science. However, elements of them can still be found in some modern studies of menstrual knowledge and attitudes (see chapter four), and the idea that menstruation is the starting point for a baby still has some currency. Such thinking remains important because it illustrates the relationship between ideas about the purpose of menstruation and gender politics. In the Hippocratic description, men and women are equal partners in reproduction. In Aristotelian thinking, it is the man who provides the important part, the 'soul', the woman's role being little more than that of an incubator. Feminist critics have observed this type of thinking – woman as 'womb-container' – in much of the discourse surrounding the new reproductive technologies (Corea, 1985; Spallone, 1994; Rowland, 1992). Similarly, the words used to describe the male reproductive system in physiological texts are often more positive than those used to describe the female system (Martin, 1989). These examples suggest that, like Aristotle, modern science attributes activity to the male part of reproduction and passivity to the female part. Looking back at Hippocratic notions reminds us that these ideas are culturally constructed. Hence, our understanding of menstruation can change to fit the dominant cultural view of gender roles.

Menstruation as heat

Laqueur (1990) identifies another metaphor or story about menstruation, which appeared in the nineteenth century. He writes:

Menstruation, which had been a relatively benign purging of plethora, not unlike other forms of corporeal self-regulation common to men and women, became the precise equivalent of oestrus in animals, marking the only period during which women are normally fertile.

(Laqueur, 1990: 213)

The metaphor of menstruation as heat, or oestrus, had its roots in nineteenth-century developments in natural and medical sciences. Three broad theoretical perspectives were particularly influential. First, Darwin's *Origin of Species*, published in 1859, proposed a progressive and hierarchical relationship between humans and animals, and paved the way for animal models of human physiology (and later, psychology). Second, concepts of micro-organisms and the notion of cells, fundamental to life but invisible to the human eye, raised the possibility of new metaphors for disease (King, 1963). In the context of reproduction, these 'cell theory' ideas allowed the concept of a microscopic human egg, for example, to become possible. Third, Thomas Laycock published an influential series of papers in *The Lancet* between 1842 and 1844, outlining his theory of periodicity. He argued that human (and animal) physiology is governed by a 'vital periodicity', or a number of externally and internally driven rhythmic processes. In a reproductive context, the metaphor of cyclical physiological fluctuations led to a different perspective on menstruation. Anatomical studies identified the existence of egg cells in the ovaries of dogs and pigs, and elegant experimental manipulations demonstrated that, for these animals, eggs were released for fertilisation on a regular basis during oestrus or heat. Since oestrus is often accompanied by a bloody discharge, it wasn't long before theorists began to consider the possibility that menstruation and oestrus are analogous (Laqueur, 1990; Medvei, 1982).

Raciborski (1842) wrote that menstruation is analogous to 'animals in their rutting season', and cited data from fifteen conceptions to suggest that menstruation is the most favourable time for impregnation. Girdwood, in the same issue of *The Lancet* (1842), uses evidence from post-mortem examinations of ovaries to suggest the same thing. He found that the number of cicatrices (scars) on the surface of the ovary increased with age, and showed an exact correspondence with the number of menstrual periods the woman had experienced. He suggested that each scar represented the release of one egg from the ovary, and that the agreement between number of scars and number of menstrual episodes demonstrated that the two were related. For these writers, and the many others who published similar views at around this time, the important finding was that women are spontaneous ovulators, i.e. ovulation happens regardless of sexual activity, rather than reflex ovulators (like rabbits) who release eggs in response to sex.[16]

These theories combined earlier ideas of menstruation as a time of fertility with ideas about spontaneous ovulation, and hence were very powerful. As recently as 1923, Marie Stopes was recommending abstinence from sex during menstruation as a form of contraception. As we shall see in chapter two, these theories were important, not only because their application may have inadvertently caused more pregnancies than it prevented, but also because of their behavioural implications. For most female mammals, oestrus is associated with particular behaviours – suggesting to many, that women too might become 'heated' or slightly mad during menstruation.

Menstruation as failed reproduction

In the twentieth century, the dominant metaphor for menstruation is one of 'failed reproduction'. This metaphor can be traced back to the realisation that ovulation and menstruation are not coincidental in humans, and to the isolation of the 'female' hormones, oestrogen and progesterone. These discoveries occurred during the period which Borell (1976) calls the 'heroic age of reproductive endocrinology', that is 1890–1930, and have been well documented (Corner, 1943; Medvei, 1982; Gruhn and Kazer, 1989; Oudshoorn, 1994). Ovulation, although invisible, is viewed as the central and important function in these accounts, rather than menstruation. Hence, most medical texts and health education books describe an intricate and complex hormonal feedback system designed to support ovulation and the preparation of the uterus for pregnancy (e.g. Lein, 1979; Phillips and Rakusen, 1989).

Modern scientific theories of menstruation suggest that it has no purpose, occurring only as a by-product of an inefficient reproductive system. It is a waste product with no function, representing only the woman's failure to achieve a pregnancy (see Martin, 1989; Laws, 1990), as this definition demonstrates:

> The fall in blood progesterone and estrogen which results from regression of the corpus luteum, deprives the highly developed uterine lining of its hormonal support; the immediate result is profound constriction of the uterine blood vessels, which leads to diminished supply of oxygen and nutrients. Disintegration starts, the entire lining begins to slough, and the menstrual flow begins, marking the first day of the cycle.
>
> (Vander *et al.*, 1980: 501)

By this account, menstruation is an epiphenomenon of the female reproductive cycle, resulting from a failure to conceive. The female reproductive system is designed to produce children. If pregnancy is not achieved, then the uterine lining must be shed to allow preparations to be made for the next 'pregnancy opportunity'. Emily Martin suggests that the metaphor of production which is found in textbook accounts of the female reproductive system makes a negative perception of menstruation inevitable. She writes: 'Menstruation not only carries with it the connotation of a productive system that has failed to produce, it also carries the idea of production gone awry, making products of no use, not to specification, unsaleable, wasted, scrap' (Martin, 1989: 46). She points out that no other bodily functions are described in such a negative way, although they

18

also create 'waste products'. In particular, the production of spermatozoa in the male reproductive tract is usually described in very positive terms (e.g. 'amazing'), despite the 'waste' of millions of sperm in every ejaculation.

This view of menstruation can lead to the conclusion that it is positively harmful, an idea which echoes those of Soranus in the second century AD. For example, Dennis (1992) writes: 'Contrary to generally accepted opinion, frequently repeated menstrual cycles represent an unphysiological condition. . . . Exposure to this unphysiological condition may result in any number of medical conditions' (Dennis, 1992: 487). Descriptions of the relative scarcity of menstruation in non-industrialised cultures, which are assumed to represent our 'natural' state, are used as evidence to support the unhealthy and redundant nature of Westernised menstruation (e.g. Short, 1984), in direct contradiction to the discussions of osteoporosis and heart disease which argue that menstruation is necessary for prolonged good health.

Menstruation as awesome

The association of menstruation with both fertility and blood makes it powerful in many stories and a source of dread or awe (see Horney, 1932). Many writers argue that menstruation is literally awesome on the grounds that it is surrounded by behavioural proscriptions, rituals and taboos in many cultures. These are seen to arise from the belief that menstruating women have either natural or super-natural power, or are vulnerable to supernatural forces. The majority of accounts describe this power as negative or destructive, the familiar idea of menstruation as 'a curse', but recent feminist interpretations of anthropological literature suggest that the power of menstruation can be seen as a positive, life-giving force, a blessing.

Menstruation as a curse

The power ascribed to menstruation can inspire dread. The appearance of blood without injury is in many societies a fearful and dangerous event, which must signify a dreadful misdeed by womankind. The theme of menstruation as a punishment for an original crime or a reminder of human, and especially female, imperfection is a common one, and has been described by many writers (e.g. Harding, 1989; Delaney et al., [1976] 1988; Golub, 1992).

The description of menstruation as 'the curse' is often interpreted as a reference to its origin as described in the book of Genesis.[17] As Cadden (1993) points out, this does not make menstruation a sin, but it is a regular reminder of human imperfection, and has been seen as a significant event because of this in all Judaeo-Christian cultures, particularly in the Middle Ages. This is far from the only description of menstruation as punishment for a sin. For example, Paula Weideger (1976) quotes an ancient Indian myth in which Indra kills the demi-god Visvarupa with a thunderbolt, but is freed from the shame of his murder by sharing his guilt between the earth, the streams, the rocks and women. Freed from the murder, Indra lives happily, whilst women menstruate every month. In this myth, the man's guilt is projected on to women and he is liberated.[18] In other stories, woman and menstruation occur together after the original man is punished for a crime by having his genitals cut off. Hence, woman is a castrated man and menstruation is a reminder or symbol of her castration.

Many anthropological accounts describe societies in which women withdraw during menstruation to special menstrual huts or lodges, which may also be used during bleeding after childbirth (Ploss *et al.*, [1865] 1935; Frazer, [1890] 1922; Crawley, 1902). From the perspective of menstruation as a curse, menstrual huts are seen as evidence that women in these societies are considered to be dangerous and 'untouchable' during menstruation – literally taboo (e.g. Harding, 1989). During menstruation, the woman is open again to the influence of super-natural forces and must be protected. Men, too, must be protected while her bleeding occurs. Hence, in most cultures, including postmodern industrialised cultures, sexual intercourse is taboo during menstruation (Paige and Paige, 1981; McNeill, 1994). For example, in the book of Leviticus, intercourse during menstruation is clearly forbidden, for reasons which appear to have more to do with a curse than with hygiene (see below): 'And if a man shall lie with a woman having her sickness, and shall uncover her nakedness; he hath discovered her fountain, and she hath uncovered the fountain of her blood; and both of them shall be cut off from among their people'[19] (Lev. 20:18). Practices such as the service for the churching of women after childbirth in Anglican and Roman Catholic religions are also cited as evidence that modern taboos about vaginal bleeding relate to a spiritual vulnerability and not just to literal uncleanness (Harding, 1989; Keith, 1978). Hence, it is argued, the colloquial description of menstruation as a curse is not just a historical legacy, but reflects a deep subconscious belief in the dangerous nature of women around menstruation.

Religious injunctions have less influence for most modern women than they did in the Middle Ages. However, many authors argue that the idea of menstruation as a curse remains influential, as seen in the taboo of silence and secrecy which surrounds it and the feeling of shame so often associated with it. For example, Treneman (1988) argues that although adverts for menstrual products appear to be breaking this bond of silence surrounding menstruation, they in fact reinforce secrecy and shame by working from an assumed shared knowledge of the anxieties and taboos related to it. While they seem to promise an active, liberated lifestyle, the adverts never mention menstruation itself. They fuel concern that our secret will be found out, emphasising the possibility of 'leakage' or bulky towels showing through tight trousers, telling us that we can even wear white shorts during menstruation, individually wrapping towels so that no-one will know even if the contents of our handbags are spilt. We do not, in fact, become Lycra-clad roller-skating 'liberated' women by using these products, Treneman argues, but are increasingly anxious about menstruation and unable to acknowledge the reality of it. With all these wonderful products to help us, what possible excuse could there be for leaking or being incapacitated by menstruation?[20] In other words, shame sells, and will continue to sell whilst the taboo around menstruation persists.

Menstruation as a blessing

More positive descriptions of the power of menstruation are found in accounts of cultures which are matriarchal and/or goddess-worshipping. Some archaeologists have argued that the existence of menstrual symbolism provides evidence that goddess-worshipping cultures existed (Gimbutas, 1969). For example, over two hundred Palaeolithic figurines have been found, almost all of which (99 per cent) represent women at all stages of life, and which were originally decorated in red ochre, thought to symbolise the colour of life – menstruation (Rice, 1981). Gimbutas (1969) argues that the existence of these figurines suggests that a goddess tradition existed in ancient cultures, which were probably matriarchal, and that in these cultures menstruation may have been seen as a powerful and sacred symbol of life and fertility. Evidence of this understanding of menstruation can also be found in ancient Greek mythology and ritual (Shuttle and Redgrove, 1986). The Thesmophoria, or annual women's autumn festival, has been described as 'nothing else but the periods of the Greek women elevated to an annual festival' (Kerenyi, 1975). Similar positive accounts of the power of menstruation can be found in descriptions of modern cultures. For example, Barbara Walker (1983) writes that among the Ashanti, girls are more prized than boys because they carry the sacred blood or *mogya*, and among the Chiricahua Apache, singing, dancing and feasting continues for five days in celebration of a young woman's menarche.

In positive accounts of menstruation, menstrual blood itself is a magical and fertility-enhancing substance. Examples of the use of real or symbolic menstrual blood in fertility rites, as a fertiliser, a love potion or a powerful healing agent, can be found in many cultures. Pliny describes a number of remedies given to him by a medical woman, Salpe, a native of Lemnos, among which menstrual fluid is recommended as a cure for malaria and for many types of sores (Mead, 1977), while in the Middle Ages it was used as a cure for leprosy (Crawfurd, 1915). Women of Pliny's time also recommended including threads soaked in menstrual blood in bracelets worn to protect against fever, or using it to massage the soles of a patient's feet to reduce fever (Crawfurd, 1915). Esther Harding (1989) describes the Mother Goddess in India, who is thought to menstruate. At these times, statues of her are hidden and bloodstained cloths are displayed. These cloths are then highly valued and used as treatments for numerous illnesses. Shuttle and Redgrove (1986) suggest that women in ancient Greek culture used menstrual blood as a fertiliser, mixing it with seed corn before planting it. They go on to argue that menstrual blood might also have been used for laying scent trails for hunting,[21] giving huntresses an advantage and explaining the adoption of Artemis, the goddess of the new moon, as the

21

patroness of hunters. Similarly, they suggest that Greek women may have withdrawn to 'menstrual huts' during menstruation, to allow them to use their 'menstrual magic' to promote the earth's fertility, through meditation, and sometimes blood-shedding or sacrificial rites. This wisdom and magical quality was not necessarily lost at the menopause. Barbara Walker (1983) describes Tantric rites which were often controlled by older women, who were thought to be the wisest people of all because they retained their 'magic blood' every month rather than menstruating.

Modern versions of this view can be found in anthropological accounts of Native American traditions, in which women are thought to be at their most spiritually and physically powerful during menstruation. Nootka women from the Pacific Northwest retreat to a 'moonlodge' during menstruation, where they play games, talk, rub each other's backs to ease menstrual pain and generally enjoy themselves. In addition to this, they sit on special moss padding, allowing their menstrual blood to go back to the Earth Mother – a modern version of the ancient Greek promotion of earthly fertility (Cameron, 1984; Owen, 1993).

The heightened but positive spirituality associated with the notion of menstruation as a powerful blessing is also found in modern non-industrialised cultures. For example, a Yurok woman from North California described her menstrual beliefs thus:

> A menstruating woman should isolate herself because this is the time when she is at the height of her powers. Thus the time should not be wasted in mundane tasks and social distractions, nor should one's concentration be broken by concerns with the opposite sex. Rather, all of one's energies should be applied in concentrated meditation to find out the purpose of your life and toward the accumulation of spiritual energy. . . . The blood that flows serves to purify the woman, preparing her for spiritual accomplishment.
>
> (Buckley and Gottlieb, 1988: 190)

The idea of menstruation as a blessing has had little explicit credence in Western thinking for many centuries, although, as seen above, many women describe the feeling of oneness with others and closeness to nature as positive aspects of menstruation. Empirical studies which investigate positive feelings around menstruation also suggest that some Westernised women feel more creative, energetic and powerful before and during menstruation (Logue and Moos, 1988; Stewart, 1989; Chrisler et al., 1994). The concept of blessing has been rediscovered by feminist (particularly ecofeminist) writers both within and outside academia with the political aims of self-empowerment and liberation of women from the dominant negative stories about menstruation (e.g. Owen, 1993; Chrisler et al., 1994).

Karen Horney (1931a, 1932) has argued that the association of menstruation with fertility and women's ability to give life is envied by men and dreaded by them because it makes women powerful. Taboos and rituals were a necessary invention of patriarchal cultures, therefore, in order to control women's power. The most extreme example of this was the persecution and killing of witches, which has been described as 'nine million menstrual murders' (Shuttle and Redgrove, 1986). Control, however, is no cure for envy and Bettelheim (1955) argues that rituals developed in which men attempted to wrest the ability to give life away from women, so that male puberty rites which involve incisions to the penis and blood-letting imitate menarche. If this ritual failed to grant men the magical capacity of procreation, then further revenge might be taken on women in the form of female circumcision – as retribution for the pain the men had experienced through subincision. In other words, 'menstrual envy' could be as powerful a reason for controlling women as menstrual disgust.

Health and hygiene

In addition to all the stories already outlined, menstruation is commonly thought of as a source of weakness or disability with implications for health and/or as a hygienic crisis. These ideas are often interlinked, but I will begin by considering writing that links menstruation and health.

Menstruation as a health crisis

Health can be conceptualised as a state of balance or equilibrium in the body (see Stainton-Rogers, 1991; Helman, 1991a). Medical and scientific accounts which adopt this view see any bodily discharge, including menstruation, as a means of maintaining fluid balance in the body and preventing the potentially harmful accumulation of excess nourishment. In Hippocratic thinking, to maintain a state of health the body needs to achieve a balance between extremes of hot and cold, moisture and dryness, etc. (see Medvei, 1982). The point of equilibrium was thought to vary with age, gender and geographical circumstances. So a different balance might be needed in a hot climate than in a cold one, for instance. As women's seed was contained within a bloody substance, the possibility arose of the build-up of an excess of blood or fluid. This was thought to be dangerous to the woman's health because it would disturb the body's equilibrium. Hence, regular menstruation is necessary to purge the body of excess blood and to maintain good health. These ideas were expanded upon by Aristotle (384–322BC) and his followers, who argued that girls did not menstruate because they were sexually immature, pregnant women used all excess nutriment to feed the foetus and therefore didn't have any excess blood to lose, while lactating women were thought to convert menstrual fluid into milk for the baby. Hence, menstruation is only necessary among sexually mature women who are neither pregnant nor breast-feeding.

The Roman physician Soranus of Ephesus (AD 98–138) considered the question of the relative importance of the roles of menstruation in reproduction and health (Medvei, 1982; Soranus [transl.], 1956). Soranus argues that menstruation cannot be solely for the maintenance of health, because women who do not menstruate are often perfectly healthy. It clearly has a role in childbearing because

> [nature] did not bestow menstruation on those who are not yet able to conceive, like infants, nor on those who are no longer able to conceive, as is the case in women past their prime, but extinguished this activity upon the termination of its usefulness.

> (Soranus, 1956: 24)

He concludes that the major role of menstruation is a reproductive one, and argues against the Hippocratic idea that frequent menstruation is healthy or plays a role in regulating fluid balance under normal circumstances. Only if an excess of fluid has built up, so that the woman is already ill, is menstruation advantageous, he argues. Otherwise the blood loss may be harmful, particularly if a woman is naturally weak.

A nineteenth-century version of Hippocratic ideas is found in John Power's theory of female economy, published in 1821. In his view, the female body acts as a co-ordinated and purposeful unit, the goal of which is to bear children. In Power's theory, the accumulated blood must be released regularly if pregnancy does not occur, hence menstruation (see Moscucci, 1993). The belief in a state of hyperaemia (excess blood) before menstruation was also known as the theory of plethora (e.g. Barnes, 1886). If the excess blood could not escape through menstruation for one reason or another, then bleeding was expected to occur in another part of the body. This was described in the medical literature as 'vicarious menstruation'. So, for instance, Michael Ryan writes in *A Manual of Midwifery* (1841):

> the menstrual secretion may be vicarious, and issue from the surface of the vagina or vulva, or from ulcers on any part of the body. This is the case, perhaps, when a pregnant woman continues to menstruate regularly. This deviation is occasionally observed, and also when there is a vicarious discharge from the urethra, rectum, stomach, intestinal canal, air passages, or any part of the tegumentary surface of the body.

> (Ryan, 1841: 66)

All of these ideas are expressed clearly in a paper, 'On vicarious menstruation', delivered to the British Gynaecological Society by Robert Barnes, in 1886. In this paper he argues that 'the immediate purpose of menstruation is to discharge the superfluous material and energy prepared for the missed pregnancy' (p. 154), and that both lactation and gestation are substitutes for menstruation. He then goes on to describe several cases of bleeding which he attributes to vicarious menstruation. For example,

> M.A., age 30, single. A stout strong woman, admitted complaining of distressing soreness of stomach and pain in the left shoulder, extending

down the arm, which was rigidly flexed; the least attempt to move it caused great pain. After being ill a month she vomited a large quantity of blood. She was carried to bed fainting. Vomiting of blood recurred every month.

(Barnes, 1886–7: 164)

As well as patients vomiting blood, he also notes cases of 'blood-sweating', nose-bleeds (epistaxis), oozing of blood from the nipples, bleeding from the eyes, ears or throat, coughing blood, and bleeding from skin lesions, all occurring either at the same time as menstruation or cyclically in the absence of menstruation.

He identifies three possible causes for vicarious menstruation. The largest group he attributes to a mechanical obstruction of normal menstruation, requiring the excess plethora to find an alternative outlet. In these cases, he argues that removal of the obstruction is necessary to cure the condition. A second group are those women who have an 'unhealthy surface or organ' (for example, a leg ulcer or stomach condition). In these cases, it may be easier for the excess blood to find its way out through the damaged surface than through the uterus and vagina. Intervention is by healing the lesion and attracting the blood back to uterus either by attaching leeches to the vulva (or elsewhere) or by stimulating the uterus with iodine or hot water injections.[22] The third group are those in which 'the menstrual disturbance is traced to nervous influences, emotional or reflex' (p. 176). These women, he implies, are experiencing hysterical vicarious menstruation, and he suggests only that the 'constitutional derangement' must be corrected in these cases, without suggesting a mechanism for doing this.

The discussion following Barnes' paper shows that such ideas were controversial. For instance, Dr Wilks is reported as saying that none of the cases of so-called vicarious menstruation stand up to an investigation, usually failing to demonstrate periodical bleeding. Barnes is criticised for relying on second-hand accounts and being imprecise in his observations. The idea of vicarious menstruation was a powerful one, though, and its possible psychological implications were explored with disastrous effects by Sigmund Freud and Wilhelm Fliess in their treatment of Emma Eckstein (see Lupton, 1993; Masson 1985).

A modern version of the idea that menstruation has a protective function, necessary for good health, has been proposed by Margie Profet (1993). She suggests that menstruation (and other forms of uterine bleeding) protect the womb and reproductive system from pathogens carried by sperm. Hence, regular menstruation is a valuable and natural function, independent of ovulation, which protects women from infection. She observes that uterine bleeding usually occurs as the first outward sign of infection; women who are not menstruating regularly have higher rates of vaginal and uterine infections than those who do; and menstruation occurs more regularly among humans than other apes, as does 'recreational' sexual activity. She offers a different rationale, but with the same conclusions that Hippocrates drew – regular and moderate menstruation is necessary for health, at least for those who are heterosexually active.

The idea of a build-up of blood (or nourishment) which must be released also finds currency in modern theories. For example, most textbooks describe the accumulation of blood in the uterus as nourishment for a foetus, and Strassman (1996) has argued that menstruation occurs because it is less costly, in terms of metabolic energy, to shed and renew the uterine lining than to maintain it in a state suitable for implantation.

The practical implication of this reasoning for women is that menstruation is to be encouraged and seen as healthy. The Hippocratic texts contain many remedies and suggestions for maintenance of regular menstruation (see Cadden, 1993). This idea has been particularly persistent, with concerns about 'menstrual retention' and/or amenorrhea being expressed in many Victorian medical texts, and the widespread prescription (and presumably use) of emmenagogues, drugs or herbal concoctions to 'bring on' menstruation (Shorter, 1983). Advertisements for remedies in the nineteenth century suggest that the Victorians were not concerned with menstruation itself or any pain associated with it, but were concerned about the unhealthy effects of retaining menstrual blood, i.e. of not menstruating. Hence, remedies are marketed to relieve 'obstruction' (Shuttleworth, 1990). Studies with modern women similarly suggest that the perception of menstruation as a cleansing or purgative function which is healthy is widespread (Snow and Johnson, 1977; Martin, 1989).

While menstruation may be necessary for health, the menstruating woman is widely perceived as ill or debilitated (Vertinsky, 1990). Soranus' ideas that menstruation could harm 'weak' women can also be found in Victorian concerns that menstruation may deplete the body's resources, and predispose women, particularly 'delicate' women, to ill health. (see chapter two). In Victorian writing, menstruation is generally considered hazardous only for middle- and upper-class women. Working-class women, seen as being constitutionally stronger, were not thought to be affected by it (Ehrenreich and English, 1973; Cayleff, 1992). It seems that Soranus' ideas about the purpose of menstruation have combined with notions of a hierarchical evolution taken from Darwin's ideas in the popular imagination. The idea that menstruation itself is a time of sickness or illness, though, is a widespread and familiar one. Menstrual euphemisms include 'sickness' or being 'poorly', for example, and women are often described as incapacitated or ill during menstruation. These ideas will be discussed in more detail in the next chapter, and coincide with the growth of medical influence and the medicalisation of reproductive functions throughout the nineteenth and twentieth centuries. The conjunction of the ideas of menstruation being itself a form of illness but also necessary for health remind us again that cultural views surrounding it often place women in a no-win situation. By menstruating regularly women are protected from serious ill health in the future, but the price is monthly sickness. A modern equivalent of this discourse is found in discussions of heart disease or osteoporosis, in which regular menstrual cycles (described in terms of hormone levels) or hormone supplements are hypothesised to protect women from developing the disease (Colverson *et al.*, 1996; Coope, 1989).

Menstruation as a hygienic crisis

The association of menstruation with blood has not only influenced its interpretation as a powerful spiritual time, but has also resulted in its description as a state of pollution. The idea of menstruation as 'dirty' is widespread, and some versions of this view depict menstruation as physically (rather than spiritually) poisonous as well. These ideas are often associated with the view of menstruation as a curse, and have been well documented by other writers (e.g. Delaney *et al.*, 1988; Golub, 1992; Stephens, 1961).

The classic expression of this point of view is found in the book of Leviticus, the third book of the Pentateuch,[23] which is concerned particularly with cleanliness and hygiene (Eadie, 1874). In Leviticus, any discharge – or 'issue' – from man or woman is seen as unclean. The regulations relating to menstruation are clear:

> And if a woman have an issue and her issue in her flesh be blood, she shall be put apart seven days: and whosoever toucheth her shall be unclean until the even. And every thing that she lieth upon in her separation shall be unclean: every thing also that she sitteth upon shall be unclean. And whosoever toucheth her bed shall wash his clothes and bathe himself in water, and be unclean until the even.
>
> (Lev. 15:19–22)

At the end of menses, women were required to wash their bodies by total immersion either in a natural stream or a specially constructed bath called a *Mikweh*.[24] Mikweh were widespread across Europe in the nineteenth century (Shorter, 1983; Ploss *et al.*, 1935).

The concern about cleanliness is also found in many cultures in the form of proscriptions about the activities in which women can engage during menstruation. In particular, many societies forbid the preparation of food during the days of bleeding, for fear that the food will be spoilt. Shorter (1983) describes folklore in the Sologne district which forbade menstruating women to touch salted pork or to approach a newly killed pig. In this area it was believed that menstruating women could cause mayonnaise to curdle and flowers to lose their scent. Similar restrictions applied in Hungary, where menstruating women were not allowed to make preserves, pickles or sauerkraut, nor to bake bread. Frazer (1922) gives several instances of menstruating women being seen as unclean, amongst which is this one:

> Among the Bribri Indians of Costa Rica a menstruous woman is regarded as unclean. The only plates she may use for her food are

banana leaves, which, when she has done with them, she throws away in some sequestered spot; for were a cow to find them and eat them, the animal would waste away and perish. And she drinks out of a special vessel for a like reason; because if any one drank out of the same cup after her, he would surely die.

(Frazer, 1922: 208)

The toxic nature of menstruating women was not without its uses, however, since it could be harnessed as a pesticide for plagued crops (Crawfurd, 1915). The conviction that the touch of menstruating women is poisonous persisted into the twentieth century, resulting in a series of experimental studies of 'menotoxin' (Macht, 1943; see chapter two).

While women in modern societies are not excluded from food preparation during menstruation, most women feel that they should change their behaviour in some way and menstruation is often associated with ideas about dirt and cleanliness (Snow and Johnson, 1977; Paige and Paige, 1981; McNeill, 1992). As with the shamefulness of menstruation, modern ideas about its toxicity or uncleanness can be found in advertising for menstrual products. Berg and Block Coutts (1994) argue that products are promoted on the grounds that they will make menstruation invisible, but also that they will keep women 'fresh and dry', with an emphasis on hygiene and absence of odour. These products are often labelled 'feminine hygiene' in pharmacies and supermarkets, equating menstruation with an absence of cleanliness. It is interesting to note that other 'sanitary products', e.g. babies' nappies, are not labelled in this way. A shelf labelled 'baby hygiene' seems ridiculous.

SUMMARY

The purpose of this chapter was to outline some of the many ideas about menstruation in Western cultures. Menstruation itself, it seems, is a variable experience, often unremarkable, occasionally traumatic, sometimes painful. Women's experiences of menstruation are not all the same, and neither is every menstrual period the same for any woman. Despite this variability and a large number of euphemisms for menstruation, we have very little to say about how menstruation feels or what it is like to menstruate. What we can say reflects what Lovering (1995) calls the 'dominant menstrual discourse'. We can say that menstruation is messy, painful and unpredictable. And sometimes it is. The silence about the many experiences of menstruation which are none of these things, though, perpetuates the myth that menstruation is always like that. This idea that all women are liable to suddenly and unexpectedly start gushing blood is a pretty horrifying one.

Perhaps it is not surprising that so many myths and stories have grown up about menstruation. The reality of menstruation – the evidence which would limit the power of this mythology – is enmeshed within a web of secrecy and shame. It is not polite to talk about menstruation or to let it show. So there is nothing to contradict the myth, except personal experience.

The 'science of woman' might be expected to say more about the reality of menstruation than the myth. Yet, despite centuries of debate and controversy, we still do not know why women menstruate or what it is like to menstruate. We know more now than ever before about the mechanism of menstruation and the connection between menstruation and reproduction. We know how often women menstruate, the amount of fluid and blood lost, and what people will or won't do during menstruation, but we don't know why women menstruate, or whether it is healthier to menstruate or not. We know very little about the phenomenology of menstruation or the relevance of the sorts of cultural ideas described in this chapter to women's lives. Perhaps these are questions which cannot be answered, but it is more likely that these are questions which have not been asked. And perhaps the reason that they have not been asked is because the myth of menstruation serves a powerful political purpose. As Sophie Laws has argued, menstruation is a political issue. The association of menstruation with femininity makes it a central (even if unspoken) concern in the ongoing controversy of body politics. In the twentieth century, the influence of menstruation in discussions of gender has expanded beyond the days on which bleeding actually occurs to encompass the whole menstrual cycle. It is stories about menstruation like those discussed in this chapter, which set the scene for 'scientific' studies of the relationship between menstrual cycle and women's feelings and behaviour, that will be examined in chapter two.

2

A HISTORY OF MENSTRUAL PSYCHOLOGY

ORIGINS: THE NATURE OF WOMAN

As we have seen in the previous chapter, menstruation is not only a biological phenomenon, but also a socially constructed one. Many differing interpretations of menstruation can be made, and different theories or concepts of menstruation are popular in different societies and periods in time. Most of these concepts of menstruation have implications for our understanding of women's experience or behaviour. For instance, if menstruation is seen to be healthy, then by implication it is a positive feature in women's lives and has a beneficial effect on well-being. Absent, delayed or scanty menstruation from this perspective might be expected to cause physical harm or psychological distress. This reasoning is followed by John Millar (1861) in *Hints on Insanity*, where he attributes 'mental derangement' among young women to amenorrhea, and recommends 'establishment of the periodic discharge' to accomplish 'complete mental recovery'. The curse is a more familiar concept of menstruation in Judaeo-Christian cultures, with its attendant implication that women are weak, sickly or even mad around menstruation. It is these assumed implications for women's behaviour, experience and abilities which make menstruation both a hot topic in gender politics and a subject of interest to psychologists. The purpose of this chapter is to tell the story of the origins and development of empirical scientific research about menstruation and women's well-being, psychological state or behaviour. This research did not begin in psychology and has not only been carried out by psychologists. Predominantly, gynaecologists and psychiatrists have been called upon to explain women's experience, but researchers from a wide variety of different disciplines have been involved, including nursing, psychology, sociology and anthropology. So, this is by no means a history of academic psychology – and psychologists are in the minority. All of these researchers are asking questions about the effect of menstruation, or the menstrual cycle, on how women feel, think or act (and occasionally vice versa).

The story begins in the middle of the nineteenth century. In post Industrial Revolution Europe and North America a new wave of feminism was breaking. At the same time, science was becoming fashionable and medicine a respected and authoritative profession (Moscucci, 1993). The latter half of the nineteenth century was a time of great social change and intellectual debate, with two of the most controversial issues of the time being the 'woman question' (Showalter, 1992; Bland, 1995) and human evolution (Easlea, 1981). Some women were demanding access to higher education, the professions and the electorate. Should they be allowed in? If they were allowed in, what might be the effect on the children they might have – would the 'superior' races be strengthened or weakened by the education of women? Suddenly, the nature of woman, always a perplexing topic for male writers and thinkers, was an intellectual 'growth industry'. What is 'woman'? The eyes of the new scientists turned on the mysterious 'other' and set about investigating her (see Moscucci, 1993).

Questions about women's character and behaviour were not new, of course. From Aristotle to Emile Zola, from Pliny to Alexander Pope, women have been seen as psychologically different from men, as mysterious and difficult for men to understand. In particular, women have been seen as fickle, unstable and prone to madness or demonic possession (see Chesler, 1972; Showalter, 1987; Ussher, 1991; Russell, 1995). There is no shortage of descriptions of women's character or theories about why women are different from men. As Freud noted, 'Throughout history people have knocked their heads against the riddle of the nature of femininity' (quoted in Morgan, 1989: 239). In 1919, Alfred Schofield, a distinguished Harley Street psychiatrist, wrote that 'a woman's mind remains the greatest mystery of the race', and in 1926 Bernhard Bauer asked:

> Is not the mind of woman a great eternal question mark? Remember the myth of the Sphinx. Was it chance that the Sphinx was represented with the upper half of a female body and with a female face of such extraordinary beauty? Did not this symbol alone represent the epitome of all that was puzzling?

> (Bauer, 1926: 119)

These men may not entirely agree about what women are like, varying in their degrees of misogyny, but they all agree that woman is different from man, and that efforts should be made to understand her. For Schofield women's minds should be investigated because 'ignorance by men on the subject leads to serious results, and to great injustices. To England, the mind of a woman today is an asset of untold and increasing importance' (Schofield, 1919: 6). For Dr C. Willett Cunnington, writing in 1950, the rationale is less benign. For him, it is necessary to understand women in order to 'hold our own against them' (Cunnington, 1950: flyleaf). For many, such as Freud, it is the alleviation of women's distress, in the form of hysteria or depression, which is the motive for investigating feminine psychology.

For most theoreticians, the explanation for the perceived emotional and behavioural differences between men and women was seen to lie in the balance between mind and body (Stonehouse, 1994; Bland, 1995). The most obvious physical difference between most women and men is the capacity of women to

31

conceive and bear children, and this is seen by many as the *raison d'être* of woman – her destiny and ultimate purpose. It is also seen by most authorities as a vitally important task, which must not be disrupted (see comments below on women's education). Expressions of this view are numerous, and found in the writing of both male and female theorists. So, for example, Eliza Lynn Linton writes in 1891:

> Be it pleasant or unpleasant, it is none the less an absolute truth – the *raison d'être* of a woman is maternity. For this and this alone nature has differentiated her from man, and built her up cell by cell and organ by organ. The continuance of the race in healthy reproduction, together with the fit nourishment and care of the young after birth, is the ultimate end of woman as such; and whatever tells against these functions and reduces either her power or her perfectness, is an offence against nature and a wrong done to society.
>
> (Linton, 1891: 80)

Hence, it is argued, nature has decreed that the needs of women's bodies should predominate. Women behave in the way they do because their minds cannot escape this biological imperative, no matter how much they may try to be civilised. The behaviours which are attributed to this biological imperative differ throughout history, but the logic is the same. For example, in the seventeenth century, women were seen to be driven by a desire for sex, and the voracious, insatiable sexual appetites of women are often commented on (Laqueur, 1990). In the nineteenth century, on the other hand, women's behaviours are interpreted as expressions of their desire to attract a husband and care for children (and/or enable others to do so – what Weininger (1906) called the 'match-making instinct'), rather than to be sexually active *per se*.[1] Men, by this reasoning, are less concerned with the physical aspects of reproduction, and so their behaviour is the result of rational thought and logic, and is literally civilised in a way that women's behaviour can never be. The idea that women's (or female)[2] behaviour is biologically driven (or 'embodied'), while men's is intellectually driven, is implicit in almost all discussions of gender and psychology, both past and present (Jacobus *et al.*, 1990; Currie and Raoul, 1992). It is ultimately this concept that the various waves of feminism have challenged, and it is this challenge which stimulated the origins of empirical menstrual cycle research.

The answer to the question of *why* men and women are different (assuming that they are) is seen to lie in their differing degree of biological commitment to reproduction. The next question to concern theorists is *how* this difference comes about. What is it about women's reproductive capacity which drives or determines women's behaviour? Aristotle answered this question by inferring that male and female reproductive processes require different amounts of body heat. Men are able to convert circulating blood into a completely different substance, semen, a process which Aristotle thought would require considerably more body heat than the equivalent female creation of menstrual blood from venous blood. Women's character was attributed by Aristotle to this relative lack of heat, and constituted a biological anomaly. 'On the Generation of Animals', he wrote: 'For females are weaker and colder in nature, and we must look upon the female character as being a sort of natural deficiency'. While this idea persisted for many centuries (see chapter one), it was not the only theory of how women's ability to have children resulted in a different personality or character. As anatomical and physiological knowledge grew, theorists looked increasingly towards the reproductive organs themselves, and later the physiological mechanisms controlling reproductive functions, for the answer to this question. The normal functions of the uterus or ovaries were seen as the basis of 'normal' femininity, with abnormalities or dysfunctions resulting in madness, hysteria or physical illness. The varying concepts of menstruation mean that it is seen as a normal function by some theorists and an abnormal one by others, depending on the view of menstruation adopted.

The wandering womb

Anatomical studies by the ancient Greeks, and earlier, had established the existence of the womb or uterus, and had shown that it had a role in childbearing (Corner, 1943; Medvei, 1982; Gruhn and Kazer, 1989). The womb was not, however, thought to be fixed within the body, but loose and able to move around within the abdominal cavity. For the ancient Greeks, the symptoms of hysteria were thought to be caused by the wanderings of the uterus (*hyster*) in the abdominal cavity. The symptoms could be alleviated, it was thought, by attracting or repelling the uterus upwards or downwards into its 'normal' position by use of sweet- or foul-smelling salts (McKay, 1901). The association of hysterical symptoms with femininity and particularly the uterus persisted into the nineteenth century (Showalter, 1987) with recommended treatments directed specifically at the uterus (see below).

The perceived importance of the uterus in femininity is seen in the prominence it is given in early anatomical drawings (Poovey, 1989; Martin, 1989). Representations of female internal anatomy show a uterus considerably out of scale with the rest of the body until late in the nineteenth century, reflecting the views of W. Tyler Smith in 1847 that the uterus is 'the largest, and perhaps the most important, muscle of the female economy' (Smith, 1847: 544). Another physician, Hubbard, addressing a medical society in 1870, explained that it was 'as if the Almighty, in creating the female sex, had taken the uterus and built up a woman around it' (quoted in Wood, 1973: 29). The uterus was seen to be closely connected to the central nervous system, so that any shock to the system might upset reproductive functions or even damage or mark an unborn baby (Smith Rosenberg and Rosenberg, 1973; Crawfurd, 1983). Ann Wood (1973) notes that 'doctors in America throughout the nineteenth century directed their attention to the womb in a way that seems decidedly unscientific and even obsessive to the modern observer' (Wood, 1973: 28). The typical symptoms of a uterine disorder, according to William Byford, a physician writing in America in

1864, are weight loss, peevish irritability and any of a range of 'nervous disorders' ranging from 'hysterical fits of crying and insomnia to constipation, indigestion, headaches and backaches' (quoted in Wood, 1973:29). Like the ancient Greeks before them, these physicians focused their remedies on the uterus itself. Their remedies might involve manual investigation and manipulation of the uterus, the application of leeches to the vulva or neck of the uterus, injections of various substances (e.g. water, milk and water, linseed tea) into the uterus, or as a final resort, cauterisation, usually by the application of nitrate of silver. Cauterisation was clearly the most dramatic of these, leaving the uterus 'raw and bleeding' in successful cases and causing severe haemorrhage and pain in unsuccessful ones. By the 1880s it had largely been abandoned as barbaric, with 'rest cures'[3] becoming an increasingly fashionable treatment for hysteria (Wood, 1973; Showalter, 1987).

Overriding ovaries

In the late nineteenth century, medical and intellectual thought was greatly influenced by anatomical discoveries and the ongoing debate between science and religion. Darwinian ideas about the origin of the species reopened discussion about the critical differences between humanity and 'the beasts'. In particular, late nineteenth-century thinkers and writers were concerned to demonstrate the superiority of white men in the hierarchy of the species. This was achieved chiefly by the belief that white men could control their bodies with their minds. Even the most supposedly instinctual of functions, sexual desire and behaviour, were thought to be controllable among white men by willpower. Black men were 'closer to the animals' and less able to control their instinctual 'urges', while women were seen as being ruled by their bodies.[4] At this time, though, the discoveries of gynaecology and endocrinology had changed ideas about the organ responsible for controlling women's minds and behaviour. The ovaries were seen as the dominant organs rather than the uterus. For example, the obstetricians Robert and Fancourt Barnes (father and son) wrote in 1884, 'the active or dominant organ of the sexual system is the ovary' (quoted in Bland, 1995: 63), and Dr W.W. Bliss (1870) remarked that 'the influence of the ovaries over the mind is displayed in women's artfulness and dissimulation' (quoted in Ehrenreich and English, 1973: 34). Hence, nineteenth-century ideas about women are dominated by what Ehrenreich and English (1973) call the 'psychology of the ovary'.

The shift of influence from the uterus to the ovary was incorporated neatly into discussions of the relationship between menstruation and women's wellbeing. Although the importance of the ovaries in reproduction had been demonstrated, ovulation was still thought to occur during menstruation. Hence, most writers simply replaced 'uterine activity' with 'ovarian activity' in their discussions of women's mental state, attributing madness to menstruation in both cases (see Jalland and Hooper, 1986; Skultans, 1975). So, for example, Henry

Maudsley wrote in 1873: 'The monthly activity of the ovaries . . . has a notable effect upon the mind and body: wherefore it may become an important cause of mental and physical derangement' (Maudsley, 1873: 87).

So until the late nineteenth century a woman's reproductive ability was located firmly in the uterus, and the womb was thought to govern her personality. As the role in reproduction of the ovary and, later, hormones became clearer, these structures were identified as the source of femininity. This change is seen in the psychological research too. Early studies were concerned with the role of menstruation itself in women's well-being, implying a connection with the uterus, while later research investigated the effect of the menstrual cycle, suggesting a link with the ovaries and hormones. This was an important shift because it changed the type of questions which researchers asked and the expectations which were held about studies. If popular ideology suggests that the uterus is the source of female madness, for instance, then research focuses on the feelings that women have when the uterus is 'active', i.e. during menstruation and pregnancy. If the ovaries are seen as important, then behaviour or feelings around ovulation will be the concern of researchers (which became inconvenient only when it was realised that ovulation and menstruation do not happen at the same time).

The identification of a continuous rhythm of hormonal changes underlying reproductive physiology raised problems for theorists – it is not immediately obvious that one part of the cycle is more hormonally 'active', or potentially dysfunctional, than another. The problem of which part of the cycle to focus on was solved in the 1920s, immediately following the discovery of oestrogen and progesterone (see chapter six), by the definition of 'premenstrual tension' to describe the feelings women report before a period. So it is no longer menstruation or ovulation which make women different from men, but women's hormones. Similarly, it is no longer dysfunctional menstruation or dysfunctional ovulation which cause women to become mad, but dysfunctional hormones. In modern discussions of women's behaviour during the reproductive years (and particularly around the menopause) it is a hormonal discourse which dominates, and not a discourse about menstruation or ovulation. The story of research about the menstrual cycle and well-being is influenced not only by gender politics and the 'woman question', but also by the developments and discoveries of anatomists and physiologists. In both cases, it has been theory-driven, testing preconceived and stereotypical ideas about women's experience, rather than epidemiological or theory generating (see chapter three).

Menstruation and madness

As ovulation and menstruation were thought to be coincidental by many researchers and clinicians until the early twentieth century (Stopes, 1923; Jalland and Hooper, 1986), theoretical ideas about whether the ovary or the uterus had more influence on women's nature had little impact on early empirical research.

The behavioural effects were thought to be the same, whether they were caused by the release of an egg or the loss of menstrual blood. In the nineteenth-century discourses surrounding the origins of empirical research, menstruation was thought to affect women's minds and behaviour in two ways. First, menstruation, or more particularly its absence, could drive women mad or make them hysterical. Second, the presence of menstruation caused a drain on the 'female economy' which meant that women would be mentally weak and vulnerable whilst menstruating, or could risk damaging their health by excessive mental activity. Both of these ideas had a major impact on the development of research, and will be considered in turn in a little more detail.

The association between 'madness' and menstruation itself or obstructed menstruation has a long history (see chapter one). In his *Natural History*, written nearly two thousand years ago, Pliny (AD 23–79) refers to menstruation as 'this pernicious mischief', suggesting that menstruating women can turn wine sour, blight crops and dull mirrors by their poisonous touch. In later centuries, the presence or absence of menstruation was associated with numerous physical and mental disorders. In seventeenth-century medical writing, menstruation was thought to occur either to purify women's blood, following Hippocratic thinking, or to purge the body of excess blood, or plethora, as Aristotle suggested (Crawfurd, 1981; 1983). In either case, the absence of menstruation drives women mad – by allowing impurities to build up or excess plethora to accumulate. It was thought that this blood would move back from the uterus to the brain, 'causing melancholy and troubling her spirits. The idle fancies produced in her head might even incline her to suicide' (de Loier, 1605, quoted in Crawfurd, 1981). Numerous remedies are available from this time to encourage menstruation to occur, known as emmenagogues (Shorter, 1983; Shuttleworth, 1990).

In the nineteenth century, regularity of menstruation is still seen as important, and irregular or 'obstructed' menstruation as a hazard to physical and mental health. Menstruation itself makes women irritable and 'capricious', but if it is suppressed disaster may follow, as Henry Maudsley points out in a continuation of his comment quoted above.

> Most women at that time [during menstruation] are susceptible, irritable, and capricious, any cause of vexation affecting them more seriously than usual; and some who have the insane neurosis exhibit a disturbance of mind which amounts almost to a disease. A sudden suppression of the menses has produced a direct explosion of insanity; or, occurring some time before an outbreak, it may be an important link in its causation.
>
> (Maudsley, 1873: 87)

Thus insanity could be attributed to an episode of 'suppressed menstruation' in the past, even if the woman was menstruating normally at the time of diagnosis. Not surprisingly, then, according to Bucknill and Tuke (1874), uterine disorders and suppressed or irregular menstruation accounted for 10 per cent of all female admissions to asylums.

The supposed dangers of amenorrhea or 'improper' menstruation were not only a concern for doctors. Popular advertisements and self-help guides in the nineteenth century encouraged women to keep a close watch on their menstrual functions, always on their guard for any irregularity (Shuttleworth, 1990; Wood, 1973). These irregularities could of course be remedied by the use of the 'female corrective pills' being advertised. Medicines to control the quality and regularity of menstruation and to treat obstructions were common during the nineteenth century and some remedies became household names, such as Lydia Pinkham's Vegetable Compound (Burton, 1949; Shuttleworth, 1990). If such remedies were not effective, though, women – particularly upper- and middle-class women – were encouraged to seek medical attention.[5]

This belief that 'disordered menstruation' could cause temporary insanity can also be found in nineteenth-century judicial decision-making. For example, Martha Brixey, 'the Greenwich murderess', a domestic servant who was accused of murdering one of her employer's children in 1845, was acquitted on the grounds of 'insanity probably arising from obstructed menstruation' (Smith, 1981: 155). Amenorrhea, or 'disordered menstruation', was also used as a miti- gation for less serious crimes. At Carlisle Quarter Sessions in 1845, Ann Shepherd was acquitted of stealing a fur boa because of temporary insanity caused by suppressed menstruation, and acceptance by the magistrates that her conduct was 'periodically erratic' (Smith, 1981). In 1896, Mrs Castle, a wealthy American, was acquitted of shoplifting in London because she was said to be suffering from kleptomania, a condition thought to result from suppressed menstruation (Shuttleworth, 1990). The association of insanity with menstrual dysfunction persists in modern judicial decision-making. Within the hormonal discourse of twentieth-century Britain, though, it is not dysfunctions of menstru- ation which are thought to cause temporary insanity, but dysfunctions of hormones in the form of premenstrual tension or premenstrual syndrome (Eagan, 1985; Boorse, 1987; Houlgate, 1987; Kendall, 1992; and see chapter six). The retention of menstruation was viewed as both a cause and a possible effect of madness (Shuttleworth, 1990; Skultans, 1975). Thus menstruation made women prone to madness, but madness itself could also cause menstrual disruption.

Women, work and education

It was not the possible association between menstruation and madness, however, which triggered scientific and ultimately psychological interest in female cyclicity, but the heated debate concerning the 'woman question', and particularly the controversy about education for women, which raged on both sides of the Atlantic in the middle and later years of the nineteenth century (see Showalter, 1992).

Free, compulsory state education did not become widely available in Britain until the 1870s. Before this time, education depended on social class, parental income and parental attitude. Although some girls were sent to school and/or otherwise educated, many were not (Kamm, 1965; Perkin, 1993). Most universities did not admit women until late in the century (Kamm, 1965; Perkin, 1993). The issue of education for girls was taken up with great fervour by many feminists of the time, who saw it as a key means for women to become employable in higher status occupations and able to support themselves financially – a means of escape from the enforced dependency and 'legalised prostitution' of marriage (e.g. Hamilton, [1909] 1981; see Tomalin, 1977; Spender, 1982). However, not everyone agreed that girls should be educated, and the campaign for women's education (especially higher education) was a long and bitter one (see Kamm, 1965). Among the many arguments used to oppose education were those which inferred dangers to women's reproductive health through intellectual activity. These drew principally on notions of the 'female economy' (see chapter one) and the biological suitability of women's bodies for motherhood (Moscucci, 1993).

The 'human economy' view of physiology held that the human system can only work efficiently by directing energy to one function at a time. Effective digestion could only occur, for example, if the body and mind were otherwise at rest (see chapter one). Since the most important organ in the 'female economy' was seen to be the uterus (or later the ovaries), it is not surprising that menstruation was thought to be an energy-demanding process. Menstruation weakens and disables women by its demands on the limited 'female economy'. So, for example, the psychiatrist George Man Burrows wrote in 1828:

> Every body of the least experience must be sensible of the influence of menstruation on the operations of the mind. . . . the functions of the brain are so intimately connected with the uterine system, that the interruption of any one process which the latter has to perform in the human economy may implicate the former.
>
> (Burrows, 1828: 146)

The specialisation of function argument was justified largely on the basis of sex differences in the sizes of the pelvis and the skull. The larger size of the pelvis in women was thought to indicate a female specialisation for reproduction, while the larger skull size in men indicated a specialisation for intellectual activity. Pelvimetry in women was seen as complementary to craniometry in men as a measure of evolutionary progression and a means of classifying races and species (Moscucci, 1993). Large pelvises (which were of course found among relatively wealthy, white women) were thought to indicate a higher level of evolution and a greater suitability to childbearing. It was exactly these women who, according to such theories, were the most suited to pregnancy, the most likely to produce healthy (and highly evolved) children, and therefore to ensure the continuing progression of humanity towards an evolutionary ideal. From a eugenic point of view, these women should be encouraged to have children, while women with smaller pelvises (typically poorer women) should not. These were, however, exactly the women who were demanding education and emancipation. So, not surprisingly, writers of the time suggested that education could damage the pelvis because the stooping position necessary for study would constrict the blood vessels, and sedentary habits weaken the body and interfere with the development of the pelvis. Such pelvic damage could also result in menstrual problems. Dr A.F.A. King warned in 1895 that 'the method of education in the schools was a large factor in producing menstrual disorders'. Ultimately, Cook (1895) complained, 'with an overstimulated brain and a weakened body, what, if any, progeny is to be expected from her?' (both quoted in Cayleff, 1992: 230–231).

These two ideas were brought together in two influential essays published in the 1870s. In America, Edward Clarke, professor of Materia Medica at Harvard University, published a book called *Sex in Education: or, a Fair Chance for the Girls* in 1873. In the same year, Henry Maudsley, an eminent British psychiatrist and editor of the *Journal of Mental Science*, published a similar book, *Sex in Mind and Education*, and an essay, summarising his book and with the same title, in the *Fortnightly Review* of April 1874. Both these doctors believed that intellectual activity during menstruation (especially in the years following puberty) would damage the reproductive system and could potentially cause sterility (Bullough and Voght, 1973). This would not only prevent women from fulfilling their 'natural' function, but could even wipe out the human race. Clarke drew on case studies to argue that 'the [reproductive] system is then peculiarly susceptible; and disturbances of the delicate mechanism . . . by constrained positions, muscular effort, brain work, and all forms of mental and physical excitement, germinate a host of ills' (Clarke, 1889, quoted in Harlow, 1986: 40). As the reproductive system was thought to be particularly sensitive during menstruation, any kind of brain work at that time was particularly detrimental, and any damage caused, they argued, was incurable.

These ideas were extremely influential and popular, with Clarke's book going through seventeen editions in thirteen years (Bullough and Voght, 1973; Showalter and Showalter, 1970; Ehrenreich and English, 1973; Wood, 1973; Blake, 1990). They were popularised by T.S. Clouston who wrote a lengthy series of articles for *Popular Science Monthly* in 1883 and 1884, summarising (and exaggerating) the dangers of education to women. According to these articles, 'overstimulation of the female brain causes stunted growth, nervousness, headaches and neuralgias, difficult childbirth, hysteria, inflammation of the brain, and insanity' (quoted in Bullough and Voght, 1973: 72).

These ideas were profoundly anti-feminist and created a crisis for those campaigning for secondary education for girls (Blake, 1990; Perkin, 1993) who published numerous rebuttals. In America, a collection of essays by distinguished educators and public figures, edited by Julia Ward Howe, was published in 1874, arguing that education improves women's health and especially their menstrual health (Delaney *et al.*, 1988). The most vehement and active responses to Clarke and Maudsley, however, came from women who were struggling to obtain access to medical qualifications. It has been argued that Clarke, in particular, published his ideas specifically to block the ambitions of such women (Bullough and Voght, 1973; Blake, 1990). The most celebrated of these rebuttals was from Elizabeth Garrett Anderson, at the time a medical student at Edinburgh University. She was asked to write a response to Maudsley's article by Emily Davies and Frances Buss on behalf of the recently founded Girls' Public Day School Trust (Blake, 1990). Her article, which was published in the May 1874 issue of the *Fortnightly Review*, includes a scathing attack on Maudsley's argument that women are periodically handicapped by menstruation (L'Esperance, 1977). She writes:

> when we are told that in the labour of life women cannot disregard their special physiological functions [i.e. menstruation] without danger to health, it is difficult to understand what is meant, considering that in adult life healthy women do as a rule disregard them almost completely. . . . Among poor women, where all available strength is spent upon manual labour, the daily work goes on without intermission, and as a rule without ill-effects. For example, do domestic servants, either as young girls or in mature life, show by experience that a marked change must be made in the amount of work expected of them at these times unless their health is to be injured? It is well known that they do not.
>
> (Anderson, 1874: 582)

Clarke had an answer to this contradiction in his argument that it is 'brain work' rather than physical work which damages the reproductive system. He argued that girls working in factories suffer less than schoolgirls (in his view) because they 'work the brain less. . . . Hence they have stronger bodies, a reproductive apparatus more normally constructed, and a catamenial function less readily disturbed by effort, than their student sisters' (Clarke, 1873). As Emily Martin (1989) points out, his case studies completely disregard the often appalling working conditions which women experienced in factories, offices, the retail trade or domestic service.

The furore about women's access to work and education was the immediate stimulus for empirical studies of the menstrual cycle. As with almost all of the research which followed, these studies were politically motivated, designed to demonstrate that women were or were not incapacitated by menstruation. They were concerned almost entirely with the effect of menstruation on cognitive and physical abilities and long-term health. The concern about the relationship between menstruation and madness was not to enter empirical research until the combined influences of psychoanalysis and endocrinology came into play in the early twentieth century.

TRENDS IN EMPIRICAL RESEARCH 1870–1995

The story of the research which investigates women's well-being and the menstrual cycle begins, then, with practical concerns. In particular, two questions fuel the research. Are women driven mad by menstruation, and are women fit to work during menstruation? As the years have passed, the specific concerns of researchers have changed, and shifts have occurred in which aspects of the cycle are the focus of study. However, these are the two themes which are clear in all the research which is described in this book. The social and practical nature of the research questions asked, as well as their importance in gender politics, means that research into the psychology of the menstrual cycle has been influenced by social and political events. For example, the demand for female labour during wartime stimulated research into the effects of menstruation on work (Harlow, 1986). Political pressures have influenced not only the questions asked but also the interpretation (and acceptability) of the answers obtained (Fausto-Sterling, 1992). Hence, menstrual cycle research is often a story of rediscovery. Studies whose findings don't fit with the ideology of their time are difficult to publish and remain obscure, only to be rediscovered by researchers asking the same questions many years later. So, for example, Barbara Sommer (1992) writes at the beginning of a chapter about cognitive performance and the menstrual cycle:

> previous reviews had indicated that the menstrual cycle has virtually no impact on objectively measured cognitive performance (Sommer 1982, 1983), a conclusion similar to that of Hollingworth's dissertation in 1914, of Lough's dissertation in 1937, and of Seward's 1944 review article in *Psychological Bulletin*. Nevertheless, at the end of 1988, it was news.
>
> (Sommer, 1992: 39)

The story of research into mood, cognition and the menstrual cycle is not a typical scientific story of small painstaking studies joining together into a coherent whole, usually likened to the gathering of pebbles into a mountain. It is in itself a cyclical phenomenon, perhaps even a circular phenomenon. Above all, the lesson of menstrual cycle research is that science is socially constructed, both in terms of the questions which are asked and the answers which are heard

It was noted at the beginning of the chapter that researchers from a wide range of disciplines have been concerned with menstruation. Research into the effects of menstruation or the menstrual cycle on mood and emotion (latterly, premenstrual syndrome and menstrually related depression) has largely been the province of psychiatrists and gynaecologists, while investigations of cognitive or behavioural experiences across the cycle have interested psychologists. However, there is no perfect relationship between the background of the researcher and the subject of their research. More influential in the choice of research question has been the rationale and motivation of the researcher. Jane Ussher (1992b) has described four types of researcher in modern menstrual cycle research: the rational reductionist, the liberal feminist hero-innovator, the radical feminist dissenter and the accidental tourist; and with a little imagination these different research motivations can be seen throughout the history of the research field. The 'rational reductionist' is 'committed to identifying the causal links between behaviour and cyclical phenomena and to exposing the relationship between hormones and behaviour within a rigid positivistic paradigm' (Ussher, 1992b: 152). The presence of a cyclical pattern, or distress surrounding menstruation, is a necessary assumption of this type of research, which has dominated twentieth-century investigations, with a particular emphasis on the identification of biological (or psychosocial) factors causing the so-called 'premenstrual syndrome'. Liberal feminist hero-innovators are concerned about the negative stereotypes which surround menstruation and are 'determined to provide empir-ical evidence to refute the claims that menstruation is deleterious' (Ussher, 1992b: 146). They have usually been trained in biomedical or psychological research methods, and use experimental techniques to 'prove' that menstruation has little or no effect on mood or behaviour. The radical feminist dissenters criti-cise both of these points of view. They argue that the attribution of women's distress to reproductive functions is socially constructed, and that 'any research that investigates menstrual cycle phenomena reinforces the ideology that menstruation is debilitating' (Ussher, 1992b: 151). From this view, both reduc-tionist and liberal feminist research is ideologically flawed. The fourth category of researcher identified by Ussher is the accidental tourist, who 'regards menstrual cycle phase as yet another (in)dependent variable . . . that is unprob-lematic ideologically' (Ussher, 1992b: 153). It is another variable to include in an analysis, rather as gender is often included. All four of these groups have contributed significantly to menstrual cycle research, but their contributions are most marked in the study of 'premenstrual syndrome' (see below).

The following part of the chapter will outline the development of different lines of research and attempt to indicate the events which have triggered growth and decline in particular areas. The studies themselves will be described in more detail in chapters four to six; the purpose of this outline is to illustrate the cyclicity of menstrual psychology research, and perhaps to inspire new research questions.

Feminism, science and industry 1870–1920

In the late nineteenth century, gynaecology, the 'science of woman' (Moscucci, 1993) was developing fast. Gynaecology had a wider remit than it is usually accorded today. Moscucci (1993) argues that nineteenth-century gynaecology had two aspects. The first was a concern with understanding the physical and reproductive aspects of woman – her anatomy and physiology, for example. The second was a concern with the description of the 'natural' state of woman – the female equivalent of anthropology. Methodical and 'scientific' research was largely restricted to these areas, and while medical men published discussions of feminine psychology which often appeared to be scientific and objective, these were usually based on subjective interpretation of clinical impressions.

Most of the medical research between 1870 and 1920 investigated the physiological mechanisms underlying the menstrual cycle. The history of these scientific discoveries is a fascinating one and has been well documented (Medvei, 1982; Corner, 1943; Gruhn and Kazer, 1989; Short, 1984; Laqueur, 1990; Moscucci, 1993; Oudshoorn, 1994). Although we have learned a great deal about the biochemistry and neurohormonal aspects of the cycle since then, our modern understanding of the physiology of the cycle has changed little from that which was emerging at the end of this period.

While some medical men endeavoured to understand the nature of woman by investigating the physical functions of femininity, others turned their attention to the study of woman as a race. The best known of these studies is *Das Weib*, which appeared in 1885 (Ploss *et al.*, 1935). Studies like this contain little which could be called psychology. They are detailed accounts of the rituals, beliefs and legends which surround women's lives in various cultures, but say little about how women themselves interpret them or how they think or feel.

In this period, there were several studies concerned with menstruation and work or cognitive performance. Some of these could be described as from a rational reductionist perspective, while others are early examples of feminist empiricism. The first public enquiry into the relationship between work and menstrual dysfunction was conducted by Dr Azel Ames in Massachusetts, and published as *Sex in Industry: A Plea for the Working Girl* (Ames, 1875). Ames observed the tasks performed by and working conditions of women in six female-dominated industries, and gathered reports from doctors, employers and supervisors about their menstrual problems. In his report he describes the long working hours and unhealthy conditions experienced by these women, and associates this with the high rate of menstrual problems reported by their supervisors and doctors. He didn't see the conditions themselves as inhumane or responsible for women's suffering, rather he used ideas of the 'female economy' to argue that women are physiologically incapable of coping with the simultaneous mental and physical demands of the industrial process. The result of this overtaxing of limited female resources, he argued, is a diversion of energy away from the vital reproductive functions, and hence a disruption of menstruation. Rather than suggesting changes in the working conditions to which women were exposed, he recommended that women's employment in industry should be limited.

The first study from a liberal feminist perspective was published by Mary Putnam Jacobi. She was an American woman who had been active in the campaign for women to gain entry to the medical profession, and who was among the first women to achieve this status (Blake, 1990). Although she was not a psychologist, her book *The Question of Rest for Women During Menstruation*, published in 1877, argued for the use of empirical and scientific methods to investigate women's experiences of menstruation, and raised many of the issues and questions which feminist scientists are still grappling with over a hundred years later. She surveyed 286 women and found that 54 per cent had no menstrual problems, while the remainder reported at most moderate menstrual pain. She argued on the basis of this evidence that enforced rest (or assumed weakness) during menstruation was the result of custom and men's wishes, and not a physiological requirement (Blake, 1990; Cayleff, 1992). This study was supported by several studies of general health amongst college-educated women which showed either no change or a general improvement in health (Bullough and Voght, 1973). For example, Clelia Duel Mosher studied menstruation among college women between 1890 and 1920. She found a greater incidence of menstrual difficulties in the 1890s, which she initially attributed to a self-fulfilling prophecy. These girls, she argued, were taught to expect that they would be sick during menstruation and therefore perceived a greater number of problems. Given the emphasis in the popular and medical literature on remedies for problematic menstruation (see above), this seems a reasonable conclusion. However, she also found a correlation between reported menstrual difficulties and style of dress. In 1894, women wore tight corsets, constricting their waists to an average of 20 inches, and heavy clothing (skirts and petticoats weighing 15lb). By 1915, skirts were shorter, petticoats fewer and waist measurements increased by 40 per cent. By this time 68 per cent of the women she sampled reported no menstrual difficulties, compared to only 19 per cent in 1894 (Mosher, 1916; Bullough and Voght, 1973). These studies suggest that menstrual problems may have more to do with physical conditions than mental activity. The absence of rest during menstruation, according to these writers, was not causing profound reproductive or psychological difficulties.

Although these studies largely contradicted the assertions of writers such as Clarke (1873) and Maudsley (1874), it was the opinions of these men, rather than the evidence, which formed the views of the next generation of authorities, such as G. Stanley Hall, Havelock Ellis and Sigmund Freud (Bullough and Voght, 1973; Smith Rosenberg and Rosenberg, 1973; Cayleff, 1992). Each of these theorists argued that women *must* be incapacitated by menstruation. Ellis (1894) observed that women are 'periodically wounded in their most sensitive spot' (Ellis, 1894: 284), and recommended that, instead of one day of rest per week, women should take all four days during menstruation. This advice was echoed by Hall (1908), who dismissed the statistical studies as inaccurate, and clearly connected menstruation to mental exercise. He argued that girls should be educated separately from boys, in schools in the country with plenty of space for exercise and privacy, in which the 'monthly Sabbath' could be observed during which 'idleness be actively cultivated'.

It was in this atmosphere that the first truly psychological study was conducted. Leta Stetter Hollingworth was born in 1886 and after an early career as a high-school teacher obtained an MA (1913) and PhD (1914) in educational psychology from Teacher's College at Columbia University, studying under Edward Thorndike among others. She was concerned with intelligence and cognitive ability, and particularly with the contemporary assertions that women's abilities were in some way inferior to men's (Hollingworth [1943] 1990). In her PhD research, she directly tested the hypothesis that women are less competent or less able to work during menstruation. She tested both men and women on a variety of measures of psychomotor and mental ability, finding no evidence for a menstrually related rhythm in women's performance or abilities. Leta Stetter Hollingworth, like Mary Putnam Jacobi, can be called a 'liberal feminist hero-innovator'. She was tremendously encouraged by her findings and by the potential of science for challenging the myths about women's abilities. In the conclusion of her thesis, she writes:

> It seems appropriate and desirable that women should investigate these matters experimentally, now that the opportunity for training and research is open. Thus, in time, may be written a psychology of women based on truth, not on opinion; on precise, not on anecdotal evidence; on accurate data rather than remnants of magic.
>
> (Hollingworth, 1914)

Unfortunately, her optimism precluded the possibility that science might itself be used to establish particular 'truths'. As Linda Kreger Silverman (1992) notes, if Hollingworth were to observe modern society she might be surprised to learn that, fifty years after her death, the 'woman question' is still unresolved.

War, peace and hormones 1920–1965

The period from 1920 to 1965 marks the transition between nineteenth-century and twentieth-century concerns. In particular, there is a shift during this period away from the uterine and ovarian discourses of the Victorians to a new hormonal discourse – although the language of the 'raging hormone' was not to take hold until the 1970s. This shift is most clearly demonstrated by a move away from menstruation as a focus of research interest and towards the recognition of 'premenstrual tension'. The world wars and economic depression in the first part of this period caused a dramatic shift in the questions being asked in all aspects of psychology, and menstrual psychology was no exception. In particular, the need for women to work in 'heavy' industries while men were fighting led to renewed interest in menstruation and work in the years from 1920 to 1950, but a marked lack of interest in this area from 1950 onwards. The battles for women's access to education and enfranchisement had largely been won by the 1930s, and the 'problem which has no name' (Friedan, 1963) was not to emerge until the 1960s, sparking a new wave of interest in menstruation. The growth of psychology as a distinct discipline during this period – particularly the growth of applied psychology (Myers, 1929) – was significant, as was the separate development of psychoanalysis (Lupton, 1993) and later psychosomatic medicine (see Engel, 1967).

As experimental psychology became established as a discipline alongside the professions of educational, occupational and clinical psychology, the now familiar institutions and indexes were founded. One of the most useful of these for the purposes of following developing interest in particular areas within psychology is *Psychological Abstracts*, first published in 1927 by the American Psychological Association. It was initially a collection of summaries of articles of interest to psychologists, sent in on a voluntary basis by society members; later it became a more systematic collection of psychological literature. In its first year, 2,730 abstracts appeared, of which 3 were concerned with aspects of menstruation. By the 1990s, there are between 30,000 and 40,000 abstracts each year, with around a hundred menstrually related papers. *Psychological Abstracts* includes the abstracts of papers appearing in some medical journals as well as psychology journals – for instance *Psychosomatic Medicine* and the *Journal of Psychosomatic Research* – so, although it is not a comprehensive index of research literature, it covers most of the field of interest to this book. The growth in interest in menstrual cycle psychology is shown by the increasing number of papers on the subject in *Psychological Abstracts* (see Figure 2.1). In the early period, interest was fairly stable, increasing dramatically in the 1980s. What were these early research papers concerned with?

The relationship between menstruation and work continues to be of interest in this period, influenced, as noted above, by the need for women to work in non-traditional occupations during the war years, and by the growth of industrial and applied psychology. So, for instance, a report by the Industrial Fatigue Research Board was published in 1928, describing two experimental studies of simulated work performance across the menstrual cycle (Sowton *et al.*, 1928). The results of this study, which involved daily testing of 29 women on two forms of number-checking test for four to six months, were more equivocal than those of Hollingworth. Of the 18 women who completed the study, the researchers found that performance during menstruation was unaltered in 5 women, better than usual in 4 women, and worse than usual in 9 women (see chapter four). By the 1940s, the concern is more explicitly job-related. So, for example, Holtz (1941) asks whether women should fly aeroplanes while they are menstruating, concluding that women with 'healthy' menstrual cycles are perfectly safe pilots. By 1944, Georgene Seward concluded in her influential review in *Psychological Bulletin* that extensive experimental studies had shown no evidence of a consistent cognitive impairment associated with menstruation. In the later 1940s and 1950s, occupational researchers shift their attention away from the competence of women during menstruation, to the possibility that particular types of work or working conditions might be associated with menstrual dysfunctions (e.g. Hesseltine, 1944; Burnell, 1944; Varney, 1944). At this time the cause of the menstrual dysfunction was seen to lie with the woman's inherent weakness or inability to cope with the working environment, rather than with any occupational hazards. So, although women may be perfectly competent workers, these studies reflect a concern reminiscent of the 1870s, that they will damage their reproductive systems as a result. Not until the 1970s did researchers start to

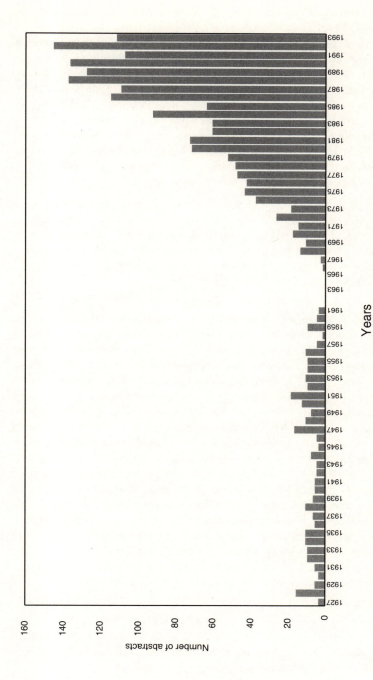

Figure 2.1 Menstrual cycle related abstracts, 1927–1993

Note: The number of abstracts relating to menstruation or aspects of the menstrual cycle (keywords: premenstrual tension/syndrome, dysmenorrhea, menorrhagia, menopause, menstrual cycle, menstruation), appearing in *Psychological Abstracts (PA)* from 1927 to 1993. The number of menstrually related abstracts as a proportion of all entries reaches a maximum of 0.39 per cent in 1988.

suggest that working conditions might be the problem, rather than women themselves (see Harlow, 1986).

Another strand of research in the 1920s and 1930s which reflected a continued interest in nineteenth-century concerns about menstruation was the series of studies, conducted principally by David Macht and his (usually women) colleagues in Baltimore, into the nature and properties of 'menotoxin'. These pharmacologists were interested in the folkloric pollution belief that the touch of menstruating women could be poisonous to plants or other animals (see Laws, 1990). This research was inspired by Professor Bela Schick's observations, published in 1920, of the effect on flowers of being handled by menstruating women. Fluhmann (1956) describes the origins of the search for menotoxin in a story which evokes a vivid picture of research in the 1920s:

> Some thirty years ago Professor Schiff, a distinguished pharmacologist, had a secretary who carefully placed a rose in a small vase on his desk every morning. The observing scientist was intrigued by the fact that several days each month the flower faded very rapidly. He kept a note of these days and on comparing notes with his assistant found that they corresponded with the days of her menstrual periods.
>
> (Fluhmann, 1956: 4)[6]

Macht and his colleagues were at the time investigating the effects of various drugs and chemicals on plant and animal tissues at the plant physiology laboratory at Johns Hopkins University, and used the same procedures to investigate menotoxin. In the first experiments, they grew plants hydroponically, in solutions which contained samples of blood serum, blood plasma, saliva, sweat, tears, milk and other unspecified secretions from either a menstruating woman or the same non-menstruating woman. They found that the plants exposed to the fluids from the menstruating woman were 'definitely retarded in growth', so went on to examine the effects on animal tissues. Later studies found 'menstrual toxin' to be toxic to goldfish and to depress maze-running behaviour in rats, but were inconclusive about the effects of menotoxin applied to male genitalia (in circumcised and uncircumcised guinea pigs). In a review of the area, Macht (1943) refers to a large number of studies and researchers, but is remarkably quiet about the implications of his findings (although he does suggest that the avoidance of sex during menstruation, as decreed in Leviticus and elsewhere, may be well founded). He suggests that menotoxin is closely linked to the female sex hormones, and may be responsible for psychopathological symptoms occurring around menstruation. In a modern reworking of menstruation as hygiene theories, he argues that:

> In the female organism there is a periodic accumulation, under the influence of ovarian secretions, of certain substances essential to the furtherance of fertilization and implantation of the ovum. Failure of this excretion, usually controlled by the menstrual flow, leads not only to the retention of the poisons but to many pathologic symptoms.

(Macht, 1943: 301)

A contradictory theory was put forward by O. and G. Smith (1950), who suggested that menstrual toxin may originate from the uterus itself, rather than from the ovaries. This flurry of interest in menotoxin, and the almost hysterical concern about its absorption through the penis, diminished in the light of several contradictory studies (e.g. Bartelmez, 1937), particularly a paper by Zondek (1953) which found that the toxic properties of menstrual blood could be eliminated by antiseptics. He argued that it was bacterial action after the collection of menstrual fluid which made it toxic and not menstruation itself. His fellow gynaecologists seem reluctant to abandon the idea of menotoxin, though. Israel muses that 'despite Zondek's objection to the existence of such a toxin, it provides an attractive theory to explain the premenstrual intoxication of women' (Israel, 1959: 179).

Throughout the 1920s, there was speculation about the existence of one or more ovarian hormones in the medical literature. Allen and Doisy (1923) identified 'an ovarian hormone', which was later named oestrin by Parkes and Bellerby in 1926. The hormonal action of progesterone was not discovered until 1929 (Corner, 1943). These discoveries created great excitement, not only among clinicians but also among pharmaceutical companies, who were keen to develop uses for synthetic hormones. By the late 1930s, drug companies such as Bayer and Schering were already circulating physicians with information about 'sex hormone therapy' (e.g. Bayer, 1938; Schering, 1941). From a gynaecological perspective, premenstrual tension was first described as a hormonal dysfunction by Robert Frank in 1929 and 1931 (see chapter six), and quickly attributed to an imbalance or deficiency in female sex hormones. By the early 1940s, a number of small and uncontrolled studies had demonstrated a dramatic efficacy of 'natural' and synthetic progesterone in the treatment of PMT (e.g. Israel, 1938; Greenblatt et al., 1941). As time progressed, theories developed about the process by which hormonal fluctuations might lead to psychological distress, and studies testing new treatments based on these theories were published (e.g. Greenhill and Freed, 1941; Morton, 1950). By the 1950s, studies were revealing conflicting findings, a problem which was attributed to methodological problems and the possibility that Frank's concept had been too simplistic. Tension, such authors argue, is not the only experience reported by women premenstrually and a broader definition is needed. The concept of PMT enlarged to premenstrual syndrome (or premenstrual tension syndrome) after the Second World War (e.g. Rees, 1953; Greene and Dalton, 1953) and researchers set out to investigate how many women experienced premenstrual symptoms and their consequences (e.g. Pennington, 1957; Dalton, 1960, 1961; Kessel and Coppen, 1963)

The interest in links between menstruation and madness began to grow in this period, particularly in response to the discovery of hormones and the development of psychosomatic medicine. By the end of this phase, the interest of psychiatrists and psychoanalysts too was focused around premenstrual experiences, but at the beginning it was the psychological reactions to menstruation itself which were of concern. So, for example, Hirschmann-Wertheimer (1927) is concerned with reciprocal relationships between 'menstruation and the mind', and identifies two main types of woman on the basis of twenty-four questions about women's dispositions and ability to work during menstruation and their affective reactions to it. The first type is the 'woman who endeavours to attain her womanly occupation as wife and mother, the other . . . emancipates herself from that calling but in her periods thinks forcibly of it and thus develops a divided disposition' (*Psychological Abstracts*, 1928). This paper represents a continuation of the nineteenth-century idea that it is a psychological or constitutional weakness in women which causes them to experience menstrual dysfunctions if they step outside the traditional role, rather than the occupational hazards which they face. The hypothesis that women who adopt a non-traditional role (or have an 'unfeminine personality'), or experience psychological conflict about the role they should adopt, will experience more period pain or PMT is a recurrent theme in both psychoanalytic[7] and psychological papers during this period. So, for example, Karen Horney (1931b) attributes PMT to unconscious conflicts about the desire for a child which are triggered by the physical signs of impending menstruation, and Claude Daly (1935) describes a *menstruationskomplex* in similar terms (Lupton, 1993). By the 1950s and 1960s, psychologists had begun to investigate the role of personality and sex-role socialisation in the experience of, initially, dysmenorrhea but later PMT or PMS, with mixed results (e.g. Levitt and Lubin, 1967; Coppen and Kessel, 1963). Psychiatric (rather than psychoanalytic) interest in PMT or PMS did not really become established until the 1960s, when the simple hormonal explanations of women's experiences began to be questioned (e.g. Janowsky *et al.*,1966).

A final theme which emerges at this time is interest in women's periodicity, that is, in the study of the menstrual cycle as an example of a biological rhythm which may influence levels of arousal or physical states. As long ago as 1840, Thomas Laycock introduced the notion of rhythm or cyclicity in health and illness. His ideas were developed by Wilhelm Fliess among others, and through him influenced Freud's thinking (see Sulloway, 1980; Lupton, 1993). In industrial psychology, interest in optimal work rhythms was extensive between 1920 and 1965, although interest was directed predominantly towards daily (circadian) rhythms and the practical implication of the identification of the best timing for rest pauses to maximise efficiency (e.g. Knight, 1929). Leta Stetter Hollingworth's work was used to emphasise an absence of menstrual cyclicity in cognitive functions (Hollingworth and Poffenberger, 1918; Seward, 1944). Interest in emotional periodicity or cyclical fluctuations in behaviour, though, continued. Marie Stopes (1918) was among the first to suggest a monthly rhythm in women's sexual interest, a topic which has continued to intrigue researchers into the 1990s (see McNeill, 1994; chapter five). A number of other studies in the 1930s and 1940s investigated day-to-day fluctuations in women's emotions and well-being and related these to the hormonal cycle, using a variety of methodologies (e.g. Chadwick, 1933; Seward, 1934; McCance *et al.*, 1937; Benedek and Rubinstein, 1939a, 1939b; Altmann *et al.*, 1941; see chapter five and Sherman, 1971). These researchers are not exclusively concerned with the effect of menstruation itself on women's well-being, but in the 'interaction of endocrine and mental functions' (McCance *et al.*, 1937) and their findings will be discussed in chapter five. They represent the shift towards a hormonal explanation for all types of experience, not just distress or disorder, and they are generally concerned with ordinary women rather than those who are requesting help from a clinician.

Someone who combined an interest in the menstrual cycle with a psychoanalytic rather than endocrine interpretation of causal mechanisms is Mary Chadwick (1933). Her book *Women's Periodicity* is concerned with emotional fluctuations across the whole cycle, and she is interested in menstruation only as one aspect of a rhythm which affects every day of a woman's life. However, she does see menstruation as 'the climax of the rhythm, the highest point of the curve, since it generally provides the culminating point of tension' (Chadwick, 1933: 114–115). The psychological symptoms which women may experience around menstruation are, she argues, varied, and may have been 'unconsciously borrowed or imitated from somebody else who was known in childhood', or are 'a revival of some illness or psychological disturbance from which the patient suffered in childhood or during adolescence'. Another source of origin, she suggests, for menstrual pain particularly, is female masochism (Bonaparte, 1953) which may lead women to overexert themselves during menstruation and thereby worsen their physical discomfort. The idea that menstrual pain or PMT is self-induced features repeatedly (although usually in a less explicit form than this) in psychosomatic research until the 1970s, and its legacy has been an ongoing distrust of psychological research into the menstrual cycle by the popular media and women themselves (Walker, 1995b). Chadwick's work is a forerunner of research into the menstrual cycle, rather than menstruation itself, which is a feature of the next period of research.

The period from 1920 to 1965 was not a particularly fertile one for menstrual psychology. However, it was a time in which the issues which would preoccupy the next generation of researchers were identified. Most remarkable in this period is the virtual absence of feminist research outside the specifically work-related fields. Although many of the people working at this time were women, notably the analysts, they seemed largely unconcerned with the social implications for women of their findings. The influence of menstruation in women's lives is either denied, as in the case of industrial psychology, or related to the maternal drives which are seen to define femininity, as in the case of the analysts. Most psychologists were simply uninterested in or ignorant of menstruation. As Lupton (1993) suggests, menstruation is so taboo it is not even considered as a factor. At the end of this phase, we are left with the impression that menstruation is toxic, both to the woman herself and to others, that menstrual pain results from daring to challenge women's 'natural' role or unconscious masochism, and that while women may be able to work during menstruation they are liable to hormonal dysfunctions which make them over-emotional and unreliable premenstrually.

Biological rhythms and feminist empiricism 1965–1984

The 1970s saw a substantial growth in menstrual cycle psychology research (see Figure 2.1), stemming largely from three interacting influences. First among these is the new wave of feminism emerging in the late 1960s and early 1970s. This influence produced a new interest in women's experiences for their own sake and a critique of the medicalisation of reproduction. Suddenly, menstruation was of interest, and women both inside and outside academic institutions began talking and writing about their experiences. Products of these activities were books such as *Our Bodies Ourselves* (Boston Women's Health Book Collective, 1978; British edition Phillips and Rakusen, 1989), *The Curse* (Delaney *et al.*, 1988) and *Menstruation and Menopause* (Weideger, 1976),[8] historical papers about medical attitudes towards menstruation (e.g. Showalter and Showalter, 1970; Wood, 1973; Bullough and Voght, 1973) and consideration of the menstrual cycle in the new psychology of women texts (e.g. Bardwick, 1971; Sherman, 1971). A new awareness of the implications of medicalisation for women led some psychologists to ask new questions about menstruation and to challenge the biologically reductionist assumptions of medical research. A new generation of mostly North American liberal feminist hero-innovators (Ussher, 1992b) had emerged, including women such as Diane Ruble, Mary Brown Parlee, Jeanne Brooks Gunn, Judith Rodin, Randi Koeske, Barbara Sommer and Karen Paige Erickson. The task which these researchers set themselves was to challenge not only the folklore surrounding menstruation, but also the assumptions of (predominantly psychosomatic) medical research, using the methods of science in general and psychology in particular, in the same way that Leta Stetter Hollingworth had done fifty years before.

Two further strands of influence, in the early 1970s particularly, were the concern with biological rhythms in psychology and the development of sex differences research (e.g. Maccoby and Jacklin, 1974). Applied psychologists had become increasingly interested in the effect of circadian rhythms on human performance. These researchers, concerned particularly with aspects of cognition, developed increasingly sensitive measures of arousal and performance, applying them to the study of the menstrual cycle (e.g. Asso, 1978; Asso and Beech, 1975; Patkai *et al.*,1974). The debate around sex differences research was (and continues to be) heated, with most of the effort and energy spent on studies of intelligence and specific cognitive abilities in men and women. The development and political motivations of this research have been described elsewhere (e.g. Fausto-Sterling, 1992). Some researchers, however, turned to psychological studies of the menstrual cycle to shed light on assumed sex differences. This was one of the chief motivations of De Marchi (1976), for example, who in describing the rationale for a two-year study of the psychophysiology of the menstrual cycle notes an interest in 'the menstrual cycle itself and the implications it has for sex differences and mood changes' (De Marchi, 1976: 279).

Within this period, a concern with the normative experiences of women across the menstrual cycle continued. These studies were usually justified on the basis of the contradictory findings of previous studies, or as an attempt to provide comparative data for the clinical studies concerned with premenstrual syndrome. Most of these studies required daily self-reports of mood and well-being, and sometimes regular hormone measures over at least one menstrual cycle. Participants in most of these studies were young women, usually college students. Examples of these studies include Wilcoxon *et al.* (1976), Ablanalp *et al.* (1979a, 1979b), Zimmerman and Parlee (1973), Englander-Golden *et al.* (1978), Little and Zahn (1974); their findings are discussed in chapter five. The growing use of the oral contraceptive pill meant that many women were experiencing artificial 'menstrual' cycles, and several of these studies investigated the possibility that the experiences of these women might be different (e.g. Paige, 1971; Morris and Udry, 1972).

PMS research continued during this time, and by now had become the subject of most of the papers published in the field. Most of these studies were conducted from a biomedical or psychosomatic perspective and were concerned to test new and adapted theories of the causes of premenstrual syndrome. Studies of possible endocrine factors in PMS continued, becoming more sophisticated as measures of circulating hormones were developed (e.g. Backstrom and Carstensen, 1974; Backstrom and Mattson, 1975; Backstrom *et al.*, 1983). New features in this period are the association of PMS with depression, leading to (or justifying) a greater psychiatric involvement, and the development of questionnaires to identify PMS and methodologies to investigate it. The link with depression was to be crucial for the future development of PMS research, and the ultimate inclusion of premenstrual dysphoric disorder in DSM IV in the 1990s. While psychiatrists have always been interested in premenstrual mood states, this is the first period in which there are as many articles in psychiatric journals as there are in gynaecological ones. The reason for this is the increased concern about the levels of depression among women (see, for example, Brown and Harris, 1978). The possibility that 'the occurrence of affective symptoms premenstrually may indicate a susceptibility to develop clinical depression' (Wetzel *et al.*,1975) led to a renewed research interest, both among clinicians seeking inspiration about the causes of PMS and among those looking for an appropriate model of depression to use in clinical trials. Hence, for example, a number of studies investigate monoamine oxidase levels during the cycle, especially in women with PMS (e.g. Feine *et al.*, 1977; Belmaker *et al.*, 1974; Gilmore *et al.*, 1971). Monoamine oxidase inhibitors formed the basis for the new generation of anti-depressant drugs emerging in the 1970s.

A concern with the identification and measurement of premenstrual experiences led to an increased involvement of psychologists in this area in the 1970s.

The early epidemiological studies had produced varied estimates of its prevalence, based on assessments of differing combinations of 'symptoms' in questionnaires designed for each study. The resulting confusion was attributed, as has consistently been the case in PMS research, to inaccurate or unscientific methods (e.g. Moos, 1968; Parlee, 1973). As a result, some effort was spent in the design of standard questionnaires to assess menstrual or premenstrual experiences. The best known of these is the Moos Menstrual Distress Questionnaire (Moos, 1968; Moos *et al.*, 1969), but there were others, such as the Menstrual Symptom Questionnaire (Chesney and Tasto, 1975). A number of studies followed, developing, testing and criticising these measures (e.g. Rouse, 1978; Markum, 1976; Sampson and Jenner, 1977; Parlee, 1973; Parlee, 1974). In addition to this concern about the measurement of PMS, researchers began to show concern about the methodology of menstrual cycle research in general (see chapter three) and to point out its lack of scientific rigour (e.g. Koeske, 1981). The notion that the truth about menstrual cycle experiences will emerge if only we can get the methodology right began in the 1970s, and led not only to concerns about measurement but also to concerns about the best ways of testing treatments for PMS. The first randomised controlled trials of treatments were conducted in the 1970s (e.g. Silbergeld *et al.*, 1971; Sampson, 1979).

Finally in this period is the development of social psychological research concerned with attitudes towards menstruation and expectations about menstrual experiences. Most of this research was conducted by psychologists who were keen to demonstrate that social factors as well as biological ones determine women's experience. Most of them are concerned with the expectations held by adolescent girls (and boys) about menstruation (e.g. Clarke and Ruble, 1978; Golub and Harrington, 1981; Brooks *et al.*, 1977). Others use social psychological research about the effect of expectations on behaviour and self perception (e.g. Schachter and Singer, 1962; Rosenthal and Jacobson, 1968) to develop and test a social cognition model of menstrual and premenstrual symptoms (Ruble, 1977; Ruble and Brooks Gunn, 1979; Rodin, 1976; Koeske and Koeske, 1975; Schneider and Schneider-Düker, 1974). Another, and related, group of studies investigated the attitudes of adult men and women towards menstruation, and their needs from a health education perspective (e.g. Brooks *et al.*, 1977; Dunham, 1970; Snow and Johnson, 1977).

Throughout the 1970s, the increased acceptance of discussion about menstruation and acknowledgement of women's experiences led to an increase in the number of women identifying themselves as PMS sufferers. These women turned to medical practitioners for help, and a number of specialist clinics were set up in Britain and North America. Most women, though, would be seen by non-specialist gynaecologists, psychiatrists or general practitioners. For these women, and their doctors, there was a dearth of readily accessible and easily digestible information about premenstrual experiences. The only books which fitted this description in the late 1970s were those by Dr Katharina Dalton, in particular *The Menstrual Cycle* (1969) and *Once a Month* (1978). Not surprisingly, she was hailed as a heroine by feminists and non-feminists alike, and her theory that premenstrual symptoms are caused by an imbalance or deficiency of progesterone became very popular. Her views equally fitted the hormonal discourse familiar to both medical and lay readers and the 'women's experiences are real' discourse developing in the new women's movement. By the end of this period, voices were being raised against her work from both groups, on grounds of inappropriate methodology from medical researchers (e.g. Sampson, 1979) and promotion of the medicalisation of women from radical feminists (e.g. Laws *et al.*, 1985). By the 1990s, the credibility of her early research in academic circles was running low. For many women, though, she is still perceived as the only person in authority who is concerned primarily with real, individual women (rather than women in general or abstract terms), who understands their experiences and who offers hope of a 'cure' for what they perceive as a disease. This continues to make her a popular figure in the media and a powerful inspiration for the self-help movement.

The period from 1965 to 1984 sees menstrual cycle research and PMS research become established in psychology, psychiatry and gynaecology. Research in these disciplines largely appears to be independent. There is some overlap between gynaecological and psychiatric research, although – with some notable exceptions – few studies could be said to be interdisciplinary. There is much less evidence of a dialogue between psychological research, generally concerned with normative experiences, and medical research. Some papers have had a considerable impact on medical research (e.g. Parlee, 1973; Ruble, 1977) but this is more in the context of a concern about methodology rather than the development of theory. Similarly, there is very little dialogue between either psychologists or medical scientists and other researchers in the social sciences (e.g. historians, sociologists and anthropologists). Towards the end of this period, Mary Parlee (1981), reviewing the field from a psychologist's point of view, is optimistic about the development of psychological theory in menstrual cycle research, but points to the need to fill in the numerous gaps – particularly the gaps regarding individual and subcultural differences between women. She concludes by observing the different perspectives of the various researchers asking questions about the menstrual cycle, and argues that the cross-disciplinary gaps need to be transcended to allow further progress. Whether this is possible is, she notes, 'an open question'. So, at the end of this period, researchers from the different disciplines are largely 'ploughing their own furrows'. A fragile psychology of the menstrual cycle is growing beside the more robust medical research, but is still at the 'problem-finding, question-formulating' stage rather than a problem-solving or theoretical stage.

PMS hysteria 1985–1994

Menstrual cycle research grew steadily during the 1970s and early 1980s, but suddenly increased dramatically in volume in the mid-1980s (see Figure 2.1).

The main trigger for this was the use of PMS as a defence, or at least a mitigating factor, in two murder trials in the early 1980s (Eagan, 1985). Suddenly,
PMS was in the news, arousing the interest of researchers who might be classed
as 'accidental tourists' (Ussher, 1992b), but also galvanising both biomedical
researchers and radical feminist social scientists. The output of psychologists who
have been, by and large, liberal feminists, committed to what Sandra Harding
(1991) calls 'feminist empiricism', has continued, but has made little impact on
the public perception of menstrual cycle research.

The concern of medical researchers with the development of questionnaires
and techniques to measure premenstrual symptoms was increased by the
publicity surrounding the trials. The need now became the identification of the
'true' PMS sufferer from women whose experiences were not specifically
menstrually related, or not severe enough to justify medical attention (e.g. Hart *et
al.*, 1987; Schnurr, 1989; Metcalf *et al.*, 1989a; Morse and Dennerstein, 1988;
Rubinow *et al.*, 1986). This activity was particularly pronounced among psychiatric researchers, who were concerned about the inclusion of PMS in the
Diagnostic and Statistical Manual of Psychiatric Mental Disorders (DSM).
Diagnostic criteria were identified (see Gise *et al.*, 1990; Gold and Severino,
1994), and PMS was included as 'late luteal phase dysphoric disorder', a topic
for further study in the appendix of DSM IIIR, published in 1987. This sparked
a series of new studies testing and developing the diagnostic criteria (e.g. Gallant
et al., 1992a; 1992b), and more debate about the nature and causes of PMS, and
whether it should be included in the main text of the next edition of DSM. After
heated discussions, it was included in DSM IV as 'premenstrual phase dysphoric
disorder'. This discussion and research into the nature of PMS has led to speculation that there may be not one premenstrual syndrome but several (e.g. Gise,
1988) and questions about the validity of the concept (e.g. Bancroft *et al.*, 1993;
Bancroft, 1993). The majority of biomedical research continues, though, as if
PMS were a simple, unitary condition. Aetiological studies have investigated
numerous possible causal mechanisms in the last ten years, with an increasing
emphasis on links between premenstrual dysphoria and clinical depression (e.g.
Warner *et al.*, 1991; Mackenzie *et al.*, 1986; Halbriech and Endicott, 1985), and
the role of neuroendocrine factors in PMS (e.g. Dinan and O'Keane, 1991).
Studies with a greater gynaecological than psychiatric orientation continued to
examine the efficacy of various forms of exogenous oestrogen (as 'patches' or
implants) and progesterone, as well as hysterectomy and surgical or medical
ovariectomy (e.g. Schmidt *et al.*,1991; Metcalf *et al.*, 1992; Dennerstein *et al.*,
1986). Interest in diet, nutritional supplements and exercise as treatments for
PMS also grew in this period, in response to a growing 'self-help' movement.[9]

Non-medical researchers continue to investigate normative menstrual cycle
experiences over these ten years, although such studies are very much in the
minority. The continuation of this research owes much to the development of
new journals concerned with women rather than with illness, for example
Psychology of Women Quarterly and *Health Care for Women International*, and the

Society for Menstrual Cycle Research, founded in 1977, which provides a forum for presentation and discussion of a range of research from a broadly liberal feminist tradition (e.g. Taylor and Woods, 1991; Dan and Lewis, 1992). Most of these studies investigate the claim that all women experience significant premenstrual changes (e.g. Slade, 1984; Jarvis and McCabe, 1991; Ainscough, 1990), generally suggesting that premenstrual debilitation is not universal. These researchers are also keen to demonstrate the extent of menstrually related changes in relation to other cyclical patterns, such as fluctuation over days of the week (e.g. McFarlane *et al.*, 1988), and to investigate the variability of experience between individuals and between cycles (e.g. Walker, 1994a). Positive experiences are investigated (e.g. Logue and Moos, 1988; Stewart, 1989) and the wider context of women's lives is also considered, predominantly within the context of stress research and the conceptualisation of menstruation as a stressor (e.g. Collins *et al.*, 1985; Gannon *et al.*, 1989; Choi and Salmon, 1995b). Demonstrations of expectations surrounding menstruation continue (e.g. Walker, 1992b) and the effect of manipulating expectations is tested (e.g. Olasov and Jackson, 1987; Chrisler *et al.*, 1994). Theoretically, there is a move towards 'integrated' models of menstrually related mood, which bring together biological, psychological and social components into one framework (e.g. Ussher, 1992b). The essence of this line of research is that it is reactionary. Studies are designed to challenge negative views of menstruation in both medicine and the popular media. So, not surprisingly, this research shows a similar concern with the premenstrual phase of the cycle rather than the cycle as a whole, even in studies which emphasise that they are not concerned with PMS. Little of either this or the gynaecological/psychiatric research considers the physical experiences (e.g. breast tenderness, dysmenorrhea, headache) which women report around menstruation and how these may interact with emotional or cognitive states; the emphasis is clearly on the explanation of depression and irritability.

This decade is significant too for the development of a radical feminist critique of science in general and the concept of PMS/PMT. One of the most eloquent expressions of the political implications of the concept of PMS for women is that of Sophie Laws, Valerie Hey and Andrea Eagan (1985). Cyclical change is not denied in these critiques – what is questioned is the construction of these fluctuations as evidence of sickness, and the description of PMT/PMS as a disease. Who needs PMT, Laws (1985) asks, and who benefits from its existence? The beneficiaries, she argues, are not the majority of women, whose anger or physical pain is dismissed as the result of PMT – 'it's just the time of the month' – or who are exposed to a variety of treatments whose long-term side-effects are unknown. Rather, the beneficiaries are, specifically, drug companies and others who sell remedies to women and, generally, patriarchal society which attributes any 'inconvenient' female behaviour to her hormones, rather than having to deal with the realities of women's lives or experiences (which may involve change for men themselves). The question we ask ourselves, she argues, 'should not be: do I have PMT? It should be: why have the changes I am used to going through with my menstrual cycle become intolerable to me?' (Laws, 1985: 58). This type of criticism has allowed a new form of menstrual cycle research to develop. Studies which deconstruct cultural notions of femininity and menstruation begin to emerge in this period (e.g. Ussher, 1989; Nicolson, 1992; Martin, 1989; Laws, 1990; Johnson, 1987; Rittenhouse, 1991; Rodin, 1992), as do studies which investigate the meaning of menstruation and PMS/PMT in women's lives by talking to women rather than measuring their mood state (e.g. Martin, 1989; Swann and Ussher, 1995). Unlike liberal feminist research, these studies question the usefulness of traditional positivist methodologies for describing or under-standing women's experience, and are moving towards the development of a new feminist social science (see Morawski, 1994).

CONCLUSIONS

This chapter has shown that menstrual cycle research is not a recent phenomenon, and that it has been influenced at every stage by cultural ideas about menstruation and gender politics. Early studies were concerned to demon-strate that women are not incapacitated by menstruation, and modern liberal feminists still design studies to test the assumption that we are. The invention, or discovery, of a new syndrome, PMT, allowed the belief that women are ruled by their reproductive capacities to persist in a modern form. The fact that many women do experience distress, whether menstrually related or not, led to problems both for those who believe that hormones lie at the root of women's 'problems' and for those who don't. Evidence of this is seen in the media debates about the existence of PMT (see Walker, 1995b) in which 'doctors' are seen as arguing that PMS exists and is a disease, while 'psychologists' or 'feminists' are said to believe that PMS does not exist and is 'all in the mind'. The 'yes, it does; no, it doesn't' argument about whether menstruation affects women adversely (either in the form of debilitation or as madness) is alive and kicking over a hundred years after Edward Clarke published his 'gloomy little specter'[10] of a book.

3

METHODS IN MENSTRUAL CYCLE RESEARCH

One of the few things about which menstrual cycle researchers of all perspectives agree is the methodological complexity of their chosen task. Whether the researcher is bewailing the difficulty of PMS diagnosis or berating statistics linking menstruation with poor work performance, lack of rigour in methodology is a universal attribution for inconclusive findings. Deviation from the currently advocated ideal is the most common reason for rejection of findings which fail to concur with the author's thesis. This is not only true of menstrual cycle research, of course; it is a frequent occurrence in science. However, the 'methodological minefield' of menstrual cycle research is commented upon in almost every review of the subject, and often accorded more space in discussion than the findings of the research (see Fausto-Sterling, 1992). Indeed, several authoritative reviews are devoted to the subject of methodological complexity in menstrual cycle research (e.g. Koeske, 1981; Rubinow and Roy-Byrne, 1984; Brooks Gunn, 1986; Halbriech and Endicott, 1985). The aim of this chapter is to describe the major methods used by menstrual cycle researchers and to outline the issues which the use of these methodologies has raised.

With the exception of those scientists concerned exclusively with the physiology of the menstrual cycle, the majority of questions being addressed by menstrual cycle researchers are, broadly speaking, psychological. They are concerned with whether the menstrual cycle has an effect (direct or indirect) on thoughts, feelings and actions. The approach taken to answering this question by most psychologists and biomedical researchers has been a positivist one, grounded in the methods and principles of what has become 'traditional' science. This approach depends fundamentally on measurement and quantification of the phenomenon which is to be established and explained. Once this has been achieved, questions about causal mechanisms are addressed. The phenomenon which clinicians and psychologists are attempting to describe and explain differs, but the methods they have used to investigate it are very similar. Clinicians and biomedical researchers have been concerned to describe and explain a dysfunctional state occurring in the days before and/or during menstruation. Psychologists, on the other hand, have been concerned with the relationship between physiological and psychological states throughout the menstrual cycle. These two purposes often overlap: psychologists are sometimes concerned with dysfunctional states and medical researchers are occasionally interested in 'normal' states, for example. Studies within the positivist tradition can be divided into four broad categories: descriptive, correlational, quasi-experimental and experimental (Rosenthal and Rosnow, 1991). In all four, methodological questions are raised about what to measure, how often, and what to do with the data which is collected as a result of the research, so these issues will be discussed first. The measures used are principally of cognitive state, mood and well-being, and physiological aspects of the menstrual cycle. The question of whether any of these approaches has brought us any nearer to an understanding of how individual women feel, either just before menstruation or at any other part of the cycle, and why researchers still feel dissatisfied with the measures used, will be addressed in chapter seven. This chapter will simply review the various measures and techniques which have been used and aims to provide a guide through the 'methodological minefield'.

MEASURES OF PSYCHOLOGICAL STATE

The first problem facing the menstrual cycle researcher asking, from a positivist perspective, whether women's mental and physical state is affected by the menstrual cycle, is what to measure and how. As almost any human physical, emotional or cognitive state has been attributed to menstruation, it is a puzzle to know where to start. One group of researchers, predominantly psychologists, have followed in the footsteps of Leta Stetter Hollingworth, and have investigated cognitive functioning during the cycle. These researchers have used a wide variety of standardised and unstandardised psychological tests to measure sensory ability, memory, perceptual functions, information-processing ability, hand-eye co-ordination and so on.[1] The other group of researchers, predominantly clinicians or psychologists concerned with women reporting menstrual distress, have been concerned with the assessment of mood and well-being during the cycle. This group, to a greater extent than the cognitive function group, have focused on the measurement of mood and physical state before or during menstruation. The measures they have used and invented have often been designed to discriminate between the presence or absence of psychological distress, such as depression, in the premenstrual days. These can be used either to differentiate between those women whose premenstrual experiences warrant clinical attention and those whose do not (in the view of the clinician), or to demonstrate that one part of the cycle is quantitatively different from another on measures of distress, either within an individual or across groups of women. It is in the area of mood measurement that menstrual cycle research methodology has become most complex. In particular, the number and variety of measures used to assess well-being has grown disproportionately. It is hard to resist the interpretation that researchers criticise the measures used by others when the results do not fit their own preconceived ideas. So, those who feel that most women are unaffected emotionally by the physiological process of menstruation argue that the methods used by those who believe that most women are, are biased, imprecise or insufficiently rigorous. In the other direction, the detailed and painstaking methods of those who wish to demonstrate that the menstrual cycle is not a major influence for most women are criticised as requiring unethical amounts of data collection, and the participation of an unrepresentative and highly motivated educated middle-class volunteer sample. Both sets of criticisms are equally valid. The many measures used in menstrual cycle research range from the almost flippant retrospective symptom check list to the detailed completion of batteries of questionnaires daily for three months or more (see Table 3.1). The key features of these are outlined below (see also Budieri et al., 1994).

Retrospective questionnaires

As indicated earlier, most of the heated debate in menstrual cycle research methodology has focused around how to measure mood and well-being, and particularly how to differentiate between 'distress' and 'normal' states. Researchers are inordinately concerned with, as Mitchell et al. (1991) put it, 'recognizing PMS when you see it'. Early menstrual cycle studies used a variety of techniques to investigate women's experience across the cycle. For example, Benedek and Rubenstein (1939a, 1939b) correlated daily psychoanalytic sessions, usually based on dream analysis, with physiological assessments of the ovarian cycle. This degree of systematic investigation was rare, however, and most studies based the assessment of distress on clinical impression and the spontaneous accounts of women requesting treatment (e.g. Frank, 1931; Israel, 1938; Morton, 1950). By the 1960s, these approaches were being criticised for their lack of objectivity and emphasis only on clinical samples, and a number of studies were designed to assess the prevalence of premenstrual symptoms in the general population using questionnaires (e.g. Pennington, 1957; Coppen and Kessel, 1963; Kessel and Coppen, 1963). These studies were themselves criticised for lack of rigour by researchers who pointed out that the questionnaires they had used asked only about a limited range of premenstrual experiences, and had not been designed following psychometric principles. They assess, for instance, only the occurrence of particular states, and not their degree of severity. The first attempt to devise a premenstrual symptoms questionnaire using psychometric principles was made by Rudolf Moos and his colleagues in the late 1960s (Moos, 1968; Moos et al., 1969). The instrument which resulted, the Menstrual Distress Questionnaire (MDQ) remains the most widely used single instrument in menstrual cycle research, although much modified and extensively criticised (see Richardson, 1990).

The original version of the MDQ contains a list of 47 experiences, each of which women are asked to rate for severity on a 6-point scale. The 'symptom' list was obtained from a literature review of 'menstrual cycle symptomatology' and open-ended interviews with an unspecified number of women about their

Table 3.1 Questionnaires used to assess mood and well-being

Specific retrospective	Specific prospective	Non-specific prospective
Moos Menstrual Distress Questionnaire (MDQ) Moos, 1968	MDQ ('Today' form) Moos et al., 1969	Profile of Mood States McNair et al., 1971
Premenstrual Assessment Form (PAF) Halbriech et al., 1982	PAF Daily Rating Form Halbriech et al., 1982	Multiple Affect Adjective Check List (MAACL) Zuckerman and Lubin, 1965
Premenstrual Rating Scale (PMRS) Steiner et al., 1980	Patient Self Report Symptoms Calendar Plouffe et al., 1993	Beck Depression Inventory Beck et al., 1961
Menstrual Symptom Questionnaire (MSQ) Chesney and Tasto, 1975	PRISM Reid, 1985	State-Trait Anxiety Inventory ('State' form) Spielberger et al., 1970
Menstrual Health Questionnaire Warner and Bancroft, 1990	Calendar of Premenstrual Experiences (COPE) Mortola et al., 1990	Green-Nowlis Mood Adjective Check List Nowlis, 1965
Menstrual Attitude Questionnaire Brooks, Gunn and Ruble, 1980	Daily Symptom Rating Scale Taylor, 1979	Hamilton Depression Scale Hamilton, 1967
	Washington Women's Health Diary Mitchell et al., 1994	Carroll Depression Scale Feinberg et al., 1981
	Menstrual Symptom Severity List Mitchell, Woods and Lentz, 1991	Emotions Profile Index Plutchik and Kellerman, 1974
	Daily Well-Being Form Mansfield et al., 1989	Eight State Questionnaire Curran and Cattell, 1976
	Daily Life Experiences Questionnaire Schechter et al., 1989	Depression Adjective Checklist Lubin, 1967
	PMT-Cator Magos and Studd, 1988	Thayer Activation–Deactivation Check List Thayer, 1967
	Utah PMS Calendar Speroff et al., 1984	Differential Emotions Scale IV Izard et al., 1974, cited in Boyle, 1985
	Daily Self Report Questionnaire Ripper, 1991	Taylor Manifest Anxiety Scale Cattell and Scheier, 1961

menstrual experiences. In addition a number of experiences which were not expected to vary across the cycle were included as control items. These were taken from an index of menopausal symptoms (Moos, 1968). The final question-naire was completed by '839 wives of graduate students at a large western university' (Moos, 1968), who rated the severity of each of the 47 experiences in the menstrual, premenstrual and intermenstrual phases of both their most recent and 'worst' menstrual cycle. After collecting this data, Moos factor analysed the scores and produced a set of 8 factors, which became subscales of the question-naire. These were labelled pain, concentration, behavioural change, autonomic reactions, water retention, negative affect, arousal and control, and accounted for 46 of the items on the questionnaire. Scores on the remaining item, 'change in eating habits', did not correlate consistently with any of the 8 factors. Moos found a statistically significant difference between the reports of symptom severity in the different cycle phases for 6 of the subscales, but not for arousal or control. He also reported the prevalence of mild/moderate and strong/severe symptoms in the different cycle phases. The prevalence of mild/moderate levels in the premenstrual phase ranges from 1.2 per cent for 'suffocation' (a control item) to 39.2 per cent for irritability (a negative affect item). Strong/severe reports were obtained from between 0.1 per cent (suffocation) and 13.0 per cent (irritability) of women in the same phase (see chapters four and five). Later versions of the MDQ have been modified to incorporate a 4-point scale rather than the original 6-point scale, and a daily rating form has been produced. In addition, many researchers have modified the instructions and title of the MDQ in studies, to reduce its perceived negative bias or to disguise the researcher's interest in menstrually related experiences (e.g. Slade, 1984).

From a psychometric perspective, the MDQ is criticised for inadequacies in scale construction and the factor analysis which produced subscales (Richardson, 1990). The sample used to validate the MDQ was relatively large but remarkably homogeneous in terms of age (mean 25.2 years, standard deviation 3.9) and years of education (mean 15.2, standard deviation 1.7). The only reported demographic factor which varied in the group was the number of children the women had, but even in this respect the group was very similar, with 472 of the 839 women having no children. Not surprisingly, the scores and factor structure of the questionnaire differ from Moos's original findings if an older, treatment-seeking group of women is sampled (e.g. Morse and Dennerstein, 1988). From a feminist perspective, the MDQ is criticised for its emphasis on negative experi-ences, such as depression and irritability, and the possibility of stereotypical reporting of experiences retrospectively (e.g. Parlee, 1974). From a clinical perspective, the MDQ is criticised either because it is too long or because it is too short. Steiner et al. (1980) argue that the MDQ is inadequate because it covers a broad range of phenomena and is 'less helpful in measuring the particular changes which occur in PMTS (premenstrual tension syndrome)' (Steiner et al., 1980: 178). Hence, they constructed a new checklist-type scale, based on the MDQ but containing a list of 36 questions to be answered yes or no (e.g. 'Have you gained five or more pounds during the past week?', 'Do you feel confused?') which they called the Premenstrual Rating Scale (PMRS). In addition to this, a 10-item observer-rating scale was devised for the clinician to use for diagnosis of what they call 'premenstrual tension syndrome' (PMTS). The PMRS has not been widely used in research, although on the basis of a factor analysis of it John Condon argues that it may be a useful measure of 'pure' PMS (Condon, 1993). While Steiner and his colleagues were concerned about the length and complexity of the MDQ biasing diagnosis, Uriel Halbriech, Jean Endicott and their colleagues (e.g. Halbriech *et al.*, 1982; 1985) were unhappy about its brevity. In their development of the Premenstrual Assessment Form (PAF), they argue that 'a greater variety of items and descriptive specificity was needed to increase the sensitivity for differentiating among different types of changes'(Halbriech *et al.*, 1982: 48). As a result the PAF is over twice as long as the MDQ, with 95 items included in the final version.

The PAF is an increasingly popular questionnaire in menstrual cycle research. Its purpose, like the PMRS but unlike the MDQ, is to identify levels of premenstrual change or distress which are clinically important – that is, which are thought by the clinician to warrant therapeutic intervention. Primarily, it is intended as an initial screening instrument for clinical use, or for allocation of women to different groups for research purposes. It is often used as the only means of diagnosis, although its authors intended that it should be just one of a number of different clinical assessments (see Halbriech *et al.*, 1985). Its authors criticise both the MDQ and the PMRS for their assumption that there is a single premenstrual syndrome which combines different types of premenstrual change. Halbriech and Endicott argue that there may be different types or dimensions of 'premenstrual changes', which are obscured by squashing 'symptoms' together into a single dimension. They also criticise other scales for failing to provide a cut-off point distinguishing between levels of distress which are of clinical importance and those which are not, and for focusing on absolute levels of experience in different parts of the cycle rather than on the degree of change in experiences from one part of the cycle to another. Hence, the ideological basis of the PAF is quite different from that of the MDQ or PMRS, and it is fundamentally a psychiatric rather than a psychological measuring instrument.

The initial pool of items from which the PAF is derived was identified using similar techniques to those of Moos and his colleagues. A pool of 200 items was selected from the research literature and existing questionnaires, added to by Halbriech and Endicott, on the basis of their own clinical experience, and a group of 40 'female staff members'. This pool was reduced to 150 by combining items that 'apparently described the same type of change' and reduced again on the basis of item analysis and intercorrelations after the questionnaire had been completed by 154 women. Relatively little information is given about this group of women. They were all experiencing regular menstrual cycles and not taking oral contraceptives. They were recruited from among medical centre staff (69) and student nurses (85), with average ages of 34 years and 24 years respectively

(Halbriech *et al.*, 1982). These women represent a wider age range than those in Moos's sample, but it is difficult to assess their educational level and no information is given about the number of children they had or other social or demographic characteristics. The sample size is also relatively small for reliable psychometric questionnaire development.[2] The 95 PAF items are rated for their 'level of change during the last three premenstrual periods' on a scale ranging from 1, indicating not applicable or no change from usual level, to 6, indicating extreme change. Hence, the woman herself indicates whether the degree of change which she experiences premenstrually is tolerable or not, rather than this being inferred, as in the MDQ, by calculating the difference between ratings of the amount of an experience felt in different phases. Items vary from 'have headaches or migraines' to 'feel depressed' or 'tend to "nag" or quarrel over unimportant issues'.

The PAF can be scored or analysed in at least three different ways. For psychiatric diagnosis, a woman can be assigned to one or more of several typological categories. These range from 'general discomfort syndrome' to 'major depressive syndrome', and include 'increased well-being syndrome' (see Table 3.2). The decision about which PAF items should be considered indicative of which 'syndrome' was based on psychiatric criteria, not on statistical analysis of questionnaire scores. Hence, not surprisingly, the authors recommend that assignment to a particular diagnosis should be based on psychiatric interviews and daily ratings as well as PAF scores, and outline specific diagnostic criteria for each of them (Halbriech and Endicott, 1982; Halbriech *et al.*, 1985). In addition to this typological classification, the PAF can be scored on the basis of 'unipolar summary scales'. These 18 subscales are of items which were found to be inter-correlated and/or have high alpha coefficients of internal consistency between them (Halbriech *et al.*, 1982); the PAF was not factor analysed because the validation sample of 154 was too small. The subscales are shown in Table 3.2. These quantitative scores can be used, they suggest, in correlational studies of menstrual well-being. Finally, they point out that some women report apparently contradictory premenstrual experiences – for example, reporting both increased and decreased energy. To take account of this, they combined several of the PAF items into 7 bipolar constructs (see Table 3.2). They indicate that 'subjects who rate items descriptive of changes in both directions are tagged as having "bipolar" changes and not given a summary score on either pole of the bipolar continua' (Halbriech *et al.*, 1982: 50).

The PAF has been less criticised than the Moos MDQ, partly because the vogue for retrospective questionnaires has been overtaken by a fashion for prospective assessment and particularly daily ratings of well-being (see below), diverting the attention of researchers and critics. It is, as Richardson (1990) notes, a psychiatric questionnaire designed to identify particular 'syndromes' with criteria based more on clinical judgement than statistical principles. As such, many of the criticisms of it relate to the conceptualisation of menstrual experiences in psychiatric terms (see chapters five and six). A major concern with

Table 3.2   Subscales of the Premenstrual Assessment Form

Typological categories	Unipolar summary scales	Bipolar continua
General discomfort syndrome	Low mood/loss of pleasure Impulsivity	Psychomotor activity (agitated–retarded)
Water retention syndrome	Endogeneous depressive features Organic mental features	Appetite (increased–decreased)
Fatigue syndrome	Lability Signs of water retention	Sleep (increased–decreased)
Autonomic physical syndrome	Atypical depressive features General physical discomfort	Sexual interest and activity (increased–decreased)
Major depressive syndrome	Hysteroid features Autonomic physical changes	Energy (increased–decreased)
Minor depressive syndrome	Hostility/Anger Fatigue	Goal-oriented activity (increased–decreased)
Anxious syndrome (not depressed)	Social withdrawal Impaired social functioning	Mood (depressed–increased well-being)
Irritable syndrome (not depressed)	Anxiety Miscellaneous mood/behaviour changes	
Impulsive syndrome	Increased well-being Miscellaneous physical changes	
Increased well-being syndrome Impaired social functioning Organic mental features		

Source: Adapted from Halbriech *et al.* (1982)

Note: Either of the depressive syndromes can be classified with subtypes of endogenous features, atypical features, hysteroid features, agitated anxious features, hostile features and/or withdrawn features.

the PAF is that it identifies large numbers of non-complaining women as having 'syndromes' (see Youdale and Freeman, 1987; Yuk *et al.*, 1990; Christensen and Oei, 1995a). In a study of 133 women who had responded to an advertisement asking for volunteers *without* menstrual or premenstrual problems to act as a control group for PMS research, only 27 (20.3 per cent) failed to meet criteria for one of the negative PAF syndromes (Yuk *et al.*, 1990). This underlines concerns of feminist researchers that women with 'normal' cyclical fluctuations may be labelled as psychiatrically ill, and raises questions about the usefulness of the PAF as a diagnostic instrument when used in the absence of other clinical assessments. The majority of studies which use the PAF, however, do not assign women to typological categories, but use total numbers of experiences rated or total scores to differentiate between levels of premenstrual symptomatology. For example, Gise *et al.* (1990) took the number of symptoms rated 5 or 6 as an index of severity, finding that 50 per cent of a sample of 79 women requesting help from a PMS clinic had 31 or more 'severe' or 'extreme' changes on the 95-item PAF. This reduces the number of women receiving a diagnosis, but given that the PAF contains positive as well as negative items and acknowledges the bipolarity of some women's experience, it is difficult to interpret such global scores. For many researchers, the PAF seems to be used as a sort of 'insurance' measure, among a battery of other instruments, with little consideration or analysis of the scores obtained. This contrasts with studies using the MDQ, which almost always report subscale scores at least, and often involve detailed critique of the scales (e.g. Parlee, 1974; Morse and Dennerstein, 1988). This may be a consequence of its length, which precludes reporting of scores for individual items or even summaries of the 18 'subscales'. A shortened 10-item version of the PAF has been developed by Sharon Allen and her colleagues (Allen *et al.*, 1991), based on a factor analysis of the 20 most frequently reported PAF items in a sample of 217 women taking part in a smoking cessation trial. The shortened PAF contains 3 subscales: affect (3 items), water retention (3 items) and pain (3 items), and so the emphasis is on physical states rather than psychological well-being, which may explain its lack of use in the psychiatric research literature.

The MDQ and the PAF are the most frequently used retrospective questionnaires to assess experiences around menstruation. Others which appear in the literature are the Menstrual Symptom Questionnaire (MSQ – Chesney and Tasto, 1975), the Menstrual Health Questionnaire (MHQ – Warner and Bancroft, 1990) and the Menstrual Joy Questionnaire (MJQ – Delaney *et al.*, 1988). The MSQ was designed primarily to assess menstrually related pain and to distinguish between 'spasmodic' and 'congestive' dysmenorrhea. It was developed using appropriate psychometric procedures on two samples of female students at Colorado State University. The result is a 25-item questionnaire, with 12 items loading on a 'congestive' dysmenorrhea factor and 12 on a 'spasmodic' dysmenorrhea factor. Chesney and Tasto (1975), following Dalton (1969), define 'congestive' dysmenorrhea as 'a variation or a symptom of the premenstrual syndrome with dull, aching pains accompanied by lethargy and depression prior to the onset of menstruation' (Chesney and Tasto, 1975: 237), so, as would be expected, there is considerable overlap between some of the items on the MSQ and the pain scales of the MDQ and shortened PAF. Subsequent studies of the MSQ with much larger samples, however, have failed to replicate the 2-factor structure which they obtained (Webster *et al.*, 1979; Webster, 1980; Stephenson *et al.*, 1983; Monagle *et al.*, 1986), finding either six or seven factors which are not unlike those of the MDQ. For example, Monagle *et al.* (1986) labelled their 6 factors premenstrual negative affect, menstrual pain, premenstrual pain, gastrointestinal/prostaglandin, water retention and asymptomatic. Clinical work, too, has suggested that the distinction between 'congestive' and 'spasmodic' dysmenorrhea is not aetiologically meaningful. While these two types of dysmenorrhea may be conceptually spurious, the MSQ may be a useful alternative retrospective measure to the MDQ if pain and physical state are the focus of interest.

The MDQ, PAF and MSQ are all designed along more or less psychometric lines, with the aim of identifying clusters of experiences which might represent different aspects of a premenstrual syndrome or syndromes. Researchers who are not interested in or convinced by the conceptualisation of menstrual experiences which these instruments imply have used questionnaires which are analysed on an item-by-item basis, hence avoiding assumptions about the syndromal nature of menstrually related experiences. These questionnaires are usually untitled. Typical of them is the Menstrual Health Questionnaire, designed by Pamela Warner and John Bancroft (Warner and Bancroft, 1988; 1990; Bancroft and Rennie, 1993; Bancroft et al., 1993). This questionnaire is not a psychometric instrument and does not attempt to measure or diagnose a 'premenstrual syndrome' or syndromes. It was designed to assess the prevalence of premenstrual and menstrual experiences (or 'symptoms') in a large-scale survey of readers of a British women's magazine. The list of experiences assessed is reminiscent of the items found in the MDQ or PAF; the differences lie in the style of rating and the form of analysis. The women are asked to rate each of the 27 'symptoms' on a 0–5 scale at three different points in their last menstrual cycle (the week before menstruation, during menstruation and the week after menstruation), and the data are analysed item by item, rather than as subscale scores. There are many questionnaires of this type in the literature, and they provide interesting descriptive information about women's retrospective accounts of their experience (e.g. Andersch et al., 1986; Taylor et al., 1991; Jorgensen et al., 1993; Kessel and Coppen, 1963; Boyle et al., 1987; Richardson, 1989). As with all retrospective questionnaires, they can be accused of bias (see below and Richardson, 1990), and findings from them are difficult to interpret because they differ from other reported questionnaires. The emphasis on experiences usually thought of as negative, such as depression and pain, is the key shortcoming of most of these questionnaires. Studies including positive items have found that these will be endorsed in addition to the negative ones (see Stewart, 1989; Logue and Moos, 1988; Chrisler et al., 1994). This has been most dramatically demonstrated by Joan Chrisler and her colleagues (Chrisler et al., 1994), who asked undergraduate students to complete both the MDQ and the Menstrual Joy Questionnaire (MJQ). The MJQ was devised by Delaney et al. ([1976] 1988) as a satirical comment on the overwhelming negativity of most menstrual cycle questionnaires. The MJQ uses the same format as the MDQ, but asks respondents to rate themselves on 10 positive items: high spirits, increased sexual desire, vibrant activity, revolutionary zeal, intense concentration, feelings of affection, self-confidence, sense of euphoria, creativity and feelings of power. The MJQ is neither a psychometric instrument nor widely used. It is, however, a salutary comment on the content of most retrospective questionnaires.

An influential criticism of all types of retrospective questionnaire has been that they are subject to response biases as a result of stereotypes, expectations, poor memory or intercycle variability (Richardson, 1990; Gannon, 1985; Parlee,

1994). The earliest empirical demonstration of this was reported by Mary Brown Parlee in 1974. She asked both men and women students to complete the MDQ, asking them to rate each item according to 'what women experience', rather than 'what you experience', as in the original instructions. The women in Parlee's study rated each of the items in a very similar way to those in Moos's (1968) sample. When the symptom scales were rank ordered according to the amount of 'change' between premenstrual or menstrual and intermenstrual phases, correlations of 0.95 and 0.98 were found between the rankings of women in both studies. Parlee then compared the men's ratings, which cannot be based on direct experience, with those of the women in her study, finding a correlation of 0.88 for both the premenstrual–intermenstrual change scores and the menstrual–intermenstrual change scores. The equivalent correlations with the women in Moos's study were 0.95 and 0.90 respectively. Comparisons of absolute scores in each phase showed that men's ratings indicated greater 'symptom severity' in each of the phases for all of the symptom scales, but that the pattern of scores was remarkably similar between the men and the women. Parlee suggests that a stereotype of menstrual experience may be influencing both the men's and the women's accounts in this study, and, given the similarity of their scores with those of the women in Moos's study, may also have been influencing his findings. This paper, together with Diane Ruble's study demonstrating increased 'symptom' reporting amongst women who were led to believe that they were premenstrual compared to those who were not (Ruble, 1977), has been remarkably influential in menstrual cycle research. This work has not only triggered a number of studies examining stereotypes about menstrual experiences (e.g. Walker, 1992b) and the effects of expectation on paramenstrual symptom reporting (e.g. Olasov and Jackson, 1987; AuBuchon and Calhoun, 1985; Chrisler et al., 1994), but has also convinced both medical and nonmedical researchers that prospective rather than retrospective data collection is needed in menstrual cycle research.[3] So strong has the prospective measurement dictum become that papers advocating some use of retrospective questionnaires are liable to provoke a critical response.[4] Hence, there has been a shift away from questionnaires towards prospective and daily measures.

The final measure which should be mentioned in this section is the Menstrual Attitudes Questionnaire (MAQ – Brooks Gunn and Ruble, 1980). This, as its name suggests, is not designed to measure physical or emotional well-being during the cycle, but the nature and strength of attitudes towards menstruation. It was developed as a consequence of the research described above, demonstrating the existence of stereotypes and expectations about menstruation. The original questionnaire was based on a sample of 191 young women students (average age 19 years), and the factor structure was replicated in a separate sample of 154 women students. The MAQ consists of 33 items which load on to 5 factors. These factors represent attitudes towards menstruation as debilitating, positive, predictable, bothersome, and as having no effects (Brooks Gunn and Ruble call this factor 'denial'). Each item on the MAQ is rated on a 7-point scale.

This questionnaire has been widely used as a 'routine' measure of menstrual attitudes (e.g. Olasov Rothbaum and Jackson, 1990; Brooks Gunn, 1985) but, as was the case for the MSQ, its factor structure has not always been replicated (e.g. Strauss *et al.*, 1987; Dye 1991). The questionnaire has also been criticised for including questions about the respondents' own feelings and experiences together with questions about the experience of women in general, possibly compromising its validity (Müller, 1991).

Prospective measures and daily ratings

Daily ratings of mood and well-being have been used in menstrual cycle research since the 1930s (e.g. McCance *et al.*, 1937; Benedek and Rubenstein, 1939a, 1939b; Altmann *et al.*, 1941). However, studies of this level of detail became less popular in the 1950s, as the development of questionnaires became the vogue. Now, retrospective questionnaires have lost favour in menstrual cycle research, and the majority of studies use either prospective or daily measurement. The crucial difference between these approaches and the retrospective one is that the state of the woman is assessed at the time of completing the questionnaire or test, rather than at some point in the past. Whereas retrospective studies are almost always cross-sectional, comparing the ratings of a number of women on a questionnaire or test which each has completed only once, prospective studies can be either cross-sectional or longitudinal, or may combine aspects of both. For example, Ramcharan *et al.* (1992) administered the 'Today' version of the MDQ (see below) once only to 6,232 women in the city of Calgary, and compared the prevalence of MDQ 'symptoms' at different points in the cycle by identifying each woman's cycle phase at the time of completion. This type of cross-sectional prospective study is relatively unusual; more often a prospective approach is synonymous with a longitudinal one.

The number of times during a cycle that a woman's state is measured varies, too, from two or three times to daily, across one cycle or several months. In studies of cognitive function , daily ratings are unusual because of the time-consuming nature of the tasks and the likelihood of practice effects. So, these studies usually sample performance at two or four points in the cycle (see Sommer, 1992, for a review). Among studies of mood and well-being, the criterion of confirmation of PMS (or LLPDD/PMDD – late luteal phase dysphoric disorder/premenstrual dysphoric disorder) through observation of two months of daily ratings specified in DSM IIIR and DSM IV has been influential. In recent years studies concerned with PMS have usually incorporated two months of daily ratings, even if the data obtained is not reported. This raises the question of what a daily rating means. For example, should women complete daily ratings to represent an average of their experiences during the day, or to describe their feelings at the time of completing the form? Studies vary in the instructions given to women on this point, although most ignore the issue. Diurnal variation in mood has been observed in menstrual cycle research (e.g. Rubinow *et al.*,

1984), leading some researchers to control for time of day effects on diary completion by asking women to fill in their forms at the same time each day, usually in the evening (e.g. R. Smith *et al.*,1995). Others have argued that the best way of avoiding diurnal and other systematic influences on diary completion is to randomly sample feelings across the day, asking participants to complete a diary when they are 'bleeped' – a technique called the 'experience sampling' method (Hamilton and Gallant, 1990; LeFevre *et al.*, 1992). This technique itself may cause difficulties since participants are always completing the diary in response to an irritating stimulus or interruption – a phenomenon which has been commented on in 'mainstream' emotion research.[5] Whichever method is used, it is difficult to know exactly how respondents are using the daily ratings, and how much inter-individual variability there is in their completion. My own studies with women using daily visual analogue scales suggested a degree of response drift over time, which it is difficult to take account of in analysis (see Walker, 1994a), and my impression was that some women were putting a great deal of thought and effort into diary completion while others were more lackadaisical. This raises the issue of what to do if a diary is missed. In some studies, participants are allowed to complete a missed diary on the following day (e.g. McFarlane and Williams, 1994); in others, any kind of retrospective data is excluded and participants are asked to submit blank diaries for days they have missed. Rarely, though, are researchers explicit about how they dealt with this missing or recalled data in their statistical analysis – or how much missing data was considered to exclude a participant from the study altogether (see analysis, below).

The widely used retrospective questionnaires have been modified to be suitable for daily or prospective assessment. The MDQ-T form (T stands for 'Today'), for instance, is identical to the retrospective MDQ apart from the inclusion of different instructions. The Daily Rating Form (DRF) version of the PAF is, however, much shorter (21 items). In addition to these a wide range of 'purpose-built' and nonspecific questionnaires have been used to assess menstrual cycle related states. The rationales for the use and development of these instruments fall into two categories. The first group are concerned with the validity of the measures being used. For example, standard mood measures, such as the Multiple Affect Adjective Check List (MAACL), are often advocated because they avoid the negative bias inherent in measures designed specifically to assess premenstrual or menstrual states. Similarly, widely accepted clinical rating scales, such as the Spielberger State-Trait Anxiety Inventory (STAI) or the Beck Depression Inventory (BDI), are justified on the grounds of investigating the similarity (or not) of menstrually related mood states with those associated with other psychiatric diagnoses (e.g. major depressive disorder).[6] The second group of rationales are concerned with study compliance. These researchers are concerned either with the ethical difficulties of asking women to complete lengthy questionnaires on a daily basis (e.g. Smith and Schiff, 1989) or with the need to ensure that as many women as possible complete the full study schedule.

Studies using this rationale choose measures which are as brief and easy to complete as possible (e.g. Schnurr *et al.*, 1994; Rubinow *et al.*, 1984); however, to date there has been no empirical demonstration that daily questionnaire length has an effect on study compliance.[7] The choice of shorter measures may have as much to do with the researcher's desire to reduce the amount of data generated as it does with a concern for the demand being made on the study participants.

No matter whether the study uses a nonspecific questionnaire or a brief, purpose-built one, issues of reliability and validity of the measures used are rarely addressed. Mood adjective checklists may be valid and reliable instruments for occasional use, but that does not mean that they are suitable for repeated daily completion over a lengthy time period. Similarly, few studies which use specially designed daily ratings forms describe their reliability or validity. This is particularly true of visual analogue scales (VAS), which have become very popular in menstrual cycle research. A visual analogue scale is a horizontal line, usually 100mm in length, with both extremes labelled. The respondent draws a vertical line at some point along the VAS to indicate how close she feels herself to be to one of the extremes. Visual analogue scales can be 'unipolar' or 'bipolar'. In the unipolar case, the extremes of the VAS are labelled with maximum and minimum intensities of a single experience, such as happiness. In the bipolar case, the extremes of the line are labelled with opposite types of experience, such as depressed–happy (Gift, 1989; Monk, 1989). Visual analogue scales were introduced in the 1970s as a quick and easy means of rating mood states, with high sensitivity to small fluctuations in mood, and without the limitations of response set which may occur if the same numerical scale is being used repeatedly (e.g. Aitken, 1969; Zealley and Aitken, 1969; Luria, 1975). They also have the advantage of producing data which can be treated as parametric for statistical purposes, unlike Likert-type scales which, strictly speaking, provide ordinal data which should be treated as nonparametric. They have been tested for repeated use, have demonstrated reliability in this context (Monk, 1989) and are advocated by a number of menstrual cycle researchers who have validated them against other scales (e.g. O'Brien, 1987; Casper and Powell, 1986; Rubinow *et al.*,1984; Sanders *et al.*, 1983; Wells *et al.*, 1989). Visual analogue scales seem the ideal solution to the problems of measurement in menstrual cycle research. They are not without problems, however. First, studies rarely take into account the effect of 'response drift' over time or the likelihood that ratings on consecutive days will be highly inter-correlated. Second, because the extremes of the scales are defined according to the individual's experience, they are relativistic. If a woman has used the full range of the VAS and then experiences more joy, for example, than she has ever experienced before, she cannot mark it on the scale. This relativism also makes the comparison of scores on the same scale between individuals difficult to interpret (McNeill, 1992). Third, some people have difficulty using visual analogue scales – not everyone finds it easy to conceptualise their experience along one dimension (Gift, 1989). Fourth, the scores obtained on VAS are usually expressed in millimetres, ranging from 0–100, but it is unlikely that we can really grade how we feel so accurately. This type of measurement also means that statistically significant differences can occur between groups (or cycle phases) on the basis of very small scale differentials. It could be argued that VAS are a more sensitive measure than, say, Likert-type scales, but the degree of sensitivity may not be psychologically meaningful. Such conceptual difficulties may be particularly important in longitudinal studies, becoming compounded over time. Finally, while VAS may be quick for the respondent to complete they can be time-consuming and fiddly for the researcher to score, involving measurement in millimetres for each scale and increasing the likelihood of errors. Visual analogue scales may reduce the 'risk' of stereotypical symptom reporting with which so many researchers are preoccupied, but that does not make them the perfect measurement tool.

The main concern with VAS and other daily ratings is the choice of what dimensions to measure. A wide variety is found in the literature (see Table 3.3 and Budieri *et al.*, 1994), with the number used in any study varying from 1 per day (e.g. Rubinow *et al.*, 1984; Schnurr, 1988; Cowdry *et al.*, 1991) to 63 per day (e.g. Abraham *et al.*, 1985b). Most studies use between 8 and 12 (e.g. Sanders *et al.*, 1983; Walker and Bancroft, 1990; Wells *et al.*, 1989). Whether or not the researchers are explicitly concerned with identifying a premenstrual syndrome, this reduction in the number of items used for daily ratings results in an emphasis either on those experiences which are of particular interest to the researcher (for whatever reason) or on those experiences which might be expected to vary across the cycle. These expectations, of course, derive from the previous retrospective literature and cultural stereotypes, both of which have a negative bias. Hence, most studies using daily ratings (on numerical scales or VAS), whether they are based on versions of retrospective questionnaires or 'purpose-built' daily diary formats, share the criticism of negative emphasis and the possibility of creation of expectations and self-fulfilling prophecies. To some extent, this criticism is addressed by the use of single bipolar global mood scales, such as the one used by Cowdry *et al.* (1991), with extremes labelled 'best I've ever felt' and 'worst I've ever felt'. Many researchers feel uncomfortable with such global measures, however, either because they may obscure subtle changes in specific mood states (e.g. the 'bipolarity' described by Halbriech and Endicott, 1985, see above), or because they may disguise individual differences in 'symptom' experience, or because the researcher has a theoretical interest in the relationships between and configuration of particular mood or physical states.

The question of who should choose which dimensions to rate on a daily basis, the researcher or the participant, is also raised. Some researchers, usually clinicians, ask the women in the study to rate their own choice of experiences, for example their 'five worst symptoms' (Magos and Studd, 1988). The resulting variations in choice of scales between studies makes comparison between them difficult and comparison with studies of non-menstrually related experiences almost impossible. The list of scales in Table 3.3 is also remarkably similar to descriptors used in studies of gender stereotypes (e.g. Bem, 1974; Hill *et al.*, 1994)

Table 3.3 Dimensions used in daily rating scales

Unipolar mood	Bipolar mood	Physical state
depression	happy–unhappy	breast swelling/tenderness
irritability	exhausted–energetic	abdominal distension
feelings of hopelessness	confident–lacking in confidence	swelling of face, hands, etc.
lack of initiative	tense–calm	pelvic or low abdominal pain
withdrawal	friendly–hostile/irritable	backache/back pain
argumentativeness	confused–mentally alert	headache
cheerfulness	placid–irritable	hot flushes
outgoingness	good spirits–poor spirits	constipation
tiredness	changeable mood–stable mood	food cravings
mood	dominant–submissive	fluid retention
crying/weepiness	lighthearted–depressed	period pain
ability to work	bungling–competent	nausea
interest in work	stable–moody	menstrual bleeding
sleep quality	trusting–suspicious	acne
appetite change	creative–unimaginative	craving sweets
anxiety	confident–vulnerable	craving salty foods
restlessness	randy–disinterested in sex	binge eating
jitteriness	efficient–inefficient	weight gain
tension		fainting
active aggression		energy
sexual interest		stomach pain
well-being		
mood swings		
depressed libido		
cheerful and happy		
depressed and unhappy		
relaxed		
brisk		
apprehensive		
efficient		
gloomy		
stressed		
avoidance of social activity		
impaired relationships		
anger or impatience		
sadness		
bitchiness		
emotional lability		

and provides an interesting commentary on the feelings and behaviours which are considered 'normal' or acceptable for women in white Western cultures (see Nicolson, 1995). If it is assumed that the aim of any intervention is to shift women towards the 'positive' ends of these scales, then it seems that women are optimally supposed to be stable, trusting, happy, energetic, confident, placid, creative, mentally alert and 'randy', among other things! All of these fit with the notion of woman as nurturer of or carer for husband and family, with the exception of changes in the ability to work (if 'work' is assumed to mean paid employment outside the home), and it is interesting to note that feminist researchers have shown particular interest in this area (see Sommer, 1992). Some researchers have attempted to solve the problems of negative bias, global versus specific state measurement and length of rating scales in daily measurement studies by using two-dimensional scales or grids to measure current mood state (e.g. Cohen *et al.*, 1987; McFarlane *et al.*, 1988), or by focusing on pleasant events and positive experiences (e.g. Wilcoxon *et al.*, 1976). However, these are relatively rare.

Non-questionnaire measures

Techniques other than questionnaires or rating scales have been used to assess mood and well-being during the cycle. The most widely used alternative is a clinical interview, which continues to be used generally in research using DSM IIIR or IV criteria (see Gold and Severino, 1994) but was the only measure used in many early studies of menstrual experience (e.g. Frank, 1931), sometimes supplemented with case history material and physical assessments (e.g. Morton, 1950; Israel, 1938). A small number of studies are based on daily interviews with participants and measures of physiological status, producing detailed case study material (e.g. Altmann *et al.*, 1941). Psychodynamically oriented studies have also used non-questionnaire material, such as daily psychoanalytical sessions (Benedek and Rubenstein, 1939a; 1939b) and content analysis of regular free-association speech samples using the Gottschalk Verbal Anxiety Scale (e.g. Ivey and Bardwick, 1968; Paige, 1971) or the Gottschalk-Gleser Free Association Test (Vila and Beech, 1980).

Another means of inferring mood, well-being or cognitive state is by observing behaviour. A number of studies have assessed suicide or attempted suicide in relation to menstrual cycle phase (e.g. Wetzel *et al.*, 1971a; 1971b). Other behaviours of interest have been school (particularly exam) or work performance (e.g. Dalton, 1960; 1968) and clinic attendance (Crowther, 1994). In an interesting recent study, women were asked to make selections for an evening's viewing from television programme schedules at different phases of the cycle (Meadowcroft and Zillmann, 1987), while the relationship between menstrual cycle phase and social interaction has been assessed by observations of women in group situations at different cycle phases (Hood, 1992). Sexual arousal in response to erotic material has also been assessed at different phases of the cycle by use of vaginal plethysmography, and the type and frequency of sexual behaviour has been monitored, although, as would be expected, by self-report rather than direct observation (see McNeill, 1994).

One of the aims of traditional science is objectivity: from this perspective, all these observational measures can be criticised on the grounds that the observer may bias the ratings of the behaviour observed. It is difficult, for instance, for the researcher to be unaware of the cycle phase of the participant, although efforts are made to control for this (e.g. by separating data collection from data analysis). More subtle influences may come into play here, though, since the researcher defines the cycle phases to be observed in the first place (see below). More subtle still may be the effect of the presence of the observer or interviewer on the behaviour or responses of the participant, and the nature of the relationship which develops between them, especially if observations are repeated over time. It would be almost impossible, for instance, for the researcher to practically disguise the purpose of the study or their menstrual cycle interest. In cases where the data are being collected by others, for example on exam performance or suicide, it may be difficult to ensure their accuracy or completeness. However, given the inferences which are often made about women's behaviour on the basis of studies using self-report questionnaire data, it is disappointing that there are so few studies which actually adopt observational or behavioural measures to lend weight, or otherwise, to their conclusions.

MEASURING THE MENSTRUAL CYCLE

Menstrual cycle research is not only about mood, well-being and cognitive state, although issues about how to measure these dominate the methodological literature. It is also about the menstrual cycle, which raises another series of less frequently aired measurement issues. These relate not only to the definition of the cycle in temporal terms and what counts, for research purposes, as a menstrual cycle, but also to the question of which (if any) physiological measures are considered to define the menstrual cycle. In early studies, it was the fluctuations of ovarian hormones which were thought to define the cycle physiologically, and researchers focused on measuring or manipulating the hormonal state. During the 1980s and 1990s, attention has shifted away from circulating ovarian hormones and towards either cycle definition and measurement in solely temporal terms or investigation and measurement (or inference of levels of) neurochemicals.

Defining the cycle

The menstrual cycle is defined in physiological texts as the number of days from the beginning of one menstrual period to the next. Unfortunately, as outlined in chapter one, menstruation and menstrual cycles do not always fit the neat assumptions underlying this definition. In my own research, women often found it difficult to identify the first day of menstruation, particularly if their periods followed the 'gradual onset' pattern described by Snowden and Christian (1983). Are days of 'spotting' before the full menstrual flow part of menstruation or not? Similarly, if a woman experiences some days of 'spotting' at the end of a period, is this menstruation or not? In practice, most studies probably include all consecutive days on which bleeding occurs as menstruation, ignoring the variability between women and cycles which this implies. Similarly, variation in cycle length is commonly ignored in menstrual cycle research, and attempts are made to recruit women whose cycles are as close as possible to those in the textbooks by excluding those who report 'irregular' cycles, those who have borne a child or stopped using oral contraceptives recently and those who are approaching the menopause. Even after all these controls, cycles of less than 21 or more than 35 days are usually excluded from analysis. Hence, the definition of the menstrual cycle which is being used in research studies does not include all menstrual cycles.

In longitudinal studies using daily ratings of well-being, the time between one menstrual period and the next is usually divided up in some way into 'cycle phases', the number of which varies between studies from 3 to 14 (4 and 7 are the most common). The names given to these phases often reveal the assumption being made by the researchers that particular physiological states prevail at particular times. The most obvious example of this is the common practice of cycle division on the assumption that ovulation has occurred, as revealed by cycle phase names such as 'follicular', 'ovulatory', 'luteal', 'preovulatory', and 'postovulatory' (e.g. Slade, 1984), which is not appropriate unless the researchers have evidence that cycles studied were indeed ovulatory.[8] The studies which define cycle phases on the basis of measured endocrinological criteria are few and far between (e.g. Schechter et al.,1989; Sanders et al., 1983; Ablanalp et al.,1979b).

In most studies, endocrinological criteria are not available, so the researcher(s) must either find a way of analysing the cycle without imposing phases (e.g. Sampson, 1979; Sampson and Prescott, 1981; Magos and Studd, 1986), or define phases on usually arbitrary criteria. As Erin McNeill (1992) notes, there is some debate and a great deal of inconsistency about the appropriate way to divide the cycle up into phases. She writes: 'Generally, phases are determined arbitrarily with regard to the timing of menstrual bleeding based on the clinical impression of the timing of cyclical symptoms, in order to "capture" symptoms in one phase, and exclude them from others' (McNeill, 1992: 107). This certainly seems to be the case for Dalton's phase criteria – in which the 6 days of menstruation and the 14-day premenstrual phase form almost two-thirds of a 28 day cycle. This is contrasted to a 7-day 'intermenstrual' phase (Dalton, 1984; see Ainscough, 1990, for a critique). The problem of differing cycle lengths between and within women is approached in one of four ways by researchers trying to identify phases. The most frequent method is to ignore some of the daily ratings, selecting only small sections for comparison, the most popular being a premenstrual segment and a follicular phase or postmenstrual segment, although some studies also include a menstrual phase (e.g. van den Akker and Steptoe, 1985; Englander-Golden *et al.*, 1978). These segments are usually of 5 or 7 days in length (e.g. Christensen and Oei, 1989; Endicott *et al.*,1986; Both-Orthmann *et al.*,1988; Gise *et al.*,1990). The mood ratings on those days are averaged to produce a score for each phase, and the degree of difference between them may be used diagnostically. A second and similar method is to collect prospective data only on predefined cycle days. For example, Goudsmit (1983) and van der Ploeg (1987) asked women to complete questionnaires only on days 12, 18, 22 and 26 (counting the first day of menstruation as day 1). A third technique is to include all of the data collected and to specify the length of one or two of the phases, but to leave the other(s) variable to accommodate different cycle lengths. So, for example, Walker and Bancroft (1990) define the seven days before menstruation as the 'premenstrual' phase, and the seven days after the end of menstruation as the 'postmenstrual' phase, allowing all days of bleeding to be the 'menstrual' phase and the remaining days to be the 'intermenstrual' phase. This type of division, with variations in the precise length of the fixed phases, is widely used (e.g. Graham and Sherwin, 1992; Walker, 1994a). A fourth technique is to standardise all cycles to the same length mathematically by stretching or squeezing the data, and then imposing cycle phases (e.g. Hart *et al.*, 1987; Slade, 1984). In these studies, cycles are always standardised to 28 days, although the phase definitions thereafter vary.

Physiological measures

Apart from menstruation, the physiological event which is seen to define the cycle is ovulation. Hence, a number of studies attempt to identify whether ovulation has occurred and when, using vaginal swabs (e.g. Benedek and Rubenstein, 1939a; 1939b), basal body temperature (e.g. Herrera *et al.*, 1990), the 'symptothermal' method (e.g. Hart and Russell, 1986), assays of blood or urine for progesterone (e.g. Trunnell *et al.*, 1988; Sanders *et al.*,1983), commercially available ovulation detection kits which identify the preovulatory surge in luteinising hormone (LH) (e.g. Sveinsdottir and Reame, 1991), or ultrasonic visualisation of the ovary (e.g. McNeill, 1992). The reliability and sensitivity of these techniques varies, with basal body temperature used alone being the least reliable (Kesner *et al.*, 1992; Moghissi, 1992).

Ovarian hormones are the next most commonly assessed physiological measure of the menstrual cycle. As with mood and well-being, there is a wide variety of circulating reproductive hormones to choose from, for example oestrogen, progesterone, testosterone, prolactin, luteinising hormone, follicle stimulating hormone (FSH). These usually circulate not only in their 'pure' form but also as a variety of metabolites, any of which might have relevant physiological activity, and either 'free' in plasma or 'bound' to protein molecules, altering their activity (Hillier, 1985). The choice about what to measure may in part be determined by the body fluid to which the researcher has access – that is, blood, urine or saliva. Most studies which use plasma samples measure oestradiol-17ß, which is the predominant oestrogen, and progesterone, rather than their precursors or metabolites. Studies using urine or saliva samples measure excreted metabolites (e.g. oestrone glucuronide, pregnanediol glucuoronide) and estimate the total daily production of a particular hormone rather than the amount circulating at any one time (e.g. Sanders *et al.*,1983; Walker, 1988; McNeill, 1992). Any of these will give an index of ovarian activity if they are assessed regularly enough, but single samples are rarely very informative even if the researcher is only interested in whether ovulation has occurred (Landgren *et al.*, 1980; Collins *et al.*, 1979; Steele *et al.*, 1985). The pulsatile nature of gonadotrophin and progesterone secretion (Crowley *et al.*, 1985; Steele *et al.*, 1986) and diurnal variations in circulating hormone levels (Veldhuis *et al.*, 1988; Younglai *et al.*, 1975) also complicate ovarian function assessment, making standardisation of time of day of sample collection vital if plasma samples are being used.

The measurement of ovarian hormones on a regular basis is dependent on the development of appropriate assay technologies. Samples are assayed using either radioimmunoassay (RIA) or enzyme-linked immunosorbent assay (ELISA) techniques.[9] Until the 1970s, these assays were available only for plasma, necessitating repeated blood sampling to monitor cyclical fluctuations in hormones. The earliest urine assays were hardly more convenient, since they required collection of all urine passed in a 24-hour period. The demonstrations that the ovarian cycle can be accurately assessed by use of the hormone–creatinine[10] ratio mean that smaller urine samples (e.g. 30ml early-morning urine samples) can be utilised, easing the burden of hormone assessment for participants. Each assay is slightly different, and samples are assayed against a set of standards allowing coefficients of variation to be calculated both within each assay (intra-assay coefficient) and between the different assays used to assess all the samples in a study (inter-assay coefficient). These coefficients describe the reliability of the assay in the same way that alpha coefficients describe the internal consistency of a questionnaire, for instance. In longitudinal studies, it is generally the case that more samples are collected than can be analysed in a single assay, so the degree of variability between assays is a crucial determinant of the trustworthiness of the data. If the coefficients are too high then the data is meaningless, as Trunnell, Turner and Keye (1988) mournfully point out in a footnote to their paper comparing hormone levels between women 'with and without PMS':

The authors are indebted to an anonymous reviewer who suggested that we report both interassay and intraassay coefficient of variation from our lab. After calculating each intraassay coefficient of variation, it was felt that the estradiol variation was too high and not within acceptable limits. We therefore made the decision to exclude this data here. It is our hope that this will serve as a warning to future researchers to examine both within-subject and between-subjects variation in any RIA kits to be used.

(Trunnell *et al.*, 1988: 431)

As assay technology has become more sophisticated, so the definition of the crucial physiological aspects of the menstrual cycle has shifted away from fluctuating oestrogen and progesterone levels towards gonadotrophins, LH and FSH, originating in the pituitary gland (e.g. Coulson, 1986), their respective releasing hormones, specifically luteinising hormone–releasing hormone (LH–RH) (e.g. Facchinetti *et al.*, 1993a), and catecholamines and neurotransmitters (e.g. Odink *et al.*, 1990; Veeninga and Westenberg, 1992). Assays for these are equally subject to variation, although the coefficients are rarely included in study reports.

Almost all menstrual cycle studies make some inference about the relationship between mood or well-being and physiological state. Yet the most significant observation about physiological measures in comparison to measures of mood and well-being is their comparative rarity and the lack of discussion of them in the menstrual cycle research literature. The size of this section in comparison to the previous section on measures of well-being is testimony not to the fact that hormones (for example) are easier to measure than moods – they are certainly not – but to the fact that most menstrual cycle studies have not considered it necessary to measure them at all. The reasons for not measuring hormone levels (or other indices of physiological state) are generally pragmatic – these are expensive procedures, and techniques which most menstrual cycle researchers do not have access to. Depending on the perspective of the researcher, non-measurement can be justified on the grounds that the link between psychological states and the endocrinology of the menstrual cycle is either so obvious that it does not need to be demonstrated, or so spurious that it does not warrant attention. The absence of even the most basic measurement, of ovulation for instance, in studies which infer a biochemical basis for women's experience underlines the assumptions about hormone–behaviour relationships in women which permeate all menstrual cycle research (see chapters one, two and seven).

STUDY DESIGN

Scientific approaches

Studies in the positivist tradition either attempt to describe a phenomenon under study or test hypothetical explanations for a phenomenon. The explanatory models from which these hypotheses are derived are usually the product of inductive thinking on the part of the researcher, while the hypothesis-testing aspect of the research involves deductive logic (see, for example, Salmon, 1973). Because of this, studies in this tradition are not usually designed to generate theories; rather, the preconceived theory drives the data collection. Sometimes the theory driving the research is explicit, but more often in menstrual cycle research, as I have suggested already in chapter two, it is implicit. This approach results in three main groups of study designs: descriptive studies, usually taking the form of surveys or observational research; correlational studies, which investigate the possibility of a relationship of some sort between the variables of interest; and experimental or quasi-experimental studies, which test cause–effect relationships between variables. All of these are found in menstrual cycle research in either 'pure' or – more often – hackneyed forms.

The earliest descriptive studies of menstrually related experiences are those based on clinical descriptions and case studies (e.g. Frank, 1931; Horney, 1931b; Israel, 1938; Morton, 1950). Large-scale epidemiological surveys or descriptive studies have formed only a very small part of menstrual cycle research. A number of studies have examined the prevalence of particular experiences around menstruation (e.g. Pennington, 1957; Kessel and Coppen, 1963; Moos, 1968; Sheldrake and Cormack, 1976) or have tried to estimate the prevalence of premenstrual syndrome (e.g. Andersch *et al.*, 1986; Woods *et al.*, 1982; Ramcharan *et al.*, 1992). Psychologists have investigated the prevalence of particular attitudes towards menstruation (e.g. Brooks Gunn and Ruble, 1986; Dye, 1991; Scambler and Scambler, 1985), although usually in relatively small samples (less than 500), and most recently have examined the frequency of particular coping strategies used by women in relation to menstrually related experiences (e.g. Choi and Salmon, 1995a). In addition to these frequency-oriented accounts are a number of descriptive studies which try to identify the nature of premenstrual experiences rather than the number of women who experience them. These are usually focused around the factor analysis of a particular questionnaire (e.g. Richardson, 1989; Moos, 1968; Condon, 1993). All of these studies share the methodological difficulties of every large survey. First, they are dependent on appropriate measurement, which as I've shown is problematic, and second the estimates of prevalence they produce are only meaningful in the context of the sample assessed. Many of these studies are based on 'convenience' samples of, for example, students (e.g. Timonen and Procope, 1971; Sheldrake and Cormack, 1976) or clinic attenders (e.g. Rouse, 1978; Boyle *et al.*, 1987). Even when the sample studied is randomly selected from the general population of a particular district, it is often relatively small (e.g. Woods *et al.*, 1982, *n* = 179; Taylor *et al.*, 1986, *n* = 530). So, it is difficult to know what to make of their findings, and estimates of premenstrual 'symptom' prevalence vary widely. These studies, too, are limited because of their focus on the premenstrual days. Other parts of the cycle are only sampled to contrast with these, leaving the frustrating feeling of a story only half told.

Correlational studies usually investigate the relationship between one or other aspect of menstrual cycle physiology and a measure of mood or well-being. Studies of cognitive function rarely employ sufficiently frequent measures to be considered correlational – they are more likely to be quasi-experimental (see below). Truly correlational menstrual cycle studies include the early work by Benedek and Rubenstein (1939a; 1939b) in which daily assessments of emotional state were 'correlated' with daily physiological measures, although these comparisons were not made statistically. Modern studies which could be considered as correlational are those which relate cycle day to mood using various forms of time series analysis, such as trend analysis or sine wave analysis (e.g. Magos and Studd, 1986; Sampson and Prescott, 1981; Livesey *et al.*, 1989) or those which relate mood and physiological measures taken at the same time (Walker, 1988). These studies are not designed to test causal relationships, but simply ask whether there is a relationship between well-being and physiological state. In other words, would knowing a woman's hormone levels or menstrual cycle day allow us to predict with any accuracy the mood she is in (or vice versa, of course)? This question implies that the relationship between menstrual cycle and mood is not a perfect one – other factors might be expected to influence either biochemistry or well-being – and almost necessarily implies a consideration of the menstrual cycle within the context of the rest of women's lives. Given the cultural milieu, then, it is not surprising that studies employing correlational or multiple regression techniques to predict women's state are absent from the literature.

Correlational designs are used more frequently to predict other aspects of menstrually related behaviour – for example, who will label themselves as having PMS (e.g. Warner and Bancroft, 1990) or who will seek help at a PMS clinic (e.g. Christensen and Oei, 1995a). Correlations are also conducted between various putative aetiological factors and perimenstrual distress. Researchers have investigated the relationship between menstrual distress scores and aspects of personality, menstrual attitudes, 'femininity', life stresses and many others (see chapters four and five).

Experimental studies hypothesise that one variable, which is manipulated, will have an effect on another, which is measured. The procedure usually involves either a counterbalanced repeated measures design or the comparison of groups of randomly allocated participants. In this way, experimenters endeavour to minimise the 'error' resulting from individual differences. There are a number of true experiments in menstrual cycle research, most of them falling into the realm of social psychology. For example, studies in which the expectations of participants about the purpose of the study are manipulated, and their subsequent ratings on menstrual health or distress questionnaires are measured, are true experiments (e.g. Ruble, 1977; Olasov and Jackson, 1987). Similarly, studies in which stereotypes are assessed by asking participants to respond to randomly allocated vignettes depicting a woman in one or other cycle phase are experimental in nature (e.g. Koeske and Koeske, 1975; Walker, 1992b).

The majority of menstrual cycle research, though, uses a quasi-experimental approach. That is, studies are designed as though they were experimental, but participants are not randomly allocated to groups. It is not possible, for example, to randomly allocate women to 'PMS' or 'non-PMS' conditions, and neither is it possible to randomly allocate women to cycle phases or counterbalance the order in which cycle phases are experienced! However, because of the conviction that there must be a causal relationship between the menstrual cycle and women's emotional experience, and because the direction of that relationship is perceived to be from the physiological to the psychological rather than vice versa, the menstrual cycle is treated as though it were an independent variable, and studies are designed to be quasi-experimental rather than correlational (see Koeske, 1981). This is true in both biomedical and feminist approaches to the cycle (e.g. Wilcoxon *et al.*, 1976). Essentially the majority of studies concerned with menstrual cycle test the hypothesis that the cycle has a causal effect on whichever state is of interest. This may or may not be the case, but in light of evidence which suggests that a variety of psychological factors can disrupt menstrual function (e.g. Russell, 1972; Halmi, 1982; Shangold *et al.*,1979; Iglesias *et al.*,1980; Shangold, 1985) and that menstrual cycles may be susceptible to influences outside the woman herself (e.g. McClintock, 1971; Graham, 1991; Weller and Weller, 1993), it seems shortsighted in the least to assume that the only relationship between them is unidirectional, linear and causal. Nonetheless, this is what is wittingly or unwittingly implied by the majority of studies which divide cycles into phases and compare scores between phases using ANOVA.[11] This assumption is explicitly tested when researchers compare groups of women who differ on some hormonal criterion, for example women who are currently using oral contraceptives with those who are not (Paige, 1971; Walker and Bancroft, 1990), women before and after medical or surgical suppression of ovarian function (e.g. Muse *et al.*,1984; Casper and Hearn, 1990), or women experiencing different forms of oestrogen and progesterone replacement therapy after ovariectomy (e.g. Watson *et al.*, 1989).

Social constructionist approaches

As has already been indicated, the overwhelming majority of the research relating to psychological aspects of the menstrual cycle has used 'the scientific method'. That is, it has been conducted within an empiricist epistemology, with an emphasis on the collection and statistical analysis of numerical data. Numerous critiques of the assumptions of this approach and its suitability for understanding human psychology have been published in recent years (e.g. J. Smith *et al.*, 1995; Potter and Wetherell, 1987; Morawski, 1994; Gergen, 1985). As a result of this criticism, a variety of different research epistemologies and methodologies have developed and are continuing to develop, most of which shift the emphasis away from reductionism and quantification towards the collection and analysis of qualitative material – that is, verbal, written or pictorial representations of experience rather than numerical representations (see Henwood and Nicolson, 1995). Those empirical studies which have adopted a different epistemological stance can be broadly categorised as social constructionist and feminist standpoint approaches, although there is overlap between them. These have as yet had little impact on menstrual cycle research, but their methodology and assumptions will be briefly outlined here.

One of the key strands of positivist epistemology is the assumption that human beings are passive organisms. From this perspective, if we know every-thing about an individual's personality or beliefs and their situation, then their behaviour will be entirely predictable. This assumption can be seen clearly in the methodologies chosen by traditional scientists and feminist empiricists in menstrual cycle research, described above. Although any particular research study may be concerned with only one or two aspects of the person, such as the amount of stress she is experiencing or her ovarian hormone levels, the assump-tion is that if we could measure and describe all of the factors which are thought to have an impact on menstrually related behaviour, then we could predict premenstrual absenteeism, suicide attempts or whatever precisely. This assump-tion is made explicit in multidimensional biopsychosocial models of PMS (see chapter six). A social constructionist epistemology challenges this assumption (e.g. Sarbin and Kitsuse, 1994). From this perspective, human beings are active agents who organise and interpret information, whether from their own internal states or from the outside world, in an attempt to make sense of reality. What we do then is a response to our particular construction of events and circumstances, and is not necessarily predictable either from our behaviour in the past or from some fundamental aspect of ourselves. Rather it is the *meaning* of a situation to us which is of key importance. As Henwood and Nicolson (1995) note, 'meanings – including lay and scientific knowledge of the world – do not merely reflect the world as it exists, but are produced or constructed by persons and within cultural, social and historical relationships' (Henwood and Nicolson, 1995: 109). This approach has developed within sociology, and is found in particular in the work of the Chicago school (e.g. Goffman, [1959] 1969), symbolic interactionism (Mead, 1934; Hewitt, 1994) and ethnomethodology (Garfinkel, 1967), all of which have been particularly concerned with the understanding of social prob-lems (see Schneider, 1985). In psychology, the search for the meaning attached to events and situations as a way of understanding human behaviour has become more popular in recent years, particularly in social psychology, as a means of resolving the 'crisis' which many writers perceive in social psychology, created from its decontextualisation of human experience (see, for example, Parker, 1989; Morawski, 1994).

Once the human being has been conceptualised as an active agent for whom the meaning of situations is important – a meaning which may itself be created through social interaction – then the research questions and research methodolo-gies of traditional science are no longer appropriate. It makes no sense to position the researcher as an objective and value-free outsider, and the reduction of human experience to numbers seems artificial and unnecessarily limiting. Social constructionist researchers therefore usually collect qualitative data, which is analysed qualitatively, in an attempt to identify cultural or personal meanings. The research question is usually of the form, 'What is the meaning of x to y?', where x is the phenomenon in question and y is the person or group of people of interest. As most social constructionist research has been conducted in sociology and anthropology, y has most frequently been a particular culture or sub-culture.

In menstrual cycle research, social constructionist approaches have been applied to the phenomena of PMS and menstruation, with research questions concerning the meaning of PMS in Western cultures (e.g. Rodin, 1992; Johnson, 1987; Swann and Ussher, 1995; Walker, 1995b) or the meaning of menstruation to men or women within a culture (e.g. Laws, 1990; Martin, 1989). Studies in this vein often take a historical perspective, investigating representations of menstruation, for instance, in the nineteenth century (e.g. Shuttleworth, 1990; Rodin, 1992) or in contemporary culture through advertising (e.g. Berg and Block Coutts, 1994; Block Coutts and Berg, 1993; Chrisler and Levy, 1990; Treneman, 1988) or 'popular' media reports (e.g. Eagan, 1985; Rodin, 1992; Walker, 1995b). These researchers are not interested in counting how many people hold particular views, because they assume that any one individual might express any of a number of different views depending on their circumstances; rather, they are concerned with the meaning or meanings which a phenomenon may have. The approaches they take to this research question vary: in psychology, the most popular are discourse analysis (Potter and Wetherell, 1987) and grounded theory (e.g. Henwood and Pidgeon, 1992).

Feminist standpoint research

Late twentieth-century feminism has many definitions and many forms. Fundamental to all of them are the commitment to an understanding of women's experience from women's perspective and a concern with power differentials between people, particularly, in this respect, between those who claim to speak on behalf of others and those who are spoken for. In menstrual cycle research, the majority of feminist-inspired studies have adopted the methods and practices of traditional science, either because the researchers believe that this is the only way in which their findings will be taken seriously by the 'establishment', or because they believe that feminist concerns will transform 'bad science' into 'good science' (see, for example, Fausto-Sterling, 1992; Harding, 1991). There has been a considerable debate, however, among feminists both within and outside academia about whether positivist research can ever be truly feminist (see, for example, Stanley and Wise, 1983; Harding, 1991; Morawski, 1994; Griffin, 1995). These feminists are concerned about the inherent imbalance in power relations between the researcher and the researched in 'science'. The scientist, for example, decides what the research question is, whose answers to it are relevant, the precise form in which the question should be asked and the 'correct' interpretation of the responses. No matter whether the person being researched is called a 'participant' or a 'respondent', they are still a 'subject' in this power relationship, with no influence over how the data are collected or interpreted and, in many cases, no knowledge of the outcome of the research. Similarly, women's experiences are rarely of interest in their own right but only as a secondary phenomenon. In menstrual cycle research, for example, women's premenstrual experiences are investigated because they are thought to be symptoms of disease or to interfere with work or domestic functions, not because how women feel is of intrinsic interest.

For some feminists, any kind of research which is about other people is anathema to feminist principles. For others, academic research is thought to be a possibility, but not in the form of positivist science. Feminist standpoint research (FSR) has developed from within this strand of critique. Chris Griffin (1995) argues that FSR is characterised by: (i) an emphasis on the importance of experience, particularly women's experience, as the focus both of 'data collection' and of theory generation; (ii) the concept of the researcher as accountable both to the research participants and to feminists in general; and (iii) a reflexive perspective on research – that is, a 'self-conscious awareness of the ways in which what counts as "knowledge" and the whole process of research are structured by relations of dominance around gender, race, class, age and sexuality' (Griffin, 1995: 120). Hence, there are many similarities between FSR and social constructionist research: they both imply qualitative data and analysis, and they both emphasise the subjectivity of the researcher. The key difference is in the explicit political grounding of FSR, and the concern for 'collaboration' with and acknowledgement of all those who are engaged in the research enterprise. In FSR, the research is being done for the research participants rather than for the researcher or the funding body; it is to them that the researcher is accountable.

In menstrual cycle research, although there have been several radical feminist critiques of PMS in particular (e.g. Laws et al., 1985), there have been very few empirical studies which could fit the description of FSR. Emily Martin's research (Martin, 1989; 1990) and Paula Weideger's early studies (Weideger, 1976) are exceptional in this regard, and even these could be criticised for lack of accountability and reflexivity. Similarly, Vieda Skultans' study of menstruation and menopause in a Welsh mining village in 1970 (Skultans, 1970) and Scambler and Scambler's studies of women's menstrual beliefs in London in the 1980s (Scambler and Scambler, 1985; 1993), share a concern with women's experience for its own sake and are based on qualitative data analysis and broadly feminist ideology, but they are neither demonstrably accountable to the women who took part nor obviously reflexive. Sophie Laws' research is driven from a feminist standpoint but is concerned with men's experiences of menstruation. In part this lack of research may reflect the difficulty of FSR; however, there is a need for more good quality feminist standpoint research in relation to menstruation and menstrual experiences.

CONCLUSIONS

The methods used to investigate the menstrual cycle which have been described in this chapter certainly substantiate the statement made at the beginning that menstrual cycle research is a 'methodological minefield'. The dominant scientific methodology is full of contradictions and biases, many of which have been empirically challenged by feminist psychologists. The methods used by researchers reflect the cultural meanings attached to menstruation (see chapter one) and the historical context within which research has occurred (see chapter two). Menstruation has been associated with 'health' and more often 'illness', placing the investigation of menstrually related experiences within the realms of medicine and medically related disciplines such as nursing and, often, psychology. The preoccupation of the illness-related disciplines with the identification and treatment of disease has resulted in a large range of methodologies concerned with the diagnosis of PMS/LLPDD/PMDD, and relatively few methods for investigating the full range of women's experience. Feminist empiricists have challenged the validity of these methodologies by demonstrating the influence of cultural stereotypes and sexist biases. By and large, however, these findings have been incorporated into mainstream menstrual cycle research as additional methodological requirements rather than being seen as a challenge to its foundations. The dominant research question continues to be, 'Does the menstrual cycle affect behaviour/experience?' or, more often, '*How* does the menstrual cycle affect behaviour/experience?' The possibility of designing an empirical study to investigate this question while observing all the criteria which distinguish a 'good' study makes menstrual cycle research more of a challenge to creative ingenuity now than it was at the turn of the century, although not one which appears to daunt researchers judging by the steady increase in published reports.

The feminist empiricist approach to menstrual cycle research has certainly led to refinements in research methodology. In this way, feminists, and particularly feminist psychologists, have had a significant impact on scientific research. Concerns about whether or not to disguise the purpose of a menstrual cycle research study (and how to disguise it well), and how to avoid stereotypical reporting, disturb the sleep of even the most reductionist bio-medical researchers. Undoubtedly the science in this area has become 'better' as a result of the studies and exhortations of feminist psychologists. The question which remains for me is whether our knowledge or understanding of the psychological aspects of menstruation or the menstrual cycle has improved. In other words, have we been altruistically spending our energy on the improvement of medical science, in the hopes that women's treatment will be better as a result, while neglecting the questions which as social scientists we are uniquely placed to address? This question can only be approached by a consideration of the findings of modern menstrual cycle research which follows in chapters four and five.

4

COGNITIONS AND THE
MENSTRUAL CYCLE

Research concerned with the menstrual cycle has two broad themes. The first is a concern with the relationship between menstruation (or cyclical hormones) and women's ability to think or work. The second is a concern with the relationship between mood or well-being and the menstrual cycle. It is the second theme which has been more closely related to modern preoccupations with PMS. The first theme, though, is the older one, leading directly back to the nineteenth-century worries about menstruation and education. This chapter will describe the research concerning the relationship between the menstrual cycle and cognition, while the next looks at the menstrual cycle and well-being. The research in both of these chapters is concerned with women in general, and not necessarily those who perceive themselves to have PMS. The question of whether these women are or are not different psychologically, physically or experientially from women who complain of (or are diagnosed as having) PMS or an equivalent will be considered in chapter six. Much of the research described in this and the next chapter is justified (by its authors) on the grounds that it may give some insight into the aetiology of PMS, although some is concerned specifically with the 'pure' investigation of the variety of women's experience. All of these studies address the question of whether menstruation or the menstrual cycle affects mood, well-being or the ability to think or make judgements. Some take the question further and ask how any such effects might occur.

Cognitive psychology is broadly concerned with mental processes – thinking, memory and perception, for example. In this chapter, I have added psychophysiological studies and studies of social cognitions (e.g. attitudes and beliefs) to the more 'traditional' cognitive psychology. They are all linked by a common concern with the relationships between the menstrual cycle and cognitive function, either directly or indirectly. So, for example, psychophysiological studies investigate cyclical fluctuations in sensory processes or arousal, which might indirectly link the neuroendocrinology of the menstrual cycle to task performance or ability to think. The logic is that it may not be reaction time *per se* which changes over the cycle, for example, but visual or auditory sensitivity. Similarly, it may not be task performance which changes, so much as arousal. Studies of attitudes and beliefs about menstruation follow a similar logic and similarly have tended to see these as mediators between biological changes during the menstrual cycle and either ability to work or mood. It is not the hormonal changes themselves which affect ability to concentrate, for example, but the stereotypical beliefs about menstruation held by menstruating women (and their observers) which lead performance or mood around menstruation to be perceived as inferior to that at other times. As well as adding to the understanding of cognition and the menstrual cycle, then, these social cognition studies provide a bridge between this chapter and the next.

COGNITION AND TASK PERFORMANCE

Studies of the relationship between the menstrual cycle and women's ability to think or work competently have been a feature of the research field since the beginning of the twentieth century (see chapter two). There have been numerous studies in this area, and they have been reviewed several times, almost always resulting in the conclusion that, for most women, the menstrual cycle has little or no noticeable effect on cognitive function (see Sommer, 1973, 1982, 1992; Gannon, 1985; Richardson, 1992; Asso, 1983; Golub, 1992). Despite this, the belief that it must have an effect is strong, so studies continue, using ever more complex and detailed tests of ability and making headlines when non-significant findings are reported (e.g. Sommer, 1992; Golub, 1992; Choi, 1995). Because of this, the cognitive research will be summarised briefly here, but as space is limited the interested reader is referred to reviews by Barbara Sommer (1973, 1982, 1992), John Richardson (1992, 1995) and Kimura and Hampson (1994) for more detailed accounts.

Cognition

Cognitive functions include thinking, memory and information processing, and have been assessed across the menstrual cycle largely through the use of a wide range of laboratory tests. Sommer (1992) classifies these tasks as measures of complex cognition, simple cognition and social cognition. Measures of complex cognition include critical thinking tests, written tests on lecture content and academic examinations. Tests of simple cognition are a great deal more varied. Sommer groups them into measures of abstract concept formation, breaking set, immediate and short-term memory, simple arithmetic, verbal skills, visuo-spatial ability, simple rote speed tasks, simple decisions, frustration tolerance and flexibility, time-interval estimation and motor co-ordination. Social cognition includes measures of the accuracy of perception of other people's facial expression or behaviour. Clearly, psychologists have left few stones unturned in the search for a measure of cognitive function which will demonstrate a cyclical effect.

As in all areas of menstrual cycle research, the findings of these studies vary. Some demonstrate cycle phase effects and some do not. Those which do find phase effects do not always support the stereotype of premenstrual or menstrual performance decrements either. For example, Hampson and Kimura (1988) report improved manual and drawing skills premenstrually, while Graham and Glasser (1985) found a significant positive correlation between measured luteal phase pregnanediol levels and performance on subtraction and time-estimation tasks. However, the overwhelming weight of evidence suggests that, for women as a group, performance on cognitive tests is not significantly affected by menstrual cycle phase. Since these conclusions are always based on averages across a varying number of women, the variability between women is hard to assess. Some women may perform very well premenstrually but less well at other times, and others vice versa. The assumption here, as in most menstrual cycle research, is that all women will experience the same response to fluctuating hormones. The conclusion that there is no cycle phase effect means that cognitive psychologists have debunked the cultural myth of universal premenstrual or menstrual deficit. This is a politically important conclusion, but only a first step in understanding the range of female experience. It is to be hoped that the next eighty years of research will not see a continued repetition of the questions Leta Hollingworth was asking in 1914.

Doreen Kimura and Elizabeth Hampson (Hampson and Kimura, 1992; Kimura and Hampson, 1993, 1994) have begun to develop this research beyond a concern with whether menstruation or the premenstrual phase of the cycle is associated with cognitive deficits. They argue that both men and women experience cyclical fluctuations in cognitive functions, and that these fluctuations are associated in both sexes with changes in sex hormones (i.e. oestrogen and testosterone). In a series of studies they have tested the hypothesis that task performance on 'feminine' tasks (e.g. verbal fluency, verbal articulation, perceptual speed and accuracy, fine motor movements) and 'masculine' tasks (e.g. spatial rotation and manipulation, mathematical reasoning) is related to levels of oestrogen and testosterone respectively, in both men and women. They argue that performance on neutral tasks – that is, tasks on which men and women obtain consistently similar average scores – is not related to sex hormone levels. To test their hypothesis, they have compared women's test performance at times in the menstrual cycle when oestrogen levels are high (i.e. the mid-luteal phase) and times when oestrogen levels are low (i.e. the early menstrual/follicular phase). Similarly, they have compared men's test performance at different seasons, or between groups of men with different testosterone levels.[1] By testing these hypotheses they are criticising the existing menstrual cycle literature for drawing on too wide a range of tasks, and for focusing on phases of the cycle chosen for their relationship to menstruation rather than to endocrine parameters. They also link studies of cognition and the menstrual cycle explicitly to the contentious literature on sex differences in cognition.[2] The findings from their studies so far support their hypotheses. Hormone-related fluctuations are not found on tests which are 'gender neutral' but are found among both men and women on 'feminine' tasks and 'masculine' tasks. So, for example, women performed better on manual dexterity tasks ('feminine' task) in the high-oestrogen mid-luteal phase than in the low-oestrogen early menstrual phase (Hampson and Kimura, 1988; Hampson, 1990), while Gouchie and Kimura (1991) found that men with lower than average levels of testosterone performed better on spatial and mathematical tasks than men with high testosterone levels. Among women, the effect was reversed. Women with higher than average testosterone did better on these 'masculine' tasks than women with lower than average testosterone levels. No differences in relation to testosterone levels were found on tasks which do not usually show a sex difference or which women on average perform better.

These studies are interesting because they shift concern away from the stereotypical assumption of a menstrual decrement in performance, and because they emphasise the links between cognition and sex hormones in both men and women. However, they also represent an example of another stereotype – that is, the tendency to attribute differences between men and women to reproductive hormones. They are problematic for all of the reasons that sex differences research is problematic. For example, these studies aim to explain differences in cognitive performance between men and women and make generalisations about superior female performance on some tasks and superior male performance on others. In reality there is a considerable overlap of men's and women's performance on these tasks. It is not the case that all women obtain better scores on verbal fluency tasks, for example, than all men – although small but consistent differences are found in average scores. The focus on sex differences rather than sex similarities can result in distortion of the findings, not necessarily by the researchers who conducted the studies but by those who make use of the research. Similarly, these studies do not address the relevance of any hormone-related changes. Although statistically significant differences may occur, are these large enough for women and men to be aware of them? Do they actually make any difference in everyday life? This resurgence of interest suggests that the story of cognition and the menstrual cycle is not yet closed. Studies are certainly needed to replicate and extend Hampson and Kimura's findings. If they are replicated, then the potential for such findings to be used against women – on the grounds of the menstrual cycle (rather than menstruation) affecting performance – will remain.

Work performance

Actual work performance is more difficult to measure than laboratory-based tests of cognition, not least because gaining access to workplaces (and the agreement of workers themselves) is often pragmatically and politically fraught. So there are fewer of these studies, and the areas of work on which they focus are limited. Their benefits in 'real-world validity' are also balanced against disadvantages such as the absence of physiological assessments of the cycle or control over the conditions in which the work is performed. The areas of work on which researchers have focused are academic performance, athletic performance and repetitive factory-based production work.

A concern with the relationship between menstruation and academic work, triggered by the entry of women into higher education, provoked the original scientific interest in menstrual cycle research in the nineteenth century (see chapter two), so it is interesting to note that John Richardson justifies his study of student learning and the menstrual cycle, published in 1989, on the grounds of understanding the implications of menstruation for 'nearly 380,000 women enrolled as students in courses of higher education in the United Kingdom, and at least one million more engaged in non-advanced further education' (Richardson, 1989: 215).[3] On a more pragmatic level, researchers employed in higher education have relatively easy access to students and academic work. These studies usually assess performance in tests or exams by comparing the cycle phase and scores either of different women on a single exam ('between subjects' design) or of the same woman on repeated tests over one or more cycles ('within subjects' design), with the former design being more popular. Almost all of these have failed to demonstrate a consistent effect of menstrual cycle phase on performance (e.g. Walsh *et al.*, 1981; Sommer, 1972; Richardson, 1988, 1989; Bernstein, 1977; Asso 1985–86). The only research which supports the hypothesis of a menstrual or paramenstrual decline is that of Dalton (1960, 1968), who found lower performance in schoolgirls' weekly work and standardised exams immediately before and during the first days of menstruation. These data are usually discredited by other researchers, though, on the grounds that they were not analysed statistically (see Gannon, 1985).

Similar findings are reported for both athletic and industrial performance. Erdelyi (1962) reported that 42–48 per cent of female athletes tested showed no change in performance across the menstrual cycle, while 33 per cent performed less well than usual around menstruation and 13–15 per cent performed better than average. This concurs with self-report data from 66 top women athletes at the Tokyo Olympic Games (Zaharieva, 1965), 17 per cent of whom said that they felt their performance was worse than usual while they were menstruating, and 15 per cent of whom thought it was worse premenstrually. In both studies, the largest group of women are either unaffected by menstruation or perform better than average then.

Industrial performance has been subjected to more rigorous and extensive scrutiny than either athletic or academic work, although most of this research was carried out before the Second World War. Seward (1944) reviewed this research and concluded that there was no evidence to suggest a universal or systematic paramenstrual deficit in work performance. Since then, researchers have shown little interest in this area, and some studies have shown phase effects (e.g. Smith, 1950a, 1950b; Farris, 1956), although not necessarily a paramenstrual deficit. Farris (1956), for instance, studied the daily output of 7 women in a shell-loading factory, whose work involved weighing powder, placing it in the shells and stacking the packed shells in boxes of 24. These women were paid on a piece-work basis, so were motivated to produce as much as possible, and their work showed performance peaks on days 4, 12 and 25 of the menstrual cycle – that is, around mid-cycle and the paramenstruum. Redgrove (1971) conducted extensive studies of 20 women for between five months and a year, collecting daily performance measures. Eight of these women worked in a laundry, sorting and pressing white lab coats, and were paid according to the number of coats processed; 9 were punch-card operators, paid on a bonus system based on the number of cards punched per hour each week, and 3 of the women were secretaries, who typed a set piece each day for at least twelve months. These women had no financial incentive to type quickly or accurately, but Redgrove notes that two of them 'worked in the same office and competed with each other to see who could work fastest' (p. 228). The data were analysed individually, and of all these women only two, both typists, showed any menstrual cycle-related fluctuations. For these women 'high performances tended to occur in the late premenstruum and early part of the menstrual periods, whilst slow performances were recorded in the early pre-menstruum and late menstruum' (p. 230). In other words, the women were working more effectively at the times when common belief would have us think they should be doing less well. Redgrove attributes this to over-compensatory effort on their part, making the important point that in the real world (and maybe in lab experiments too), we rarely work 'flat out', even under piece-work conditions, so we may be able to work harder than usual at times when we believe or perceive ourselves to be 'off colour'.

The research relating to cognition and work performance, then, seems to provide a fairly clear answer to the question of whether women's work is adversely affected by menstruation or the menstrual cycle. That answer seems to be no. There are two possible reasons for this. The first is that for most women the menstrual cycle simply is not associated with fluctuations in cognitive ability. The second is that for many women it is, but that in most situations the changes are small enough for the woman to compensate for them (see Cockerill *et al.*, 1994). Active compensation can explain the absence of phase effects, while over-demanding or unfamiliar tasks which prevent compensation can explain the occurrence of paramenstrual deficits, and over-compensation can explain paramenstrual enhancement of performance. Such a theory can also account for the discrepancies between women's self-reports of lower concentration, etc., premenstrually and their objective performance.

These two possible reasons for the absence of universal menstrual cycle phase effects on cognition imply different strategies for future studies. If the findings result from the absence of 'real' menstrual cycle fluctuations, then the best advice would seem to be to draw a line under the research and turn our attention to more useful matters. If the findings result from compensatory efforts, then further studies of cognition across the menstrual cycle may be warranted but, as John Richardson (1992) argues, these should be driven by a theoretical interest in the processes of human cognition, and not by a practical or political interest in women's work performance.

PSYCHOPHYSIOLOGICAL PROCESSES

If it is assumed that cyclical changes do occur in task performance or cognition, the next question is: how do they occur? What mechanism might cause these changes? From a biopsychological point of view, candidates for such a mechanism may be found in psychophysiology. The menstrual cycle can be conceptualised as a biological rhythm, similar in function and effect to circadian rhythms (e.g. Dye, 1992; Asso, 1983, 1992). Researchers who take this perspective have looked for evidence of cyclical fluctuations in central psychophysiological processes, such as sensory sensitivity, and autonomic arousal, because these types of variation occur in response to other biological rhythms. The fluctuations which occur may not be directly noticeable to the person experiencing them, unless the rhythm itself becomes disrupted, as in the case of 'jet lag', for example. However, it is often suggested that they may have implications for cognitive performance or emotional experience.

Sensation

Studies of fluctuations in sensory processes across the menstrual cycle have focused on all five sensory modalities and pain perception. As is true of almost all sensory research, vision has received most interest, but olfaction too has been extensively investigated because of the assertion that menstrual/ovulatory synchrony may result from olfactory detection of pheromones between women (see Weller and Weller, 1993). Methodological differences between these studies are both a strength and a weakness. Measuring the same phenomenon in different ways and obtaining similar results would strengthen conclusions based on studies of different types (i.e. triangulation of data). Variable studies which also produce variable results are almost impossible to interpret, and it is for this reason that methodological differences between studies are usually referred to critically in the literature. The differences between studies of sensation and perception are similar to those in other areas of menstrual cycle research (see chapter three): that is, differences in designation of menstrual cycle phases, timing of measurement, choice of 'subjects' and 'controls', and choice of which aspect of the sensory process to measure. The latter, for example, raises some interesting issues in olfaction research – which odours are we interested in and why? Despite these difficulties, the majority of reported studies suggest that menstrual rhythms in sensory processes do exist, although their relationship to fluctuations in ovarian hormones is unclear.

Studies of vision have used various indices of visual sensitivity, but most frequently visual acuity tested under either light-adapted or dark-adapted conditions (e.g. Scher *et al.*, 1981). Visual acuity is tested by asking people to identify detail in a visual stimulus, for example letters of different sizes, as in the familiar optician's eye-test, or the direction of lines in gratings of different widths. Visual sensitivity may be tested by measuring the reaction time to the onset of a light stimulus, the time between two flashes of light which the subject reports seeing as one (two-flash fusion threshold – TFFT) or the flicker frequencies of a number of lights at the point at which the subject perceives them to fuse (critical flicker fusion threshold – CFFT), although both TFFT and CFFT are more properly conceptualised as measures of visual information processing rather than sensory sensitivity (see Dye, 1992).

Results of these studies have suggested that there is no change in visual sensitivity across the cycle in light-adapted women (Scher *et al.*, 1981), but that dark-adapted women do experience fluctuations in sensitivity (Diamond *et al.*, 1972; Ward *et al.*, 1978; Scher *et al.*, 1981). Similarly, night vision has been reported to be more sensitive at mid-cycle (Barris *et al.*, 1980). Johnson and Petersik (1987), using time series analysis techniques although only over thirty-two days, demonstrated fluctuations in visual contrast sensitivity in two menstruating women compared to two non-menstruating controls, and Wuttke *et al.* (1975) found that women respond more quickly to a flicker of light in the luteal phase of the cycle, although others have not observed phase differences (Jensen, 1982). TFFT has been reported as lowest in the premenstrual phase in almost all published studies (e.g. Diamond *et al.*, 1972; Braier and Asso, 1980; Asso, 1986). In contradiction to this, CFFT has been found to be highest premenstrually (Dye, 1992). Visual acuity has also been found to fluctuate across the cycle (Diamond *et al.*, 1972; Scher *et al.*, 1981; Scher *et al.*, 1985). These studies provide good evidence that visual abilities fluctuate measurably during the cycle. They are not very helpful, though, about the precise pattern of that fluctuation. Some studies find one peak of sensitivity, although not always in the same part of the cycle as others, while other work suggests a bi-modal pattern. Similarly, the studies say little about the practical significance of these fluctuations. They may be measurable and statistically significant, but are they sufficiently large to be meaningful in everyday life? Are all women the same, or do we have our own idiosyncratic rhythms? Clearly, the standard injunction that more research is needed is appropriate here if the detail of the rhythm (or rhythms) is of interest.

Similar comments could be made about olfactory sensitivity, which requires even more rigorous testing conditions than vision. While it is relatively easy to produce a dark room to test visual thresholds, a totally smell-free room is more of a challenge. Similarly, the choice of odours to test is more varied. A study of 32 women (12 using oral contraceptives), tested regularly during the cycle on seven 'primary' odours (ethyl-butyrate, eucalyptol, (-ionon, menthol, acetic acid, scatol and thiophene), showed no demonstrable fluctuations in perception or recognition thresholds (Herberhold *et al.*, 1982). Most menstrual cycle researchers, however, are not interested in olfactory sensitivity *per se*, but in sensitivity to substances which may act as chemical messengers between people, i.e. pheromones. Hence, Herberhold's study would be criticised for inappropriate choice of test odours. Most researchers who investigate cyclical fluctuations justify their choice of odours by referring to Le Magnen's studies of sex differences in odour sensitivity (Le Magnen, 1948; 1952), selecting only those to which women are more sensitive. The most frequently investigated odour is exaltolide, a 'musky smelling substance found in male urine', to which Le Magnen suggested women were more sensitive at mid-cycle. His findings with exaltolide have been replicated in later studies (e.g. Vierling and Rock, 1967; Good et al., 1976), and similar peaks of sensitivity to other odours have been reported at mid-cycle.[4] It seems that women are particularly sensitive to the odour of both roses and male urine around the time of ovulation – although these studies do not indicate how these smells are evaluated.[5] Doty et al. (1981, 1982) found similar fluctuations in sensitivity in a small group of oral contraceptive users, suggesting that ovulation is not the key mechanism in this process. Some odours seem to be easier for women to detect around menstruation rather than mid-cycle. Elsberg et al. (1935) reported that women were more sensitive to benzene, coffee and camphor 24–28 hours before menstruation than at other times. Similarly, Doty et al. (1981) found peaks in sensitivity to furfural during the latter days of menstruation and in the mid-luteal phase, as well as mid-cycle. As with studies of vision, it is difficult to identify patterns of cyclicity because tests are rarely conducted frequently enough or over a sufficiently long time. Strictly speaking, data collection over one menstrual cycle, however extensive, is not enough to demonstrate a cyclical effect reliably, in the same way that repeated measurement over one day would not be considered adequate demonstration of a circadian rhythm (see Sollberger, 1965; Kendall, 1976). It is important to remember, too, that demonstrating a cyclical sensitivity to a small group of odours does not suggest that the olfactory system is itself cyclical, only that – for whatever reason – we are more responsive to some odours at some times. As with vision research, more studies are needed to investigate the meaningfulness of current findings in the context of real life. The odours presented experimentally are usually in a more concentrated form than those experienced 'normally', and are certainly less contaminated by other odours or information from other senses. Do these findings generalise outside the laboratory?

In comparison to studies of vision and olfaction there have been relatively few studies of audition, taste or touch, and it is far more difficult to see clear similarities between them (see Parlee, 1983). Several studies have suggested that menstrual cycle fluctuations can be observed in auditory sensitivity (e.g. Henkin, 1974; Mehta et al., 1977; Tobias, 1965; Swanson and Dengerink, 1988; Becker et al., 1982), but other studies have not demonstrated this effect (Haggard and Gaston, 1978; Schubert et al., 1975; Grieze-Jurgelevicius et al., 1990). Similarly, studies differ in their comparison of oral contraceptive (oc) users and normally cycling women. Wong and Tong (1974) found that both groups showed menstrually related fluctuations in the ability to discriminate between two consecutive sounds (the auditory equivalent of two-flash fusion), although overall pill users were more sensitive than non-users. However, Becker et al. (1982) and Swanson and Dengerink (1988) found that oc users did not show the same cyclical pattern as non-users. In the study by Grieze-Jurgelevicius et al. (1990), it was the normally cycling women who did not experience menstrually related fluctuations in auditory sensitivity, while the oc users did have lower thresholds postmenstrually than at other times. In this study, the oc users were more sensitive overall to five of the six tones used, regardless of cycle phase.

Taste is difficult to study independently of olfaction, but the few researchers who have attempted it have shown menstrual cycle fluctuations in the subjective pleasantness of sugar solutions (Aaron, 1975; Wright and Crow, 1973) and the detection threshold for salt (Henkin, 1974). A more recent study examined sucrose thresholds at three points during the menstrual cycle for 14 normally cycling women compared to 13 men tested at similar intervals (Than et al., 1994). The men's thresholds remained stable across the three testing points, but the women showed significantly lower thresholds in the preovulatory phase (days 8 to 12 of a 28-day cycle) compared both with the men and with themselves at the other two points. There is no clear pattern to these findings and, as Parlee (1983) notes, no speculations have been offered about the mechanisms which may underlie them. In the light of the growing research interest in cyclical food cravings and eating patterns (e.g. Cohen et al., 1987; see chapter five), it may be informative to replicate and develop these findings.

Tactile sensitivity, too, has received little investigation, with the only reports published suggesting a lower sensitivity to touch premenstrually and a higher sensitivity around ovulation/mid-cycle (Herren, 1933; Henkin, 1974). Sensitivity to pain, on the other hand, has attracted more attention, largely resulting from assertions – made before the discovery of prostaglandins – that dysmenorrhea might have psychogenic origins (see chapter five). As is characteristic of this area, while a number of studies have demonstrated cyclical fluctuations in sensitivity to pain stimuli, the pattern of these fluctuations is unclear (Parlee, 1983). Some researchers find increased sensitivity to pain at mid-cycle (e.g. Goolkasian, 1980) while others report lowest sensitivity to pain at this time (e.g. Warren et al., 1979) and yet others describe a bi-modal pattern (e.g. Robinson and Short, 1977). Robinson and Short (1977) were concerned with breast sensitivity, which was assessed at the nipple, areola and cutaneous breast tissue using a pricking pain-threshold technique. The nipple was, not surprisingly, found to be the most sensitive part of the breast, but all parts were more sensitive to this type of touch at mid-cycle and menstruation than at other times. A similar study also found a peak of sensitivity during the luteal phase (Hilgers et al., 1981). However, these researchers do not comment on the levels of premenstrual breast tenderness or breast pain experienced by the women in their samples, which may confound measures of pain sensitivity. The mechanisms suggested to account for these fluctuations in sensitivity relate either to peripheral processes, i.e. generalised oedema stretching the skin (e.g. Millodot and Lamont, 1974), or to changes in the central nervous system (e.g. Procacci et al., 1972).

In summary, then, the majority of studies of sensory sensitivity suggest that fluctuations do occur during the menstrual cycle (see Asso, 1983; Parlee, 1983). There is a bias here, of course, because studies which do not show a cyclical fluctuation are likely to languish in filing cabinets rather than being published (this is true throughout menstrual cycle research). The widely differing methodologies and cycle phase designations mean that quantitative techniques, such as meta-analysis, cannot be meaningfully applied to these studies, and conclusions about the size and pattern of fluctuations are difficult to draw. In addition, researchers have generally focused on only one cycle, thereby failing to demonstrate a rhythmic effect, but showing differences only between two or more different timepoints. In a telling comment on Herberhold *et al.*'s paper, which found no cyclical fluctuation in olfactory sensitivity, Richard Doty remarks that 'it is frequently important that the data matrix of such studies be normalized to counteract the effect of marked inter-cycle variability. Data not carefully normalized will often mask subtle changes across the cycle' (Doty *et al.* 1982: 350). This is a little ambiguous, but the author's comment that 'sets of data were evaluated for one cycle therefore no inter-cycle variability had to be considered' suggests that in the context of the discussion, variability in olfactory sensitivity between the same phase of different menstrual cycles is being referred to (rather than variability in menstrual cycle length *per se*). 'Marked' inter-cycle variability would seem to contradict the notion of a fundamental biological rhythm, but would help to explain the variability in research findings in this area.

Nervous system activity

Chronobiologists are interested in nervous system activity (or 'arousal') as an index of biological rhythms; researchers from a biomedical perspective are searching for a biochemical basis for 'dysfunction', while social psychologists are concerned with the possibility that differing attributions for heightened arousal premenstrually may explain different patterns of 'symptom' reporting. It is surprising, then, that there are relatively few studies which directly investigate cyclical changes in either central or autonomic nervous system arousal, although there are many which speculate about them. One reason for the lack of studies is the difficulty of investigation in this area – how can we know that the central nervous system (CNS) or autonomic nervous system (ANS) is aroused or activated? CNS activity can be assessed in a variety of ways – subjectively, using self-report questionnaires such as Thayer's Activation–Deactivation Adjective Checklist (Thayer, 1967), or objectively, by observation of EEG or TFFT/CFFT (Dye, 1992; Asso, 1983). ANS arousal is assessed by more peripheral measures, such as skin conductance, blood pressure, heart rate, respiration rate and hand steadiness. Autonomic responses to stressors induced at different points in the menstrual cycle have also been used to examine ANS activity. Studies using these techniques have produced a variety of results.

Increases in CNS arousal have been identified premenstrually on self-report measures (Parlee, 1980; Ussher and Wilding, 1991), and EEG alpha rhythms have been found to be accelerated during the luteal phase (Wuttke *et al.*, 1975). Cortical responsiveness as measured by CFFT has also been found to increase premenstrually (Dye, 1992). All of these suggest heightened central arousal or activation just before menstruation. On the other hand, the majority of studies suggest a decrease in cortical activity premenstrually using a variety of measures (Braier and Asso, 1980; Asso and Braier, 1982; Kopell *et al.*, 1969; Asso, 1986; Grant and Pryse-Davis, 1968; Klaiber *et al.*, 1974; Belmaker *et al.*, 1974; Solis-Ortiz *et al.*, 1994). Increased CNS activity around ovulation is a more consistent finding, however (Dye, 1992; Asso, 1983), raising the possibility of a bi-modal rather than sinusoidal pattern for some measures of arousal.

Studies of ANS activity present an even more confusing picture. Asso (1983) notes that 'appraisal of the work on the ANS is complicated . . . because of the fragmentation of autonomic responses and of the wide variety of responses within and among individuals' (Asso, 1983: 49). So, different measures of ANS activity taken at the same time in the same women may suggest conflicting conclusions (e.g. Little and Zahn, 1974; Ussher and Wilding, 1991). This was accommodated for by Wineman (1971) who produced a composite score based on salivary output, sublingual temperature and skin conductance to estimate overall autonomic balance. This procedure indicated lower ANS activity in the luteal phase than during menstruation or the follicular phase. Other studies suggest an overall increase in ANS activity premenstrually, however (Asso, 1978; Uno, 1972; De Marchi and Tong, 1972; Bell, 1976; Kuczmierczyk and Adams, 1986; Ussher and Wilding, 1991; Choi and Salmon, 1995b). Similarly, a number of studies show no cyclical fluctuations in these measures (Friedman and Meares, 1978; Kopell *et al.*, 1969; Little and Zahn, 1974; Slade and Jenner, 1979).

ANS responses to induced stress at different points in the cycle are not entirely consistent either, although this has become a very popular experimental paradigm in menstrual cycle research. Marinari *et al.* (1976) found that adreno-cortical responses to stress were significantly greater during the premenstrual phase than at mid-cycle in a small group of normally cycling women. This effect has been replicated with a variety of measures (Hastrup and Light, 1984; Ladisich, 1977; Tersman *et al.*, 1991; Fishman *et al.*, 1994), but an equal number of studies have found that ANS responses to stress do not differ across cycle phases (Ablanalp *et al.*, 1977; Stoney *et al.*, 1990; Girdler *et al.*, 1993; Choi and Salmon, 1995b). Self-reports of perceived stress do change, however, with women rating themselves as more stressed after the same task in the premenstrual phase than they do earlier in the cycle (Choi and Salmon, 1995b). Since this was observed in a study which found no difference in ANS responses between cycle phases, it suggests either that the self-reports were influenced by expectations, or that these women were able to compensate for the stress they felt and limit their autonomic response (e.g. by deliberately trying to relax during the test); alternatively, the measures of ANS activity used were not measuring what the women felt to be a stress response. This point does raise an important methodological issue – the persistent difference between self-reports of subjective state in menstrual cycle research and objective measures. Georgene Seward commented on this in her literature review published in 1944, noting that self-reports usually indicate a cyclical effect while objective tests do not. Fifty years later, though, we still have few convincing explanations for this phenomenon which do not privilege one form of information over the other.

So, studies of arousal provide a complex picture. Louise Dye (1992) argues that 'the prevailing impression appears to be one of increased ANS activity during the premenstrual phase' (p. 77) – although the precise nature of these fluctuations and their relationship to CNS arousal remains obscure. Theoretical conceptualisations reconcile these difficulties by suggesting that there are a number of partially independent but interacting arousal systems which can account for the wide variety of experiences women report, and then go on to implicate fluctuations in arousal in a wide variety of other menstrually related phenomena (see Asso, 1992; Ussher, 1991; chapter six). While there is plenty of evidence here to justify that position, there is just as much which does not, and fluctuations in arousal seem to be every bit as variable as those in sensory processes.

SOCIAL COGNITIONS

Social cognition is defined by Fiske and Taylor (1991) as 'the study of how people make sense of other people and themselves' (Fiske and Taylor, 1991:1). In menstrual cycle research, the social cognitions which have most often been of interest are the beliefs, stereotypes and attitudes of menstruating women about or towards menstruation, although a few studies do investigate the views of other groups, such as men. The research described in this section reflects many of the cultural constructions of menstruation described in chapter one, as they are expressed in the questionnaire and interview responses of men and women studied by social scientists. From a social psychological point of view, they have been of interest as possible causal factors in the self-perception and reporting of experiences around menstruation as 'symptoms' (see chapter five). From a social cognition perspective, the presence of strong social stereotypes about menstruation and/or the premenstrual phase could give rise to the cognitive heuristics and biases which affect all judgements of the actions of self and others, e.g. illusory correlations, availability heuristics, fundamental attribution errors, etc.[6] Even before social cognition theory became established in the 1970s, it was argued that negative attitudes towards and beliefs about menstruation might be the root cause of either menstrual pain or paramenstrual depression and irritability (McHugh and Wasser, 1959). This approach is often perceived as implying that menstrually related experiences are 'all in the mind', and dismissed with irritation by both radical feminists and biomedical researchers. For many earlier studies, this irritation is well justified; it is, after all, no more logical to suggest that negative attitudes towards menstruation cause pain or distress than it is to say that the experience of problematic periods causes a negative attitude towards menstruation, as we shall see below. The social cognition studies, though, such as those conducted by Diane Ruble, Jeanne Brooks Gunn, Randi

Koeske, Mary Parlee and others, are more concerned with the difference between retrospective and prospective accounts of menstrual experience than they are with explaining women's experience *per se*. These studies ask why retrospective questionnaires invariably produce inflated reports of symptomatology in comparison to similar measures used prospectively, and locate the answer in social cognitive mechanisms. The experimental evidence relating to this theoretical approach is discussed in chapters three and five. This chapter is concerned with the content of the cognitions which these researchers have uncovered, rather than in the question of whether cognitions have behavioural or experiential implications.

Menstrual knowledge and beliefs

What do most people know or believe about menstruation? A number of studies have investigated modern beliefs about menstruation, often in the spirit of anthropological enquiry (Snow and Johnson, 1977) or in an endeavour to improve menstrual health education for adolescents (Abraham *et al.*, 1985a). Ignorance about the physiological and phenomenological reality of menstruation might be expected to be a significant feature of cultures in which menstruation is surrounded by secrecy and euphemism. To some extent, empirical research suggests that this is the case, especially for young people. Kathryn Lovering (1991) in her study of 11 and 12 year olds in Britain found that one in ten of the boys and one in twenty of the girls denied having heard of menstruation when she asked them about it. Abraham *et al.* (1985a) report a study of 1,377 young Australian women aged 14–19 years and representative of the general population. The average score of these women on a menstrual knowledge questionnaire was 10, from a possible maximum of 30. In particular, these women were unsure about the timing of ovulation, when pregnancy is most likely to occur, and the contents of menstrual discharge. Only 15 per cent of them could accurately estimate the average volume of menstruation (about 80 ml), for example. The question of precisely how women are supposed to measure the volume of their own or other women's menstruation is not considered by these researchers as mitigating their ignorance.

Studies of menstrual beliefs and folklore are full of 'fancy that' phenomena. For example, Paige Erickson (1987) describes findings from a national North American survey of menstrual beliefs and attitudes – the Tampax Report, published by Ruder and Finn (1981). She notes that two-thirds of the sample thought that women should conceal the fact that they are menstruating, while half of the sample believed that women have a different scent during menstruation and a quarter agreed that women look different at this time. She went on to point out that:

> 24 per cent of men and 18 per cent of women thought it harmful to bathe or swim while menstruating; and 34 per cent of men and 24 per cent of

women believed menstruating women should restrict their physical activities. Men, however, are much more likely than women to say that menstruating women do not function well at work (89 per cent vs. 66 per cent), and there are even some who believe that women should stay away from people while menstruating (12 per cent of men and 5 per cent of women).

(Paige Erickson, 1987: 176)

These findings are similar to those of Snow and Johnson (1977) who investigated the 'menstrual folk beliefs' of 40 women enrolled as patients at a public clinic in Michigan. The authors report that most of these women were 'ignorant of the real function of the menstrual cycle', but 'offered a variety of folk beliefs to explain it'. The major theme running through these beliefs was an association between menstruation and bodily cleanliness (see chapter one). Like the Welsh women in Vieda Skultans' study (see below), these women described menstruation as a time when the body is open to allow the flow of blood, thereby risking the possibility that dangerous substances might enter it. Dangerous substances included cold air, water, 'germs' or disease, and penises – hence the belief that menstruating women should avoid situations in which they might encounter these (e.g. funerals, swimming, bathing, 'catching cold', penetrative sex). Some of these substances were seen as dangerous because they might stop the menstrual flow, causing the accumulated blood to collect and haemorrhage elsewhere, e.g. in the brain or lungs. Some foods were also avoided for this reason (e.g. citrus fruits, tomatoes, green leafy vegetables).

One of the largest studies of menstrual beliefs was the World Health Organization-funded study of patterns and perceptions of menstruation (Snowden and Christian, 1983). This study involved over 5,000 women in ten countries and collected information about their menstrual experiences, such as the length, frequency and amount of bleeding, as well as their menstrual beliefs (see chapter one). The questions about menstrual beliefs have recently been analysed in more detail (Severy et al., 1993). In this analysis, most of the variance in the data was accounted for by women's ratings on 11 questions or statements about menstruation. These included: 'a woman should avoid washing her hair while she is menstruating', 'it is necessary for a woman to have menstruation to feel completely feminine' and 'a woman who does not menstruate cannot have children'. When the scores on these scales were cluster analysed, 9 different groupings of menstrual beliefs were found. These different belief profiles demonstrate the diversity of views held by women about menstruation, with each different belief pattern being held by a relatively small proportion of women, ranging from 4.68 per cent to 19.17 per cent of the total sample (see Table 4.1). The interesting point about this study is that while many women may hold the same belief, e.g. that hair-washing should be avoided during menstruation, they hold it in combination with a variety of other beliefs. The combination of beliefs may be associated with a particular 'theory' of menstruation, and logical in that context (see below). This study is also important because it demon-strates a relationship between menstrual experiences and menstrual beliefs. For example, women whose periods were perceived as 'difficult' were more likely to be found in belief profiles 1 and 6. Both of these agree that they would take something to stop their periods if they could, and disagree that menstruating more than they already do would be 'better', although they differ on all other belief items. While some may argue that particular beliefs about menstruation increase the likelihood that it will be perceived as 'difficult', it is equally possible that heavy, painful or unpredictable periods lead some women to believe that they would be better without them!

Some researchers suggest that menstrual beliefs may be explicable in terms of 'folklore', and imply that women are 'ignorant' if they fail to describe menstrua-tion in terms which match those in current medical texts (i.e. in terms of ovulation, fertility and 'no big deal'). The imperative, as Snow and Johnson (for example) declare it, is to prevent these folk beliefs from interfering with what medical professionals believe to be healthy behaviours (e.g. attending for 'smear' tests, using effective contraception, eating vegetables) by identifying and educating those people who hold them. Do we have to describe cultural beliefs about menstruation as 'ignorant' and 'unhelpful'? Folklore may be influential, but Severy et al. (1993) suggest that it is not the only factor determining women's beliefs about menstruation. Whether or not women are 'ignorant' of medical knowledge about menstruation, they are not ignorant about their own experi-ence, and this seems to be related to the beliefs they express and the meaning that menstruation has. In this respect, it is generally the researchers who are ignorant. The implications of these beliefs need not always be seen as negative, either. Margie Profet's analysis of menstruation as a means of cleansing the reproductive tract and preventing infection suggests that some of these beliefs might serve a useful purpose, and the behavioural changes which women report may also serve a purpose as coping strategies to alleviate menstrual pain or discomfort (Choi and Salmon, 1995a). For example, 16 per cent of a sample of 342 British women reported 'avoiding certain foods' and 20 per cent 'avoided people' in order to cope with menstrually related changes (Choi and Salmon, 1995a). One alternative interpretation is that the behaviours which women asso-ciate with menstruation are similar from one generation or culture to the next, but the justification for them changes. Now we describe them as 'coping strate-gies for menstrually related changes' whereas previous generations described them as ways of promoting healthy blood loss and avoiding the entry of 'dangerous' substances into the body. In either case, they may not be as 'igno-rant' or 'unhealthy' as medical texts often assume.

Premenstrual expectations and stereotypes

Parlee's critical study of the Moos Menstrual Distress Questionnaire, published in 1974, was the first empirical demonstration of the existence of stereotypical

Table 4.1   Endorsement of each of 11 belief items by 9 belief profiles

Belief items	Belief profiles (1–9)								
	1	2	3	4	5	6	7	8	9
Number of women (total = 5,196)	518	996	243	466	542	577	642	668	544
A woman should avoid washing her hair while she is menstruating	x	√	√√	x	√	x	x	√	√
Menstruation is like being sick	x	√	√	√	x	x	x	x	√
A woman who does not menstruate cannot have children	xx	√	√	√	x	√	√	x	√
A woman should avoid intercourse/sex while she is menstruating	xx	√	√	√	x	√	x	√	√
It is necessary for a woman to have menstruation to feel completely feminine	xx	√	x	√	√	x	√	√	√
Menstruation is dirty	x	√	x	√	x	√	x	√	x
When a woman is menstruating she should take fewer baths than usual	x	√	√√	x	√√	√	x	x	x
When a woman bleeds outside the time of her normal menstrual period she is sick	x	√	x	x	x	√	x	√	√
When a woman is menstruating she should take more baths than usual	√	x	x	√√	x	x	√	√	x
If you could be given something to stop your periods, would you use it?	√	x	√	√	x	√	x	√	x
Would it be better for you to bleed more than you do?	x	√	√	x	√	x	√	√	x

Source: Adapted from Severy *et al.* (1993: 10), © The Haworth Press. Reprinted by permission.
Note: x = disagree, xx = strongly disagree, √ = agree, √√ = strongly agree

beliefs about women's premenstrual and menstrual experiences. In this famous study, men and women were asked to complete the retrospective Moos MDQ on the basis of 'what women experience'. The ratings made by men and women of experiences in the premenstrual, menstrual and intermenstrual phases of the cycle were remarkably similar, suggesting either a very accurate knowledge of female cyclicity by the male participants, or else the existence of a stereotype of menstrually related experience which both groups accessed when completing the questionnaire. This is not to say that the experiences women describe at any point in the cycle are not real (although it is often interpreted this way), simply that when filling in questionnaires women may report those experiences which fit the stereotype and not those which don't – research participants generally attempt to give the researcher what they think he or she wants to hear (social conformity/desirability effect). This effect has been replicated in several studies, suggesting the existence of a stereotype of menstrual cycle related experiences (or implicit theory about the effect of menstruation on mood) which influences expectations and premenstrual symptom reporting (Englander-Golden et al., 1978; Olasov and Jackson, 1987; AuBuchon and Calhoun, 1985; Walker, 1992b; McFarland et al., 1989; Chrisler et al., 1994).

Although these studies imply that stereotypes exist, and explore 'symptom' reporting after manipulating expectations, few researchers have investigated the content of such stereotypes. Studies using the MDQ, or parts of it, suggest that women believe that the menstrual cycle affects pain, water retention and negative affect, reporting typically higher levels of all of these around menstruation for women in general (Brooks Gunn and Ruble, 1986; McFarland et al., 1989). In a study of Scottish undergraduates, Yvonne Hill and I investigated stereotypes of the 'premenstrual woman' and the similarity or difference between that and other gender stereotypes (Hill et al., 1994). We asked 75 men and 197 women to rate four 'target' people on a list of mood adjectives. They rated 'self', a 'typical man' (TM), a 'typical woman' (TW) and 'a typical woman premenstrually' (TWP). The women participants were also asked to rate 'self premenstrually'. Nine adjectives were chosen from the PMS literature, and were presented with appropriate antonyms, so that an equal number of 'positive' and 'negative' adjectives were rated. The adjectives were: tense/relaxed, tired/energetic, distracted/able to concentrate, inhibited/uninhibited, lethargic/alert, under the weather/on top of the world, aggressive/peaceful, depressed/happy, and irritable/calm. They were rated on unipolar 7-point scales with extremes labelled 'not at all' and 'very'. In this group, gender stereotypes were quite clear. Overall, the 'typical man' was rated as more relaxed, energetic, uninhibited and 'on top of the world' than the 'typical woman', but also more irritable, distracted, aggressive and lethargic. Typical men and typical women were rated as being equally happy, although typical women were rated as significantly more depressed. So, while men and women are seen as being different, it is not the case that the 'typical woman' is being given high scores on all of the negative dimensions and the typical man is being given high scores on positive dimensions, or vice versa. The 'typical woman premenstrually', in contrast, was given more extreme and more negative ratings than either TM or TW on all of the adjectives, by both men and women. The most extreme scores were given to 'irritable', 'tense', 'under the weather' (all at the 'very' end of the scale) and their antonyms, 'relaxed', 'calm' and 'on top of the world' (all at the 'not at all' end of the scale). It seems that, in this group at least, the TWP stereotype is a hybrid of the worst aspects of both men and women. She is more irritable and aggressive than the typical man, but also more tense and depressed than the typical woman. These descriptions bear close similarity to the depictions of PMS in media and press reports (Chrisler and Levy, 1990; Rittenhouse, 1991; Walker, 1995b), suggesting that such imagery has spilled over into generalisations about all (or 'typical') women. Further research is needed, though, to investigate how such stereotypes are used in everyday life – for example, how are women identified as being 'premenstrual', or is it the case that a woman who appears to be irritable is assumed to be premenstrual? This possibility has concerned feminist writers (Laws *et al.*, 1985; Stoppard, 1992), but still awaits empirical investigation.

Attitudes towards menstruation

In Western cultures, menstruation is a private and usually hidden experience, surrounded by euphemism and a subtle menstrual 'etiquette' (see Laws, 1990). The attitudes towards menstruation expressed in medical literature are profoundly negative, usually describing menstruation as a 'loss' or failure of reproduction, or omitting any discussion of 'normal' menstruation and focusing only on dysfunctional or abnormal states (McKeever, 1984; Laws, 1990; Martin, 1989). Descriptions of menstruation in popular media, and particularly advertising for menstrual products, similarly emphasise the need for secrecy and avoidance of leaks or mess (Ernster, 1975; Treneman, 1988; Berg and Block Coutts, 1993, 1994; Block Coutts and Berg, 1993). In the context of this negativity, it is not surprising that researchers have been curious about the attitudes women hold towards menstruation as a function, and whether these attitudes have behavioural implications.

The first empirical study of menstrual attitudes was reported by Gelolo McHugh and Judith Wasser in 1959. They asked 200 students in two women's colleges to complete a brief open-ended questionnaire, which included the question, 'Just how do you feel about menstruation?' From their responses, 48 statements of attitudes towards menstruation were obtained, ranging from 'menstruation gives me a feeling of pride' to 'menstruation revolts me'. This is an interesting study, but unfortunately, the authors do not investigate the frequency with which the attitude statements are endorsed, or consider their factor structure. Twenty of these statements were used by Frances Dunham (1970) in a study of 189 introductory psychology students. She chose statements so that 'on inspection some seemed to represent a neutral or approach attitude and others, an avoidance attitude toward menstruation' (p. 208) – in other words on the grounds of face validity rather than psychometric procedure. Nine of the statements were described as 'positive' and 11 'negative'. The students rated each of the statements on a 4-point scale labelled 'very true', 'moderately true', 'moderately untrue', 'very untrue'. In scoring, these were assigned weights of 1, 2, 4 and 5 respectively, with 3 being given to missing scores. The mean scores of the young women in this study show that their attitudes towards menstruation are predominantly positive. The lowest mean score (1.13) was associated with the item 'menstruation is a normal biological function', and the average score for the 9 positive items for the whole group was significantly lower than that for the negative items (28.92 compared to 45.38), suggesting that these students were more likely to agree with the positive statements than the negative ones. The negative items which these women did agree with related to inconvenience and pain, i.e. 'menstruation is a terrible nuisance' , 'I resent it because of the pain' and 'menstruation interrupts my activities'.

These findings were largely supported by Brooks *et al.* (1977), who asked 191 undergraduate women to complete 7-point rating scales indicating how much they agreed or disagreed with 46 statements about menstruation. The origins of these statements are not given, so it must be assumed that the authors generated the statements themselves. They were, however, 'constructed to represent five categories: beliefs about physiological and psychological concomitants of menstruation; styles of dealing with menstruation; menstrual-related effects on performance; and general evaluations of menstruation' (Brooks *et al.*, 1977: 290). Factor analysis of the scale produced 5 different attitude dimensions: menstruation as a psychologically and physically debilitating event; as a positive event; as a bothersome event; as an event whose onset can be predicted and anticipated; and as an event that does not and should not affect one's behaviour. The presence of these different factors suggests that menstrual attitudes are multidimensional, rather than falling somewhere on a single positive–negative dimension as had previously been thought. These items and scales then became the Menstrual Attitudes Questionnaire (see chapter three). As in Dunham's study, items from the 'positive' scale were most frequently agreed with. Women were said by the authors to agree with a scale if their mean score for the items loading on that factor fell between 4.0 and 7.0. By this definition, 77 per cent of the women agreed with the 'positive' scale, in response to items such as 'menstruation provides a way for me to keep in touch with my body' and 'menstruation is a reoccurring affirmation of womanhood'. The next most popular scales were 'bothersome' (59 per cent agree) and 'predicted and anticipated' (54 per cent agree), with only 32 per cent agreeing that menstruation is debilitating and 12 per cent denying any effects of menstruation. The MAQ has now been used in several studies, although not all of them report the subscale scores. Results from three of these studies are shown in Table 4.2. The pattern of these results supports the original finding that positive or neutral statements about menstruation are most frequently endorsed. The young men studied by Brooks Gunn and Ruble (1986) rated menstruation as significantly more debilitating than did young women, and older women studied by Olasov Rothbaum and Jackson (1990) emphasise the predictability of menstruation rather than its positive or neutral aspects. It may be that the younger women in Brooks Gunn and Ruble's studies were sufficiently close to menarche to be influenced by discourses about 'becoming a woman', which may have become less significant for older women. The purpose of Olasov Rothbaum and Jackson's study was to investigate the relationship between religious belief and religiosity and menstrual attitudes. Their findings suggest that there is little difference between groups of practising Orthodox Jewish, Protestant or Roman Catholic women. The only significant differences between them occur on the 'bothersomeness' scale: Protestants and Jewish women who do not attend Mikvah rated menstruation as more bothersome than Mikvah attenders or Catholic women, thus challenging the assumption, made by many writers about menstruation, that religious rituals surrounding it will increase the negativity of attitudes towards it. Unfortunately, all of the women in this study were members of 'organized religious congregations', and there is no secular group for comparison purposes.

The MAQ has been criticised by some authors because it includes questions both about the woman herself and about women in general (Müller, 1991) and because it assumes a simple, bipolar, positive–negative response to menstruation (Rierdan and Koff, 1990; Morse et al., 1993). It also omits questions about sex and sexuality, which may be a significant factor in attitudes towards menstruation, especially for older women. A number of new questionnaires and adaptations have been developed to address these concerns. The Adolescent Menstrual Attitude Questionnaire (AMAQ), for example, avoids simple bipolar dimensions and uses wording appropriate for either premenarcheal or postmenarcheal adolescents (Morse et al., 1993; Morse and Kieren, 1993). For older women, a German version of the MAQ has been developed by Bernhard Strauss and his colleagues, which includes questions about the degree to which menstruation interferes with or disrupts sexuality (Strauss et al., 1987; Strauss et al., 1990; Dye, 1991). Factor analysis of this set of questions also produces 5 factors, supporting Brooks Gunn and Ruble's proposition that menstrual attitudes are multidimensional. Three of the factors are very similar to those of the MAQ, i.e. 'menstruation as a debilitating influence on performance', 'positive view of menstruation' and 'denial of the effects of menstruation'. The two slightly different factors are 'menstruation as a disturbance of sexuality' and 'menstruation as a disturbance of psychological state', the second of which overlaps with the MAQ 'predictable' scale. The development of this questionnaire involved a much wider variety of women in terms of age, occupation and reproductive experience than the Brooks Gunn and Ruble questionnaire, so it is possible that the different factors reflect not only cultural differences in attitudes towards menstruation, but also age or experience-related changes. The existence of cultural differences in attitudes is also supported by Hardie and McMurray's study of menstrual attitudes among Australian undergraduates (Hardie and McMurray, 1992). In this study, too, questions about the effect of menstruation on sexuality were added to the MAQ, and endorsed by the respondents. The young women in this study rated menstruation as more bothersome than did the North American women, although their scores on other scales were similar. Women over 30, or who had borne children, were excluded from this study, and menstrual attitudes were found to be related to the women's sex role ideology (see chapter 6).

A number of studies have investigated the effect of age or menstrual experience on attitudes towards menstruation by studying adolescent women (before and after menarche) and their mothers. Clarke and Ruble (1978) asked premenarcheal (n = 18) and postmenarcheal (n = 18) girls about menstruation. Neither group felt very comfortable talking about it, and 9 out of 18 who had experi-

Table 4.2   Mean scores on the Menstrual Attititude Questionnaire subscales
in reported studies

Study	Sample	Mean age	Debili-tating	Both-ersome	Positive/ Natural	Predict-able	Denial of effect
					MAQ subscales		
Brooks, Ruble and Clark, 1977	191 students	19.3 yrs	3.39	4.18	4.64	3.79	2.73
Brooks-Gunn and Ruble, 1986	156 students	20.0 yrs	3.61	4.65	4.51	4.98	3.17
Brooks, Gunn and Ruble, 1986	83 men students	20.0 yrs	4.45	4.13	4.55	5.04	2.83
Olasov Rothbaum and Jackson, 1990	18 Jewish Mikvah attenders	36.7 yrs	1.33	1.54	2.86	3.52	1.43
Olasov Rothbaum and Jackson, 1990	23 Orthodox Jewish	40.1 yrs	1.36	2.47	2.89	4.09	1.48
Olasov Rothbaum and Jackson, 1990	35 Protestant	35.2 yrs	1.15	2.21	2.81	3.44	1.83
Olasov Rothbaum and Jackson, 1990	45 Roman Catholic	36.9 yrs	1.06	1.59	2.88	3.81	1.67
Hardie and McMurray, 1992	351 students	20.2 yrs	3.19	5.36	4.31	4.70	2.81
Hardie and McMurray, 1992	183 students	18.8 yrs	3.43	5.18	4.42	5.04	2.69

Notes: All samples are women unless otherwise stated
Items are scored on 1–7 scales, where 1 is labelled 'disagree strongly' and 7 'agree strongly'.
Scores in the Olasov Rothbaum and Jackson (1990) study were presented as mean totals for each scale. They have been transformed here by dividing by the number of items per scale, i.e. debilitating 12, bothersome 6, predictable 5, positive 5, denial 7.

enced their first period were worried that 'someone would know when they were menstruating'. Postmenarcheal girls also indicated significantly greater general dislike towards menstruation than premenarcheal girls, although about a quarter of the total group agreed that 'menstruation is something to be happy about'. So these girls seem to be ambivalent about menstruation. In a later study Brooks Gunn and Ruble (1982) asked 48 schoolgirls to complete a 12-item 'adolescent form' version of the MAQ. In this sample, the positive items were most frequently endorsed and menstruation was rated as significantly more debilitating by the premenarcheal girls than the postmenarcheal ones, contradicting the earlier findings. Since both of these studies involve small samples it is difficult to draw conclusions about the impact of menarche on menstrual attitudes. In the longitudinal part of Brooks Gunn and Ruble's study, however, girls who evaluated menstruation as negative while they were premenarcheal were more likely to report severe premenstrual pain, water retention and negative affect on the MDQ after they had begun to menstruate. Morse and Kieren (1993) similarly

109

found qualitative differences between the attitudes of 860 premenarcheal and 1,013 postmenarcheal Canadian girls who completed the AMAQ. In this study, the length of time a girl had been menstruating was significantly related to her acceptance of menarche, openness about menstruation and the ease of living with menstruation. There were also significant correlations between self-reports of menstrually related symptoms (e.g. backache, tender breasts and mood changes) and negative feelings about menstruation, acceptance of menarche and living with menarche. These relationships suggest, as in the previous studies, that the reality of menstruation is not as bad as premenarcheal girls fear, but that experiencing a variety of menstrually related symptoms does influence attitudes towards menstruation.

Stoltzman (1986) investigated the menstrual attitudes of adolescent girls (aged 15–16 years), their friends and their mothers, using a 32-item questionnaire, with some similarities to the MAQ. The adolescents in this study were more likely than their mothers to view menstruation as debilitating, bothersome and unsanitary, and less likely to view it as a positive event. They were also less worried about menstrual hygiene and more likely to talk about menstruation openly than their mothers. These differences may reflect changes in the physical experience of menstruation with maturity, or they may be the result of cohort effects and cultural changes in menstrual product availability and advertising, for example. Significant correlations between physical aspects of menstruation (heaviness, cycle length, regularity, etc.) and menstrual attitudes, measured by the MAQ, were found in a sample of 156 women students at three colleges in New Jersey (Brooks Gunn, 1985). Women who rated their periods as 'heavy' perceived menstruation as more bothersome, more debilitating and less predictable, and were less likely to deny that it had any effect than women who rated their periods as 'light'. Similarly, women who described their periods as 'irregular' rated menstruation as more bothersome and debilitating and less deniable than women who rated their periods as 'regular'. Further multivariate and longitudinal studies are needed to disentangle the influences of culture, cohort, physical experience, age, sex-role and other factors on menstrual attitudes.

All of the studies described so far have used questionnaires to measure women's attitudes towards menstruation. Although they have conceptualised menstrual attitudes as multi-dimensional, they still retain the positive–negative dimension, and the dimensions are conceptualised as independent from one another (justified by factor analysis). In studies using all of these questionnaires, one group is described as being 'more negative' than another on particular dimensions, for example, and the relationships between different dimensions for groups or individuals are rarely examined. It is difficult to obtain a clear impression from these studies of the coherence or meaning of menstrual attitudes. Qualitative researchers have approached menstrual attitudes from a slightly different direction, showing a greater concern with older women and the variety of menstrual experience than with the misconceptions and education of menarcheal women.[7] These studies suggest that menstrual attitudes are rather more complex than positive/negative distinctions suggest, but reflect a coherence which questionnaire studies obscure. Vieda Skultans (1970), for example, interviewed 18 50-year-old women in a Welsh mining village in 1970, using a broadly psychodynamic approach. She found that women could be divided into two groups on the basis of their menstrual beliefs and attitudes. One group consisted of women who believed that menstruation is healthy, and therefore wanted to lose as much blood as possible during menstruation and to continue to menstruate for as long as possible. Menstruation was seen to be 'natural', a means of losing 'bad blood' and a means by which 'the system rights itself'. These women tended to see menstruation as a time at which women are particularly vulnerable and exposed to danger, especially if the flow should be obstructed in any way. It was these women who were concerned about bathing or washing their hair during menstruation in case the period should 'go away', as a result of which they might 'go funny'. Women in this group described themselves as feeling bloated, slow and sluggish if their periods were lighter than usual, and as feeling 'really great' after a heavy period. In contrast, the other group saw menstruation as damaging their health. They were fearful of 'losing their life's blood' and hoped for an early menopause. These women described menstruation in what Skultans calls 'quasi-scientific terms', not making a fuss about it and carrying on as usual. Their views are exemplified in her description of 'Mrs Thomas' (a pseudonym).

> Mrs Thomas possesses no theories whatsoever about the value of menstruation or the need to lose menstrual blood. She says she cannot wait to stop menstruating because she is losing such a lot. She said: 'I'm sure I'm no better in health by seeing them.' Menstruation to Mrs Thomas is an unmitigated source of annoyance and discomfort. Prior to and during menstruation, Mrs Thomas feels extremely weak, suffers from sick headaches, dizziness and vaginal irritation. A hysterectomy would not worry her in the least, in fact, she thinks it would provide a welcome relief.
>
> (Skultans, 1970: 645)

In a more recent study, Annette Scambler and Graham Scambler interviewed 79 women aged between 16 and 44 years, drawn from the registers of two outer London health centres (Scambler and Scambler, 1985). From their responses they identified three broad categories of attitude towards menstruation. They label their categories 'acceptance', 'fatalism' and 'antipathy'. Women who were thought to express acceptance described their periods as 'normal' or 'a part of life's process'. Some of them referred to menstruation as 'healthy' or 'feminine', although the authors comment that 'these women, however, often seemed to feel their attitudes were somehow "deviant" – that they "ought" to be more negative' (p. 1066). The 'fatalism' group saw periods as a 'nuisance' but a necessary evil, an 'essential part of being female'. The 'antipathy' group were unambiguously negative about or hostile towards menstruation, describing it as 'unhealthy', 'unclean', 'messy' and perceiving it as problematic. Scambler and Scambler note that 'not surprisingly' a higher proportion of those women expressing antipathy towards menstruation also complained of a high level of symptom distress. This group appear to be more negative towards menstruation than the women in Skultans' study, although this may be an artefact of the context in which they were studied, their relative youth and the apparent negative expectations of the researchers. The women were interviewed after completing a 6-week health diary; during the interview they were also asked about 'their perceptions and past and present experiences of menstrual disorders'. In the same session, they completed a Moos MDQ and a questionnaire 'designed to find out which menstrual symptoms they would advise women to take to a doctor'. The study was concerned with the apparent under-reporting of menstrual complaints to medical practitioners, and possible reasons for it, and the medical context may have elicited more of the 'negative' statements about menstruation, which the women themselves note are what they feel they 'ought' to say. This situation may have elicited different comments from Skultans' interview, which considered menstruation in the context of sex roles. She was concerned with the 'woman's attitudes to her husband and to "men" generally, to menstruation and the cessation of menstruation'. Skultans' women may also have been more positive about menstruation because they were older and approaching or experiencing the peri-menopausal stage of their lives. Perhaps the imminent loss of menstruation made them more amenable towards it. There are also cohort differences between Skultans' group, who were 50 in the late 1960s, and Scambler and Scambler's group, who were between 16 and 44 in the early 1980s, and cultural differences between women in a small Welsh mining community and a new housing estate on the outskirts of London. Finally, none of these researchers discuss their own attitudes towards menstruation, or the effect that these might have either on the comments elicited by participants or on the analysis of the interviews.

A qualitative study which reconciles some of the differences between the two studies described above is reported by Emily Martin (1989). She interviewed 165 women in Baltimore. They were drawn from three 'life-stages', i.e. youngest (puberty to childbearing age), middle (childbearing and childrearing age), oldest (menopause and postmenopause), and all social groups. Forty-three per cent of the interviews were with 'working-class' women, 57 per cent with 'middle-class', and 28 per cent of the whole sample were black women. Martin took an anthropological approach to these women's lives, although her study is based on interviews rather than fieldwork in an effort to gain insight into what their reproductive bodies mean to North American women. These women saw menstruation not as a private function only relevant in home settings, but as something which was part of their lives at work and school too. They describe menstruation as a 'hassle' and are concerned about its 'messiness' because they experience a variety of practical difficulties in keeping it secret while at work. It is testament to the effectiveness of American menstrual etiquette that Martin notes that none of the women blamed their practical difficulties on the inadequacy of work and workplace design (e.g. the lack of supplies of menstrual products in most workplaces, the intolerance of frequent trips to the bathroom or 'menstruation leave'), but instead blame menstruation itself. The 'difficulties' themselves could have a positive side: restrictions on activities during menstruation could allow women to escape temporarily from unpleasant or disliked tasks. Thus the negative aspects of menstruation could be seen to have a positive aspect. In the same way, the positive feelings which these women describe could be bittersweet for some women. The main positive feeling they associated with menstruation is that it defines them as women, connecting it with the ability to have babies. However, the women themselves had very varying feelings about this capacity. As Martin says, 'The woman who wants to bear children, the woman who is a lesbian and does not have sex with men, and the woman who does not want to bear children have vastly different relationships to the potential functions of those [female reproductive] organs' (Martin, 1989: 111). And, as one of her interviewees remarks: 'There should be celebration around menstruation. If done right it could be wonderful! But what would you be celebrating? The ability to bear children? You know there's the whole uselessness part of it, too, if you decide not to bear children' (p. 111).

When these comments are borne in mind, it becomes apparent that researchers have themselves labelled which statements about menstruation are considered to represent 'positive' attitudes and which to represent 'negative' ones – usually in the light of cultural and biomedical images of it. In reality, it seems not to be the case that women are either negative or positive towards one or several aspects of menstruation, as the existing questionnaire studies imply, although even in interviews responses consistent with this can be elicited (e.g. Scambler and Scambler's study). More detailed analysis of qualitative data suggests that the positive–negative dimension is not a meaningful one, and the scores obtained on such scales do not reflect ambivalence. Rather, menstruation is a feature of women's lives, and women's feelings about it are dynamic, depending on their work, domestic and reproductive circumstances and who they are talking to, as well as the physical experiences associated with it. Cultural attitudes towards menstruation, as expressed through popular and medical literature, rarely represent this dynamism, focusing instead on 'failed reproduction' and loss of blood, both of which are 'negative' in the context of Western cultural stereotypes of femininity (see Laws, 1990).

CONCLUSION

This chapter has considered the research relating both to menstrual cognitions and to the relationship between the menstrual cycle and cognitive processes. Neither of these areas is straightforward to research, and both are characterised by negative assumptions. It is assumed that women are 'ignorant' if their beliefs about and knowledge of menstruation do not match those of the dominant medical model. It is assumed that attitudes towards menstruation are antipathetic, and it is assumed that menstruation has an incapacitating effect on cognitive function. What the findings of these studies tell us is that such generalisations are unfounded. Women's beliefs about and attitudes towards menstruation are diverse, and the relationship between the menstrual cycle and cognitive processes is similarly variable. For the majority of women the menstrual cycle does not seem to have an externally observable effect on cognitive processes, or else has an effect which can easily be compensated. The work of Hampson and Kimura suggests that there may be subtle oestrogen-related fluctuations in functions at which women on average perform better than men on average. Even if the size of these is sufficient to be noticeable to women themselves (rather than just statistically significant), it seems unlikely that they have an effect on work performance or intellectual ability. Neither are they related to menstruation, since Hampson and Kimura investigate parts of the cycle with differing oestrogen levels, rather than phases defined in relation to menstruation. Similarly, for the majority of women, menstruation evokes a number of beliefs and attitudes, many of which cannot simply be labelled as 'positive' or 'negative'. Most women do not seem to hold a single attitude towards menstruation, but a range of interrelated attitudes – towards menstrual pain, the purpose of menstruation or menstrual hygiene, for example – which change over time and with circumstances. The strength of these attitudes and their affective component (e.g. how positive or negative they are) seems to be related to factors such as the experience of pain or heavy periods. For young women in particular, the experience of menstruation is associated with less 'negative' attitudes. Premenarcheal fears appear to be unfounded for the majority of women (although that is not to imply that menarche is necessarily an easy experience – see Lovering, 1995). Stereotypes of both menstruation itself and the effects of the menstrual cycle on cognitive function and emotion are strong in Westernised cultures, however. The majority of people observe the menstrual sex taboo, for instance, and can describe the mental state of the 'typical woman premenstrually'. So, while women's cognitive abilities may not fluctuate dramatically across the cycle, the beliefs and attitudes of both women and men may influence the perception of mental and physical states around menstruation. At the very least, the existence of these stereotypes makes menstruation and the premenstrual phase noteworthy or 'different' from the rest of the cycle, making it more likely that experiences at that time will be noticed or remembered. Similarly, the existence of stereotypes means that particular behaviours can be attributed, by ourselves or others, to the effects of the menstrual cycle – whether or not such an attribution is appropriate.

5

MOOD AND WELL-BEING

Both the research literature and the popular press contain assertions about the prevalence of 'normal' premenstrual experiences among premenopausal adult women. These assertions reflect the cultural beliefs and stereotypes about the effects of menstruation and hormonal fluctuations on the female psyche (see chapters one and two), but are they supported by good research evidence? Is there a relationship between behaviour or well-being and menstruation or the menstrual cycle? As already outlined, research investigating this question is both methodologically complex and epistemologically limited (see chapter three). Researchers have addressed the question in two ways, from the perspective of 'normality' or 'abnormality'. The logic runs like this: if the menstrual cycle causes fluctuations in mood or well-being, then this will reveal itself in a menstrually related pattern in assessments of ordinary women's psychological state, which they report themselves or is observed by others. This is logical as it stands, but does not mean that a correlation between particular mood states and menstruation implies a causal link between them. A causal relationship between mood and the menstrual cycle is only one possible explanation for a correlation between the two, should one be demonstrated, but most researchers conveniently forget that 'correlation does not imply causality'. A second line of reasoning runs like this: if the menstrual cycle causes fluctuations in mood or well-being, then this will be demonstrated in pain or distress occurring at regular points in the cycle. Again, this is a correlational statement which is widely used to imply a causal relationship. The first syllogism has resulted in numerous studies of mood and well-being during the 'normal' menstrual cycle or, in theory at least, the full range of menstrual cycle-related experiences, results of which will be described in this chapter. The second has inspired attempts to diagnose, measure and treat dysfunctional states, such as PMS, LLPDD and PMDD, which will be described in chapter six. In both cases, the overwhelming interest of researchers is in women's experience immediately before or during menstruation, with information about other parts of the cycle generally collected only as a comparison. The research is also limited by an emphasis on measurement of 'negative' experiences, such as pain and depression.

The menstrual cycle is an endless rhythm, and, except during pregnancy, is ever-present from menarche to menopause for the majority of women. It might then be expected that any conceivable emotional or physical state will be reported or investigated in menstrual cycle research. However, this is not the case, and researchers have focused on a relatively narrow range of experiences. The areas which have attracted most interest are those of depression and anger or irritability, but studies of sexuality and the menstrual cycle are also numerous, and some research is concerned with physical experiences during the cycle.

MOOD AND EMOTION

Mood and emotion in relation to the menstrual cycle became topics of research interest only after the description of premenstrual tension in the medical and psychoanalytic literature of the 1920s and 1930s (e.g. Frank, 1929, 1931; Horney, 1931; Chadwick, 1933), so it is difficult to disentangle studies of PMT and PMS from those more generally concerned with mood and the menstrual cycle. In this section, I am only concerned with those studies which have drawn samples from a general population, and not those which have deliberately recruited women who believe that they have PMS or are seeking help for it. These latter studies are discussed in the next chapter. Three groups of studies fall into this section – prevalence studies, which ask how many women experience a variety of mood states at different cycle points, rhythm studies, which ask whether individual women experience fluctuations in mood across the cycle, and behaviour studies, which ask whether women act differently in different cycle phases. These questions are not conceptually different: they all fundamentally assess the possibility of a correlation between mood and the menstrual cycle, but they do imply different research strategies. Prevalence studies have generally employed epidemiological principles, surveying large groups of women who are representative of a particular population and assessing either their current state, which is then related to menstrual cycle phase, or asking them to report their experiences at different parts of the cycle retrospectively. Longitudinal studies investigate a smaller group of women prospectively, usually with daily assessments of mood and sometimes physiological state. Sometimes these are analysed as correlational studies, although more often they are treated as though they were quasi-experimental designs (see chapter three). Behaviour studies focus on either direct or indirect observations of women's actions, without necessarily involving the woman herself (for instance, research may be based on hospital or other official statistics). Researchers have been particularly interested in suicidal, parasuicidal and antisocial behaviour.

Prevalence studies

Prevalence studies have focused on experiences reported in the days before menstruation, and as a result are closely associated with studies of PMS (see chapter five). They began in the late 1950s (e.g. Pennington, 1957), and have generally been based on retrospective reports from either 'convenience' samples of women, such as students (e.g. Mao and Chang, 1985; Sheldrake and Cormack, 1976; Timonen and Procope, 1971) or clinic attenders (e.g. Rouse, 1978; Boyle *et al.*, 1987); or women selected as representative of the general population of a particular city, district or country (e.g. Andersch *et al.*, 1986; Woods *et al.*, 1982; Taylor *et al.*, 1986). The measures used have been either the established retrospective menstrual distress questionnaires (e.g. the MDQ or PAF), or checklists designed for particular studies. Some studies have asked only about 'symptoms' around menstruation (i.e. before and during), and/or have not asked women to indicate the degree of severity of the 'symptoms' they report (e.g. Sheldrake and Cormack, 1976; Pennington, 1957; Mao and Chang, 1985). It is these studies which tend to produce high prevalence estimates. If women are asked in a retrospective questionnaire whether they ever feel irritable around menstruation, for example, it is likely that most will say yes – hardly a surprising finding given that the premenstrual and menstrual days can account for between a quarter and a half of a menstruating woman's life. Without estimates of severity, the occurrence of mood states at other times or regularity of occurrence in the premenstrual days, and clear definitions of cycle phases, it is difficult to relate these observations to either menstruation or the menstrual cycle. On the basis of this type of study, Pennington (1957) concluded that 95 per cent of a sample of 1,000 young women at high school or college had experienced at least one 'symptom' before or during menstruation (including physical symptoms). Since dysmenorrhea is most prevalent amongst young women, his findings are hardly earth-shattering, and tell us little about menstrually related mood or physical experiences. However, the figure of 95 per cent has proved compelling and is often quoted in press reports about PMS (see Chrisler and Levy, 1990; Walker, 1995b; chapter six). In more rigorous studies, and studies which focus on the prevalence of particular states such as irritability or depression, much lower prevalence rates are found. The major prevalence studies have been reviewed by Camille Logue and Rudolf Moos (1986, 1988), who estimate that approximately 40 per cent of Western women experience some degree of perimenstrual mood or physical change, although only 2–10 per cent report severe 'symptoms'. Although most of these changes are classed as 'negative'[1] (e.g. irritability, depression, breast tenderness), Logue and Moos note that between 5 per cent and 15 per cent of women surveyed report 'positive' changes around menstruation, such as increased excitement, energy or activity, heightened sexuality and improved performance on some tasks.

The mood experiences most commonly assessed in large-scale epidemiological samples are those which form the negative affect subscale of the MDQ, i.e. loneliness, crying, feeling sad, restlessness, anxiety, mood swings, irritability, tension. Of these, rates for irritability and depression are most commonly reported by researchers (see Table 5.1). In general population studies (e.g. Woods *et al.*, 1982; Andersch *et al.*, 1986; Kessel and Coppen, 1963; Taylor *et al.*, 1986), approximately 40–70 per cent of women report some degree of irritability premenstrually, with 3–12 per cent of them reporting severe levels. Rates of depression premenstrually are generally lower, mild or moderate premenstrual depression being reported by around 30 per cent of the women in these studies and severe depression by around 2–7 per cent. Rates for student samples are similar for depression, but a little lower for irritability, at around 30–40 per cent (Moos, 1968; Sheldrake and Cormack, 1976; Schuckit *et al.*, 1975). Not all of these studies assess mood experiences right across the cycle, but those which do find evidence that irritability and depression are not confined to the premenstrual phase. Woods *et al.* (1982), for example, found that 39 per cent of women report mild irritability during menstruation and 14 per cent continue to report mild irritability in the rest of the cycle (the equivalent rates for 'severe' irritability were 11 per cent and 3.5 per cent). Similar rates are reported for depression. Moos (1968) in his study of 839 'wives of graduate students' noted that 10 per cent of women reported irritability and 9 per cent depression in the week after menstruation (compared to 52 per cent and 43 per cent in the week before). So, these studies seem to support the widely accepted view that mood cyclicity is a feature of the menstrual cycle for some proportion of women, probably around 40–50 per cent depending on which aspect of mood is studied. Critics of the negative bias in these studies are reassured by the findings summarised by Logue and Moos (1988) and later studies (e.g. Stewart, 1989) that positive experiences can occur premenstrually, in an equally cyclical fashion.

The major problem with all of these studies is their reliance on retrospective reporting. This is problematic for two reasons: first, because of the influence of stereotypes and expectations, and second, because questionnaires differ in what they ask women to report – experiences during their most recent cycle (e.g. MDQ) or the last three cycles (e.g. PAF) or a 'typical' cycle. Both of these have been shown to influence 'symptom' reporting (e.g. AuBuchon and Calhoun, 1985; Parlee, 1974; Logue and Moos, 1986), and hence prevalence rates. So the estimates obtained from retrospective studies are of limited validity, and many researchers have turned to longitudinal prospective studies to address the question of whether mood is related to the menstrual cycle.

Longitudinal studies

An immense amount of research effort has been spent on the investigation of day-to-day fluctuations in mood and well-being amongst non-clinical samples of women, beginning in the 1930s (e.g. McCance *et al.*, 1937; Benedek and Rubenstein, 1939a; 1939b) and continuing today (e.g. McFarlane and Williams, 1994). The aim of these studies, by and large, has been to find out whether women, as a homogeneous group, experience mood fluctuations which can be accounted for by the menstrual cycle. As noted in chapter three, most of these studies adopt a quasi-experimental approach, collecting daily self-report questionnaire data and then comparing average scores in different menstrual cycle phases. Many of the studies have used all or part of the MDQ, although some

Table 5.1   Percentage prevalence estimates for irritability and depression across the
menstrual cycle (retrospective studies)

Study	Sample size	Irritability			Depression		
		Prem	*Mens*	*Rest*	*Prem*	*Mens*	*Rest*
Woods *et al.*, 1982	179	44 m/m 12 s/d	39 m/m 11 s/d	14 m/m 3.5 s/d	30 m/m 7 s/d	30 m/m 5 s/d	17 m/m 2 s/d
Andersch *et al.*, 1986	854	72m/m 3 s/d	-	-	34 m/m 2 s/d	-	-
Kessel and Coppen, 1963	465	42	8	2	38	10	1
Taylor *et al.*, 1986	530	65	37	3	43	22	4
Moos, 1968	839	39 m/m 13 s/d	40 m/m 8 s/d	9 m/m 1 s/d	33 m/m 10 s/d	28 m/m 7 s/d	7 m/m 2 s/d
Sheldrake and Cormack, 1976	3323	32.5	22	-	31	15	-

Note: Prem: premenstrual days; mens: menstrual days; rest: remainder of the cycle; m/m: mild or moderate; s/d: severe or disabling

have used other mood adjective checklists (see chapter three). The number of women studied ranges from 7 (Parlee, 1982) to 167 (McCance *et al.*, 1937), and the majority of them are young, white, English-speaking students (with some exceptions – e.g. McFarlane *et al.*, 1988, 1994; Walker and Bancroft, 1990). Almost all of these studies have compared premenstrual and menstrual cycle phases with a 'mid-cycle', 'postmenstrual' or 'remaining days' phase. Despite this homogeneity, research findings still show the variability that has become familiar throughout this chapter. Some studies suggest that the menstrual cycle has no appreciable effect on mood (Slade, 1984; Swandby, 1981; Ablanalp *et al.*, 1979a; Englander-Golden *et al.*, 1986; Ainscough, 1990; Laessle *et al.*, 1990; Patkai *et al.*, 1974), while others do find significant differences between cycle phases on a variety of mood measures (Walker and Bancroft, 1990; van den Akker and Steptoe, 1985; Olasov and Jackson, 1987; Taylor, 1979; Sampson and Jenner, 1977; Choi and Salmon, 1995b). How can this variability be explained?

There are a number of possible explanations. Parlee (1982) noted that when she analysed the data obtained from her participants individually, the menstrual cycle was not a significant factor, but when the women were grouped together a cycle effect was apparent. In other words, the faint influence of the menstrual cycle for each individual became amplified when they were combined. If this were the case, then studies with larger samples would be expected to demonstrate stronger cyclical effects, but this is not always so. For example, Pauline Slade (1984) found that 'negative affect' measures were not related to the menstrual cycle in a study of 118 women, whilst Sampson and Jenner (1977) drew the opposite conclusion with a group of 19. An alternative explanation is that women who know they are taking part in a study of the menstrual cycle

119

report their experiences differently from women who do not, resulting in the expected fluctuations in 'aware' conditions, but not in studies which disguise their purpose. Experimental investigations of this hypothesis have again found conflicting effects. In some, women who are aware of the menstrual focus of the study do report more depression and irritability premenstrually than matched 'unaware' women (e.g. Englander-Golden *et al.*, 1986; Olasov and Jackson, 1987; AuBuchon and Calhoun, 1985), but in others they do not (e.g. Markum, 1976; Gallant *et al.*, 1991). Similarly, van den Akker and Steptoe (1985) found no differences in symptom reporting between women who had guessed the purpose of their disguised study and women who had not. A third explanation for variable findings is that women themselves are variable. While some may experience fluctuations which fit the stereotypical pattern, others may experience a steady state, or a menstrual cycle-related pattern with peaks at other points. Depending on the balance of experiences within a sample of women, these may cancel out and produce a non-significant phase effect, or else a number of women with the same pattern may 'drive' the data and produce the expected pattern. My own research (in collaboration with John Bancroft) supports this idea (Walker and Bancroft, 1990; Walker, 1994a).

We collected daily ratings on eight visual analogue scales (including measures of mood, irritability, energy and tension) from 109 British women, aged between 18 and 35 years and recruited from a pool of respondents to a national magazine survey about menstrual health. We were interested in the effect of ovulation – or rather the absence of ovulation – on menstrual and premenstrual experiences, so we deliberately approached a group of oral contraceptive users, and selected from the pool of magazine respondents, for comparison, a matched group of women who were not using oral contraceptives. In the final sample, there were 61 pill users and 48 women using other forms of contraception. They collected daily ratings for two or more cycles, which were then averaged across cycle phases. When we did this, the expected pattern emerged: significant cycle phase effects with lowest mood and energy occurring premenstrually, together with highest levels of tension and irritability (see Figures 5.1 and 5.2). Later, I became interested in whether consecutive menstrual cycles are the same in terms of mood change, and went back to this data, but this time analysed each cycle separately rather than averaging them together. When I did this, I found that a variety of different patterns were hidden in the data. So, for example, in the first cycle, 21 per cent of the pill users were less irritable before menstruation than after, 28 per cent did not change very much between those two points and 51 per cent were more irritable premenstrually than postmenstrually. This type of pattern was true of all the moods I measured. In addition to this I found that the same woman could report quite different premenstrual experiences in consecutive menstrual cycles. This was not an epidemiological study, so the proportions of women experiencing different patterns of change are fairly meaningless. What it does suggest is that by averaging across women I had obscured the variety of different patterns they were experiencing. The same is probably true

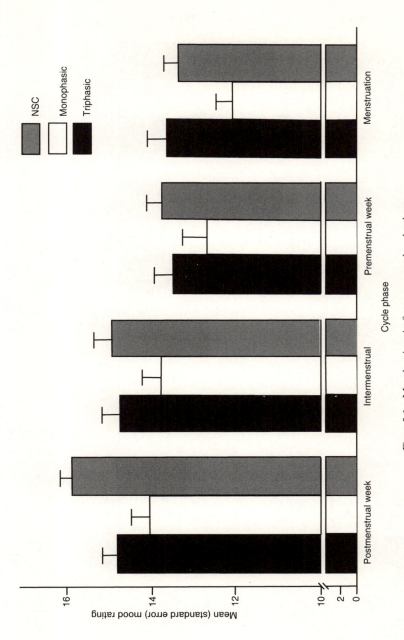

Figure 5.1 Mood ratings in four menstrual cycle phases

Note. Mean ratings made by women on daily visual analogue scales of mood, averaged within cycle phases. Ratings can range from 0 (very unhappy) to 20 (very happy). The matched groups of women were using either phased-dose oral contraceptives (triphasic, $n = 29$), combined oral contraceptives (monophasic, $n = 35$) or other, nonsteroidal forms of contraception (NSC, $n = 57$). See Walker (1988), Walker and Bancroft (1990), Walker (1994a) for study details.

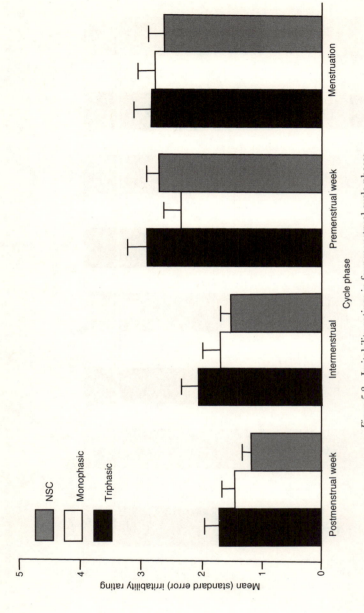

Figure 5.2 Irritability ratings in four menstrual cycle phases

Note: Mean ratings made by women on daily visual analogue scales of irritability, averaged within cycle phases. Ratings can range from 0 (not at all irritable) to 10 (extremely irritable). The matched groups of women were using either phased-dose oral contraceptives (triphasic, $n = 29$), combined oral contraceptives (monophasic, $n = 35$) or other, nonsteroidal forms of contraception (NSC, $n = 57$). See Walker (1988), Walker and Bancroft (1990), Walker (1994a) for study details.

of applying a rigid or hormonally defined cycle phase definition. Variability of menstrual cycle experiences between women is not a finding restricted to this study, but has been observed by other researchers using different methodologies (e.g. Rossi and Rossi, 1977; Hart *et al.*, 1987).

So it seems that the variability in longitudinal studies of mood and the menstrual cycle can be explained by a combination of artefact, culture and individual differences. As researchers, our questions have been driven by stereotypical beliefs rather than a value-free curiosity, so we have only investigated one possible menstrual cycle pattern, biasing our findings by our choice of what to measure, when to measure it and how to analyse the findings. We have then added to the confusion by telling our participants that the study is about the menstrual cycle, thus increasing their vigilance in reporting experiences premenstrually (if we don't tell them, of course, then experiences which they attribute to menstruation may be screened out of self-reports as unimportant or irrelevant). Finally, we have assumed that all women have the same experience at the same time in the cycle, and that this experience is the same in each of an individual woman's menstrual cycles. The conclusion from all of these studies must be that we know little about whether the menstrual cycle influences mood – studies of one or two cycles are simply not enough to demonstrate such an effect statistically, as noted above. We do know a tremendous amount, though, about how women feel in the week before and during their periods compared to other parts of the same cycle. These suggest that some women do experience more 'negative' mood states around menstruation than at other times, but some women do not. Those women who do may not experience 'negative' states before every menstrual period, and even if they do these may vary in intensity from one cycle to the next. Finally, 'negative' states are not experienced only around menstruation, neither are they the only experiences women report then. It is possible (and normal) to be happy in the week before menstruation, and in the same way, depression after menstruation is not uncommon.

Most of the research described above can be criticised for looking at the menstrual cycle out of the context of the rest of women's lives. Even if a statistically significant mood change does occur between the premenstrual phase and other days, what does that mean in most women's lives? Is it noticeable? How does it compare to other cycles or events which affect mood? How are any premenstrual changes experienced in women's lives? Several studies have now examined the menstrual cycle in the context of other rhythms, notably the social cycle of day of the week (Rossi and Rossi, 1977; Englander-Golden *et al.*, 1986; McFarlane *et al.*, 1988; Mansfield *et al.*, 1989; Ripper, 1991; McFarlane and Williams, 1994), and have compared women's and men's experiences of cyclicity. These studies have usually been conducted over a longer period (40 days to 18 weeks), although still not long enough for good time series analysis, and the data are usually analysed by means of cycle phase averages (across cycles) and analysis of variance. In general, these studies have found that both men and women experience cyclical changes in mood; for example, McFarlane and Williams

(1994) note that cyclicity was more common in their sample of 60 women and 10 men than stability, with two-thirds of both groups experiencing at least one menstrual phase, lunar phase or day of the week which was markedly negative or positive relative to the others in that cycle. These studies have also consistently shown greater variation across days of the week than across the menstrual cycle. So, these findings suggest that while 'negative' (or 'positive') states may occur premenstrually, and are very real for those women who experience them, for most they are more comparable to the 'Monday blues' than they are to a major depressive disorder. Other researchers have pointed out that, although significant fluctuations may occur across the cycle, these are generally very small in terms of the amount of the scale they represent (Golub, 1976; Gannon, 1985; Bisson and Whissell, 1989). For example, a second look at the cycle-related fluctuations shown in Figure 5.1 reveals that they represent a change of only one or two points on a 10 (irritability, tension) or 20 (mood, energy) point scale.[2] Ripper (1991) also notes in her study, which used bipolar scales, that although women's scores shifted away from the 'positive' pole in the premenstrual phase, they did not cross the midpoint into the 'negative' end of the dimension. In other words, these women were not miserable, just a little less happy than usual.

One context which has been placed on the investigation of mood and the menstrual cycle is not the one of women's lives, but the context of depressive disorder. One of the motives underlying much of this research (and especially PMS research, see next chapter) is a desire to explain and understand why depression is diagnosed more frequently among women than men. A consequence of this has been an emphasis on global mood states, averaged by the women themselves in the form of daily ratings. Yet everyday experience is generally not like this. Any particular day might include moments of joy, contentment, anger or sadness, and it is difficult to know how these different emotion episodes are combined together into a single daily score. Is it possible to 'deconstruct' global mood states in menstrual cycle research? One way in which researchers have tried to do this is by assessing positive and negative affect separately, using scales devised for assessment of the full range of 'normal' mood states (e.g. Boyle, 1992; Ripper, 1991; Choi and Salmon, 1995b). These studies tend to show that positive affect fluctuates across the cycle more than negative affect. Another approach is to look at emotion episodes separately rather than merging them together into one global state. Previous research has suggested that people may describe themselves as depressed or unhappy if the number of angry or sad emotions they experience in a day outweighs the number of happy ones (Oatley and Duncan, 1994) – in other words, if the balance of emotions shifts. Elaine Duncan, Mary Dorward and I asked a group of 12 women to keep daily emotion diaries for five weeks, recording not their overall 'mood' during a day, but each separate episode of emotion. They were asked to describe what triggered it, how they felt at the time, and what they would call the emotion. This is a preliminary study, but the findings lend some support to the idea of a shift in emotional balance across the cycle. All of these women experienced episodes which they described as 'happy' in all phases of the cycle. In addition, they experienced angry, sad or fearful episodes in all cycle phases. As a group, though, the balance did change in different cycle phases, with, for example, more angry episodes occurring premenstrually than at other times (Duncan *et al.*, 1995). All of these contextual studies suggest that for most women who do experience menstrually related shifts in mood, these are relatively small, and represent a less happy state than usual rather than a plunge into abject misery. That is not to say that a small group of women do not experience very distressing mood states premenstrually (which might be called PMS), simply that most menstruating women do not.

Behavioural studies

There are many behaviours which might be attributed to particular moods or emotional states – laughing, crying, violence to self or others, changing eating patterns, sexual activity, spending time with others or alone, and so on – and some studies have focused on objective measures of these behaviours, rather than subjective mood assessment, to investigate menstrual cycle-related phenomena. A number of studies have assessed suicidal or parasuicidal behaviour as a function of the cycle, usually on the basis of hospital admissions or calls to suicide helplines. There are even more methodological problems in studies of suicide and the menstrual cycle than in other areas (see Wetzel and McClure, 1972), chief among them being biases in subject selection and problems with identification of cycle phase at the time of the event (especially in completed suicides). Most of these studies indicate an increased risk of suicide and suicide attempts in the second half of the cycle, usually immediately before or during menstruation (see Wetzel and McClure, 1972). The study by MacKinnon *et al.* (1959) is usually cited as one of the best concerning completed suicides, because the accuracy of menstrual cycle phase designation at time of death is better than most. They examined the uteri of 102 women who had died as a result of accident, suicide or disease, to determine their cycle phase at the time of death. Of these, 60 deaths occurred in the early-midluteal phase (between one and two weeks before menstruation), not in the immediate premenstrual phase. Their figures suggest that this pattern was true for deaths from suicide and disease, but not for accidents. Convincing as these studies may be, there are problems with the interpretation of them. The first is that they have rarely used statistical analysis to assess the differences between cycle phases, so that it is difficult to know whether the increases are really more than might be expected by chance. Second, they rarely take account of cycle irregularity. As Linda Gannon (1985) points out, most studies exclude from analysis women who could not recall the date of their last period, biasing the sample towards regularly menstruating women. They also fail to take account of the possibility that a woman whose period is late may believe that she is pregnant, a factor which may have a greater effect on her behaviour than her 'real' premenstrual status. Third, the effect of stress or life events on menstruation and the menstrual cycle is not accounted for (Parlee, 1975). Since these women were probably stressed before they died or attempted suicide, their cycles may have been disrupted or hormonally unusual as a consequence, rather than a cause, of their suicidal behaviour. Birtchnell and Floyd (1974) accounted for some of these deficiencies in a study of 76 consecutive attempted suicides. They found no significant difference between the number of women who were actually premenstrual or menstruating at the time of the suicide attempt and the number who would be expected to be paramenstrual by chance, after making an allowance for cycle irregularity. They also note that 13 of the women in their sample were either pregnant or beyond the expected date of their next period at the time of the attempt, suggesting that social reasons might be as important as physiological ones for some women.

The incidence of anti-social behaviour has also been studied around menstruation, particularly criminal activities. Katharina Dalton (1961) found that, of 156 regularly menstruating women admitted to a London prison after being arrested for theft or prostitution within the previous twenty-eight days, 76 (49 per cent) were in the 'paramenstruum'[3] at the time the alleged crime was committed. This study has been extensively criticised for its lack of appropriate statistical analysis (Sherif, 1980) and for Dalton's failure to differentiate between crimes which may be impulsive, such as shoplifting, and those which require premeditation or organisation, such as embezzlement. Dalton's findings are supported by Morton *et al.* (1953), who found that 26 out of 42 women sentenced for violent crimes had committed the offence in the premenstrual week (although this study too is methodologically flawed – see Parlee, 1973; d'Orban, 1983), and by d'Orban and Dalton (1980), who found that 22 women out of 50 consecutive admissions to a British remand prison were paramenstrual at the time of their crimes, which in this case all involved violence against property or people. This contrasts with a study of 200 shoplifters which found no relationship between the offence and menstrual cycle phase (Epps, 1962). These studies do seem to suggest that women who commit crimes may be more likely to do so (or to be caught for doing so) before or during menstruation than at other times of the cycle. It is very important to keep these figures in perspective, though, as the vast majority of crimes involving violence are committed by men (see Laws *et al.*, 1985). These figures do not suggest that women are more likely to commit crimes when they are premenstrual than when they are not, but that women who commit crimes are more likely to be premenstrual than not. The designation of a woman as premenstrual is no less problematic in these studies than it is in studies of suicide, and, as in most of those studies, none take account of cycle irregularity or the potential effects on menstrual functions of the stress involved in the commission of, or apprehension for, a crime. A well-designed and carefully analysed study is badly needed in this area.

Clinical observations have also been made of women admitted to psychiatric hospital on an emergency basis. One index of the severity of their behavioural disturbance or agitation is the likelihood of their seclusion away from other patients. In a carefully designed study, Kees van Heeringen and colleagues (1995) found no association between menstrual cycle phase (determined by oestrogen and progesterone monitoring) and the likelihood of seclusion. This suggests that agitation and 'acting out' type behaviours are no more likely among women admitted to hospital in the luteal phase than at any other time.

Other aspects of behaviour have been subjected to laboratory tests rather than 'real world' investigation. For example, Kathryn Hood (1992) observed women's participation in a single-sex discussion group every week for four weeks, rating their assertiveness, nonverbal behaviour and participation style. She found that the menstrual cycle had no effect when the groups were engaged in a task, but in the 'free interaction' section at the end of each discussion group, women initiated conversations more often when they were at mid-cycle than when they were menstruating. Hood labelled the effect she observed 'menstrual quietude'. Her finding of context-specific effects is an important one, and supports the idea that women can 'compensate' for any change in mood or emotion which they experience around menstruation. The observation that female yellow baboons are more likely to spend time alone in trees when they are menstruating than when they are not (Hausfater and Skoblick, 1985) has been seen to add weight to Hood's observation, and to suggest that women seek solitude and time for contemplation around menstruation, withdrawing from social activities (Golub, 1992).

In another study of social type behaviours, Jeanne Meadowcroft and Dolf Zillmann (1987) asked women in different cycle phases to select TV programmes for an evening's viewing and to rate their enjoyment of a series of cartoons and excerpts from TV programmes. The women could choose from a battery of 27 programmes, varying in length between thirty and sixty minutes, and including 10 comedies, 7 game shows, and 10 drama programmes. They had to choose enough programmes to fill a three-hour schedule. The authors found that women in different cycle phases appreciated humour and comedy in the programmes and cartoons they saw to the same extent, but that, when given a choice, women in the premenstrual and menstrual phases of the cycle selected more comedy programmes for their evening's viewing than women at mid-cycle. Meadowcroft and Zillmann suggest that women may deliberately choose programmes to 'cheer themselves up' premenstrually, and hypothesise that differences may also be found in choice of music or other forms of entertainment across the cycle.

Consistent with these latter findings are studies of the coping strategies which women adopt to deal with (or compensate for) menstrual cycle changes. Precilla Choi and Peter Salmon (1995a), for example, in a study of 342 women recruited through a variety of workplaces and 'social' locations (e.g. GP waiting-rooms), found that 52 per cent 'tried to see the positive side of things', and 32 per cent 'told myself things to make me feel better', which seem consistent with Meadowcroft and Zillmann's comedy choices, while 20 per cent 'avoided people', supporting Hood's observation of 'menstrual quietude', although conceptualising it as a coping strategy rather than a 'symptom' of cyclicity. Many more coping strategies were reported by these women, including keeping busy (62 per cent), talking to people (51 per cent), taking exercise (41 per cent) and eating more (40 per cent) or avoiding certain foods (16 per cent). As Choi and Salmon warn, care must be taken in observational studies to distinguish between behaviours which occur as a result of how women feel premenstrually, and those which are deliberately adopted as a means of coping with pain or other menstrually related experiences.

Clearly, the research does not support the concept of universal premenstrual irritability or depression, even at a 'mild' or 'normal' level. However, the evidence provided by these studies that some fluctuations occur is sufficient for researchers to investigate explanatory models. Explanations for fluctuations in mood across the menstrual cycle usually imply a fundamental hormonal or biochemical mechanism, overlaid by (or contextualised within) social and psychological mechanisms. It follows that the majority of models of 'normal' menstrual cycle-related changes (as distinct from PMS which will be described in the next chapter) are broadly 'biopsychosocial'. The two major approaches within psychology have been psychophysiological and social psychological. The psychophysiological approach conceptualises the menstrual cycle as a biological rhythm, similar to the circadian rhythm, which is associated with a variety of fluctuations in CNS and ANS arousal (Asso, 1986; 1992). Different levels of arousal are associated with different physiological and psychological states – for example, one level of arousal may be described as anxiety, another as excitement, a third as boredom, a fourth as relaxation. Hence, if the menstrual cycle is characterised by altering states of arousal, it will also be characterised by changing mood and well-being.

Social psychologists have turned to social cognition theories for possible explanatory mechanisms for menstrual mood experiences (e.g. Ruble and Brooks Gunn, 1979; Koeske and Koeske, 1975; Rodin, 1976). These theorists have pointed out that beliefs and expectations about menstruation and menstrually related experiences can influence women's reports of their current state and their premenstrual 'symptoms' (see chapter four). Ruble and Brooks Gunn (1979) argue that there is extensive evidence of cultural beliefs that the menstrual cycle affects mood and well-being; however, physiological factors cannot account for the strength of these beliefs. In other words, prospective studies of mood across the cycle, and studies which measure hormonal or other biochemical factors, fail to demonstrate that women's emotions are affected by menstruation to the extent that culturally we believe that they are. What might account for this difference? They argue that biased information processing can lead both to altered self-perception and to stereotypical reporting of menstrual symptoms. The existence of cultural beliefs may lead us to define and label states of premenstrually occurring arousal in a particular way. As Schachter and Singer (1962) demonstrated, descriptions of subjective states are influenced by a variety of external factors, including the behaviour of others around us, expectations about how we should behave and so on (just as arousal on hearing that someone has died is more likely to be labelled as 'grief' or 'sadness' than the same physiological state on hearing that someone has been born). Hence, we may label feelings differently when they occur premenstrually from when they occur at other times. When we are asked to report experiences retrospectively, Ruble and Brooks Gunn argue, two sets of information are referred to. The first is information about physical or psychological states we have experienced. The second is information about cycle phase. As they note, 'a woman must then decide, from these two sets of information, if she feels or behaves differently during the premenstrual or menstrual phase of the cycle' (Ruble and Brooks Gunn, 1979: 182). Processing this information is subject to all of the biases that have been identified in the general information-processing literature (Fiske and Taylor, 1991), such as illusory correlations, information salience, connotative meaning of information, selective bias and so on. These types of bias operate whenever we process social information, and in this case are likely to produce a stereotypical description of paramenstrual experiences. The research conducted by these social cognition theorists tends to support such an analysis. For example, Koeske and Koeske (1975) showed that negative moods were attributed to menstruation, but positive ones were not, supporting the idea that the negative connotations of menstruation affect 'symptom' perception. Similarly, Brooks Gunn (1985) reported higher negative symptom ratings among women whose menstruation was salient because of heavy bleeding than among those whose menstruation was less salient. (This was true of Catholic but not Protestant women, suggesting a cultural rather than biological mechanism.) Hardie and McMurray (1992) have argued that asking women about menstruation may make their social identity as women more salient and encourage self-stereotyping as a 'typical' woman. The form which such self-stereotyping takes, they argue, will depend on the sex-role ideology of the particular woman, i.e. what she thinks a 'typical woman' is like. They have demonstrated a relationship between sex-role ideology, self-stereotyping and menstrual attitudes, but have yet to apply the analysis to premenstrual symptom reporting.

So, is mood affected by the menstrual cycle? The answer from these studies would seem to be yes and no! Epidemiological studies based on retrospective accounts elicit reports of cyclicity from around 50 per cent of women surveyed, depending on which mood or emotional state is examined. Longitudinal studies are more equivocal. Some have failed to demonstrate any significant menstrual cycle-phase effects, others have suggested that rhythms are present if women are considered as a group, but that they are less clear in individual cases. The obvious resolution seems to be that some women do and some women do not. But if some women do experience menstrual rhythms, what proportion of the population do they represent?

Retrospective studies are unreliable and longitudinal studies are impractical for epidemiological purposes, but there is one study which tries to address this problem.[4] It is a large-scale epidemiological survey ($n = 3,793$) of randomly selected households in Calgary, Canada, in which women were asked to complete a single Moos MDQ ('Today' form) relating to their experiences over the last 24 hours (Ramcharan *et al.*, 1992). Each woman was asked to indicate her menstrual cycle phase at the time of the study by noting the date of her last period, and returning a menstrual date card at the onset of the next. They were then assigned to cycle phases by the researchers, and 'symptom' reports compared 'between subjects'. This study was concerned with the prevalence of PMS, and focuses on 'severe' symptom reports, so that its findings are limited in understanding the full range of possible menstrually related cyclicity. The researchers reason that if a measurable proportion of women experience 'negative' affective states premenstrually, then more premenstrual women will obtain high MDQ scores than women in other phases in a cross-sectional study. This was not what they found, however. Scores above 14 on the 'negative affect' scale, which has a range of 0–32, were defined as 'high', and the proportion of women obtaining high scores in each of the cycle phases was 4.2 per cent (menstrual), 6.8 per cent (postmenstrual), 4.0 per cent (mid-cycle), 3.4 per cent (early premenstrual) and 4.5 per cent (late premenstrual). These proportions were not statistically significantly different across cycle phases. Even when lower cut-off points were employed (i.e. 8 or 10), the proportion of women did not increase premenstrually in comparison to the other phases. When the researchers looked at the items which make up the negative affect scale separately, only one, restlessness, was more prevalent premenstrually, reported by 3.8 per cent of women in the premenstrual phase compared to 2.7 per cent in the mid-cycle phase, but this was not statistically significant. A significant difference was found, however, between the proportion of women obtaining high negative affect scores in the mid-cycle group (3.2 per cent) and the premenstrual group (5.1 per cent) for women aged between 30 and 39, and for women reporting stressful life events throughout the previous year (mid-cycle group 7.4 per cent, premenstrual group 20.0 per cent). These findings, like those relating work performance to the menstrual cycle, could be interpreted in a variety of ways. The first would be to say that, for the majority of women, menstrual cyclicity in mood is not a significant feature of life, the classic PMS-type pattern being experienced by only a small number of women and associated with particular risk factors, e.g. age and high life stress. Another would be to say that fluctuations for the majority of women are below the level of clinical significance, and may or may not follow the expected pattern. A variety of different cyclical patterns could cancel each other out in a study like the one described here. Whichever perspective we take, two pieces of mood data from Ramcharan *et al.*'s study, unrelated to the menstrual cycle *per se*, might be worth bearing in mind. The first is that the proportion of women obtaining distress level scores on all of the MDQ scales across all cycle phases fell steadily and significantly with age, from around 7–9 per cent at age 20–24 to less than 4 per cent by age 45–49. The second is that across all cycle phases between 3 per cent and 7 per cent of women are reporting high levels of depression, irritability, tension, etc. In other words, a significant number of women are experiencing distress which cannot be blamed on the menstrual cycle or dismissed as a consequence of 'raging hormones'.

FOOD CRAVING AND EATING

Eating behaviour and food intake have become topics of concern in Western cultures in the 1990s as levels of obesity rise and links between obesity and a variety of illnesses become clearer. Studies of what, when and why people eat are no easier to design or interpret than studies of the menstrual cycle, so, not surprisingly, when these areas are combined the degree of methodological stringency required for a study to be considered 'good' is considerable, and the criteria for a 'good' study may not be the same from the perspectives of eating research and menstrual cycle research. Nonetheless, a number of studies have investigated food intake and eating behaviour during the menstrual cycle.

Food cravings

Retrospective studies which ask women about food cravings suggest that cravings are more common premenstrually than at other times. For example, in a study of 5,546 women who had completed a retrospective questionnaire about 'menstrual health' in a British magazine, 74.3 per cent reported at least mild food cravings in the premenstrual week, compared to 56.3 per cent during menstruation and 26.9 per cent postmenstrually (Dye, Warner and Bancroft, 1995). This increase in food cravings in the week or two before menstruation has also been reported in much smaller studies which have collected daily self-reports of cravings. For example, Cohen, Sherwin and Fleming (1987) found significantly higher average daily craving scores (a composite of the number of foods craved and intensity of each craving) in the ten days before menstruation than in the ten days following the onset of menstruation among 32 undergraduates. In this study, women who were actively 'dieting' or restraining their food intake reported fewer food cravings in both cycle phases than those who were not. The majority of women studied report cravings for sweet foods, such as cakes, sweets or chocolate, although cravings for other foods have also been reported. The foods craved seem to combine elements of different macronutrient groups, e.g. fat, carbohydrate and protein, rather than suggesting a craving for a particular type of nutrient (e.g. Blundell and Dye, 1995a). They are, however, predominantly foods which are socially constructed as 'naughty but nice' – in other words they are delicious but highly calorific or 'unhealthy'. So, for example, the most frequently craved foods in one of these studies were chocolate and chocolate-chip cookies (Cohen et al., 1987).

Craving a food does not necessarily imply that we will eat it, so researchers have also turned their attention to food intake across the menstrual cycle. Moos (1968) asked women about changes in eating habit, but because this item did not load on to any of the eight factors linking the other questions he asked it disappeared from the MDQ, and is not investigated in epidemiological surveys of premenstrual experiences. The inspirational finding for researchers investigating food intake is not one relating to anything women have said, but the observation of reduced food intake in many other mammals during oestrus, i.e. around ovulation (see Cohen *et al.*, 1987). So, unusually for menstrual cycle research, these studies have focused on ovulation rather than menstruation. The definition of cycle phases in most of these studies has been crude – usually involving a comparison of the ten days before and the ten days after identified or assumed ovulation (see Cohen *et al.*, 1987). These studies have generally found the anticipated pattern of reduced caloric intake around mid-cycle compared to the premenstrual days (e.g. Dalvit, 1981; Lyons *et al.*, 1989). The difference between average premenstrual and mid-cycle caloric intake is around 100 kilocalories, hardly noticeable in an average daily intake of 2,000 kcal. More detailed studies which have examined intake of particular nutrients across the cycle are less consistent. Dye and Blundell (1995b) review thirteen studies which provide sufficient data for comparison. Amongst these, luteal increase, luteal decrease and no change are reported for all three macronutrient types (i.e. protein, fat and carbohydrate), so it is unlikely that there is a single menstrual cycle-related pattern of nutrient intake.

So if it seems that food craving and consumption may change around menstruation, the next question must be: why? Several ideas have been investigated, all of which assume a premenstrual increase in both craving and food intake – premenstrual loss of appetite is not considered to be a social problem. The two main ideas which are tested are, first, that cravings and increased consumption reflect a 'real' physiological deficiency or need resulting from hormonal or biochemical fluctuations during the cycle, and second, that they are a consequence of premenstrual depression or moodiness. In other words, they are not themselves the result of cyclical changes in physiology. Other possibilities are that reports of food cravings result from cultural expectations about the premenstrual phase – which make it more socially acceptable to admit to craving or eating 'naughty' foods such as chocolate premenstrually – or that changes in eating are part of a 'be nice to myself' coping mechanism rather than a 'symptom' of an underlying problem or disease.

As yet, there are relatively few studies testing these hypotheses, and those which exist report conflicting findings. The nature of the foods craved, together with their mixed nutritional composition, has been used as an argument against a specific physiological or metabolic explanation for cravings (see Blundell and Dye, 1995), so much of the research has focused on possible links with depression. The findings are unclear as yet, however. In the studies described in the previous paragraph, for instance, one found a significant correlation between retrospective reports of the degree of food craving and depression in all cycle phases,[5] while the other, based on prospective reports, did not (Cohen *et al.*, 1987). These studies differ in a number of ways: in their sample size (5,546 vs. 32), the age, reproductive history and 'PMS' experience of the women studied ('normal' population vs undergraduate students), the definition of cycle 'phases' and the measures used to assess both mood and food cravings, so clearly there is room for more research investigating these phenomena in more detail. Possible direct or indirect links between depression and food craving or intake premenstrually have led researchers to investigate serotonin (5-hydroxy-tryptamine, 5-HT) mechanisms as a biochemical explanation for women's experiences (see Blundell and Dye, 1995; Bancroft, 1993; and chapter six), and further investigations of this are ongoing.

There is plenty of evidence that different foods do have different social, cultural and individual meanings, and that social acceptability factors do influence what we eat when, and what we admit to eating. However there have been no direct tests of the hypothesis that reports of cravings and intake premenstrually result from a disinhibition of social constraints either on eating or on descriptions of eating. The possibility that food intake is altered to cope with other perimenstrual changes has similarly received little attention, although in the study by Choi and Salmon (1995a) 40 per cent of women 'ate more than usual' and 16 per cent 'avoided certain foods' as ways of coping with menstrual cycle changes.

Research investigating eating behaviour and the menstrual cycle is interesting, not only because it might tell us something about the relationship between these two phenomena, but also because it brings together two research areas which are both influenced by 'political' concerns. Obesity and premenstrual symptoms can both be classified as social problems in white middle-class Western societies. That is not to say that they do not exist elsewhere, or to suggest that these are not important phenomena; it is simply to point out that they have not always (and will not always) attract research attention. The increasing methodological demands of this research, with the consequent 'junking' of previous studies, is symptomatic of the research cycle described in chapter seven.

SEXUALITY

The study of women's sexuality across the menstrual cycle, like the study of eating behaviour, has been inspired by observations of other mammals. The majority of sexual activity among mammals occurs during oestrus, when the female ovulates and is 'receptive' to male advances. At a simplistic level, sexual behaviour for these animals appears to be biologically determined, although in primates particularly, non-hormonal factors can override physiological ones (Sanders and Bancroft, 1982). Not surprisingly then, given the quasi-evolutionary and biologically reductionist emphasis in twentieth-century scientific thinking, researchers have asked whether women's sexuality is equally 'driven' by ovulation. This has led to numerous studies investigating sexual desire and activity during the menstrual cycle, and several careful reviews (Sanders and Bancroft, 1982; Meuwissen and Over, 1992; McNeill, 1994; Bancroft, 1989). In common with other areas of 'sexology', female sexuality, as conceptualised by most of these researchers, means desire for or participation in heterosexual vaginally penetrative activity (Nicolson, 1993, 1994; Ussher, 1995). Although some studies investigate autosexual or masturbatory activity, very few include women who identify themselves as lesbian or bisexual, and similarly few ask about sensual or sexual activities with a partner which do not involve vaginal penetration. These studies are generally asking whether heterosexual intercourse is more likely around ovulation than at other times in the cycle.

Researchers have investigated this question in two ways. First, they have asked women to keep daily records of their sexual interest and activity and correlated these with measures of hormonal activity, and second, they have observed the effects of exogenous hormones (e.g. the oral contraceptive pill) on sexual behaviour. Most of the studies which correlate sexuality with phase of the menstrual cycle have found peaks in sexual desire and/or activity around menstruation rather than ovulation. For example, in a review of 32 studies, 17 reported increased sexual activity premenstrually, 18 postmenstrually, 4 during menstruation and 8 at around ovulation (Schreiner-Engel, 1980; see Sanders and Bancroft, 1982; McNeill, 1994). Thirteen of these studies reported peaks both before and after menstruation. Such an unexpected set of findings is explained by most commentators in terms of either methodological inadequacies or abstinence from sex during menstruation. Problems resulting from the subjective measurement of sexual behaviour and imprecise detection of ovulation are described (Sanders and Bancroft, 1982), as are biases resulting from inappropriate cycle phase definition (Kolodny and Baumann, 1979). When a more 'objective' measure of sexual arousability, vaginal photoplethysmography, is used, most studies fail to demonstrate a cyclical pattern of arousability (Meuwissen and Over, 1992). Similarly, if cycle phases are defined differently, cyclical patterns vanish (Kolodny and Baumann, 1979).

An alternative approach suggests that it is not the endocrinology of the ovarian cycle which influences sexual activity, but the reverse. That is, that women who are in regular sexual contact with men are more likely to ovulate regularly.[6] Burleson et al. (1995) have tested this hypothesis and have proposed three possible mechanisms by which sexual activity might influence ovarian function. They argue that a pheromone excreted in male sweat could influence the cycle, or else a substance in seminal fluid absorbed through the vaginal wall might have an effect, or potentially the neural processes associated with orgasm might trigger ovulation. They tested these hypotheses in a study of exclusively heterosexual couples, measuring orgasmic frequency as well as sexual activity, type of contraceptive used and time spent in close nonsexual contact (e.g. hugging, sleeping) to explore their proposed mechanisms. They did find a relationship between sexual activity patterns and ovarian function, but not in the predicted direction. Women with a high rate of heterosexual activity and celibate women both experienced a lower number of fertile cycles during the study than women with 'intermediate' sexual activity levels. In other words, the relationship between sexual activity and ovarian function may be curvilinear rather than linear. In addition, sexual activity was higher in anovulatory cycles than ovulatory ones. None of their proposed mechanisms could account for this finding, and they conclude that hormone levels predict sexual activity rather than vice versa and specifically that progesterone inhibits sexual activity. What they don't consider is the possibility that these couples deliberately chose particular sexual activity patterns, depending on whether or not they were trying to conceive. Some women are aware of ovulation because of *mittelschmerz* or changes in vaginal mucus, or changes in basal body temperature. The nature of the study meant that all of the women would be aware of ovulation, since they were all asked to measure basal body temperature and record cervical mucus changes. In this study, then, there is little doubt that the researchers were using the same assessment of ovulation as the women themselves. If we assume that most of these women did not wish to conceive, then it is hardly surprising that, since they have been given careful instructions about how to detect ovulation, they were more sexually active in those cycles which were anovulatory. At best, this is an indirect hormonal effect.

Approximately 50 per cent of men and women in Western cultures say that they avoid sexual intercourse during menstruation, for a variety of reasons (McNeill, 1992; Paige Erickson, 1987; Barnhart *et al.*, 1995). This is a behavioural factor which may explain the peak in sexual activity found in some studies after menstruation, although it is hard intuitively to see how the anticipation of menstrual abstinence, either because of a woman's own preference or that of her partner, could explain changes in arousability or activity premenstrually (Sanders and Bancroft, 1982). If menstrual abstinence is incorporated into a mathematical model which assumes that the longer the time since intercourse, the more likely it is to occur, then the probability of intercourse is found to be higher on days 6/7, 13 to 15, 21 to 22 and 28 than on any other days in the cycle (Dobbins, 1980). This pattern is entirely the result of menstrual abstinence and 'regular' sexual activity, i.e. behavioural and relationship factors, not biological ones. The existence of a menstrual taboo on sexual intercourse does suggest that menstruation affects how women express their sexuality in heterosexual encounters, but suggests that this is as likely to be through social learning mechanisms as through hormonal ones.

These 'problems' suggest, first, that the cyclical pattern observed may not be as 'reliable' as it appears because of measurement error, and, second, that it may be the result of social factors rather than biological ones. In addition to these difficulties, McNeill (1994) points out that studies of sexuality rarely consider aspects of the relationship in which women are engaged: for instance, whether this is a new relationship or a long-established one, the social context (e.g. work or family demands), the desire for conception. Any of these might influence the frequency of sexual activity during the cycle. In particular, though, different patterns might be expected in couples who are trying to conceive and in those who are not or are actively trying to avoid conception. In other words, sexuality may fluctuate in particular menstrual cycles for psychosocial reasons.

The search for psychosocial mechanisms to explain cyclicity in female sexuality is largely a consequence of the failure to demonstrate a clear role for ovarian hormones. Sanders and Bancroft (1982) note that 'there has been a consistent failure to find correlations between oestradiol and female sexuality' (p.649), although oestrogens may have a role in vaginal lubrication after menopause. Similarly no consistent effect of progesterone has been found (Bancroft et al., 1987), although it has been suggested that the synthetic progestogens in the oral contraceptive pill may account for the loss of interest in sex which some women experience during early pill use (Bancroft and Sartorius, 1990). The findings in relation to androgens, such as testosterone, in women are contradictory and suggest that they have little effect, although in some studies higher testosterone levels have been associated with more frequent masturbation amongst those women who masturbate regularly (e.g. Bancroft et al., 1983; Alexander et al., 1990; Bancroft et al., 1991; Schreiner-Engel et al., 1989). In summary, it seems that when and how women express their sexuality in heterosexual encounters cannot solely be explained in terms of ovarian endocrinology. In this area, as in others, diverse findings abound, but always the hormonal holy grail is sought. In this literature, as in the wider literature concerned with female sexuality and 'sexual problems', women are largely positioned as passive sexual participants, triggered only to sexual activity if their hormone levels are 'just right'.[7] Perhaps the only conclusion that can be drawn from these studies is that such a model is too simplistic.

PHYSICAL EXPERIENCES

While most of the concern in menstrual cycle research has been with changes in mood or cognitive state, physical changes are reported by a significant number of women before and during menstruation. The most commonly reported physical 'symptoms' are abdominal pain or cramps, swelling or bloated feelings, breast pain, headaches, backaches, acne or skin problems and weight gain, but a wide range of other physical ailments or exacerbations of existing conditions have been reported at this time, ranging from the serious, such as increased frequency of epileptic or asthmatic episodes, to more minor, such as cold sores or constipation (Magos, 1988).

Changes in medical conditions around menstruation are usually attributed to fluctuations in body systems, such as the cardiovascular system or the gastrointestinal system, in synchrony with the menstrual cycle. Magos states that over 200 physiological variables have been shown to fluctuate during the cycle, and argues that more than seventy medical conditions may be influenced by cycle phase (e.g. asthma, epilepsy, migraine, rheumatoid arthritis, infections, etc.). The implication is that these are all worsened before or during menstruation. The conditions which have attracted most interest are epilepsy, asthma and migraine, all of which many women sufferers perceive to be exacerbated before or during menstruation (see, for example, Newmark and Penry, 1980, for epilepsy;

Facchinetti *et al.*, 1993b, for migraine; Browne, 1995, for asthma). Empirical studies have largely followed the same pattern as menstrual cycle research in general. A number of studies investigate correlations between the menstrual cycle and aspects of the medical condition in question, e.g. frequency of asthma attacks, while the remainder attempt to define and diagnose a particular menstrually related condition, e.g. 'premenstrual migraine' or 'catamenial epilepsy'. The rationale for the latter is that these women will benefit from interventions which manipulate the menstrual cycle, as much as from treatments for their particular condition. Correlational studies suggest that there is a relationship between menstruation and medical conditions, but few women meet the criteria for specific menstrually related disorders. Studies of epilepsy provide a good example of this. Correlational studies, such as that of Tauboll *et al.* (1991), have found an increase in epileptic seizure frequency premenstrually. Specific 'catamenial epilepsy', though, seems to be rare. For example, Duncan *et al.* (1993) asked 40 women, consecutive attenders at an out-patient epilepsy clinic in Glasgow, to keep a seizure diary for three months, and found that only 5 showed evidence of 'catamenial epilepsy' (which they defined as at least 75 per cent of seizures each month occurring in the ten-day frame including the four days before and six days after the onset of menstruation). Nevertheless, 31 of the 40 women (78 per cent) believed that most of their seizures occurred around menstruation. Similar examples can be found in both the asthma and migraine literatures (Browne, 1995; Johannes *et al.*, 1995).

The mechanism which connects the reproductive system with other physiological functions is unknown. It is also unclear whether the mechanism which links specific menstrually related experiences, such as breast tenderness and period pain, to menstruation, and that which links other medical conditions, e.g. asthma, to menstruation is the same. It is possible that there are numerous different underlying processes, although it may be that both the menstrual rhythm and other cycles are regulated by a central 'timing' mechanism, in the hypothalamus perhaps. Whatever the mechanism or mechanisms, it is true to say that many women experience physical changes which correlate with menstruation, whether or not they are directly caused by it. These aches and pains are rarely debilitating. Despite the assertions of some gynaecology textbooks (e.g. Novak, 1965), women in general are not incapacitated by dysmenorrhea, fulltime workers taking no more days off work in a year on average than do men, for instance (Central Statistical Office, 1996; Arber, 1990; see chapter six). That doesn't mean that we should ignore menstrual aches and pains, or that they are imaginary. They are experienced by a large number of women, but have been relatively neglected by researchers in our obsession with cognitive and mood states.

Most people are aware that menstruation itself can be painful. 'Period pain' or dysmenorrhea,[8] is a well-known phenomenon, particularly common among young women. The pain is usually described as cramping, but may be a continuous dull ache. Pain often radiates from the abdomen into the lower back and thighs. It may also be accompanied by faintness, nausea, vomiting or an upset stomach. Period pain is a common experience, reported as 'moderate' by 35.8 per cent and 'severe' by 12.3 per cent of the 463 women studied by Kessel and Coppen (1963), for example. In another epidemiological study, Woods *et al.* (1982) found a 36.3 per cent prevalence of mild/moderate 'cramps' and a 16.8 per cent prevalence of severe/disabling cramps during menstruation. In the premenstrual days, approximately one-quarter of women surveyed report cramps or abdominal pain of at least 'moderate' intensity (Woods *et al.*, 1982; Kessel and Coppen, 1963). Janiger *et al.* (1972) report higher rates of premenstrual abdominal pain (54–83 per cent) in samples of women living in different countries. These women were not sampled on an epidemiological basis, so there is likely to be a bias towards women who experience pain. However, they do suggest that rates of pain are similar in different parts of the world. All of these studies are based on retrospective reports, which may also result in overestimates of pain frequency in relation to any particular menstrual period. It is generally assumed that retrospective accounts of menstrual pain are more 'reliable' than those of mood or cognitive experiences. This may be the case, although the effects of Ruble's manipulation of women's beliefs about their current cycle phase were largely seen in reports of physical experiences, particularly pain (Ruble, 1977). Menstrual pain, unlike feelings such as depression or irritability, is absent from other parts of the cycle, so its relationship with menstruation is fairly clear, even if prevalence rates may be a little exaggerated.

The majority of studies suggest a relationship between period pain and both age and childbearing, although which of these is more important is hard to determine since older women are also more likely to have had children. Severe period pain is most common in the first five years or so after menarche. Widholm and Kantero (1971) studied the menstrual patterns and experiences of 5,485 adolescent women (aged 10–20 years) and their mothers in Finland. In this study, 50 per cent of the adolescents reported pain-free periods, but 38 per cent said they sometimes had period pain and 13 per cent always experienced pain with menstruation. The length of time since menarche made a considerable difference to the prevalence of period pain. Only 7 per cent of the women whose menarche was less than a year before reported regular pain, compared to 26 per cent of the women whose menarche occurred five years before. However, among women over about 20 years, the degree of period pain declines with age. In this study, only 8 per cent of the mothers of these young women experienced regular pain. This decline of pain intensity with age and having children is reported widely (e.g. Kessel and Coppen, 1963; Woods *et al.*, 1982). In the study reported by Kessel and Coppen (1963) the relationship with parity remained significant after the effect of age had been controlled, suggesting that it is having children rather than getting older which reduces period pain, although they offer no statistics to support this. Woods *et al.* (1982), on the other hand, found that age was a more important factor than parity in multivariate analyses. It seems that both have an effect, although, as Golub (1992) points out, they do not abolish dysmenorrhea in all women – having a baby is not the universal answer to dysmenorrhea. The implication of these studies for the aetiology of menstrual pain is unclear. It is generally assumed that the effects of age and parity are physiological (see below), but there may be a psychological component too. The meaning and cognitive appraisal of pain can alter both its perceived intensity and the behaviours which are adopted to cope with it.[9] For example, an injury obtained during an exciting sports match may hurt more after the game is over than while still playing. It is possible that severe pain experiences (such as childbirth) and vivid memories of pain experiences, as well as repeated pain experiences (such as dysmenorrhea or migraine) could alter the cognitive appraisal of pain. These experiences may lead people to 'reset' their idea of what 'severe' means in relation to pain, and hence rate later experiences of the same physiological state as less severe than earlier ones. It may be that the women who have had children experience the same 'absolute' pain as the women who have not, but rate it as less severe because it is 'not as bad' as childbirth. Similarly, older women will have had more experience of period pain, possibly also influencing their perception (and self-reports) of pain severity, and are more likely to have experienced other severe pains (e.g. from accidents, migraine, etc.). Equally, these experiences may have equipped women with a range of more effective coping strategies, so that adult dysmenorrhea is easier to deal with and rated as less painful. Periods may therefore be less painful for older women and women with children, for a variety of physiological and psychological reasons.

So, what does cause period pain? For many years, menstrual pain was a medical enigma, and attributed by many authorities to psychological factors (see Golub, 1992; Gannon, 1985). This led to numerous studies correlating dysmenorrhea with menstrual attitudes, personality or rejection of 'traditional' feminine roles or femininity (see Gannon, 1985, for a review). Some of these found significant relationships and others did not. None demonstrated causal relationships. In the light of later physiological research, it seems that psychological factors do influence the experience of menstrual pain, as they do for all types of pain (Melzack and Wall, 1982; Gamsa, 1994a, 1994b; Novy et al., 1995), but they are not significant aetiological factors. In addition, as Golub (1992) points out, almost all of the psychological factors which have been investigated could as easily be affected by the experience of pain as vice versa. It is not surprising that women who report severe menstrual pain also have negative attitudes towards menstruation.

The most popular physiological explanation of menstrual pain is the prostaglandin (PG) theory (see Gannon, 1985). Prostaglandins were first identified in menstrual fluid by Pickles in 1957. They are a group of unsaturated fatty acids which are found in almost all tissues of the body, and have powerful effects on smooth muscle, blood cells, fat cells and nervous tissue. They are not stored in the body, but are produced 'on site' in tissues in response to either biochemical messages from within the body (e.g. catecholamines), other internal body states (e.g. inflammation or anaphylaxis) or external mechanical stimuli such as stretching or squeezing of muscles. There are a number of prostaglandins, but the ones thought to be of most relevance in dysmenorrhea are PGE_2 and $PGF_{2\alpha}$ (Gannon, 1985). Both PGE_2 and $PGF_{2\alpha}$ increase in the endometrium after ovulation, rising dramatically in the late luteal phase and reaching a peak on the first day of menstruation (Singh et al., 1975). Several studies have found that $PGF_{2\alpha}$ stimulates uterine activity, and that prostaglandin inhibitors can reduce it (e.g. Garrioch, 1978; Hargrove et al., 1976). Women with dysmenorrhea are thought to have either an increased sensitivity to prostaglandins, or a larger concentration of prostaglandins in the uterus around menstruation . Studies of endometrial tissue and menstrual fluid suggest that women who experience severe period pain may have up to seventeen times more $PGF_{2\alpha}$ in the uterus during menstruation than women who don't (Chan et al., 1979). Most studies evaluating prostaglandin inhibitors have reported that they are successful as a treatment for dysmenorrhea (Budoff, 1983; Gannon, 1985; Golub, 1992). High levels of prostaglandins can also be associated with gastrointestinal disturbances (see Budoff, 1983), which are often experienced by women with dysmenorrhea. All of this still leaves the question of why some women have higher levels of prostaglandin than others unanswered – or why some periods are very painful but others are not. Prostaglandin levels are influenced by oestrogen and progesterone levels, so menstruation following ovulation is more likely to be painful than menstruation in anovulatory cycles. Similarly, factors other than prostaglandin can cause or exacerbate smooth muscle contractions, such as stress or anxiety (Nicassio, 1980). There remains plenty of work to be done in understanding the causes of dysmenorrhea, but in the meantime at least there are effective remedies – prostaglandin-inhibiting drugs are effective for around 80 per cent of women who experience severe dysmenorrhea, and non-prescription drugs with anti-prostaglandin effects (e.g. aspirin) may be helpful for milder pain.[10]

As well as 'classic' period pain, women report a range of other pains before and during menstruation, which have received far less research attention. Breast pain and tenderness was reported by 28 per cent of women during menstruation and 35 per cent of women before menstruation in Moos's (1968) study, with similar frequencies reported by Woods et al. (1982). Premenstrual breast pain seems to be directly linked to some aspect of the ovarian cycle, although it is not currently clear which. In the comparison or oral contraceptive (oc) users with nonsteroidal contraceptive users described earlier, we found that women using an oc with three 'stepped' dosages of ethinyl oestradiol and L-norgestrel (triphasic pill) experienced the same pattern and intensity of breast tenderness as women using nonsteroidal means of contraception. Women using 'monophasic' type pills, that is pills which have the same dose of ethinyl oestradiol and L-norgestrel in each tablet, experienced significantly less premenstrual breast tenderness than either of the other groups (Walker and Bancroft, 1990). This is not simply an effect of changing synthetic hormone levels, though. When we looked at the data more closely, we found that 51 per cent of the monophasic users experienced some breast tenderness around menstruation in one or more of three cycles, compared to 83 per cent of triphasic users and 90 per cent of nonusers; consequently a much higher proportion had no paramenstrual breast symptoms at all (49 per cent, compared to 17 per cent and 10 per cent).[11] These results suggest that ovulation *per se* is not necessary for breast tenderness to happen, but that cyclical changes in hormone levels may be a contributory factor. Mansel and his colleagues have successfully treated cyclical mastalgia, a more severe form of menstrually related breast pain than the women in this study experienced, with bromocriptine, a drug which suppresses the activity of prolactin (Mansel *et al.*, 1980; Kumar *et al.*, 1984). Other researchers who have tested bromocriptine for PMS have also found that breast symptoms are responsive to it (e.g. Kullander and Svanberg, 1979; Andersch, 1983). Since breast tissues are particularly responsive to prolactin, and the degree of cyclical variation in prolactin varies considerably between individuals (McNeilly and Chard, 1974; Steiner and Carroll, 1977), it seems a likely candidate for the aetiology of breast pain. Horrobin (1983) argues that a deficiency of essential fatty acids around menstruation causes an abnormal sensitivity to prolactin, and hence breast pain. Such a deficiency, he argues, explains the beneficial effects of evening primrose oil (a source of gammalinoleic acid, an essential fatty acid) for premenstrual breast pain (Horrobin, 1983). A meta-analysis of the few controlled trials of EPO suggests that it is indeed effective for menstrually related breast pain, and is a safe and reliable treatment, with fewer risks than bromocriptine (Carter and Verhoef, 1994).[12]

Headaches around menstruation are also reported by about 30 per cent of women in surveys of paramenstrual symptoms (e.g. Moos, 1968; Pennington, 1957; Woods *et al.*, 1982), and yet there has been very little research into the nature or causes of menstrual headaches. Patricia Solbach and her colleagues have identified two types of headache occurring around menstruation, menstrual migraine and menstrual tension headache (Solbach *et al.*, 1991). Menstrual migraine is a one-sided throbbing head pain, which may be associated with upset stomach, sensitivity to light and irritability. Tension headache is a sensation of tightness or pressure usually in the frontal lobes or behind the eyes, and can range in intensity from very mild to quite severe. Solbach *et al.* (1991) asked 32 regularly menstruating women to keep daily records of headache activity for thirty-six weeks, and found that tension headaches occurring around menstruation are qualitatively different from those happening at other times. In this group, tension headaches during menstruation were more intense and less responsive to treatment than those at other times, although intensity at all times was fairly low, with average means less than 30 on a 100-point scale. Other research has also suggested that migraines occurring during menstruation are different from those at other times in terms of their frequency, duration, location and accompanying symptoms (Nattero, 1982), and that migraine without aura are significantly more likely to occur during menstruation than at other times

(Johannes *et al.*, 1995). The aetiology of these headache types is unknown, although falling/low oestrogen levels may be involved in menstrual migraine (Somerville, 1972; 1975). Non-pharmacological therapies, such as biofeedback, relaxation and counselling, do not seem to be effective treatments for either type of headache (Solbach, 1992; Szekely *et al.*, 1986; see also Facchinetti *et al.*, 1993b), suggesting that the cause(s) is/are physiological and not psychogenic. Recent research suggests that a shortage of serotonin may be associated with migraines; a drug called sumatriptan, which supplements serotonin, has been shown in one study to improve menstrual migraine symptoms dramatically (Solbach and Sargent, 1991, cited in Golub, 1992), although as yet it requires further clinical trials to demonstrate long-term safety and efficacy. As with all of these menstrually related physical experiences, more good biomedical and physiological research is needed to clarify the biochemistry of menstrual headaches.

Finally, this section would not be complete without some mention of the feelings of bloating or swelling which many women report, and which may be accompanied by weight gain. In Kessel and Coppen's (1963) study, 72 per cent of women reported some swelling of the stomach and abdomen, breasts, feet or ankles, although fewer women reported swelling in other studies – 35 per cent both menstrually and premenstrually reported by Moos (1968) and 45 per cent premenstrually, 39 per cent menstrually by Woods *et al.* (1982). Andersch *et al.* (1986) asked women to report swelling in different areas of the body separately, and found that 74 per cent reported at least mild abdominal swelling premenstrually, 59 per cent reported premenstrual breast swelling and 25 per cent reported swelling of fingers and/or ankles. Even accepting that these retrospective accounts probably provide inflated prevalence estimates, it seems that a great many women feel bloated or swollen before and during menstruation. These feelings are related to reports of greater body dissatisfaction premenstrually (e.g. Carr-Nangle *et al.*, 1994), although not always to measurable changes in body shape or body shape perception (see O'Brien, 1987; Carr-Nangle *et al.*, 1994). About one-third of women report a weight gain of one to five pounds (500–2500g) premenstrually (Abramson and Torghele, 1961), although this too is not always found in prospective daily weight assessments (Andersch *et al.*, 1978; Voda, 1980; see O'Brien, 1987). The feelings of swelling are usually attributed to fluid retention, which is assumed to arise through fluctuations in the sodium–potassium balance during the cycle, through some effect of ovarian hormones on the renin-angiotensin-aldosterone system which controls fluid balance within the body. Many early writers saw this as a possible aetiological mechanism for PMS (Greenhill and Freed, 1941), and studies of water and electrolyte balance attracted a great deal of research attention during the 1960s and 1970s. This research literature has been thoroughly reviewed (Reid and Yen, 1981; Rausch and Janowsky, 1982; O'Brien, 1987), and the results relating both to fluid retention mechanisms across the cycle and to the possibility that fluid retention is the 'cause' of premenstrual depression or irritability were inconclusive. The search for an aetiology for PMS moved on to more rewarding pastures, and consequently our understanding of fluid balance and the menstrual cycle has remained more or less stuck since the early 1980s.

The studies reviewed in this section have all suggested that a proportion of women experience a variety of physical 'symptoms' around menstruation, which result from the association between the ovarian cycle and other body systems, e.g. uterine prostaglandin production or the renin-angiotensin-aldosterone system. The effects on such body systems do not always result in unpleasant 'symptoms' around menstruation – the opposite can be the case. Women with rheumatoid arthritis, for example, report that their symptoms are less troublesome around menstruation, possibly as a result of anti-inflammatory effects of ovarian hormones or their synergistic effects on hydrocortisone (Magos and Studd, 1985a). Similarly, the effects are not always severe. For most women, breast tenderness, period pain and a swollen abdomen are uncomfortable rather than disabling – equivalent to the effects of exercise on an unfit body rather than a disease state. This may be why surveys of women suggest that premenstrual depression and irritability are more 'worrying' than physical changes (Warner and Bancroft, 1990), even though the physical experiences are more reliably linked to menstruation. It is certainly the case that researchers have shown very little concern about the physical concomitants of menstruation. While pain and discomfort seem to be treated by researchers (and those who provide research funding) as 'normal' aspects of menstruation, meriting only the occasional study, depression and irritability are seen as 'abnormal' and a 'social problem' worthy of considerable research effort and expenditure. Similarly, while both physical and psychological experiences are attributed to menstrual physiology and are 'just a part of being a woman', pain is something the culture is willing to put up with, but anger, depression or unpredictability of mood is something we cannot accept. This point is made even more graphically when we consider the controversy and concern surrounding PMS, the subject of the next chapter.

6

PREMENSTRUAL SYNDROME

The concept of a 'premenstrual syndrome' has dominated Western medical and psychological thinking about the menstrual cycle throughout the second half of the twentieth century. Neither is PMS simply an obscure medical phenomenon – it has become a familiar part of Western culture, a regular topic for magazines and an inspiration for cartoonists and comedians. The concept of PMS has been an important one for researchers concerned to establish a causal relationship between women's moods or well-being and the menstrual cycle (or reproductive processes). The possible relationship between reproductive neuroendocrinology and mental states, especially depression, is frequently discussed in medical journals (e.g. Pearlstein, 1995; Blehar and Oren, 1995; Hamilton and Halbriech, 1993; Steiner, 1992; Gitlin and Pasnau, 1989). If menstruation or another aspect of the menstrual cycle could be shown to cause a 'disease' or mental illness, then the relationship between women's psychology and women's reproductive ability would, from a medical perspective, shift from hypothesis to fact. PMS is not the only possibility. There are several case reports in the literature of a 'premenstrual psychosis', for example (see Severino and Yonkers, 1993). However, it is PMS which has attracted the majority of research – and there has been plenty of it. As we saw in chapter two, PMS 'hysteria' has been a significant feature of menstrual cycle research, especially in the 1980s and 1990s, and there are now hundreds of research papers concerned with it. In addition to these is the burgeoning self-help and women's health literature – part of what has been called the 'PMS industry' (Laws, 1985). Interest in this line of research is not purely academic, however. It might be possible to argue that, for most women, the question of whether the menstrual cycle is related to cyclical fluctuations in well-being is a largely academic one, having little impact on everyday life. On the other hand, the question of whether PMS exists and whether it is a disease has significant impact. It means that women may receive a medical or psychiatric diagnosis and be exposed to a wide variety of treatments, ranging from vitamin supplements to hysterectomy and ovariectomy. For some, this is a positive step – acknowledging at last that women's distress is important and offering treatment. For others, the risk of medicalisation and psychologisation of women's experiences outweighs any benefit. The purpose of this chapter is to consider whether

PMS exists as a disease or illness, and to outline the current state of research. The key question is whether the research about PMS represents the discovery of a significant disease state, or the invention of a syndrome which can be used to continue women's oppression (Laws *et al.*, 1985; Ussher, 1991; Russell, 1995). In other words, does the concept of PMS as medically and socioculturally defined bear any relation to women's experience, or are we trying to force the experience to fit the concept?

MEDICAL PERSPECTIVES ON PMS

As noted in chapter two, PMS or PMT emerged as a concept in the scientific literature of the 1930s, and has remained a firm feature of it ever since. It has been through numerous name changes and subtle conceptual alterations, but remains fundamentally the same phenomenon that Frank and Horney were describing in 1931. The scientific approach to PMS has three broad strands: attempts to measure the experiences women report; attempts to identify and define a dysfunctional or diseased state; and the development and testing of theoretical models for this dysfunction. The study of PMS originated within medicine and psychoanalysis, both of which are concerned with abnormality, and medicine particularly with disease. So from the beginning the scientific approach to PMS was not concerned with the investigation of a 'neutral' phenomenon, equivalent to plant growth in botany or muscle function in physiology, for example, but with the investigation of a disease or dysfunctional state. The women described by Frank, Horney and their contemporaries were experiencing distress for which they had sought professional help, and in both cases the menstrual cycle was proposed as a possible explanation for that distress.[1] Not surprisingly, then, the medical literature is predominantly concerned with unpleasant or distressing states, and not with positive premenstrual changes, for example. Most of the research assumes that there is a 'normal' level of menstrual cycle fluctuation – but precisely what this level is defies definition.

There may be implicit consensus within the medical profession that PMS is a dysfunction (or medical condition), but there is less agreement about what kind of condition it is. As O'Brien (1993) notes, no one specialty within medicine has taken 'ownership' of PMS, and researchers from a wide range of specialisms have been involved. The two specialties most often concerned with PMS are gynaecology and psychiatry, leading some to question whether PMS is 'really' a psychiatric or gynaecological condition (Backstrom and Hammarback, 1991). The involvement of both gynaecology and psychiatry, together with the many varieties of hybrid,[2] has resulted in the production of a large number of theories and a diverse and confusing literature. One reason for the confusion is that specialists in the two disciplines are not always talking about the same concept and their reasons for being interested in PMS are not the same. Gynaecology can be defined as the 'science of physiological functions and diseases of women' (Oxford English Dictionary, 1976), and is usually confined to conditions attributed to reproductive functions and processes. Hence gynaecologists are interested in any type of physical or emotional distress, so long as it is related in some way to the menstrual cycle. The majority of gynaecological research has adopted a broad definition of PMS (or premenstrual syndromes), concerned with the severity of symptoms and their temporal relationship to the menstrual (or ovarian) cycle, and not with the nature of the experiences women report (see Magos and Studd, 1986; O'Brien, 1987, 1993). Psychiatry, on the other hand, is generally concerned with the study and treatment of states which are conceptu-alised as 'mental disease' or 'mental illness'. Psychiatrists in general are concerned with particular mental illnesses (e.g. depression, schizophrenia, etc.), rather than the gender of the person experiencing them. However, from its earliest days more women have obtained a psychiatric diagnosis than men, prompting a concern about why this should be from both within and outside the profession.[3] In the nineteenth century, this concern was focused around the diag-nosis of hysteria (see Showalter, 1987, and chapter two); in the late twentieth century, depression is the key concern (see Nolen-Hoeksema, 1990; Ussher, 1991; Russell, 1995). It is the apparent link between women and depression which makes PMS interesting to psychiatrists. In particular, it is the idea that women may be vulnerable to depression because of their reproductive biology which makes PMS fascinating. Hence, from a psychiatric perspective, the symp-toms which women report premenstrually do matter, and only affective experiences are of interest – particularly depression (or dysphoria), but also anxiety, tension, irritability, anger and mood swings or emotional lability, as can be seen from the DSM IV[4] criteria.

So, depending upon the perspective of the authors, a wide variety of experi-ences are assessed as possible symptoms of PMS (or its equivalent), and which are focused upon depends more on the orientation of the researchers than the epidemiology of premenstrual experiences. It also means that there is little agreement between studies about which experiences are assessed. Budieri *et al.* (1994) examined 350 reports of clinical trials for PMS treatments, and found 65 different questionnaires or scales used to measure symptoms or diagnose PMS. These questionnaires and scales measured no fewer than 199 different signs and symptoms. The most frequent of these are listed in Table 6.1. The list is inter-esting for two reasons. First, because none of these experiences is measured in all of the scales. Even the most frequent, irritability, was included in only 44 of the 65 questionnaires. So there is clear disagreement among medical researchers about which experiences constitute PMS. Second, of the top 36 symptoms listed by Budieri *et al.*, none would allow the rating of any kind of positive state. On these questionnaires it seems that it is not possible to indicate that you are happy, for example, only that you are not depressed. Some researchers do use contin-uous and/or bipolar scales which allow women to indicate good moods as well as bad ones, [5] but the overwhelming impression from the literature is that positive feelings are either not possible or not worth measuring premenstrually.[6]

Table 6.1   States measured in PMS questionnaires

Irritability (44)	Headache/migraine (40)
Depression (37)	Crying easily or feeling tired (34)
Anxiety (31)	Breast tenderness or soreness (31)
Tension (31)	Mood instability or swings (30)
Pain/backache (30)	Weight gain (29)
Abdominal bloating (28)	Food craving (28)
Difficulty or lack of concentration (28)	Increased appetite (26)
Fatigue (26)	Confusion (24)
Abdominal cramps (21)	Dizziness or vertigo (21)
Forgetfulness (21)	Nausea (21)
Unsociable or avoid social activity (21)	Breast pain (20)
Restlessness or jittery (20)	Anger or temper outbursts (18)
Oedema of extremities (19)	Pain in general (19)
Insomnia (19)	Breast swelling (18)
Efficiency decreased (18)	Sadness or blues (18)
Accident prone (17)	Sexual interest changes (17)
Abdominal swelling (16)	Energetic (16)
Loneliness or feeling alone (16)	Tiredness (16)

Source: Adapted from Budieri *et al.* (1994)
Note: Numbers in brackets indicate the frequency of each item out of 65 questionnaires

Defining and diagnosing PMS

Deciding which states to measure in relation to PMS is only the first step in the diagnostic process. What sort of profile is considered to be evidence of a disease state? It is this question more than any other which has exercised medical researchers in the last two decades. The conceptualisation of PMS as a disease state immediately poses problems, as does the use of science to investigate it. A disease is an 'unhealthy condition of the body' (Oxford English Dictionary, 1976). For a state to be conceptualised as a disease, there must be a contrasting healthy state in either the same person or other people. This leads to a difficulty. PMS can be seen either as a disease of the premenstrual days, with the contrasting healthy state occurring during the rest of the menstrual cycle, or as a disease affecting some but not all menstrual cycles with the contrasting healthy state occurring in other cycles. In other words, PMS can be seen as an inevitable affliction of menstruating women, or as a dysfunctional state experienced by only some menstruating women, or as some compound of the two. Severino (1993) has used a state/trait metaphor to describe this distinction. She argues that women with PMS may be different from other women on some dimension at all points of the cycle (trait), or only at particular points, e.g. in the premenstrual phase (state). This difficulty then leads on to

147

another difficulty. Since the scientific approach places experimental evidence above all other kinds in the empirical hierarchy, it is necessary to find some way of investigating PMS experimentally (or at least quasi-experimentally). To do this, it is necessary to define a control group. If it is assumed that PMS is an inevitable affliction of menstruation, then it would be logical to look for differences between women before and after menstruation for causal factors. Women in any phase other than the premenstrual one would constitute the control group. On the other hand, if PMS is a state which only occurs in some cycles, then we need to compare the premenstrual phases of women who do have PMS (PMS+) with those who do not (PMS-) to find a causal factor. In this case, women who do not experience PMS are the control group. So, the use of control groups provides a useful key to the conceptualisation of PMS employed in experimental research. Often researchers use both premenstrual–postmenstrual comparisons and PMS+/PMS- premenstrual phase contrasts, although in recent years the latter has become more popular. This results in the largest controversy in scientific studies of PMS – how to decide whether a woman is a PMS 'sufferer' or not.

Gynaecological definitions of PMS generally avoid identifying particular symptoms as indicative of the syndrome. O'Brien (1987) notes 'pedantically, then, PMS is not a true syndrome, since a syndrome is defined as a specific collection of symptoms and signs. In PMS it is the *timing* of symptoms that is important and not their specific character' (p. 8). Even when the pedantic necessity that a syndrome should be defined on the basis of its symptoms is forgone, 'experts' have had great difficulty in producing a single definition (see O'Brien, 1987; Bancroft, 1993; Gold and Severino, 1994). Dalton (1984) based her definition entirely on 'symptom' timing – 'premenstrual syndrome is the recurrence of symptoms in the premenstruum with absence of symptoms in the postmenstruum' (p.3). The premenstruum is defined as the four days before menstruation, while the postmenstruum appears to mean a phase of seven symptom-free days some time after menstruation. This definition has been widely criticised for its focus on only one premenstrual symptom pattern – several authors assert that there are many different patterns (Abraham, 1983; Reid, 1985; Bancroft, 1993) – the absence of any criterion of symptom severity, and the requirement that symptoms must be absent for some part of the cycle. Bancroft (1993) argues that mood-related experiences, such as irritability, are 'part of normal experience, ranging in degree according to circumstances as well as temperament' (p.4), and thus to require a woman to be entirely free of irritability, for example, for at least seven days in order to obtain a diagnosis of PMS is not meaningful. Other critiques similarly express concern about the absence of a criterion of severity, and offer a variety of different criteria to improve the definition. For example, Kashiwagi *et al.* (1976) specify that symptoms should be rated both subjectively and objectively as 'moderate or severe', although they provide little guidance about what these terms might mean. Attempts have been made within gynaecology to produce a consensual definition,[7] for example, this one produced by a workshop sponsored by the Royal College of Obstetricians and Gynaecologists in Britain in 1983:

> A woman can be said to be suffering from premenstrual syndrome (PMS) if she complains of regularly recurring psychological or somatic symptoms, or both, which occur specifically during the luteal phase of the cycle. The symptoms must be relieved by the onset of, or during, menstruation; there must be a symptom-free week following menstruation.
>
> (O'Brien, 1987: 6)

Psychiatric definitions are concerned with type of experience reported as well as its timing. They are also far more concerned about the degree of change reported and measurement of symptoms. As with gynaecology, psychiatrists have attempted to produce consensual definitions and diagnostic 'tools'. One of the most influential agreements came from a workshop sponsored by the National Institute of Mental Health (NIMH) in 1983. It was this workshop which proposed that a difference of 30 per cent between premenstrual and postmenstrual mood scores should be the criterion for PMS as a clinical diagnosis (Schnurr, 1989; Rubinow *et al.*, 1984), a rule which has become somewhat of a 'gold standard' in PMS research. This workshop similarly sanctified daily ratings as the key diagnostic tool. Another highly influential (and controversial) consensual definition is that of premenstrual dysphoric disorder (PMDD),[8] developed by psychiatrists in North America, and outlined in DSM IV (American Psychiatric Association, 1994).[9] This definition requires women to experience at least one affective symptom to obtain a diagnosis of PMDD, but also includes criteria about the timing of symptoms and a judgement, albeit subjective, of their intensity. It is also considerably more complex than the gynaecological definitions, and requires prospective monitoring as 'proof' of a woman's symptomatology.

The definitions appearing in DSM have been criticised both by gynaecologists and by feminist writers because they focus on affective experiences rather than somatic ones, excluding women with purely physical premenstrual experiences from the diagnosis (O'Brien, 1987; 1993) and implying that all premenstrual experiences constitute a psychiatric disorder (Caplan *et al.*, 1992; Stotland and Harwood, 1994). Gynaecologists and feminists are united for once in their opinion that PMDD/LLPDD is only one manifestation of a broader range of premenstrual experiences. O'Brien (1993), for instance, writes that, 'Premenstrual syndrome and luteal phase dysphoric disorder have wrongly been used interchangeably' (p.1,472), echoing Caplan *et al.*'s comment that 'PMS and LLPDD are not interchangeable terms' (Caplan *et al.*, 1992: 31). This view is also held by some psychiatrists, although others see the new criteria as a refinement of the previously vague PMS.[10] Within psychiatry, not all researchers wholeheartedly support the DSM criteria. Paula Schnurr and her colleagues, for instance, have compared a number of different statistical methods for analysing the daily ratings required by the DSM criteria, achieving different numbers of 'cases' with each technique (Schnurr *et al.*, 1994; Hurt *et al.*, 1992). Similarly, although researchers may agree that daily ratings are required to establish a diagnosis, there are no stipulations about what should be measured.[11] This underlines the point made by other researchers that despite the apparent detail in the criteria there is considerable scope for variation between research groups in their interpretation of them (see Gallant *et al.*, 1992a; 1992b). It remains to be seen whether these criteria are any more successful at creating cohesion than previous attempts, or even whether researchers and clinicians are able to operationalise them. Severino and Gold (1994) in their review of premenstrual dysphorias and current psychiatric thinking about the DSM criteria note that:

> The current definition of LLPDD is, however, not fixed. It is the clearest definition we have at the present time for a state experienced by a small percentage of women. . . . As research and clinical experience provide more understanding, the definition of the condition and the recommendations for treatment will change.
>
> (Severino and Gold, 1994: 233–234)

The stage seems set for a considerable amount of further research refining and disputing the LLPDD/PMDD criteria within the psychiatric profession, with the strong possibility that this will become increasingly divorced from research in gynaecology or psychology.[12]

Researchers, then, are still faced with the problem of placing a disease-type definition on to widely variable premenstrual experiences. Some have suggested that the problem arises because there is more than one premenstrual syndrome. Leslie Gise (1988) argues that 'PMS is not a discrete entity or a specific syndrome, but a heterogeneous group of symptoms better named premenstrual changes. This is more than a semantic difference. It implies that premenstrual changes should be studied as diversified subtypes' (p. xv). The notion of premenstrual changes originates in the work of Jean Endicott and Uriel Halbriech, who identify a number of subtypes in the premenstrual assessment form (PAF – Endicott and Halbriech, 1988; Halbriech *et al.*, 1982; Halbriech *et al.*, 1985; see chapter three). Other researchers, however, have challenged this idea. Jorgensen *et al.* (1993) obtained retrospective ratings from 820 undergraduate and 485 graduate students and found evidence of different levels of severity of premenstrual experiences, but no evidence of different subtypes.[13] A form of 'subtype' which is acknowledged by most researchers is the concept of premenstrual exacerbation of an existing state or disorder. Mitchell *et al.* (1994), for instance, describe three 'perimenstrual symptom patterns' in a community sample of 296 women studied both retrospectively and prospectively. The 'premenstrual syndrome', 'premenstrual magnification' and 'low symptom' groups accounted for 142 of the women in the sample, and the experiences reported by the groups differed significantly. This premenstrual exacerbation pattern is frequently described and usually such women are denied a diagnosis of PMS or PMDD (see DSM criteria).

Then there are those researchers who argue that the whole notion of a coherent premenstrual syndrome, with or without subtypes, is too 'fuzzy', and that spending time trying to define and measure such a nebulous concept is questionable. These authors argue that women's experiences are real but better thought of as premenstrual symptoms (Brooks Gunn, 1986) or as menstrually related problems (Bancroft, 1993; 1995) rather than a syndrome. Finally, there are those who argue that what matters is a woman's perception that she suffers from PMS. These researchers categorise women on the basis of their self-diagnosis or self-identification as a woman with PMS, rather than medical or psychiatric diagnostic criteria (Warner and Bancroft, 1990; Corney and Stanton, 1991; Ussher and Wilding, 1991). The fact that women can self diagnose suggests that they have their own criteria for and definitions of PMS. However, these do not seem to match medical (and especially psychiatric) diagnostic criteria and as many as 80 per cent of women seeking help from specialist PMS clinics may 'fail to confirm' their self-diagnosis.[14] There is remarkably little clinical concern or information about what happens to these women, who are after all seeking medical help or advice. Are they referred on to other specialists, or simply discharged? The implication is that these women are 'normal' or the 'worried well', but all we know about them is that they are not experiencing changes which match fairly arbitrary diagnostic criteria. From a critical perspective it seems that definitions of PMS may act simultaneously to medicalise (or psychologise) normal experiences and to deny serious consideration to women whose experiences are somehow 'incorrect'. It is hardly surprising that many women who do seek help for PMS are dissatisfied with what they receive (see below).

Attempting to define and diagnose PMS has occupied and frustrated clinicians and researchers for twenty years. It remains the case that there is no single agreed-upon definition of PMS and that many researchers believe that all would become clear in PMS research if only one could be found. In the middle of all this comes the occasional suggestion that, rather than being abnormal premenstrually, women are actually abnormally nice and pleasant in the rest of the cycle, failing to express normal levels of anger and irritability, or that a 'postmenstrual syndrome' of euphoria is a better description than a negative premenstrual syndrome (Abraham, 1984). All of this hardly seems a good basis on which to build explanatory models or evaluate treatments, but nonetheless theories and treatments abound, as we shall see.

Theories

The number of theories of the aetiology of PMS in the medical literature appears odd at first sight, since without a clear and consensual definition of a syndrome how can a cause be identified? The logic is, however, that if a 'biological marker' for the syndrome could be identified, then women could be diagnosed on the basis of a blood test or physical examination rather than their ratings on daily mood diaries. A clear biological difference between women reporting distress (of whatever kind) and 'controls' would make further statistical work unnecessary and establish the existence of a 'real' disease, with 'proper' objective diagnostic criteria.[15] This, coupled with a steady number of women seeking treatment for PMS and, in the 1980s at least, social concern about PMS, has kept the momentum of aetiological research going. A wide variety of different mechanisms have been proposed to account for severe symptomatology, ranging from neurochemical to psychosomatic, and the evidence relating to them all has been reviewed repeatedly (Bancroft, 1993; Gold and Severino, 1994; Dinan and O'Keane, 1991). The main theories fall into four broad categories: endocrine, psychosomatic, neuroendocrine and interactive.

The endocrine theories have been most popular in gynaecology, and assert that premenstrual distress results from a dysfunction or abnormality of ovarian endocrinology. The most popular hormonal candidate for investigation has been progesterone, because it is present only in the luteal phase, but other hormones have also been considered.[16] The assessment of these hypotheses depends on a good understanding of normal endocrine processes, accurate hormone assessment (and PMS diagnosis), and well-controlled treatment trials. All of these are largely absent. The endocrinology of the menstrual cycle is far from being completely understood, despite the confident assertions of the textbooks. For example, it is only in the last ten years that researchers have realised that progesterone and LH are secreted in pulses rather than as a steady trickle (Crowley et al., 1985; Steele et al., 1986). The significance of this pulsatility is not yet understood. Similarly, it is no simple task to measure hormone levels (see chapter three). For many researchers, treatment trials are the only practicable approach. In these studies, inferences are drawn about an underlying dysfunction from the effects of artificially supplementing endogenous hormones (e.g. progesterone), or suppressing the naturally occurring cycle (e.g. by oral contraceptives or GnRH agonists).[17] Treatment trials are complicated, however, not only because of a large 'placebo' effect in PMS studies, but also because the drugs used may have non-specific pharmacological effects. Progesterone, for example, can have tranquillising or anaesthetic effects in sufficient doses.[18] Reviews of this area generally conclude that women complaining of PMS are indistinguishable hormonally from women who are not complaining, but that suppression of the menstrual cycle can disrupt a usual pattern (Walker, 1992a; Bancroft, 1993; O'Brien, 1993; Parry, 1994). A distinction should be made here between physical premenstrual changes (such as breast tenderness) and emotional ones. While ovarian hormones do not seem to be significant in premenstrual dysphoria, physical symptoms are more likely to be affected by them. For example, breast tenderness in particular seems to be less severe in anovulatory cycles (Walker and Bancroft, 1990). Studies testing endocrine theories of PMS and premenstrual dysphoria continue, however, in an enterprise which Schagen van Leeuwen (1991) likens to the search for 'an endocrine holy grail'. [19]

Psychosomatic theories originated from Horney's idea that women experiencing premenstrual distress were endocrinologically normal but psychologically different from other women. Psychodynamic theorists, such as Horney, have suggested that unconscious conflicts about pregnancy may be triggered by the physical signs of approaching menstruation, resulting in tension and irritability (Horney, 1931b; Shainess, 1961; Benedek, 1963; Bernsted *et al.*, 1984). Others have suggested that women who experience premenstrual distress may be ambivalent about their femininity or experiencing sex-role conflicts (Levitt and Lubin, 1967; Brattesani and Silverthorne, 1978; Spencer-Gardner *et al.*, 1983; Slade and Jenner, 1980; Berry and McGuire, 1972), or have a different type of personality (Coppen and Kessel, 1963; Hain *et al.*, 1970; Gough, 1975; Gruba and Rohrbaugh, 1975). Neurosis has been a popular personality characteristic for investigation (Taylor *et al.*, 1991; Mira *et al.*, 1985; Herrera *et al.*, 1990). These psychosomatic ideas had largely lost favour by the mid-1970s, for several reasons. First, psychodynamic approaches became less popular within psychiatry in general, with the shift towards the brain rather than the mind as the locus of mental illness. Second, empirical studies were equivocal and widely criticised (Gannon, 1985). Third, feminist and sociological critiques of psychiatry shifted attention towards women's life circumstances rather than their psychological processes as a source of depression (Chesler, 1972; Brown and Harris, 1978). Psychosomatic theories are very rarely mentioned in the recent medical research on PMS – although the idea that premenstrual symptoms could be 'all in the mind' persists in media reports (and this is what psychiatrists and psychologists are usually perceived to be saying). In research terms, psychosomatic theories have largely been replaced by 'sociomatic' theories – studies which hypothesise that women who complain of PMS have different life circumstances from those who do not, and particularly that their lives are more stressful (Woods *et al.*, 1995). This hypothesis is currently popular, and a number of studies have shown significant correlations between levels of self-reported stress (or indices of life events) and self-reports of PMS (Warner and Bancroft, 1990; Woods *et al.*, 1995). These are predominantly correlational studies, of course, so it is not clear whether the stress is causing the PMS, or vice versa, whether both are caused by a third unmeasured factor, or whether women who complain of PMS are more sensitive to stress or more likely to report it. The popularity of these theories and their empirical support has been a significant factor in the development of multivariate models of PMS, however, and has sparked psychological interest (see below).

Neuroendocrine theories (or psychoneuroendocrine theories) reflect the shift in psychiatry which began around the 1970s towards the brain rather than the mind as a source of dysfunction. From this perspective, the source of depression and other mental illnesses is thought to lie in a dysfunction or altered sensitivity of one or other of the many transmission systems in the brain. Hence, studies investigate a variety of neurotransmitters and other indices of central nervous system function. Since the ovarian hormones can themselves have CNS activity (McEwen, 1988; Dinan and O'Keane, 1991), neuroendocrine theories can account for PMS either as a result of different levels of ovarian hormones or as a result of altered sensitivities of neurotransmitters to 'normal' hormone levels. The research showing similar ovarian hormone levels (see above) has resulted in an increased emphasis on neurotransmitter system sensitivities, leaving the question of which neurotransmitters to investigate. This is where the perceived similarity of PMS and depression is significant. Many of the psychiatrists working on PMS saw a similarity between the symptoms of the two conditions – mood change, altered eating habits, altered sleeping patterns, etc. (Hallman, 1986) and were also concerned to explain higher rates of depression diagnoses among women. Hence the focus on women experiencing depression premenstrually, and the theory that PMS, or more specifically premenstrual dysphoria, might be linked to clinical depression. The systems investigated in premenstrual dysphoria parallel those in mainstream depression research. Currently serotonin (5-hydroxy-tryptamine, 5-HT) is the most popular candidate, and several reviews have suggested that this is the most promising field for future research (e.g. Rapkin, 1992; Bancroft, 1993).[20] Theories in this category have also suggested a role for monoamine oxidase (MAO), dopamine, noradrenalin, adreno-corticotrophic hormone (ACTH), endogenous opioids (especially ß-endorphin) and melatonin (Dinan and O'Keane, 1991; Backstrom, 1992; Parry, 1994). In addition to these, prostaglandin mechanisms have been investigated, and the renin-angiotensin-aldosterone system.[21] The functions of all of these substances are difficult to assess in humans because they are acting centrally, not peripherally. Researchers rely largely on treatment trials or 'challenge' tests to infer particular functions, both of which are difficult to interpret. As a result, none of these theories has been unequivocally supported, and the area is, as Dinan and O'Keane (1991) put it, 'strong on theory but unfortunately rather weak on fact'. Psychiatric enthusiasm for the new 'selective serotonin reuptake inhibitors' (SSRIs) and the hypothesised link between serotonin and premenstrual dysphoria (Rapkin, 1992; Severino, 1993; Bancroft, 1993) means that drugs like fluoxetine (Prozac) are likely to become the 'treatment of choice' for women reporting PMS into the twenty-first century.

Interactive or biopsychosocial theories are part of a recent shift in medical and psychiatric thinking towards a more holistic or integrated view (see Engel, 1977). These theories suggest that premenstrual changes result from the interaction between various different systems, rather than a dysfunction in any one particular system. Bancroft (1993) integrates psychosomatic, endocrine and neuroendocrine approaches in his 'three factor model' of PMS. He hypothesises that PMS results from the interaction between a 'timing factor' (involving the normal hormonal cycle and its associated fluctuating neurotransmitter levels), a 'menstruation factor' (involving processes leading up to menstruation) and a 'vulnerability factor' (characteristics of the woman such as personality or a predisposition to depression). Others see PMS or premenstrual changes as the result of interactions between biology, psychological processes and social circumstances. So, for example, Severino (1993) describes LLPDD as 'a classic biopsychosocial disorder resulting from complex interactions of biological, psychological, socioeconomic and cultural forces on women' (p.229). In a similar vein, Gotts *et al.* (1995) argue that the interactions between these different systems are so complex and intricate that PMS is effectively an idiosyncratic syndrome, with different causes and different symptoms in different women. Theories of this type are also popular within psychology (see below). These theories are interesting because they do represent a paradigm shift (Kuhn, 1962). They are intuitively appealing, but are virtually impossible to test within a hypothetico-deductive model of science. Precisely how the proposed interaction between these different systems occurs remains a mystery – not least because the 'psycho' part of the model is generally poorly conceptualised. Fundamentally, PMS is still thought of as a disease, but the recommendations for treatment are 'tailored to the individual woman', and assume a depth of knowledge of the woman's lifestyle and psyche as well as her biology. PMS becomes a disease with no specific symptoms, no specific aetiology and no specific treatment. Is this a postmodern definition of disease? It will be interesting to see the medical response to these new theories. Are truly interactive models feasible within medicine, or will 'lip service' be paid to them while researchers continue in the traditional univariate mould? If the paradigm shift is real, then can PMS continue to be conceptualised as a disease? Finally, it is important to note that these interactive models emanate largely from within psychiatry and are concerned predominantly with premenstrual dysphoria. It is unlikely that such complex models are necessary to explain premenstrual headaches or breast tenderness.

Treating PMS

The various theories of PMS imply different approaches to treatment. The best-known treatment for PMS is progesterone, administered by injection or as suppositories because it cannot be absorbed through the digestive system. Progesterone was popularised and marketed in the late 1970s and early 1980s on the basis of the personal experience of a small number of women treated by Katharina Dalton (see Eagan, 1985; Norris, 1987). At that time there were no well-controlled clinical trials to test its efficacy, and no research examining the safety of progesterone for long-term use, or its side effects. However, many women found it helpful, and a concerted publicity effort encouraged many more to demand progesterone or to see it as the only treatment for PMS. Subsequent placebo-controlled trials have shown that progesterone is effective, but no more so than a placebo (Sampson, 1979; Dennerstein *et al.*, 1985; van der Meer *et al.*, 1983; Maddocks *et al.*, 1986; see Smith and Schiff, 1989, and Maxson, 1988, for reviews), and it has fallen from favour as a treatment. So, what sort of medical treatment is currently offered to women complaining of PMS?

Recent reviews of PMS management in the medical literature acknowledge the absence of a clear aetiology and emphasise the importance of thorough investigation and careful diagnosis of PMS before embarking on treatment (O'Brien, 1993; Severino and Moline, 1995; Mortola, 1994). They then recommend three broad treatment strategies – changes in diet and lifestyle, control of the menstrual cycle, and management of specific symptoms. These categories subsume a wide range of specific treatments, with varied efficacy and side effects. Rivera-Tovar et al. (1994) have reviewed the efficacy of 31 different surgical, pharmacological, dietary and psychosocial treatments for PMS/LLPDD. Many of these are effective for relief of at least some premenstrual symptoms, but none can 'abolish' PMS without simultaneously abolishing the menstrual cycle, and both surgical and pharmacological treatments have associated risks and side effects (Mortola, 1994).

Changes in diet and lifestyle are often recommended in the alternative and self-help literature, as well as in medical clinics. These are often presented as 'common sense' approaches, and are rarely subjected to proper evaluation. For example, women may be told to reduce salt intake to minimise bloating, yet there are no studies which examine the usefulness of this strategy. Severino and Moline (1995) conclude that 'it seems reasonable to recommend limiting salt intake on the chance that temporary weight gain could be avoided', (p.75) – a harmless piece of advice for most women in this case. In some other cases, though, the practice of recommending apparently innocuous dietary treatments, 'on the chance' of doing some good, has proved less benign. Vitamin B_6 (pyridoxine) was widely recommended for PMS in the early 1980s, for example, and taken by many women in large doses, until concerns began to be voiced about its side effects and potential toxicity (Parry, 1985; Schaumberg et al., 1983). The most frequently recommended dietary supplements in the self-help literature are calcium, zinc, magnesium, vitamin A, vitamin B_6, vitamin C, vitamin E and evening primrose oil (EPO). There are very few trials of any of these treatments, although vitamin B_6 and EPO have been studied more often than others. Carter and Verhoef (1994) summarise the findings of these studies and conclude that vitamin B_6 is no better than placebo for any premenstrual symptoms and that EPO is only an effective treatment for premenstrual breast tenderness. There are too few studies to draw conclusions about the other vitamins and minerals, although they conclude that magnesium 'appears promising as a potential treatment' and that all of them (except vitamin B_6) have 'good safety profiles'. [22] Herbal remedies and homeopathic treatments have not been systematically tested. Women may also be advised to reduce their caffeine and alcohol intake, to take exercise, change their smoking habits, alter their sleep patterns, manage their stress or join a support group, any of which may be effective but all of which have only recently attracted research attention (see Rivera-Tovar et al., 1994).[23] The studies which have been conducted suggest that psychosocial interventions are effective. Relaxation, for example, seems to help women cope with physical premenstrual symptoms (Goodale et al., 1990),[24] and cognitive-behaviour therapy can be as effective as hormone-based therapies in treating symptoms (Morse et al., 1991).[25] Exercise (Prior et al., 1987), reflexology (Oleson and Flocco, 1993) and support groups (Walton and Youngkin, 1987) have also been shown to be effective interventions. Similarly, uncontrolled studies by Parry and her colleagues have suggested that light therapy and/or changes in sleeping patterns may be beneficial for premenstrual dysphoria (Parry *et al.*, 1993; Parry *et al.*, 1995). The effects of dietary changes have not been systematically evaluated. It seems that for many women, developing coping skills, gaining support from other women or adopting strategies which increase personal control over life events may be useful means of dealing with premenstrual symptoms. These approaches do not imply that women's experiences are imaginary or 'all in the mind', any more than indigestion or tension headaches are imaginary. Their success, though, does suggest that, like indigestion or tension headaches, physical experiences can be exacerbated or triggered by a particular lifestyle. The problem with all of these approaches is that they assume that women are able to take control over their lifestyle – in other words, they ignore the material and social constraints which many women may experience. Although cognitive therapy or exercise may be as effective as any of the drugs prescribed for PMS, the idea of a 'magic pill' (or magic operation) will be preferable for many women because the barriers to taking control over their lives may seem insurmountable.[26]

Means of controlling the menstrual cycle have already been mentioned, and all of these appear as forms of treatment. In particular, oral contraceptives, GnRH agonists, danazol, oestrogen implants and ovariectomy have been investigated. Danazol and oral contraceptives are the least effective of these, with the others demonstrating relatively high efficacy, although they are difficult to test in a placebo-controlled fashion because of their dramatic physiological effects. All of them, however, have risks and side effects attached. Most of the treatments which suppress the cycle cause chronically low oestrogen levels, raising concerns about bone loss and acceleration of osteoporosis as well as cardiovascular effects, although they may protect against breast, ovarian and endometrial cancers. These treatments are also associated with 'menopausal'-type side effects, such as hot flushes, night sweats, vaginal dryness, urinary discomfort, emotional lability and headaches. Exogenous hormones can also cause problems. The risks and side effects of oral contraceptives are well documented, and oestrogen too has associated risks. The particular concern with oestrogen is the heightened risk of uterine cancer, which is reduced by taking a short course of progestogen at regular intervals. This regime protects the uterus, but is associated with mild premenstrual-type symptoms and withdrawal bleeds. The therapy with the highest number of side effects is danazol. This drug causes low oestrogen levels and is associated with all the side effects that that implies, but it is also androgenic and has 'masculinising' effects. Recognised (although rare) side effects of danazol include acne, weight gain, decreased breast size, voice deepening, clitoromegaly, fluid retention, hot flushes, vaginal dryness, emotional lability, altered lipid profiles with possible implications for cardiovascular function, adverse effects on liver function, and the creation of female pseudohermaphroditism in an unborn baby. It is, however, a very good treatment for premenstrual migraine. Mortola suggests that danazol is 'a poor choice for most patients with PMS' and that conventional antimigraine treatments may be equally effective and less toxic. Other gynaecologists are less pessimistic about danazol, however. O'Brien (1993), for instance, argues that its side effects are rare and 'have probably been overstated', citing evidence that danazol can abolish symptoms of PMS in sufficiently high doses. Danazol is likely to remain one of the treatment options for women complaining of severe PMS. As well as specific side effects, the way in which these treatments are administered can cause problems. Ovariectomy (usually with hysterectomy) is a major operation with associated anaesthetic risks and potential post-operative complications. Other treatments may be administered as regular injections or implants, both of which may cause pain and local irritation. Abolishing the menstrual cycle is not without its costs, and most authors recommend the most drastic treatments only in cases of 'severe intractable PMS'. How quickly a woman comes to be seen as a severe and intractable case, however, may depend on the enthusiasm of her clinician for one or other of these treatments, and on any other menstrually related problems which she experiences (e.g. heavy periods or dysmenorrhea).[27]

Treatments for specific symptoms of PMS focus on either emotional or physical symptoms. In treating emotional symptoms, most attention has focused on two types of drug – the benzodiazepines ('tranquillisers') and drugs with serotonergic activity. The benzodiazepines have become controversial drugs because they are addictive. Dependence on benzodiazepines can occur quickly and withdrawal symptoms are a serious concern. [28] Other side effects of alprazolam, the benzodiazepine most frequently tested in studies of PMS, include hypotension, drowsiness, fatigue and lethargy, and occasionally paradoxical agitation. Alprazolam does, however, seem to be an effective treatment for premenstrual depression (with or without anxiety) if used with care (Berger and Presser, 1994; Schmidt et al., 1993; Freeman et al., 1995). Severino and Moline (1995) advocate careful selection of patients to avoid those with 'any sign of an addictive personality', gradual reduction of the drug during menstruation to minimise withdrawal effects, and regular monitoring to prevent addiction. Even then they note that alprazolam is not effective or appropriate for everyone. O'Brien (1993), writing from a gynaecological perspective, does not mention benzodiazepines as a treatment option, so it seems that although tranquillisers are still prescribed for PMS, their time as a treatment of choice is coming to an end. The 'new kids on the block' are the SSRIs, which could very quickly become the mass-market treatment for PMS. The drug which is described as 'most promising' on the basis of clinical trials is fluoxetine (Prozac), administered daily throughout the cycle or just in the luteal phase (Wood et al.,1992; Veeninga and Westenberg, 1992; Steiner et al.,1995; see Rapkin, 1992, and Severino, 1994, for reviews of the rationale). Mortola (1994) is reassuring about the risks of fluoxetine, noting that early reports of an association with suicidal or homicidal behaviour have not been substantiated. It is not without side effects, however, and for about 15 per cent of patients these are sufficient to stop them taking the drug. Side effects include agitation or insomnia, nausea and diarrhoea, anorexia and loss of interest in sex. Occasionally drowsiness may occur rather than insomnia, and in a very small number of cases changes have occurred in blood physiology (e.g. anaemia or thrombocytopenia) or liver enzymes. Mortola notes that fluoxetine has not been associated with birth defects in animal studies, but there is no human evidence about this. However great the enthusiasm for fluoxetine becomes, it is not a magic cure for PMS. As Rubinow and Schmidt (1995) point out, 40 per cent or so of women with PMS do not respond to fluoxetine or other serotonergic drugs, so the search for a universal treatment is by no means over.

Drugs to treat physical symptoms are generally those which would be used to treat the same symptom at any time of the month, e.g. conventional anti-migraine treatments, and are too numerous to describe here. The only non-hormonal physically based drugs which have been widely advocated for PMS are the diuretics (e.g. spironolactone). These have limited efficacy except for women who experience premenstrual weight gain (O'Brien, 1993; Severino and Moline, 1995; Mortola, 1994). Diuretics can also have serious side effects, especially if they are used continuously, affecting cardiac, central nervous system and gastrointestinal function as well as haemotology, and causing hypokalaemia in some cases.

This survey of treatments for PMS suggests that women have been exposed to some very powerful drugs in an attempt to alleviate premenstrual complaints. The efforts put into diagnosis and definition of PMS in the 1980s have limited this exposure to those women whose experiences match the diagnostic criteria, but it remains the case that many women may experience their effects. At a clinical level, these treatments are likely to be used on a 'trial and error' basis – beginning with those which are perceived to be relatively benign or appropriate to particular symptom profiles. For many women, the first choice of treatment will not work, and neither will the second or third, until eventually they become 'severe and intractable' cases, with ovariectomy the 'treatment of choice'. The similarities between this therapeutic approach and the strategies adopted with women diag-nosed as 'hysterical' in the nineteenth century are too close to be coincidental. That is not to suggest that clinicians are not trying to do the best for their patients. They are, and many clinicians, now as then, devote large amounts of time and effort, and devotion beyond the call of duty, to finding a remedy for the suffering of which their patients complain. The medical research relating to PMS is not consciously misogynist or misguided. However, their best efforts do suggest that looking inside the woman herself (either her mind or her body/brain) is not going to be enough to solve the 'riddle' of PMS. The truth is that women have always experienced changes in physical and emotional well-being around menstruation. The puzzle is why, in the twentieth century, these have become intolerable both to women themselves and to the culture in which they live. To answer this question, we need to consider the social construction of PMS.

THE SOCIAL CONSTRUCTION OF PMS

The biomedical model of disease which has dominated Western medicine pays scant attention, as we have seen, to the social context of the individual. If diseases are attributed to the function or dysfunction of a physiological organism, there is no need. A 'heart attack' is much the same physiologically whether the person is rich or poor, black or white, Christian or Muslim, Indian or Japanese. It has long been recognised, however, that the culture in which a person is raised or living can influence the way they express or communicate their physical or mental state. For example, an often cited study by Zborowski (1952) demonstrated differences in pain expression between Americans from Irish, Italian and 'Old American' backgrounds. Culture determines the language and behaviour which is used to express distress and the circumstances in which it may be expressed. So, while the physiological states experienced may be identical, people from differing cultures may articulate and respond to them differently.

Culture may also determine which clusters of signs and symptoms are recognised as an illness.[29] Hence, although similar physiological experiences occur across humanity, they may be described as an illness (or disorder) in some cultures but not others. Disorders which are specific to particular cultures have become known as 'culture-bound disorders' or 'folk illnesses'. Helman (1991a) describes them as 'a cluster of symptoms, signs or behavioural changes recognized by members of those cultural groups, and responded to in a standardized way' (p.234). Exactly the same experiences and behaviours may be reported in another culture, but not described or responded to as an illness. Culture-bound disorders usually have some symbolic significance or meaning within a culture. This meaning may link an individual to wider concerns (e.g. to supernatural forces) or allow antisocial or 'difficult' behaviours to be dealt with in a socially sanctioned way. There are a number of examples of culture-bound disorders in the anthropological literature. For example, *susto* (or 'magical fright')[30] is a psychological disorder which is found in many parts of Latin America (Rubel, 1977, cited in Helman, 1991a). The symptoms of *susto* are depression, loss of appetite, lack of interest in dress or personal hygiene and restlessness during sleep. Within this culture, a person is thought to consist of a physical body and one or more souls. *Susto* occurs if one of these souls has become detached from the body, either because it has been 'captured' by spirits unwittingly disturbed by the patient (in Indian accounts) or because of a sudden fright or shock (among non-Indians). Treatment involves diagnosis and then healing, usually involving massage, rubbing and sweating to remove the illness and encourage the soul to return. In this example, the symptoms are recognisable as experiences familiar in many cultures, but not always identified as a specific illness. A clear aetiological mechanism and rationale for treatment are identified, and *susto* has meaning – it links the individual experience with wider cultural understandings of body function and the supernatural. It also allows people to cope with antisocial behaviours in a socially sanctioned way. So, for example, Rubel (1977) notes that *susto* is more likely to occur when an individual is in a stressful social situation, especially when they are unable to meet the social expectations of their family. The investigation of culture-bound disorders has largely concentrated on non-Western cultures, but in recent years anthropologists and sociologists have begun to investigate the possibility that these occur in Western cultures too. A number of conditions have been examined from this perspective, including PMS.[31] In particular, Thomas Johnson (1987) and Mari Rodin (1992) argue that while premenstrual experiences are real, their construction as a disease (PMS) is culturally-specific (see also Martin, 1989; Rittenhouse, 1991; Laws, 1990). What sort of evidence suggests that PMS is a socially constructed illness?

Cross-cultural studies of premenstrual experiences

Cross-cultural studies seem the logical source of information. If women report premenstrual experiences in other cultures which are similar to those in ours, but such changes are not recognised as an illness in those cultures, then it could be argued that PMS is culturally specific. Although there are many cross-cultural studies of premenstrual symptomatology,[32] there is very little research which addresses this point. All of the currently published studies are epidemiological rather than anthropological in nature – concerned to investigate whether women in different countries have similar premenstrual experiences, or at least whether they rate their experiences in a similar way on retrospective questionnaires (usually the MDQ or a derivative). These studies suggest that the physical and emotional experiences which women report premenstrually in other cultures (or at least their responses to questionnaires such as the MDQ) are similar to those of women in North American or British studies. The number of women reporting different experiences varies, and they are not universal in any country, but feelings such as irritability, breast pain, swelling, fatigue and mood swings before menstruation are common, it seems, to a proportion of women wherever they live. However, the question of whether these experiences are always recognised as an illness is not addressed in the existing studies, most of which only describe the questionnaire ratings without any detailed description of the culture in which the women live or what these experiences mean to them.

There is some anecdotal evidence that premenstrual states are not always described or experienced as an illness or disease. For example, Rupani and Lema (1993) in their study of nurses in Kenya comment that although premenstrual symptoms are reported they do not limit work activities and very few women seek medical or other treatment for them. Similarly, Monagle and her colleagues observed a high rate of premenstrual symptomatology (using the MDQ) among a community sample of 239 Italian women, three-quarters of whom answered 'no' to the question 'Have you ever heard of premenstrual syndrome?' In addition, it is noteworthy that none of the anthropological studies conducted before PMS became familiar in Western thinking describe any type of illness state occurring before menstruation, although there is extensive discussion of menstrual taboos and myths and physical experiences during menstruation.[33]

An added complication of the cross-cultural literature is the widespread influence of English-speaking cultures, which makes it difficult to interpret some of these studies. For instance, a high proportion of English-speaking Chinese women in Hong Kong report fatigue, swelling, irritability and mood swings premenstrually on the MDQ (65–92 per cent of a sample of 66 clerical workers) (Chang *et al.*,1995). In an earlier study 50 per cent of a sample of 84 nurses said they experienced 'premenstrual tension' (Mao and Chang, 1985). Are these women describing a recognised illness? If they are, is it a Western or Chinese construction? As the authors point out, 'this method may not account for a culturally specific view of PMS. The MDQ needs to be used in conjunction with other studies that focus on Chinese women's descriptions of their menstrual experience and relevant contextual information about PMS' (Chang *et al.*, 1995: 560). This, of course, is not only true of Chinese culture. Far more contextual information is needed about all of the cultures studied if cross-cultural research is to be helpful. It also raises the possibility that studies like this may themselves be a part of the social construction process. Most of them are conducted by researchers who have observed PMS in other countries, or read about it in the medical literature, and set out to investigate whether women in their country experience it. Since premenstrual symptoms are found, the provision of health education literature[34] and sources of help for women may seem an appropriate humanitarian action, and hence women are encouraged to recognise their experiences as an illness; thus PMS becomes a universal rather than culture-bound disorder.

If studies of women in other cultures tell us little about whether PMS is a culture-bound disorder, what evidence is there in our own culture to suggest that PMS is socially constructed? Three lines of evidence from our own culture are used to argue that PMS has a meaning and symbolism which make it a culturally specific condition – medical research evidence, studies of media representations of PMS, and sociopolitical analyses of it.

There is confusion about PMS in the medical literature, as we have seen, and failure to identify a biological marker for the condition despite over sixty years of trying. Despite this inconclusive literature, research and treatment continues. The logic seems to be that while a definite physiological malfunction has not been proved, it has not been disproved either, and so it is appropriate to continue to seek one. The persistence of PMS researchers in the light of so much contradictory data and so many negative findings is remarkable, and, Rodin argues, suggests that the research is motivated by more than a scientific concern. She writes:

The fact that the medical establishment treats PMS as a legitimate disease category (by applying for research funds, proceeding with research, treating patients, and maintaining PMS clinics) despite the lack of an agreed upon definition and contradictory research findings, suggests that shared cultural knowledge, as opposed to scientific facts, informs researcher understandings of what constitutes PMS.

(Rodin, 1992: 52)

Medical research continues, and funding bodies appear willing to support applications, suggesting that PMS is seen as an important social problem. After all, it could be argued that millions of pounds and dollars have been wasted on thus far inconclusive PMS research – why should any more be spent? Yet medical PMS research is increasing, not decreasing (see chapter two), and the apparent aim of it is to treat or ease women's distress. This is unusual in itself, since a concern with women's health is not a common characteristic of medical research. Many feminist analyses of health research have described the tendency to ignore women's health issues and to omit women from relevant research, especially clinical trials of drug treatments (Rodin and Ickovics, 1990; Tavris, 1992). Premenstrual experiences are not usually life-threatening (except for the small group of women who describe suicidal feelings) and severe premenstrual symptoms may only affect 5–10 per cent of regularly menstruating women. For many centuries, these experiences have been unremarkable and barely noticed. Yet in the mid-late twentieth century, they attract medical research and media attention out of proportion to their social impact. While for many women the attention paid to premenstrual symptoms is a welcome validation of women's experience, we still need to ask why attention is being paid to them at this time. It does suggest that there is something special about PMS which distinguishes it from many other medical conditions, that PMS has a particular significance in this culture.

PMS in the media

The second line of evidence which suggests that PMS is a socially constructed disorder comes from the description of it in newspapers, magazines and books. Media descriptions of PMS are a major source of health education information for women, but they also provide a reflection of cultural preoccupations with it. There have been books and articles specifically about PMT or PMS in the popular domain since the 1950s, and, like the medical literature, press reports appear in waves. The use of PMS as a mitigation in the murder trials of Christine English and Sandie Smith in the early 1980s provoked a flood of press interest (Rittenhouse, 1991; Chrisler and Levy, 1990). Ten years later, interest was triggered again by discussion surrounding the inclusion of PMDD in the DSM IV and, in Britain, a press-released academic symposium which challenged the usefulness of the concept of PMS for understanding women's experience.[35]

The content of popular articles reflects the political perspective of the publication in which they appear, so feminist analyses of PMS do appear occasionally. The most influential articles, though, are likely to be those appearing in mass circulation publications, and these tend to present a view of PMS as a negative experience (almost always discussing premenstrual violence), which ought to be considered as a medical (not psychiatric) problem and which affects a varying number of women (5–95 per cent) (Chrisler and Levy, 1990; Walker, 1995b). Chrisler and Levy (1990) analysed popular articles published between 1980 and 1987, finding that they are characterised by 'repeated instances of inaccuracy, limited perspective, and distortion'. For example, many continue to recommend progesterone treatments despite repeated demonstrations that it is no more effective than a placebo. Similarly, most articles feature the dangerous effects of premenstrual violence, without mentioning that women commit less than 5 per cent of violent crimes. A large number of symptoms are described (131 in this study – some of which do not appear in the medical literature), and estimates of the number of women experiencing PMS ranged from 5 per cent to 95 per cent, although most articles distinguish between 'mild' or normal symptoms and 'severe' ones. They comment that it is the negative changes which make PMS dramatic – and therefore newsworthy – so, not surprisingly, these are the ones most often featured. 'Positive' changes, such as bursts of energy, increased creativity, increased sexual interest or enhanced self-confidence, are mentioned in these articles, but these occur far less frequently and are usually described as exceptional. From a social construction perspective, it is significant that PMS is newsworthy, and – in these articles – newsworthy because of the association with violence. In most of these articles it is implied that PMS is a medical condition which debilitates some (or most) women and can lead them to murder their husbands or boyfriends. As Chrisler and Levy (1990) put it, the media present a picture of 'a menstrual monster'.

Rittenhouse (1991) has examined a broader range of literature in a little more depth than Chrisler and Levy (1990), asking whether PMS can be considered to be a 'social problem'. She considered American medical, popular and feminist literature about PMS, published between 1931 and 1987, and observed changes in the way PMS has been described over time. She argues that PMS was seen as an essentially private matter and a medical problem in both popular and medical discourse before 1980. Popular descriptions of it were universally negative, inferring that all women have PMS, and describing those whose symptoms are moderate or severe as 'once-a-month witches', suffering 'monthly blues' or 'needless misery'. In these accounts, women are inherently problematic because of their menstrual cycles. After 1980, while the popular press contained the kind of material described by Chrisler and Levy, a feminist discourse emerged, challenging both it and the dominant medical description of women's experiences. These articles appeared in feminist publications, but were nonetheless influential, so that by the late 1980s, Rittenhouse argues, another shift was occurring. The medical literature was beginning to differentiate premenstrual symptoms and one or many premenstrual syndromes, recognising that not all women have the same experience, and focusing on accurate diagnosis of clinically significant symptoms. In the popular literature, the negative effects of PMS were less frequently described as inevitable or debilitating. PMS was something to be managed or coped with, and not something which should interfere with caring for a family or having a successful career. PMS and premenstrual symptoms remained confused, so that PMS could still be used to describe any degree of premenstrual change, but, she argues, 'premenstrual changes were problematized while the women who suffer from the changes were not' (Rittenhouse, 1991: 417). This was a crucial distinction – shifting the concern from 'problem women' to 'problem changes'. The feminist literature, meanwhile, had become less reactive and was developing new conceptualisations of premenstrual change. On the basis of her analysis, she argues that PMS became a social problem in the early 1980s, because of its association with murderous violence. The feminist reaction to the extreme portrayals of 'out of control' women moderated the effect of this, so that it could no longer be defined as a social problem by the late 1980s. Rittenhouse notes that 'the public debate over PMS has subsided, though there is no resolution of disagreement about what exactly constitutes PMS and its related symptoms' (p.419).

The public debate about PMS was triggered again in 1993, in Britain at least, providing a useful snapshot of current cultural views of PMS. The immediate stimulus for debate was a press-released symposium on PMS held at the British Psychological Society Annual Conference in April 1993. This symposium included papers by academic psychologists and a clinician specialising in PMS, all of which challenged the idea that PMS is a disease resulting from a simple or understood endocrine imbalance and affecting all women, advocating instead a biopsychosocial understanding of women's experience. The press release associated with the symposium, headlined 'Premenstrual syndrome – not just biology', provoked a great deal of press interest and a widespread perception that psychologists believe premenstrual symptoms to be 'all in the mind'. Headlines such as 'The man who says PMT doesn't exist' and 'PMT? It's all in the mind, ladies' were quickly followed by 'Women attack PMT study' and 'Women up in arms over Professor's claim', and later by more detailed feature articles. In the 1990s, it appears, PMS is newsworthy if its existence is challenged, and the people thought to be concerned about this are the women who are suffering. Most hurtful of all, judging by these comments, is the implication that premenstrual experiences might be imaginary or a form of mental illness. For example, Anna Reynolds writes of:

> the millions of women who spend up to 10 days each month in agony suffering up to 150 possible symptoms. . . . Those same women, many of whom have lost partners, killed their young children, killed themselves, injured someone else, lost jobs and friends through this condition, have spent a fortune on so-called treatments, only to be told that they are imagining it all.
>
> (*Observer*, 18 April 1993)[36]

The concern about recognising women's experiences as real also came from a feminist perspective, with one writer likening the perceived psychologisation of PMS to earlier medical attitudes towards period pain: 'It's all reminiscent of those good old days when we were told that period pain didn't exist, we only thought it did' (*Scotsman*, 6 April 1993). In the 1990s, it seems that Western culture is endorsing the reality of premenstrual experiences.

However, there was confusion in these articles about whether such experiences constitute a disease, and if so how many women are affected. Some writers echo the style of reporting which Rittenhouse observed in pre-1980 articles, so that in some reports PMS is seen as a common and debilitating complaint and an inevitable part of being a woman – something which women can have without being aware of it. Thus, for example, one journalist writes:

> I know a lot of women I would choose not to drive with at certain times of the month and I know a lot of other women who do not know how difficult they are to deal with at certain times of the month. These are the kinds of women who would say PMT is all in the mind yet who can at times be a positive danger to society.
>
> (*Daily Post*, 7 April 1993)

However, the majority of articles did acknowledge that PMS is not something which all women experience (exhorting self-monitoring by diary-keeping to check), and that most women cope with ordinary premenstrual changes. Estimates of how many have 'true' PMS ranged, as in the 1980s, between 5 per cent and 95 per cent. Many tips for coping were also given, mostly relating to changes in diet or to many of the self-help remedies for PMS. This encouragement to self-monitor and self-medicate is also found in advertisements for menstrual products (Treneman, 1988). The key to freedom here too is seen to lie in concealment and self-regulation. Reading between the lines, these articles seem to say that if you're careful and eat properly or take the appropriate medical treatment, no-one need ever know that you're premenstrual, for which you'll be rewarded with a successful career or family.

A number of articles also acknowledged that PMS is a gendered experience, arguing that it would have received more research attention if men suffered from it, or suggesting that men use it to invalidate women's complaints, or suggesting that women use it as an 'excuse'. Some of these comments come from a feminist perspective, but others are blatantly misogynist. For example:

> Whether it's in the home or the workplace, male eyebrows are raised patronisingly whenever a female happens to raise her voice, stamp her feet or, heaven forfend, throw a major wobbly. The fact that she probably has good reason for an outburst is ignored. The poor dear must be coming up to that time of the month, so let's be kind and ignore her unseemly tantrums.
>
> (*Western Morning News*, 7 April 1993)

Since new evidence proves that PMT is mostly in the mind and often the result of having an equally neurotic mother, I hope nobody ever says it again. And that they stop exploiting it to explain their filthy temper, sloth-fulness, inefficiency or desire for a bit of attention.

(*Daily Mail*, 7 April 1993)

These 1990s articles seem to suggest that, at least in Britain, PMS is still considered an illness and something with which the medical profession should be concerned. There are dissenting voices, though, questioning for instance the amount of money made by companies selling food supplements or over-the-counter drugs to treat PMS, as well as private clinics and book sales. There are also voices questioning a disease model as the only way of understanding women's experiences. Sue Innes writes in *Scotland on Sunday*:

For years there has been a line of research which seeks to show PMS as a contributory cause of accidents, suicide, admission to mental hospital and violent crime. Although it has been argued that in some cases this could be useful, it would be to label something which is a normal part of women's reproductive capacity as pathological. We need the complexities of PMS to be recognised, but not like this. What a choice – between non-existence and pathology.

(Innes, 1993)[37]

If women want to have their experiences taken seriously, then they must describe them as an illness in Western culture. However, these articles suggest that the trend Rittenhouse was observing towards the end of the 1980s is contin-uing. While the 'knee-jerk' reaction of the British press to a questioning of PMS was an assertion of its reality, devastating nature, universality and hormonal aeti-ology, more considered articles did question this description for all women, and did describe the changes rather than the woman herself as the problem. The metaphor which appears again and again in press reports is the one of 'Jekyll and Hyde': women becoming something other than themselves premenstrually, being taken over by an evil or unseen force, and becoming 'bad' – either antiso-cially violent or antisocially depressed. This metaphor occurs, too, in women's descriptions of PMS (see below), and in a muted form in medical terms such as 'mood swings', and the diagnostic insistence that women should be asymp-tomatic for at least some of the cycle. It is this metaphor which gives PMS its power and symbolism – linking it to moral concerns about good and bad behaviour and the tangled web of gender politics.

The politics of PMS

As noted above, the political analysis of PMS (or PMT) developed in the early 1980s as a challenge to the dominant medical and media representations of it. Aspects of this analysis have informed most of the discussion in this book; however, since it is crucial to a social constructionist understanding of PMS, the main strands will be described here. The clearest political analysis of PMS is found in the collection of essays by Sophie Laws, Valerie Hey and Andrea Eagan (1985). They analyse the medical literature, press reports of PMS and the 'PMS industry', and argue that, whoever benefits, it is not the women who complain of premenstrual symptoms. Feminist analyses of PMS are often dismissed as saying that premenstrual symptoms do not exist. In fact this is far from the case. Laws (1985), for example, writes: 'All menstruating women experience cyclic change of many kinds. . . . It is clear that some women feel these changes more intensely than others, but these changes still constitute part of a woman's being, and are not signs of sickness' (p.57). Such experiences do not have to be described as an illness, and have not always been so described. The question is why we have chosen to describe them as an illness in the twentieth century. Who benefits from this categorisation, and what purpose does it serve?

The obvious beneficiaries from a medical perspective are women, whose 'ancient woe' (Gonzalez, 1981) has finally been taken seriously by the medical profession, and who are at last being offered treatment. This treatment will 'liberate' women from their bodies, allowing us to work efficiently throughout the month and to be happy, contented 'good'[38] women. But who benefits from women behaving in this way? Laws argues that it is men (and patriarchy) who benefit. A 'good' woman, as far as the PMS literature is concerned, is one who is sweet-tempered, placid and undemanding – the 'sweet wife'[39] described in many self-help books, for instance. 'Bad' women – that is, premenstrual women – are angry, demanding, sexually 'out-of-tune' with their man[40] and improperly behaved. Invoking the label of PMT or PMS allows the 'bad' feelings or behaviour to be dismissed by both men and women, and treating the behaviour restores to the man the 'sweet little lovebird' he married. The possibility that he could have provoked a genuine grievance does not have to be addressed. The benefits to patriarchy are the maintenance of women in the family and the continuation of capitalist forms of production (see Martin, 1989). Women are encouraged to control their bodies, or deny their effects, in order to fit into a society designed by and for men.

The other major beneficiary of PMS is the 'PMS industry'. Eagan (1985) describes the growth and promotion of progesterone therapy for PMS in the early 1980s, noting the lucrativeness of this for the drug company manufacturing progesterone and the individuals promoting it – all of this at a time in which there were no well-controlled clinical trials of progesterone in the medical litera-ture and no research investigating the effects of long-term use of high doses of it. While this may be testimony to the desperation of many women to control their experiences and the effectiveness of progesterone for some, it hardly inspires confidence that the welfare of women is the primary concern of the industry. Progesterone is now less fashionable – as we have seen, partly because medical research has demonstrated that it is no more effective than a placebo. There are plenty of other treatments available, though, both on prescription and over-the-counter. The efficacy and safety of treatments has already been discussed, but it is worth noting here that there is only one paper in the medical literature evaluating the risks and benefits of PMS treatments, and that was not published until 1994 (Mortola, 1994). Similarly, there are very few studies which evaluate 'self-help' treatments or strategies such as diets or exercise, although large numbers of women use them. In a study of 1,826 women in Wellington, New Zealand, for instance, 85 per cent reported one or more premenstrual symptoms and 81 per cent of these had tried some form of self-help medication (Pullon *et al.*, 1989). So, clearly, someone is benefiting, but it may not be the majority of women who take these remedies.

If patriarchy and the PMS industry benefit from the conceptualisation of women's premenstrual experiences as illness, what is the purpose of it? Johnson (1987) argues that PMS emerged in the medical and popular literature at a time at which the status and roles of women in Western societies were changing. Women are now required to be (or desire to be) 'both productive and reproductive'. He argues that this creates numerous conflicts both for individual women and for the culture, and the PMS label provides a means of resolution. So, he says:

> PMS serves to answer this role conflict of productivity and generativity by simultaneously and symbolically denying the possibility of each: in menstruating, one is potentially fertile but obviously nonpregnant; in having incapacitating symptomatology one is exempted from normal work role expectations. Through PMS, Western culture translates the ambiguous and conflicted status of woman into a standardized cultural idiom which makes her position meaningful. It is a symbolic cultural 'safety-valve' which recognizes the need for women to simultaneously turn away from either alternative role demand.
>
> (Johnson, 1987:349)

A similar meaning is suggested by Gottlieb (1988), who suggests that PMS provides a means by which women can express their anger or protest without sabotaging their femininity. These explanations focus on the meaning of PMS for women, but the political analysis already described suggests that the symbolism of it may go further than this. While attributing anger to being premenstrual may at least allow women to express anger, as we have already seen, it is an ineffective strategy because the PMS label means that it will be dismissed. As Stoppard (1992) and others (Sayers, 1982; Hamilton and Gallant, 1990; Caplan *et al.*, 1992; Cibulas and Howell, 1995; Ussher, 1989, 1991) have pointed out, the PMS label effectively attributes women's problems to their internal state, making any consideration of the social circumstances surrounding the problems unnecessary. The label also serves to deny women any responsibility for their actions. As was seen clearly in the use of PMS as a defence, a woman can be deemed to be incapable of reason or self-control because of her premenstrual (by implication, hormonal) status. Whether or not the use of such a defence is legitimate in particular cases is not the point here. From a social constructionist point of view, what is important is the existence of the label PMS which can be used both to dismiss any form of 'unfeminine' behaviour and to deny women access to situations in which responsible actions are necessary. In other words, the label PMS has the potential to disempower all women, regardless of their actual premenstrual experiences. As such, its emergence at a time when women are demanding greater participation in public life serves a patriarchal purpose. While women themselves may use the PMS label as a means of remaining 'feminine' while also taking on masculine activities, it can always be used against them to deny access to the higher echelons of power or responsibility.

So, the PMS label can serve a purpose within the realms of gender politics. Other writers have argued that PMS also serves a moral purpose. Authors such as Rodin (1992) and Ussher (1991) have linked the discussion of PMS in the medical literature to earlier medical discussions of hysteria, arguing that PMS serves the same purpose in modern society that hysteria did in the nineteenth century. Both effectively control women, as noted above, but they also define what is 'acceptable' and 'unacceptable' behaviour for women. In other words, both PMS and hysteria serve a moral purpose. In both of these conditions, 'good' and 'bad' women are identified, and in both it is the control of 'bad' behaviour (as defined by a clinician) which is paramount. Hence in PMS studies the focus is always on the mental aspects of women's experience – the irritability, anger and depression – not on the physical aspects. A 'good' woman is patient, caring, cheerful and undemanding. A 'bad' woman is irritable, angry, self-oriented or depressed. The PMS label allows these good and bad aspects to be contrasted and discussed – most emotively through the use of the 'Jekyll and Hyde' metaphor. The social consequences of this bad behaviour are emphasised – murder and mayhem apparently result from PMS. Thus the ills of society can conveniently be placed at the feet of women who have behaved badly. The bad behaviour may not be their fault – we should feel sorry for them and try to help them – but nonetheless it is women who are thought to be behaving badly, all of which conveniently shifts attention away from the major sources of violence, both inside and outside the home.

The 'Jekyll and Hyde' metaphor so often used in descriptions of PMS suggests a third purpose to Helman (1991b). He sees similarities between PMS and the cinematic myth of the werewolf. In both cases, a human being is 'taken over' by 'the animal within'. In both cases, too, this occurs rhythmically, the werewolf and the premenstrual woman both under the control of the moon. He argues that the werewolf myth is an image of male menstruation – under the influence of the moon, the man's hairy 'animality' breaks out and he wreaks violent and (always) bloody havoc, only to return to humanity in the morning. Similarly, Helman writes:

In the models of Premenstrual Tension, created by males and by medical science, women are seen as the slaves of a cyclical moon, as violent and irrepressible when 'the hidden animal within her' emerges in its monthly rage, with fangs and flying hair, and spills its contagious blood across the ordered certainties of masculine life.

(Helman, 1991b: 76)

Myths of being taken over and the power of the full moon (or another super-natural force) can be found in many cultures as a means of explaining violence and apparently irrational behaviour. Hence, Helman argues that PMS can be used to accept the reality of violent behaviour while also excusing it. Like the werewolf, the woman wanted to be good, but wasn't able to be.

At the beginning of this section I used the notion of a culture-specific disorder to ask, along with Johnson, whether PMS could be considered as a Western example of this phenomenon. The discussion here has, I hope, convinced you that it can be. As I have already said, that does not mean that women are imagining what they feel or that premenstrual experiences should not be taken seriously. It is simply to say that PMS is more than just a 'women's health' issue. The concept of PMS taps into powerful cultural ideas, about good and bad behaviour, the causes of violence, and what is considered to be feminine. It has been defined at a time when women have become a 'problem' in the same way that hysteria became an issue during the nineteenth-century wave of feminism. Whatever the reality of women's experiences, PMS is a political construct, and the power of it makes the examination of women's actual experiences difficult. Perhaps, then, it is not surprising that women's voices are almost entirely missing from the PMS debate. The next section of this chapter attempts to piece together snippets of research to redress this balance.

WHAT ARE WOMEN EXPERIENCING?

PMS arouses controversy and debate in academic and popular literature, yet it remains the case that many women seek help for experiences which they perceive to be menstrually related, and label themselves as PMS sufferers. Help is sought predominantly from medical practitioners, especially GPs, but also from a variety of 'alternative' practitioners and self-help organisations. The wide range and commercial success of over-the-counter medicines which claim to cure or ease premenstrual complaints also suggests that, for many women, the concept of PMS strikes a chord. What is it that these women are concerned about and seeking help for?

What do women describe as PMS?

The words of women attending clinics or seeking help elsewhere remain largely undocumented, as is the case in many other areas of women's lives, but anec-dotal descriptions of severe distress can be found in press reports and self-help literature. For example, Anna Reynolds described her experience as 'living

171

through unexplained bouts of suicidal despair, raging anger, severe breast pain and backache, crippling migraines and a host of other symptoms' (*Observer*, 18 April 1993). Other anecdotal reports come from letters in which women spontaneously describe their experiences to researchers. For example, these women wrote in response to a national British magazine survey in 1985,[41]

> I feel very lethargic and disinterested in things around me. I want to be alone, not talk to anyone either on the phone or face-to-face. I can't bear being touched. Physical contact (even by my children) annoys me.

> It astonishes me how much better I feel once my period has arrived. The physical symptoms may be worse perhaps with backache and fatigue particularly for the first three days, but at least the irrational anger and distorted and depressed view of reality evaporates.

> Apart from generally feeling bad about myself/tension/depression in the few days before my period starts (and this will happen even if my period is unexpectedly early) and a bad headache just before it begins, the most pronounced pre-menstrual feeling I have is a strong desire to tidy up/pay bills/file/tie up loose ends.

(Walker, 1988: 1–2)

These descriptions suggest that the experiences which concern women around menstruation are variable. For some it is the intensity of their emotional reactions which causes distress, for others it is the effect of their feelings on family and friends, or physical changes such as headache or breast tenderness. They also suggest that there may be some premenstrual experiences for which help is not necessary, even though they represent perceptible cyclical changes – paying bills, for example.

A more systematic analysis of this type of description has been conducted by Cumming and colleagues (1994). They analysed the responses of 261 women to an open-ended question at the end of the PAF. The question asked the women to provide a 'narrative description of the differences between these two times' (i.e. premenstrual state and usual state). The sample included women who were seeking help for PMS (126 had sought or were currently seeking treatment) and women who were not, but the authors do not distinguish between their responses. Hence, for this purpose, it is a limited study. It is also limited by the means of data collection, since the open-ended question appeared at the end of a lengthy questionnaire which may or may not have influenced the way in which the women reported their experiences. The analysis, however, is interesting and suggests a great deal more complexity in women's accounts of their premenstrual experiences than the medical interpretation of them implies (see below). From the responses, Cumming *et al.* identified a logical hierarchy of distinctions about premenstrual changes. The first level was the presence or absence of changes. Once changes had been noted, they identified two further broad distinctions – between descriptions of the changes themselves and the outcomes or responses to them. Over 60 per cent of the women described not only what their premenstrual experiences were like, but also how they react to them. This was not just in terms of self-management, coping or help-seeking strategies, but was also an expression of how the premenstrual changes made them feel – for example, feeling sorry for themselves, unable to cope or depressed, because of their premenstrual state, not as a part of it.

The changes themselves were also described in a variety of ways, which the authors divide into two categories, 'temporal' and 'substantive'. Temporal statements described the timing of the experiences within the menstrual cycle, often in very specific detail: their consistency from one cycle to the next; the duration of the experiences themselves – for instance, whether the woman was persistently depressed for two or three days or prone to transient or episodic unhappy feelings; and their timing within the woman's life, for example whether the premenstrual experiences had changed over the years. Substantive statements described the type of change (what the authors call the 'axis' of change), i.e. physical, cognitive, emotional or behavioural, and its orientation towards self or others, i.e. whether the description focuses on the woman's inner state or her relationship with others. The statement, 'I feel very loving and affectionate toward my husband and have a very strong desire to make love' (Cumming *et al.*, 1994: 31), for example, was classed as oriented towards another. As well as these distinctions, substantive descriptions talked about the direction and degree of the premenstrual change. Direction statements were divided into those which described an increase or decrease in the woman's normal state, for example eating more than usual, and those which describe a switch into a completely different or opposite state. The authors comment that some of the 'most forceful descriptive terms' are used to indicate this shift, with several of the women using the 'Jekyll and Hyde' analogy which is frequently found in press reports and self-help literature as noted above. For example, respondent 148 writes, 'there is a severe change in me from one time to the other. It is like I change into a totally different person. A very miserable person that hurts all over. I seem to be in a lot of pain' (p.32).

Degree of change was the final dimension used in the descriptions. In this case, the authors note that the women do not appear to be using a continuum of change on which to describe their experiences, but rather a small range of qualitatively different absolute degrees of intensity. They label these 'just noticeable', 'moderate', 'severe' and 'extreme', and argue that they describe different kinds of experience, not just different intensities. So, with regard to premenstrual depression, for instance, they argue that statements such as the following represent not different intensities of the same depression, but different types of depressive experience.

The worst days I just wake up sad and crying and can't seem to quit, although there is absolutely no reason for crying present. I feel helpless (physically), weak (physically) and blue for no reason. The flare-ups of irritability always end in weeping (release tension). I still attend work and school though.

(Respondent 261, pp. 35–36)

I feel very depressed, almost 'out of control' premenstrually. Just started on the pill and that seems to help a bit. I have tried to commit suicide three times premenstrually.

(Respondent 20, p.36)

Questionnaire studies, using a variety of similar instruments, suggest that while women are aware of both physical and emotional changes, it is the emotional ones which are most likely to be defined as distressing. For example, in a community sample of 79 women in London, using a checklist derived from the Moos MDQ, irritability was the symptom most often rated as distressing premenstrually (38 per cent of women), followed by swelling (24 per cent), headache (22 per cent), depression (19 per cent), moods (19 per cent), weight gain (19 per cent), fatigue (18 per cent), tension (15 per cent), backache (14 per cent), tender breasts (14 per cent), pain (13 per cent) and anxiety (11 per cent) (Scambler and Scambler, 1985).

Defining yourself as a PMS sufferer and seeking treatment are not solely dependent on premenstrual experience, however. Warner and Bancroft (1990) considered the factors relating to self-identification by women as a 'PMS sufferer' among 5,457 respondents to a British national magazine survey. Sixty-one per cent of these women described themselves as having PMS, and they were compared on a variety of dimensions with women who did not. The size of the sample meant that they were able to control for the inter-relationships between factors which might be associated with PMS reporting, for instance age and number of children. After doing this analysis they found a strong association between the numbers of symptoms rated as severe (especially 'emotional' symptoms) and the reporting of PMS, suggesting that women are judging their experience against similar criteria to those used in medicine. However, there were a number of women (359) who did not describe themselves as PMS sufferers, despite rating their experiences before and after menstruation in the same way as those who did. Similarly, of the 2,763 women who did identify themselves as having PMS, 17 per cent did not report 'typical' premenstrual symptoms (although a number of these did experience one or more severe physical changes in the absence of emotional symptoms).

In this study, there were strong associations between reporting PMS and both the number of years of natural cycles and psychosocial factors. The more cycles a woman had had since the last interruption from pregnancy or oral contraceptive use, the more likely she was to report PMS, and similarly with her psychosocial factors score. This score combined ratings of perceived stress, cohabitation, happiness of relationship and type of employment (e.g. PMS reporting was more prevalent among those working part-time than either full-time workers or those without paid work). These two factors were also related, suggesting, the authors argue, that the perception of PMS results from an inter-action of biological and psychosocial factors. This finding matches with those of studies of 'risk factors' for PMS, summarised by Logue and Moos (1986). They found that women who report PMS are more likely than non-reporters to be over 30,[42] have long and/or heavy menstrual flow, a history of affective illness and high life stress. Other factors, such as personality, social class, cycle length, contraceptive use[43] and general health were not consistently related to premen-strual symptom reporting.

These descriptive and epidemiological studies tell us something about how women are feeling when they say they have PMS and the sort of demographic factors and medical history associated with reporting it in questionnaires. They tell us little, however, about the meaning of PMS in women's lives or the deci-sions which women make about seeking help. It is clear from the descriptions above that the medical conceptualisation of PMS is not necessarily the same as the lay conception of it. PMS is therefore better conceptualised as an 'illness' or state of 'dis-ease' rather than a 'disease' (Parlee, 1994; Scambler and Scambler, 1993; Severino, 1994). In social science, the term 'disease' has come to mean a biological abnormality or change linked to a medical condition, and defined as such by the medical profession. 'Illness', on the other hand, is used to refer to one or more experiences which are defined as 'symptoms' within a particular culture. Although 'illness' and 'disease' often occur together, there are circum-stances in which they become separated. These distinctions allow for situations in which a person has a disease but is not ill (e.g. during early asymptomatic stages of cancer), or is ill without apparent signs of a disease.

Menstruation itself can be perceived as an illness (see chapters one and four), and the women who used an illness metaphor to describe menstruation also obtained higher MDQ scores in Scambler's study. Not all studies of attitudes towards menstruation show a link with premenstrual symptom reporting, though, so this observation requires more investigation. It may be that the women who perceive menstruation as equivalent to an illness see other body experiences in this way, too.

PMS and women's lives

As we have seen, the portrayal of PMS in medical, self-help and popular litera-ture is as a destructive force in women's lives, preventing women from either working effectively or functioning as a 'proper' wife and mother. Katharina Dalton's books are excellent sources for examples of the pernicious and destruc-tive effect of the disease of PMS on the domestic and industrial world. According to Dalton, women with PMS are a cost to industry because of their inefficient work or absenteeism, and ruin their marriages through bad house-keeping and temperamental behaviour. This assumption that PMS has measurable and negative consequences on work and relationships is also found in the DSM diagnostic criteria – although no attention has been paid to how such criteria might be operationalised (see Gold and Severino, 1994). The empirical evidence investigating the relationship between the menstrual cycle and work does not support such a doom-laden view (see chapters two and four), with no evidence that women in general are cognitively impaired around menstruation or functionally impaired at work. Similarly, national statistics do not suggest that women who work full-time take any more time off work than men.[44] However, the type of work women do may be related to whether they report PMS. Warner and Bancroft (1990) found a higher rate of self-identification as having PMS among women working part-time than either full-time workers or women without paid work. In recent studies, stress at work is more likely to be cited as a potential cause of PMS than vice versa (Woods *et al.*, 1995).

Studies of family relationships and PMS are rare. However, several studies do suggest a positive correlation between reported severity of premenstrual experiences and marital dissatisfaction or having several small children (Coughlin, 1990; Kuczmierczyk *et al.*, 1992). The relationships of women who are not married appear to be of little interest to PMS researchers, although Warner and Bancroft (1990) observed in their sample that, among women under 25 with no children, cohabiting women were slightly more likely to report PMS than single women, while in the 25–29 age group the position was reversed. Associations between premenstrual experiences and relationship dynamics among lesbian women have not been specifically investigated. As with studies of PMS and work, recent research is more likely to conceptualise relationship difficulties as a risk factor for or potential cause of PMS, rather than a consequence (Kuczmierczyk *et al.*, 1992; Woods *et al.*, 1995).

Whatever view of PMS and women's lives is being taken in the academic literature, it remains the case that many women experience a variety of 'real' menstrually related experiences which they want to be taken seriously. However, in patriarchal Western cultures these changes are not only medicalised but also are negatively valued. A key feature of much of the self-help literature as outlined above is the negative impact that such changes supposedly have on patriarchal institutions of 'industry' and 'family'. How do these dual forces impact on women's lives? What are the consequences of attributing experiences to the menstrual cycle, either at work or at home? What are the consequences for women of the existence of a label which others can use to dismiss or belittle 'inconvenient' behaviour? How do men feel about PMS, and when do they use the term? How does the existence of the concept of PMS affect women's lives? There has been remarkably little research from this perspective. As most research has been conducted within science and medicine, this is not surprising. Most feminist energy has been spent in empirical challenges to menstrual myths. However, gradually studies are emerging in which the meaning of PMS for women and men is investigated. Notable among these are Emily Martin's (1989) anthropological study of North American women and reproduction and Sophie Laws' (1990) sociological study of men and menstruation.

Martin argues that most jobs in modern societies 'require and reward discipline of mind and body' (p.121), and that the majority of occupations (including the professions) have become deskilled. The focus in most modern work is on efficiency and productivity, not on creativity or skill. As a result, many jobs are monotonous, unstimulating and repetitive. This is particularly true of the jobs most women are engaged in, since, she argues, it remains the case that women are over-represented in less well-paid jobs and the fringes of the professions. As a result of this deskilling, many people, and especially women, are required to do work which is tedious and which necessitates subjection of the body and mind, for little reward. Martin argues that what many women are saying when they describe their premenstrual experiences in the context of either paid work or unpaid domestic work is that they are less able or less willing to tolerate the discipline required. In other words, she argues, it is not that women are unsuited to work *per se* when they are premenstrual, but rather that the kind of work most women are required to do is harder to tolerate around menstruation. She wonders whether the incidence of PMS is higher among women who are subjected to greater work discipline, noting the absence of specific research on this point. Her ideas, though, are supported by the recent findings linking PMS with 'stress' (Woods *et al.*, 1995; Gannon *et al.*, 1989; Warner and Bancroft, 1990). The solution proposed for women within the medical model is to change themselves by treating their PMS. The alternative, Martin suggests, is to change the nature of work or, as much as possible, alter the structure of work time to be more woman-friendly. Scambler and Scambler (1993) note that this solution might appear tempting but fails to take into account the double-edged sword of public acknowledgement of menstruation for women. As they point out, Dalton also recommends increased use of flexitime but adds that women should be 'assigned to less skilled jobs, such as packing and stacking, during their vulnerable days rather than remaining on tasks which are harder to remedy later, such as soldering or filing' (Dalton, 1984: 120). Undoubtedly, this is not the interpretation of flexible working practices which Martin intended – from her analysis such an interpretation might be expected to worsen irritability or tension. Similarly, the negative associations with PMS make the use of the label at work difficult for many women. It may be acceptable as an 'excuse' or reason for some kinds of behaviour (Ruble *et al.*, 1982; Walker, 1994b), only later to be used to dismiss justifiable anger – 'it's just PMS' – or to imply that a woman is unreliable. How such an admission may be used by an employer may vary according to the state of the labour market. As Scambler and Scambler put it:

> It is apparent that an employer's threshold of accommodation of a female employee's period pains or perceived monthly mood swings might vary in accordance with his need to retain her. During a phase of near full employment for local people with the relevant skills he might be more accommodating than during a phase when replacement employees are plentiful. In the first circumstance he might smooth his employee's path to

the sick role for her benefit; and in the second he might smooth her path to the sick role to her cost.

(Scambler and Scambler, 1993: 97)

Hence, it seems that reality of premenstrual experiences is only one aspect of PMS in women's working lives. Important too are the nature of the work itself and the state of the labour market, as well as prevailing views about PMS. A theme running through all of this for both Martin and Laws is the patriarchal nature of the culture we live in. They argue that work is largely constructed by and for men (even if most of the workers are women), and institutions such as marriage and the nuclear family have long been criticised as situations in which men hold most of the power. If men hold most of the power and influence in a patriarchal society, then it makes sense, Laws argues, to investigate male perceptions of menstruation and PMS. It is their views which are most likely to create the social 'rules' about PMS. In her interviews with 14 white, well-educated British men, she identified an 'etiquette of menstruation', a series of expectations which men held about how women should behave during menstruation. Breaking these rules, as with any social rules, would cause embarrassment, social sanction or ridicule. The cornerstone of this etiquette for Laws is the silence which women are expected to keep about menstruation. It is simply 'not good manners' to talk about menstruation in the presence of men (other than privately and in an intimate relationship). As a result, men find out little about menstruation. However, the men studied did seem to be aware of PMS, associating moodiness or irritability vaguely with 'that time of the month', and talking about work experiences, but more often about their intimate relationships with women. So, for example, two of them described situations at work in which they or others had attributed moodiness to PMS:

> Especially when I was working in a factory, one of the supervisors was a woman and once she got really annoyed over something that was stupid, and that was when I first . . . I was only 17 when I was working there, and I remember the bloke said, 'oh, it's just the monthlies, you know, she'll get over it' . . . 'don't worry about it'.

(Laws, 1990: 190)

> when I come to think of it, when I worked in an office where you could get on with people quite well, I suppose that we would refer to it there actually. If people were feeling quite fed up, especially people I knew a little bit, then I would say, I might well say, 'oh, is it the time of the month?' And they'd usually say yes. Sometimes no.

(Laws, 1990: 191)

In the context of their relationships, PMS was generally associated with arguments or difficulties in the relationship. For example, 'Well, she gets the tension . . . like you can always tell when she's got them because she gets really uptight, and anything you say is just wrong, and she snaps' (p.194). However,

178

some men did draw contrasts between different relationships, commenting that different women's menstrual cycles affected them differently, and not all of them saw cyclic mood change as necessarily negative. One said:

> She used to get very bad premenstrual tension. . . . It was very obvious to me after a while, once she'd explained to me what it was, because I never knew about premenstrual tension before I went out with her. She explained to me exactly how she felt . . . the way she explained it to me was that she just got very, she was very, very sensitive, and it was obvious, she could get very, very angry sometimes, but sometimes she could be very soft, she was just very sensitive.

(p.196)

These men showed awareness of many of the ideas about PMS that have already been described in this chapter and used them in their understanding of women both at work and in close relationships. They could use PMS to minimise women's behaviour, as in the example of the female supervisor, or to empathise with individual women, as in the last example. Some were aware that women's experiences should not be dismissively attributed to PMS, but many could describe circumstances in which they had heard it happen. As with women's talk about PMS, though, these men are reflecting a wider range of concepts than those seen in the medical and self-help literature, although they generally seem less sophisticated or knowledgeable about it. It is significant that, while the menstrual etiquette which Laws describes forbids discussion of menstruation itself in public, these men could talk easily about PMS and could describe public situations in which it had been talked about. One of the features of the twentieth-century scientific and popular literature has been an increasing discussion of PMS and a diminishing discussion of menstruation itself, which contrasts particularly with the nineteenth-century literature (see chapter two). PMS then becomes particularly important. It is a means by which unacceptable female behaviour can be attributed to reproductive functions without the necessity of even mentioning menstruation.

Seeking help for PMS

We often assume that there is a simple relationship between perceiving oneself as ill (or diseased) and seeking help from a physician. Surely it is the case that the more severe our symptoms, the more likely we are to seek help. To an extent this is true, but the reality is a good deal more complex than that, and there is now a growing literature concerned with why people seek professional health care, which shows that degree of symptomatology is only one of many factors influencing whether or not we visit a doctor (e.g. Briscoe, 1987; Andersen and Laake, 1983; Cameron *et al.*, 1993). It seems that people have a variety of strategies to adopt and sources of advice to utilise other than the doctor alone. We may treat ourselves, using our own understanding of our experiences, or consult with

179

family or friends (lay consultations), or seek advice from a variety of 'alternative' therapists or paramedical professionals (e.g. pharmacists), or all of these things before (and after) consulting a doctor (e.g. Meininger, 1986; see Helman, 1991a). Hence, in the context of PMS, it is likely that women consult a number of people before visiting the doctor, whether or not they perceive PMS to be an illness.

There is very little information in the literature about help-seeking in relation to PMS. Scambler and colleagues (1981) asked women to keep health diaries over six weeks and to record all of their lay and professional consultations during that time. Half of the women in the sample recorded lay consultations for menstrual symptoms (including PMS, period pain, irregular or heavy bleeding). On average there were eleven lay consultations for every one medical consultation for both menstrual and general symptoms. The people consulted about menstrual symptoms were usually family members (husband, mother, other female kin), and the women were less likely to talk to female friends about menstrual symptoms than other types of symptoms. After completing the diaries, the women were interviewed about the consultations they had made. The researchers identified three types of lay consultation for menstrual symptoms, which they describe as 'casual' (passing mentions of the subject in a conversation), 'enquiring' (requests for information or advice) and 'confirmatory' (requests for support or help) consultations. Consultations with husbands were most often of the 'casual' type,[45] while the 'confirmatory' consultations were often used to sanction or support the woman's decision to see a doctor (or other professional) about her experiences. Scambler and Scambler (1984) analysed the social networks of these women and found that women with large and active kinship networks (i.e. having four or more family members who they met or spoke to at least once a week) were more likely to have seen their GP about menstrual problems in the year before the interview than women who did not. Although this study was concerned with a range of menstrual problems and not PMS *per se*, it does paint a picture of concerned women talking to their mothers and sisters about their menstrual experiences, and being supported by them in a decision to seek professional help.

There are no good epidemiological studies of professional help-seeking for PMS, but the surveys which have been conducted suggest that many women do consult their GP about PMS. Among 658 'PMS reporters' who completed a questionnaire in a British national magazine or newspaper, 48 per cent said that they had visited their GP specifically for help with PMS within the last year (Corney and Stanton, 1991). Scambler and Scambler (1985) found that 37 per cent of the 79 women they interviewed in London had consulted a GP about menstrual problems within the last year, but 74 per cent had seen a doctor at some time for menstrual difficulties. In both of these studies, criticisms were made of the professionals' responses. For example, in the magazine survey (Corney and Stanton, 1991), some women commented that medical professionals lacked time, understanding or knowledge about PMS and some (12) felt that they had been prescribed inappropriate medication (tranquillisers). A number of them felt that their premenstrual experiences were not taken seriously by the GP – 88 commented that they had been told PMS was something 'women had to put up with', 33 had been told that PMS did not exist, 16 that it was 'all in the mind' and 12 to 'pull themselves together'. Scambler and Scambler, too, found that a proportion of the women they interviewed could be described as 'alienated' from the medical professions, feeling 'let down' by previous menstrual consultations (Scambler and Scambler, 1985). These comments are similar to those made by 83 North American women attending an evening lecture about PMS (Brown and Zimmer, 1986). All of these women had consulted one or more professionals, and 87 per cent had seen their physician about PMS. Over half felt that they had been treated 'disrespectfully', and like the British women many felt that they were not taken seriously or had been told to pull themselves together. In the Corney and Stanton study, 57 per cent of the 525 women who had consulted a GP at any time in their lives did find the consultation helpful or very helpful, and it is interesting to note that these were also more likely to be the women who had tried hormonal treatments, whether or not they helped. The authors suggest that taking premenstrual experiences seriously is the key factor if a GP is to be perceived as helpful, although it seems that getting the 'right' kind of treatment (i.e. hormones) may also be important.

In addition to the GP or primary care physician, women may also be referred to a gynaecologist, a psychiatrist or a specialist clinic, or may consult other professionals or seek help from women's groups or self-help organisations. Corney and Stanton found that approximately 40 per cent of the women who had seen a gynaecologist, psychiatrist or family planning clinic for PMS found the consultation helpful. In contrast, around 70 per cent of those who had been to a specialist PMS clinic, a homeopath or other agencies found the consultation helpful. Similarly, these women had tried a wide variety of treatments, but no one medication was found to be helpful for everyone or more helpful than the others. The only study which has assessed treatment preferences among women reporting PMS and women with other menstrual disorders suggests that the majority would prefer a treatment which 'normalised' their periods, taken in the form of tablets (Warner, 1994).

The views of women attending a PMS clinic in London have been investigated by Swann and Ussher (1995) in a discourse analytic study. The polarity of experience and self-objectification described by Cumming *et al.* (1994) were also found in these interviews, and suggest, the authors argue, that women are using a dualist discourse to describe their experience, in which the premenstrual experience is split off from the 'normal self' experience. These women talk of being 'two different people' or even of being 'taken over' or 'possessed'.[46] One of the key features of this study was the importance of the PMS label to the women attending the clinic. Although many of them described their lives as problematic, talking about violent partners, poverty and abuse in childhood, for instance, they often used a 'romantic' discourse of PMS as if a cure for PMS was the

181

equivalent of a fairytale 'knight in shining armour'. One woman sums this up by saying,

> I was in prison for fraud . . . erm and I had Charlotte [daughter] erm we split up when I was pregnant and. . . . I've had injunctions and that, he's [partner] quite violent. . . . I don't know. At the moment it's the [PMS] symptoms, everything else in my life is fine.

(Swann and Ussher, 1995: 365)

Hence, the authors argue, PMS is not just a description of physical or emotional states around menstruation, it is also a concept which has a cultural meaning and around which there are a number of discourses. These discourses can be used in the ongoing negotiation of female identity and gender relations. In the late twentieth century, ideas about gender, femininity and masculinity are in a state of considerable flux in Western countries (see Showalter, 1992). There may be times or circumstances in a woman's life when the attribution of her experiences to her 'reproductive body' is important – not only because this will allow her voice to be 'heard' but also because she may perceive this to be the only aspect of her life over which she can gain control.

PSYCHOLOGY AND PMS

In all the debate and confusion, what has psychology had to say about PMS? One of the distinguishing features of psychological research is that, by and large, an inevitable effect of the menstrual cycle on mood, behaviour or cognition has not been assumed. Psychological studies also tend to conceptualise premenstrual experiences on a continuum, varying in degree of severity between women (or phases of the cycle), rather than identifying a qualitatively different, present or absent, premenstrual disease state. There is less emphasis in psychological research on the identification of a disease state, and more on the factors which may exacerbate premenstrual changes or make them distressing. Hence, more of these studies are correlational in design, or else compare levels of mood or well-being before and after an intervention. Psychological studies are making just as many assumptions about women, their lives and experiences as medical research, although these assumptions are slightly different. The woman in psychological research is more likely to have a mind, or at least 'beliefs' and 'cognitive processes', which may mediate the effects of her fluctuating physiology. Sometimes she also has a life, although this is considered only if it is 'stressful' (either judged by the researchers as 'truly' stressful or perceived by her to be so). A mind and a life, albeit a stressful one, figure only very recently in biomedical research, and the fact that they do is some testimony to the influence of psychosocial concepts in medical research. However, even in psychological research, the implicit assumption is made that fluctuating hormones (or a hormonally related system) are ultimately the cause of premenstrual experiences. Psychological factors serve only to make them better or worse, more or less manageable. They do not cause these symptoms to occur. This limited contextualisation of woman's experience, and the hypothesis that experiences can be exacerbated by non-physiological means, makes many psychologists wary of the label 'PMS' and unhappy about the use of a disease model to describe experience. Premenstrual experiences are, however, viewed as 'real' and rooted in biochemistry, but potentially manageable through psychological interventions.

The sceptical approach, which many psychologists have taken to the disease model of premenstrual experience, and the rigorous training which many psychologists receive in hypothetico-deductive methodology have meant that the main references to psychological research in the medical literature on PMS are concerned either with 'normal' menstrual cycles or with research methodology. For example, it is largely as a result of work by Mary Parlee and psychologists like her that the effects of expectation and stereotypes on symptom reporting have been considered and that daily diary measures have become commonplace in medical research. The medical research is so dominant that this can sometimes leave the feeling that there is no distinctive psychological 'voice' in relation to premenstrual changes. Psychologists have, however, made efforts to explain the variability in premenstrual experiences, and have used a variety of theoretical approaches familiar within psychology to do so.

The earliest psychological theories sought an explanation for variation in premenstrual experiences in individual differences, such as personality or sex-role orientation. These overlapped with the psychodynamic ideas which influenced biomedical thinking in the 1960s and 1970s (see above). Trait theories of personality have been the most influential in these studies, and particularly Hans Eysenck's conceptualisation of trait 'neuroticism'. Studies investigating dimensions such as these have usually correlated scores on retrospective measures of premenstrual experiences with standard trait measures of personality, such as the Eysenck Personality Inventory (EPI) or the Minnesota Multiphasic Personality Inventory (MMPI). As a result, they have been criticised by methodologists who argue that retrospective reports are contaminated by stereotypical beliefs about premenstrual experiences, or risk the possibility of aggregated symptom reporting. In addition, many of these measures are confounded. For example, the EPI contains questions such as 'Are you moody?' which may produce affirmative responses if a woman perceives herself to experience cyclical mood fluctuations (see Gannon, 1985). This approach had become unfashionable by the late 1980s, not least because of the failure to demonstrate consistent relationships between personality variables and premenstrual experiences. More recently, researchers have become interested in the possibility that personality characteristics might differentiate between those women who seek professional help for their premenstrual experiences and those who do not. For example, Olga van den Akker and her colleagues (1995a) investigated the possibility that women with high levels of trait negative affect would be more likely to report menstrual cycle distress than women who obtain low scores on a negative affectivity scale, finding a small but significant difference in support of their hypothesis.[47]

A more sophisticated theory conceptualises the menstrual cycle as a biological rhythm, akin to circadian rhythms. Biological rhythms are 'time-dependent biological changes that recur at a particular frequency in terms of their duration and in terms of the number of oscillations they comprise' (Dye, 1992: 67). Biological rhythms originate within the body and affect all aspects of physiology. Hence, this conceptualisation of the menstrual cycle fits Magos' (1988) assertion that every system in the body changes in association with the menstrual cycle. However, biological rhythms are also sensitive to external factors – *zeitgebers* – and may become synchronised around them. The classic example of this is the synchronisation of circadian rhythms to the 24-hour clock in comparison with the longer period of free-running cycles. Different intrinsic rhythms can also influence each other, so circadian rhythms and menstrual rhythms would be expected to interact (Engel and Hildebrandt, 1974). An implicit assumption about biological rhythms is that they affect performance and nervous system activity (Oatley and Goodwin, 1971), although to what extent and in what way may depend on the particular rhythm concerned. A number of researchers have advocated this approach to menstrual phenomena, and have tested it by investigating various aspects of sensory processes and arousal or manipulating the menstrual rhythm by continuous oral contraceptive administration (Smolensky, 1980; Asso, 1978, 1983, 1992; Dan *et al.*, 1992; Asso and Braier, 1982; Dye, 1992; McNeill, 1992). From a biological rhythm perspective, a number of hypotheses have emerged to explain variability in premenstrual experiences. Some researchers have argued that premenstrual 'symptoms' may be an equivalent of 'jet lag', occurring because daily rhythms have become disrupted or desynchronised by the effects of the menstrual cycle. This is tested by investigating and manipulating factors which are known to synchronise circadian rhythms, such as daylight, stress, hours of sleep and caffeine intake (Dan *et al.*, 1992; Parry *et al.*, 1993, 1995). Others argue that the peaks and troughs of a number of rhythms converge around menstruation, predisposing women to less positive feelings. So, Doreen Asso writes:

> Premenstrually, several factors can (but do not always) together contribute to a fairly negative background climate. In addition to low central nervous system arousal and often high autonomic activation, there is activity of other neurophysiological variables, such as monoamine oxidase and endorphin; there may be fluid retention, skin problems, and so on; there is the influence of complex cognitive processes, which can include memory of past discomfort, over-concentration on changes, and attitudes to the whole cycle which can affect the experience of the premenstrual phase.
>
> (Asso, 1992: 108)

Hence, not only can individual differences in neurophysiology account for variations in premenstrual emotional experience, but so too can the degree of physical symptomatology and cognitive factors.

The third theoretical strand within psychological research comes from social psychology. These theorists view the perception of menstrual cycle fluctuations from a social cognition perspective (e.g. Ruble and Brooks Gunn, 1979; Rodin, 1976). The key evidence underlying this theory is the existence of widespread cultural beliefs about the effects of menstruation and/or the premenstrual phase on how women feel or behave. Several studies have demonstrated the existence of such stereotypes in Western cultures (see chapter four). It is argued that the existence of these cultural beliefs leads to an information-processing bias in both a woman's perceptions of her own feelings or performance, and the perceptions of those around her. Such cognitive biases occur in the judgements we make of many types of social and intrapersonal information and may take a variety of forms. For example, menstruation is itself a relatively rare and salient event for most women, hence in retrospective accounts, it is argued, an illusory correlation may occur between negative experiences (which cultural influences lead us to expect around menstruation) and the menstrual or premenstrual days (Brooks Gunn, 1985). Another source of bias may be the tendency of individuals to selectively attend to information which fits their own implicit theory of the situation and to ignore that which doesn't fit (Ross, 1977). Thus, experiences of self or others may be misattributed. Researchers testing this type of theory have manipulated expectations about cycle phase or the purpose of a study to demonstrate changes in symptom reporting (Koeske and Koeske, 1975; Ruble, 1977; Olasov and Jackson, 1987; Klebanov and Jemmott, 1992). These theories do not claim to provide a complete causal explanation for menstrual or premenstrual distress, simply to account for some of the variance in individual differences in terms of the strength of beliefs and the degree of expectation about menstrual cycle phase and experiences. So, for example, Whitehead et al. (1986) found that young women who had been encouraged to adopt a sick role during menstruation as adolescents were more likely to report menstrual symptoms to a doctor as adults, and attribute this effect to social learning. Similarly, Ruble et al. (1982) found that menstruation was an acceptable reason to give for irritable behaviour, largely absolving the irritable woman from blame. They argue that this tolerance for menstrually related behaviour serves to reinforce menstrual and premenstrual stereotypes and increase women's own perceptions of menstrual distress. Hence, women whose close family and friends believe that menstruation (or PMS) has effects on behaviour, and who knowingly or unknowingly reinforce this attribution, would be expected to report higher levels of premenstrual or menstrual distress because they have increasingly incorporated this idea into their self-perception.

The studies reviewed in chapter four suggest that the premenstrual phase of the menstrual cycle is not associated with general changes in cognitive state. However, several researchers have suggested that the cognitive processing of women with PMS differs from that of women without PMS (Reading, 1992; Kirkby, 1994; Keenan *et al.*, 1992a; Morse *et al.*, 1991; Christensen and Oei, 1995b). This cognitive model of PMS is derived from the cognitive models of depression proposed by Beck and others, and is summarised by Reading (1992). It suggests that women with PMS experience similar endocrine events to women without a syndrome, but that the way they process information or perceive bodily states may be different. The model does not specify a direction of causality, however. In other words, it is acknowledged that premenstrual mood or physical changes might cause changes in thinking or memory, or vice versa. From this perspective, the aetiology of the cognitive changes matters little. What does matter is the possibility that intervening, using a form of cognitive or cognitive-behavioural therapy (CBT), may reduce premenstrual distress or enable women to cope more easily with it. Hence, this model is important because it is the only psychological model with clear therapeutic implications. There have been few studies from this perspective; those there are have either compared some index of cognitive function between two groups identified as sufferers or not of PMS,[48] or have evaluated the effectiveness of CBT. Reading notes that, at present, 'distinctive patterns of cognitive processing, comparable to those observed in depression, have not emerged' (Reading, 1992: 697), although some researchers have found that women who achieve a PMS/LLPDD diagnosis adopt different cognitive processing strategies throughout the cycle from women who do not (Lindner and Kirkby, 1992; Keenan *et al.*, 1992a, 1992b). Studies of CBT have demonstrated a beneficial effect, which seems to be at least as powerful as progestogen treatment and sometimes better than placebo tablets (Morse *et al.*, 1989; Morse *et al.*, 1991; Kirkby, 1994; Christensen and Oei, 1995b; Stout, 1995). It is not yet clear whether this is a specific cognitive therapy effect, however, or a response to any form of psychological intervention. Neither is it clear whether any effects relate specifically to premenstrual experiences, or whether women are generally 'happier' as a result of the therapy. Cognitive models of PMS can sit comfortably within the biomedical framework. They have originated within clinical psychology, and do not directly challenge the disease model – women are still diagnosed as having a premenstrual disease. However, they advocate non-pharmacological interventions, and hence are popular with those concerned about potential side effects of surgical or drug treatments for PMS. Psychotherapies, including CBT, are not entirely innocuous, however, and may not be as effective in routine practice as they are in carefully controlled trials.[49] Even if CBT is effective, it does not imply that faulty cognitive processes are the root of the 'problem', any more than the efficacy of aspirin implies that headaches result from aspirin deficiency.

The most popular theories of PMS within psychology apply interactional models of stress to premenstrual and menstrual experiences. Interactional or transactional theories assert that 'stress' results from an interaction between external demand, cognitive appraisal of the demand and coping resources (Lazarus and Folkman, 1984; see Stroebe and Stroebe, 1995, for an introduction). Hence, a situation which is stressful for one person may not be so for another. Nonetheless, it is true to say that many situations are generally perceived as stressful, traumatic or demanding (e.g. death of a loved one, job loss, moving house, etc.), and so there is usually a good correlation between stress response and major life events or chronic daily hassles, for example. Researchers have explored three possible relationships between stress and premenstrual experiences. The first is that stress exacerbates symptoms, worsening an already present state; the second is that stress causes severe premenstrual symptoms, i.e. that women who report PMS are more stressed than those who do not; and the third is that premenstrual experiences are themselves stressful. Applying a generic interactional model, these studies have considered the potential stressors in women's lives, variability in physiological 'stress' responses to the same stimuli, and the coping strategies adopted by women. Any of these, alone or in combination, it is hypothesised, could differentiate between women who experience or perceive different degrees of premenstrual experience. Studies have suggested that, in general, physiological or emotional responses to stressful tasks do not vary across the menstrual cycle (e.g. Choi and Salmon, 1995b; Girdler et al., 1993),[50] although women who report significant premenstrual distress do seem to react differently to stressors in the luteal phase than those in the follicular phase (Girdler et al., 1993; Woods et al. 1994).[51] Women diagnosed with PMS also adopt different coping strategies in response to the stressors they experience in different phases of the cycle, whereas women whose premenstrual experiences are not seen as troublesome do not (Burrage and Schomer, 1993; Fontana and Palfai, 1994; Kuczmierczyk et al., 1994).[52] Studies considering the number of stressors experienced are less clear cut. Woods et al. (1995) found that stressors could differentiate between women with low levels of premenstrual 'symptoms' and those with any type of moderate to severe premenstrual symptom pattern. Similarly, Lee and Rittenhouse (1992) found that women who report premenstrual distress also report more physical health problems, lower psychological well-being, less satisfaction with their social life and lower levels of social support than women not reporting premenstrual symptoms. Within groups of women reporting premenstrual symptoms, however, the number of stressors predicts very little of the variance in severity of premenstrual distress (Beck et al., 1990; Heilbrun and Frank, 1989; Gannon et al., 1989), although stress levels are more strongly correlated with measures of general health (Gannon et al., 1989). It is possible that all of these interact, so that severe premenstrual 'symptoms' are perhaps better thought of as one component of a larger stress–health relationship. Whatever the relationship between scientific conceptions of stress, health and premenstrual experiences, many women who describe themselves as having PMS also talk of lives which appear to be very stressful and feel that they are less able to cope with these stressors around the time of menstruation (Swann and Ussher, 1995; Burrage and Schomer, 1993).

The shift towards biopsychosocial models of health and illness has been significant in psychology as well as medicine (see above), and in recent years a number of theorists have proposed multivariate or integrated models of menstrually related experiences (Alberts and Alberts, 1990; Miota *et al.*, 1991; Ussher, 1992a; see Walker, 1995a). These biopsychosocial models bring together concepts of biological rhythmicity or hormonal fluctuation with psychological factors, such as beliefs and cognitions, and social factors such as stressors and life circumstances. These models find their major application in treatment of women complaining of distress. They imply different causal mechanisms for individual women, depending upon the balance and interaction of the various factors proposed in the model. The balance of factors may also vary from one cycle to the next, so that one premenstrual phase may be better than the next. Hence, idiosyncratic and multidisciplinary approaches to treatment are needed. From a scientific perspective, biopsychosocial models are attractive for two reasons. First, they are almost impossible to test – it is unlikely that anyone would obtain research funds for the vast study which would be necessary to test such a model comprehensively. Second, they can be used to justify research (and intervention) from any disciplinary perspective. The problem with this approach is that the contents of each of the 'bio', 'psycho' and 'social' boxes are fairly vague, and the connections between them even more so. To argue that experience is affected by some interaction between biology, psychology and culture may represent a paradigm shift within science but lacks theoretical sophistication.

CONCLUSION

The term PMS is a medical one and has become very popular in the twentieth century. The feelings which women describe premenstrually do not appear to be a twentieth-century phenomenon, nor are they specific to Western cultures. The description of them as a disease, however, is specific to Western cultures at this particular point in history. The medical literature reveals considerable disillusion with the biomedical concept of PMS, proposing instead more complex interactive and biopsychosocial models. The majority of recent reviews observe the failure to identify any hormonal abnormality or biological marker for PMS. Attempts to define and diagnose a unitary syndrome have resulted in heated debate and recent controversial attempts to focus on a subtype of PMS – premenstrual dysphoric disorder – while some respected authorities argue that the concept of PMS is no longer a useful one for research, preferring instead 'menstrual cycle related problems' (Bancroft, 1993, 1995). Nonetheless, these clinicians are all committed to getting to the bottom of premenstrual syndrome, for the sake of their women patients.

Popular literature, on the other hand, continues to support the view of PMS as a hormonally related disease. Women must not be told that their suffering is not real, they exhort – vilifying clinicians, and particularly psychologists, who venture to suggest that hormones may not be the root of the problem. The predominant view here is that the premenstrual woman (not always limited to the premenstrual woman with PMS) is mad, bad and dangerous to know. Society must be protected from her. In most cases, women can do this for themselves – the usual suggestions are regular self-monitoring, changes in diet, exercise, general health or various vitamin or mineral supplements. In severe cases, medical (preferably hormonal) treatment may be necessary – and doctors must change their attitudes and realise that this is a serious problem. The writers of these self-help books and articles in magazines and newspapers care about women and desperately want women to get the treatment they deserve.

Psychologists, too, are convinced of the reality of women's experiences, although reluctant to describe most of them as a disease and irritated by the methodology of much medical research. Psychology begins from the perspective of 'normal' experience, and so most psychological research has investigated 'normal' cyclical fluctuations while accepting the possibility of an extreme abnormal state. Psychologists point out that medical treatments have side effects, that there is a high placebo effect in PMS studies and that many women with PMS have other problems too. So perhaps psychological interventions will help women to cope. Counselling and cognitive-behavioural therapy have both been proposed – as adjuncts to medical assessment.

A radical feminist perspective also accepts the reality of premenstrual change, although denies that it is inevitably negative. The question asked from this perspective is, 'Why have cyclical changes become problematic?' The answer is: because they represent woman's otherness and her femininity. Patriarchal systems are not designed to cope with cyclical fluctuations – men, after all, are not supposed to experience them. When women experience problems, these can be attributed neatly to a fault in their design rather than a fault in the design of society. It is easier to treat women to fit in with society than to change the structures of society to accommodate women. From this perspective, we need to challenge and change society to stop premenstrual experiences from being a problem, not continue to 'take the tablets'.

In the middle of all of these well-meaning people, who want only the best for women, are women themselves, who face a double bind. Those who experience cyclical fluctuations can only call them PMS. There is no other word to describe what they are feeling. The term PMS, though, is redolent with so much meaning that it has become a poisoned chalice. Saying you have PMS may limit your chances of promotion at work but increase the chances that your doctor will take you seriously and give you something to help. Saying that your anger is due to PMS may prevent a violent man from hitting you, but may also mean that he never takes your anger seriously. Saying that you don't believe in PMS may antagonise some women, but saying that you do may damage your political credibility with others. No wonder few researchers have had the courage to embark on qualitative studies of PMS.

From an intellectual point of view, PMS is intriguing – a 'scientific puzzle', a 'fascinating phenomenon'. The question has for too long been whether PMS exists or not. From the perspective of women's health, it matters not whether PMS exists, but whether women's accounts of their experiences are believed and safe, effective treatments are available (if necessary). The research on treatment suggests that, for most women, being able to take control over their lives would be the best cure for PMS. Women taking control over their lives is not a part of the patriarchal agenda. Hence it remains, as one journalist succinctly put it, that 'searching for a cure for PMS is like searching for a cure for being a woman' (Sussman, 1993).

7

EPILOGUE: IS THERE A PSYCHOLOGY OF THE MENSTRUAL CYCLE?

The purpose of this book is to ask whether there is a distinct psychological perspective on the menstrual cycle. Is there, and should there be, a 'psychology of the menstrual cycle'? To address this question, I have tried to place menstrual cycle research into its cultural and historical context and to examine the methods and findings of research which has investigated mood, well-being and cognitive processes across the cycle. In the first two chapters it became clear that menstruation itself is a mysterious and intriguing phenomenon in most cultures, and that numerous stories have developed to account for it. In modern Western cultures these stories are predominantly scientific in origin, although versions of these ideas can almost always be found in folklore and religious accounts of menstruation too. In most accounts of menstruation, it is associated with fertility and femininity, and as a consequence is seen to be an actual or symbolic source of women's life-giving power. The myths and legends about menstruation which gain currency in patriarchal cultures are those which limit the extent of this power, or view it as a harmful force – a 'curse' – rather than a blessing, while simultaneously seeing childbearing as the *raison d'être* of womanhood. So, women's power to give life is sacrosanct and must be protected, but menstruation debilitates her and means that she is not suited to intellectual activity or public life. Hence, stories about menstruation can serve a powerful political purpose.

The most significant feature of modern scientific accounts of menstruation is the separation of women's bleeding from their fertility. The discovery that ovulation does not occur during menstruation, and that fertility has more to do with fluctuating levels of ovarian hormones than with bleeding patterns, meant that stories about menstruation lost their political currency. It is no longer menstruation which defines femininity, but women's hormones; hence there has been a shift in research away from interest in menstruation as a source of potential debility and towards investigation of hormonal correlates of well-being, and the identification of a 'new' hormonal disease, PMS, as described in chapter two.

Having described the cultural and historical context of menstrual cycle research, I then went on to examine its methods and findings. In chapter three it became clear that most of the research in this area has been preoccupied with the identification of a disease state, rather than the investigation of women's experiences *per se*. It also became clear that the validity of many of the methods which have been used in this area can be challenged. Not surprisingly, then, the interpretation of studies which have investigated cognitive processes, mood or well-being during the menstrual cycle is complex. The studies described in chapters four and five suggest that women's experiences vary from woman to woman, cycle to cycle and across the lifespan. The menstrual cycle does not have the same effect for everyone. When women are considered as a homogeneous group and studied prospectively it seems that menstruation is clearly associated with particular physical experiences, for example pain or breast tenderness, but the association with particular cognitive and mood states is less consistent. Individual women may experience changes in how they feel across the cycle, but for most these are not externally observable and can usually be accommodated. A small proportion of women do experience marked and noticeable changes in mood around menstruation, although as yet the cause of this is poorly understood.

The research demonstrates that there have been many approaches within menstrual cycle research which could be described as psychological. In terms of the questions asked by menstrual cycle researchers, almost all of the studies could be classed as 'psychology', since they are almost all concerned with women's emotional or cognitive state. The concepts used to explain them differ, however, with some researchers seeing biochemical changes as the cause of particular states, while others see a correlation between biochemistry and well-being rather than a causal relationship, and use social or psychological concepts to explain individual differences in experience.[1] It is the latter of these which I have classed as psychological approaches to menstrual cycle research.

Psychology is itself a broad discipline, adopting a variety of different perspectives and methodologies, varying, for example, in their emphasis on nomothetic or ideographic approaches. In fact, 'psychology' might be better described as a hotchpotch of 'psychologies' (see Margolis *et al.*, 1986). Viewing menstrual cycle research from this perspective, three distinct psychologies can be identified. Two of these map easily on to Ussher's typologies of 'rational reductionist' and 'liberal feminist' researchers (Ussher, 1992b) but the third is a little different. I have called them 'mainstream', 'liberal feminist' and 'postmodern' psychologies.

The mainstream psychological approach to the menstrual cycle considers the application of theories already existing in psychology to menstrually related experiences. To date, most of this research has conceptualised the menstrual cycle as an independent variable – a physiological factor which might influence the phenomenon which is really of interest. So, for example, the menstrual cycle might be seen as one factor influencing cognitive processes. It is not the cycle itself which is of interest, but memory or problem-solving ability. More frequently, the menstrual cycle is seen as the factor which might 'explain' differences between men and women on some task. Recent work by Kimura and Hampson (1994) is typical of this approach. In many ways, these studies are closest to biomedical approaches, although they rarely assess physiological states directly. The biological state is seen as the ultimate cause of the experience, although psychological mediators may be implied, such as 'stress' or 'arousal'. So, for example, the hormonal changes of the menstrual cycle may be thought to make women more 'vulnerable' to stressful events at certain times of the month, or to be associated with changes in arousal which make particular mood states more likely. These studies generally take a nomothetic approach and use experimental or quasi-experimental methods to investigate their particular hypotheses. They have made a significant contribution to menstrual cycle research, and share many of the same concerns and methodologies as biomedical research. As a result, this research strategy is best seen as complementary to biologically reductionist medical research, rather than as an autonomous psychological perspective. There is, however, considerable potential for the development of such an autonomous psychology of the menstrual cycle based within existing psychological theory. As we saw in chapter two, very few psychologists have shown interest in the menstrual cycle or menstruation as experiences in their own right, because menstruation has traditionally been viewed as a 'health' or medical issue rather than a psychological one. With a little lateral thinking and intellectual creativity, there are many theories and perspectives in psychology which could be informative without necessarily adopting a biologically reductionist or 'illness model' perspective – for example, personal construct psychology, symbolic interactionist approaches, theories of the relationship between emotions and cognitions, and so on. Indeed, menstrual experiences could become the focus for the development of new theories of the body–mind relationship within 'mainstream' psychology, if we can see beyond the cultural construction of menstruation and start asking new questions.

Liberal feminist approaches have a long history in menstrual cycle research. Researchers from this perspective are keen to demonstrate that the menstrual cycle is not a liability for women. Hence, they are guided by an explicit political concern rather than a 'pure science' motive.[2] The aim of this research is to challenge negative perceptions of menstruation and the myths and misconceptions surrounding it: to expose, as Doreen Asso put it, 'the *real* menstrual cycle'. Researchers in this tradition have used the methods of positivist science to challenge pervasive ideas about the cycle, e.g. that all women are irritable or depressed premenstrually, or that menstruation has an adverse effect on work performance. This research has had a considerable impact – especially in the area of PMS research. It is studies from this perspective which have increased the rigour of menstrual cycle research, demonstrating the effect of expectations and stereotypes on questionnaire completion, for example. This perspective, too, has limited the use of the PMS diagnosis, by repeatedly demonstrating that cyclical changes are not universal (see chapter five for examples). Researchers from this perspective have also made efforts to contextualise menstrual experiences, to view the stressful events in women's lives or working conditions as problematic, for example, rather than hormonal changes. The efforts of researchers from this perspective have been immensely successful in terms of the political agenda on which they are based, and, given the ups and downs of feminist influence in Western thought, such efforts are still vitally important. However, it is hard to justify their approach as an autonomous psychology of the menstrual cycle. The questions being asked are almost inevitably reactionary, and the research methods used are those of traditional science in order to be acceptable to that audience. The women who take part in the research, like those in mainstream psychology, are largely passive, rarely being allowed their own voice. In a culture which did not have negative views of menstruation, these studies would have little to say.

The third approach is the most recent. I have called it 'postmodern' because it challenges the nomothetic goals and positivist methods of both the mainstream and liberal feminist psychologies. All of the studies so far conducted from this perspective have adopted 'feminist standpoint' (Harding, 1991; Griffin, 1995) or discourse analytic approaches, although postmodern approaches need not necessarily be feminist. The linking theme in all of this research is its starting point – and that is women themselves.[3] These researchers do not ask how the physiological fluctuations of the menstrual cycle affect women's moods or cognitions, neither do they challenge the existence of such relationships. From this perspective, different questions are asked – for example, what do women (or men) have to say about their experiences? How do women make sense of bodily changes? What discourses can be used, when and for what purpose? What does menstruation or the menstrual cycle mean? The methods used by researchers from this perspective are more likely to be ideographic and subjective, and make more use of qualitative data and analysis. This approach draws on an extensive history in psychology – from phenomenology and introspection, through symbolic interactionism and ethnomethodology, to social constructionism, discourse analysis and feminist methodology.[4] This approach is exciting because it is part of a paradigm shift within psychology, reflecting a change in the way that psychology conceptualises the body (see Harré, 1991; Stam, 1996; Sampson, 1996), a shift which owes much to academic feminist theorising of sex and gender (e.g. Grosz, 1994; Bayer and Malone, 1996; Woollett and Marshall, 1996). As a result, it offers the possibility of new theoretical insights – new ways of thinking. Its purpose is not to alleviate distress, nor to challenge cultural stereotypes, nor to ascertain what is causing what. Instead, the purpose is to understand the rules and meanings which frame people's lives and experience – the stories which we live by – and how they are used. This understanding allows us to suggest reasons why someone may describe their experiences in the way they do, or be distressed by the way they feel. So, for example, knowing that we live in a culture in which displays of emotion are regulated by fear of embarrassment helps to explain the meaning which the label PMS may have for some women. It may be given as a legitimate reason for an emotional outburst, both to others and to oneself. This approach seems alien to biomedical approaches, and is conceptually much closer to anthropology, literary studies, history or psychoanalysis than it is to biology or medicine. It is this 'other-ness', though, which gives it the potential to be a productive and autonomous psychological perspective.

Menstrual cycle research is entering a new phase of its development. Change is in the air, both in biomedical research and in the various psychologies of the menstrual cycle. In the biomedical, mainstream psychology and liberal feminist psychology traditions, the change is a shift towards biopsychosocial theories (see chapter six) – an acknowledgement that single cause models of well-being are too limited. While this shift is important in medicine, and offers potential for greater psychological involvement in medical research and therapy, it does not create the conditions for an autonomous psychology of the menstrual cycle. Indeed, such multivariate models almost preclude such a possibility. Changes in the wider world of social science, though, do offer the possibility of an autonomous psychology. These changes shift the emphasis towards words and meanings rather than numbers and causes. They view the person as an active participant in their own experience rather than as a passive subject. They emphasise subjectivity rather than objectivity in research. They raise new possibilities and new challenges, and the hope that psychologists at the turn of the twenty-first century will be asking different questions about menstruation from those of psychologists at the turn of the twentieth.

NOTES

PREFACE

1 However, I would not categorise myself as having PMS.
2 I did my PhD at the Medical Research Council Reproductive Biology Unit in Edinburgh, supervised by John Bancroft and Dave Peck.
3 The studies I conducted were concerned predominantly with whether ovulation is necessary for premenstrual 'symptoms' to occur. I also correlated hormone measures and mood states on a day-to-day basis. I found no differences between ovulatory and anovulatory cycles on any of the measures I used, except for breast tenderness – which was generally less frequent in anovulatory cycles (see Walker, 1988; Walker and Bancroft, 1990). Later analysis of some of this data showed considerable variability both between premenstrual phases in different cycles and between women (Walker, 1994a).
4 I'm grateful to Pamela Warner for crystallising this question for me.
5 Throughout the book my focus is on psychology as 'practised' in most English-speaking university departments, rather than psychoanalysis. See Lupton (1993) for an excellent account of psychoanalytic approaches to menstruation.

CHAPTER ONE

1 Oestrogen is not produced exclusively within the ovaries, it is also synthesised in the adrenal glands. Among menstruating women, the ovaries are the major source of oestrogen, while in postmenopausal women the adrenals provide a much smaller continuous supply of oestrogen. Men, too, have measurable levels of circulating oestrogen.
2 This is not a physiological text, and my purpose here is not to give a detailed account of the current physiological understanding of menstruation. I am more concerned with the different ways in which menstruation can be understood. An excellent description of the physiology of menstruation can be found in Profet (1993).
3 See Blodgett (1988) and Spender (1980) for discussions of the role of man-made language in suppressing female experience.
4 See Scambler and Scambler (1993) for a discussion of menstrual disorders and the factors which lead women to consult their physician.
5 Most of the original material for this book was collected by Hermann Ploss, but it was added to, edited and published after his death by Bartels and Bartels. The original edition was published in German in 1885. The English edition, edited by Eric

Dingwall, appeared in 1935 under the title *Woman: An Historical, Gynaecological and Anthropological Compendium*.

6 This is particularly true of some types of feminist science, in which practices and customs described by Frazer ([1890] 1922), Crawley (1902), Crawfurd (1915) and others are quoted as examples of the negative attitudes towards menstruation in (implicitly) less enlightened times than ours, without acknowledgement either of the Victorian context in which such customs and practices were being interpreted, or of the criticisms which have been made of the techniques used by early anthropologists to collect data, especially from women (see Weideger, 1985; Laws, 1990).

7 That is, anticipated in terms of knowing that something is going to happen, not necessarily having a clear idea of what – see Lovering (1995), Kissling (1996) for discussion of menarcheal girls' experiences.

8 See Hunter (1996) for a discussion of menopause.

9 Ambiguity about the beginning and end of menstruation is also a problem for studies of mood or well-being and the menstrual cycle if cycle phases are defined on the basis of the first day of menstruation. See chapter three.

10 Fuller accounts of the meaning of menstruation in folklore, mythology, medicine and modern culture can be found in Horney (1931a, 1932), Knight (1991), Martin (1989), Laws (1990), Moscucci (1993) and Weideger (1976), among others.

11 It has been suggested that anorexia among young women may be stimulated by a desire to avoid menstruation (see Halmi, 1982; Malson and Ussher, 1996) – a possible example of menstruation phobia. This is usually interpreted, though, as a desire to remain child-like, rather than as a phobia of menstrual fluid itself.

12 This logic implicitly assumes that Western industrialised women have 'evolved' more than !Kung women, when it may be the case that we have evolved differently. There is no way of knowing whether the !Kung experience is the same as it was for Palaeolithic women.

13 McClintock (1971) found that the menstrual onsets of young women living in close proximity tend to converge, a finding supported by a number of studies in the 1970s and 1980s (e.g. Quadagno *et al.*, 1981; Graham and McGrew, 1980) and women's self-reports (Arden *et al.*, 1996). More recently, a number of negative findings have been reported (e.g. Weller and Weller, 1995a; Wilson *et al.*, 1991), and the statistical techniques used to demonstrate synchrony have been challenged (e.g. Wilson, 1992). Recent reviews suggest that although menstrual synchrony can occur, it does not always happen (Graham, 1991; Weller and Weller, 1993, 1995b). Whether menstrual synchrony was a sufficiently robust occurrence in the Palaeolithic period to support Knight's thesis is impossible to judge.

14 That is, having the ability to create new life by themselves. Reproduction was not necessarily associated with intercourse. Stonehouse (1994) argues that the association between sex and babies in ancient times would be obscured by the length of gestation and the effects of breast-feeding on fertility. As in our own time, there would be many occasions on which sex did not result in conception and relatively few in which it did, so it would be surprising if a connection between the two were made.

15 Some writers of the time believed that the seeds which combine to become a child were made entirely from parental bone-marrow and nervous material. Pangenecists argued that this was illogical. As Anaxagoras wrote: 'How can hair come from not hair, flesh from not flesh?' (Medvei, 1982). Hence, all parts of the body must make a contribution to the seed.

16 Other scientists include Pflüger (1863), whose 'nerve theory' of menstruation was very influential. See Simmer (1977), Medvei (1982).

17 An alternative interpretation is given by Barbara Walker (1983). She points out that

the Hebrew word for blood is *dam*, which means mother or woman in other Indo-European languages (e.g. madame, damsel), and is also a curse (damn). Hence, menstruation may originally have been referred to as 'dam', which in English became corrupted to 'the curse'.

18 Weideger argues, following Freud, that it is the supernatural meanings attached to menstruation through these myths of its origin which make it taboo, rather than just concerns about pollution or impurity. See Daly (1943), Shuttle and Redgrove (1986), Lupton (1993) for further discussion of this.

19 An alternative translation of the Hebrew word *koress*, used to describe the punishment, is 'to be childless' (Brim, 1936).

20 For many women, of course, the reality of menstruation is less easily denied. Pain and/or heavy bleeding defy the promises of the advertisers, and it is not surprising that these women seek medical help for periods which are interfering with their daily lives (causing shame?) even if they are not a risk to health.

21 There is ample archaeological evidence to suggest that women were hunters as well as gatherers in ancient times (see Stonehouse, 1994; Boulding, 1976). The dichotomisation of men to hunting and women to gathering is a modern interpretation of the evidence.

22 This is reminiscent of the ancient Greek idea of a wandering womb, which could be attracted back into position by different types of fumigation (see chapter two). The mechanism by which blood was thought to travel from the uterus to the various sites of vicarious menstruation (and back) is not discussed in this paper.

23 The Pentateuch forms the first five books of the Old Testament which are attributed to Moses. It has been suggested that both Moses and his wife Zipporah were students at the medical school in Heliopolis in around 1560 BC. If so, the strong association made between bodily discharges and disease at that time may have influenced the Mosaic Laws about menstruation and other bodily discharges (Wood and Suitters, 1970).

24 Baths like this are undertaken before any major ceremony (e.g. a wedding or the Sabbath), after contact with a corpse or at the end of any form of discharge (Brim, 1936).

CHAPTER TWO

1 However, prostitution was still occasionally viewed as an expression of women's sexual insatiability, e.g. Bauer (1926). See Bland (1995) for a discussion of prostitution and feminism in the late nineteenth century.

2 Some theorists (e.g. Weininger, 1906) argue that the character of any individual man or woman is made up of both male and female elements, so that it is rare to find a woman who is solely biologically driven or a man who is entirely intellectual. For Weininger, any woman will be at least 50 per cent female in character. He argued that feminists were women with a high proportion of masculinity in their character. For Weininger, an ideal world would be achieved when 'womanliness' had been eradicated in both sexes; only then, he thought, could women be emancipated.

3 While 'rest cures' were less physically barbaric, the complete bed-rest required could be psychologically damaging. Charlotte Perkins Gilman describes its effects graphically in *The Yellow Wallpaper* ([1891] 1981), a book which, among others, was published in the late nineteenth century to expose the psychological cruelty of the rest cure (Wood, 1973). The rest cure could be a very positive experience, though, as described in Elizabeth Robins' novel *A Dark Lantern* (1905). See Showalter (1987) for further discussion of this.

NOTES

4 These ideas also lay behind the eugenic and birth control movements of the times, the purpose being to 'purify' humanity by preventing those less able to control their 'bestiality' from reproducing. See Bland (1995) for a discussion of the relationship between feminism, sexual morality, birth control and eugenics in the late nineteenth century. See Moscucci (1993) for a discussion of the development of the 'science of woman'.

5 The medicalisation of upper- and middle-class women during the nineteenth century and its continuation today has been well documented. Excellent accounts are found in Ehrenreich and English (1973), Wood (1973), Bullough and Voght (1973), Vicinus (1972).

6 The text of his book clearly names Professor Schiff, with no other identification. It is likely, though, that he is referring to Bela Schick, as the account given here and in Schick's paper are very similar.

7 The role of menstruation in psychoanalytic theory (or the reasons for its absence) is beyond the scope of this book, but is covered in detail by Mary Jane Lupton in *Menstruation and Psychoanalysis* (1993).

8 Published in Britain as *Female Cycles* in 1978.

9 There has been an explosion of self-help books and groups concerned with PMS in the last ten years. In Britain, groups include PMSHelp, the National Association for Premenstrual Syndrome (NAPS) and the Women's Nutritional Advisory Service (WNAS). Books include Carpenter (1985) and Harrison (1987).

10 Martha Carey Thomas, then president of Bryn Mawr College, wrote in 1908 that the education of her generation of women had been haunted by 'the clanging chains of that gloomy little specter, Dr Edward Clarke's book', quoted in Bullough and Voght, 1973: 80.

CHAPTER THREE

1 See Sommer, 1983,1992; Parlee, 1983, and chapter four. I have chosen to focus on measures of mood and well-being in this chapter, but each of the cognitive tests used has its own methodological requirements and vagaries, which I do not have space to review here. The interested reader is referred to Richardson (1992) for a discussion of cognition and the menstrual cycle.

2 See Rust and Golombok (1989), Kline (1993) for discussion of appropriate techniques for development of psychometric instruments.

3 See the discussion of diagnostic criteria for PMDD in Gold and Severino (1994), for example.

4 For example, Slade (1988), a letter in response to Hart, Coleman and Russell (1987).

5 Elaine Duncan, personal communication.

6 Questionnaires such as the BDI or STAI are not appropriate for daily use but are often used prospectively, for example at two or three points during the cycle, e.g. Keenan, Lindamer and Jong (1992b).

7 Compliance with daily record-keeping is a problem, though – especially in treatment trials. For example, only 37 per cent of the women studied by Gise *et al.* (1990) completed two months of daily diaries. Whether shortening the questionnaire would encourage people to continue is unclear, although it seems intuitively likely. This high drop-out rate means that study outcomes are difficult to interpret.

8 That is not to imply that dividing cycles into phases is inherently 'wrong', only that the assumption of particular physiological states, on the basis of cycle phase without hormonal assessment, is both bad science and evidence of the strength of beliefs about a biological basis for women's experience.

9 For a description of these techniques, see Chard (1987).

10 Creatinine is a nitrogenous waste product, similar to urea. The amount of creatinine excreted in a 24-hour period is approximately constant from day to day, so the amount present in a sample can be used to estimate its 'concentration'. When the level of hormone metabolite is expressed per unit of creatinine, an estimate of the total daily output is achieved, which is more reliable than the uncorrected hormone measure (Cekan *et al.*, 1986). Studies which have used this technique include Collins *et al.* (1979), Stanczyk *et al.* (1980), Metcalf *et al.* (1984), Walker (1988).

11 ANOVA can be used as a measure of correlation if researchers focus on the amount of variance explained by the ANOVA model (Rosenthal and Rosnow, 1991). I have not seen this approach taken in any menstrual cycle study to date, however.

CHAPTER FOUR

1 Testosterone levels vary both diurnally and across the seasons, allowing this hypothesis to be tested. In the northern hemisphere, average testosterone levels in men are higher in the autumn than in the spring. Gouchie and Kimura (1991) found that men with lower than average levels of testosterone performed better on spatial and mathematical tasks than men with high testosterone levels. Among women, the effect was reversed. Women with higher than average testosterone did better on these 'masculine' tasks than women with lower than average testosterone levels. No differences were found on tasks which do not usually show a sex difference or where women, on average, perform better.

2 See Fausto-Sterling (1992), Hare-Mustin and Maracek (1990), for discussions of psychological research into sex differences and the question of whether feminist psychologists should engage in such research.

3 The question seems to have been turned on its head – nineteenth-century writers were concerned with the effect of academic activity on the 'quality' of menstrual performance.

4 For example, Mair *et al.* (1978), pentadecalactone, coumarin, cinnamyl, butrate; Doty *et al.* (1982), phenyl ethyl alcohol – a 'rose-like smelling odorant'.

5 The usual evolutionarily based inference for increased sensitivity to masculine odours around ovulation is a desire for conception. This assumes that women are attracted by the smell of exaltolide as well as more sensitive to it. Why we should be more sensitive to rose-like scents at this time is harder to explain – although no doubt it could be used to explain the use of roses as an instrument of seduction, if a similar 'sensitivity equals attractiveness' assumption were made.

6 See Fiske and Taylor (1991) for a full discussion of social cognition theory.

7 Exceptions to these are Lovering (1995) and Kissling (1996), who have both interviewed adolescent women and are both concerned about preparation for menarche.

CHAPTER FIVE

1 The classification of experiences as 'positive' and 'negative' is not a straightforward one, and reflects judgements about what women are supposed to be like – see chapter three.

2 But bear in mind the conglomeration of different degrees of change described in these averages. These scores only mean that on average the amount of change is small; they do not describe the variability between women.

3 In this study, Dalton defines the 'paramenstruum' as the four days before menstruation and the first four days of menstruation itself.

4 Jarvis and McCabe (1991) also used a cross-sectional, 24-hour self-report design with a much smaller group of women students (71), using a Mood Adjective Check List. They also failed to demonstrate a significant menstrual cycle phase effect for mood variables.

5 Dye *et al.* (1995). The authors do note that premenstrual increases in food cravings also occurred in a sub-group of 379 women who rated depression at 0 in all of the three menstrual cycle phases assessed, thus agreeing with Cohen *et al.* (1987) that a reaction to depression or negative mood is not the only mechanism for food craving.

6 Cutler *et al.* (1985), Veith *et al.* (1983). See also studies on menstrual synchrony which similarly hypothesise that women's cycles are influenced by external signals – Weller and Weller (1993), for example, discussed in chapter one.

7 See Nicolson (1993), Ussher (1996), Ussher and Baker (1993) for discussions of biomedical and sexological approaches to female sexuality.

8 By convention, dysmenorrhea is described as 'primary' if it occurs in the absence of any pelvic pathology, but 'secondary' if conditions such as endometriosis are present (see Golub, 1992; Scambler and Scambler, 1993).

9 See Gamsa (1994a, 1994b) for a discussion of psychological factors in chronic pain, and Erskine *et al.* (1990) for a review of pain memory. I am not implying here that pain is 'imaginary' or 'all in the mind', only that the way we think about our pain can influence how severe we say it is on questionnaires, and how we cope with it.

10 See Budoff (1980), Golub (1992). Useful self-help advice can be found in Sanders (1985), Lark (1993).

11 Although breast tenderness was common in this sample, it was not severe. On average it was rated at about 2 or 3 on a 10-point scale at its most severe.

12 See also Mortola (1994) for a review of risks and benefits of drugs used to treat premenstrual complaints.

CHAPTER SIX

1 The simultaneous use of the term 'premenstrual tension' by both of these authors suggests either that they were well-informed about their respective research fields or that the term was already familiar in general discourse (or both).

2 A variety of terms are used to describe hybrids of psychiatry and gynaecology, e.g. 'psychosomatic obstetrics and gynaecology', 'behavioural endocrinology', 'psychoneuroendocrinology'.

3 There are numerous discussions of gender and mental health, from both psychiatric and feminist perspectives. Excellent accounts can be found in Showalter (1987) and Ussher (1991). See also chapter two.

4 The DSM IV is the fourth edition of the Diagnostic and Statistical Manual of Mental Disorders, published by the APA (American Psychiatric Association, 1994). It is a highly influential diagnostic manual in North America, but has been less important in other parts of the world. Many other countries use the WHO *International Classification of Diseases*, currently in its tenth edition (ICD-10; WHO, 1992). Premenstrual tension was included in earlier versions of the ICD, categorised under 'diseases of the genitourinary system' (N00–N94). Part of the job of the 'task force' working on the development of DSM IV criteria was to co-ordinate the contents and coding of the ICD and the DSM. Hence, the new diagnostic criteria for PMDD may be influential in both North America and other parts of the world (Gold, 1994).

5 Notable among these are David Rubinow and his colleagues (e.g. Rubinow *et al.*, 1984), John Bancroft and his co-workers (e.g. Sanders *et al.*, 1983; Walker and Bancroft, 1990), and Glen Metcalf's group (e.g. Metcalf *et al.*, 1989).

6 This may seem a trivial point. After all, isn't the purpose of medicine to relieve suffering, not to interfere in or explain happiness? The emphasis on distress thus seems entirely appropriate. The problem is that it can result in a misleading impression of the premenstrual phase. If women can experience both positive and negative feelings but are able to rate only the negative ones, then they may appear to be depressed all the time, for example, when in fact they are not.

7 By consensual definitions I mean definitions discussed and agreed upon by groups of 'experts'. These definitions represent some form of agreement between clinicians about what PMS (or LLPDD/ PMDD) is but do not always reflect empirical or epidemiological evidence.

8 In the DSM IIIR, the name 'late luteal phase dysphoric disorder' (LLPDD) was used. This was altered to 'premenstrual dysphoric disorder' (PMDD) in DSM IV since the role of luteal phase endocrinology in premenstrual experiences is unclear (see Gold and Severino, 1994).

9 The evidence discussed by the APA group working on the definition of LLPDD, and its inclusion in the DSM is included in a book edited by Judith Gold and Sally Severino (Gold and Severino, 1994), together with commentaries on it.

10 This disagreement is seen clearly in letters between Sally Severino and Barbara Parry and her colleagues (both psychiatrists) in the *American Journal of Psychiatry* in 1988. Severino berates Parry *et al.* for implying that LLPDD and PMS are synonymous in a paper published in the journal (Parry *et al.*, 1987). Parry *et al.* reply that 'it is our understanding that the term "late luteal phase dysphoric disorder" was developed to delineate diagnostic criteria for what had previously been referred to as premenstrual syndrome' (p.133).

11 As noted above, 65 different scales and questionnaires have been used to diagnose PMS or PMDD in clinical studies (Budieri *et al.*, 1994).

12 Hamilton and Gallant (1990) observe that psychologists have taken little interest in the LLPDD criteria and very few psychologists have been involved in discussions about them. They point out that psychological expertise in measurement of subjective states could be of great value in preventing both overdiagnosis and underdiagnosis of LLPDD, and in improving research methodology. The few psychologists who have been concerned have been very influential, however, in raising concerns about the validity and reliability of LLPDD (e.g. Gallant *et al.*, 1992a, 1992b; Parlee, 1994).

13 See also chapter three, and research by Christensen and Oei (1995a) which suggests that the PAF does not discriminate well between treatment seekers and non-treatment seekers.

14 Several studies have now demonstrated this phenomenon, especially in relation to DSM criteria (e.g. Gise *et al.*, 1990; Gallant *et al.*, 1992a, 1992b; Hurt *et al.*, 1992; Schnurr *et al.*, 1994). On the other hand, women in community samples may not identify themselves as having PMS, despite meeting medical criteria (Metcalf *et al.*, 1989b; Warner and Bancroft, 1990).

15 Logically, the demonstration of a biological difference between women who do report premenstrual distress and those who do not demonstrates only that they are physiologically different, not that one or other group is 'diseased'. The assumption that distress equals disease is a frequent one in psychiatry and psychology, although this is not always the case. Bereavement, for instance, may be very distressing and may even require medical or psychological intervention, but that does not make it a disease or an abnormality.

16 Oestrogen and progesterone or their metabolites have been the most popular hormones to investigate (e.g. Backstrom and Mattson, 1975; Sanders *et al.*, 1983; Dennerstein *et al.*, 1993; Schmidt *et al.*, 1994; Redei and Freeman, 1995). Others include testosterone and other androgens (e.g. Eriksson *et al.*, 1992), sex hormone binding globulin – SHBG – (e.g. Massil *et al.*, 1993), follicle stimulating hormone – FSH – and luteinising hormone – LH – (e.g. Coulson, 1986; Backstrom *et al.*, 1976; Backstrom *et al.*, 1983).

17 Gonadotrophin Releasing Hormone (GnRH) agonists are drugs which hyperstimulate the hypothalamic-pituitary-ovarian axis and prevent the LH surge associated with ovulation. As a result, both ovulation and menstruation are suppressed, in a medical (and reversible) version of ovariectomy. They are administered in the form of a nasal spray or subcutaneous implant, and trade names include Buserilin, Zoladex and Leuprolide. They have been used experimentally for PMS, but are not widely available for clinical use. Some studies claim a dramatic improvement of premenstrual symptoms (Muse *et al.*, 1984; Mortola *et al.*, 1991; Mezrow *et al.*, 1994; Brown *et al.*, 1994), although others have noted an exacerbation of typical PMS-type symptoms (Bancroft *et al.*, 1987), or the persistence of cyclicity (Metcalf *et al.*, 1994) in some women. The implications of these findings for the endocrine hypothesis are not clear because assessment of a pre-menstrual state in the absence of menstruation is difficult, and all of these studies use different statistical analyses. These drugs are unlikely to become widely available clinically because of the risk of bone loss and osteoporosis with chronic use.

18 Maxson (1988) describes a case of a woman in whom a deep sleep was induced by a single 400 mg dose of oral micronised progesterone. Doses as large as these have been used in PMS trials, and raise questions not only about the side effects of progesterone, but also about whether any beneficial effects are the result of the correction of a deficiency.

19 Studies of early luteal phase progesterone levels and progesterone and LH pulsatility among women with PMS are among recent examples of endocrine approaches to PMS (Reame *et al.*, 1992; Lewis *et al.*, 1995; Facchinetti *et al.*, 1993a).

20 Not all researchers support a serotonergic hypothesis. Veeninga and Westenburg (1992), for example, found no differences in 5-HT physiology between patients diagnosed with LLPDD and controls. Similarly, this group also found no beneficial effects of treatment with serotonergic drugs (Veeninga *et al.*, 1990).

21 The renin-angiotensin-aldosterone system controls fluid balance in the body and its activity can be influenced by progesterone. As angiotensin can have effects on mood and fluid retention is a common premenstrual symptom, this theory was very popular for a while during the 1970s. It lost favour when studies failed to demonstrate either weight gain or objectively assessed fluid retention in women with PMS (e.g. Watts *et al.*, 1985; O'Brien, 1987). In addition, no association between aldosterone levels and premenstrual symptoms was found (Munday *et al.*, 1981). A recent study has suggested that rather than experiencing an increase in fluid *per se*, women who report PMS may experience a shift of water from the intracellular to the extracellular spaces, resulting in a bloating sensation (Tollan *et al.*, 1993). This requires further research but may spark a revival of interest in this theory. In the meantime, the enthusiasm for diuretics as a treatment for PMS remains undiminished, despite the lack of evidence that they are effective (Dinan and O'Keane, 1991).

22 See also Chuong and Dawson (1992) for a review of the rationale of many of these treatments.

23 Some studies do suggest that these strategies are effective, although whether through specific neuroendocrine mechanisms or general improvement in health/well-being is unclear. They all assume that women are able to take control of their lives. It would

be interesting to know how many women are able to maintain changes in diet and exercise, for instance – certainly many women experience difficulty with taking regular exercise.

24 For relaxation therapy to be effective, women need to be properly trained in its use and practise regularly. Some studies of relaxation have used audiotapes or have combined relaxation training with other techniques, so it is difficult to assess their findings. Goodale *et al.* (1990) demonstrated beneficial effects in a well-controlled intervention. Morse *et al.* (1991) report a less sustained effect, but used an audiotape to induce relaxation at home. Oleson and Flocco (1993) have demonstrated a beneficial effect of reflexology aimed at muscle relaxation.

25 Morse *et al.* (1991) demonstrated a beneficial effect of cognitive coping-skills therapy which was sustained over the three months of the study. The comparison treatments (dydrogesterone and relaxation using audiotapes) were initially effective but effects were not maintained. Other studies have shown beneficial effects of a variety of cognitive approaches (e.g. Christensen and Oei, 1995b; Reading, 1992; Slade, 1989; Morse *et al.*, 1989; Kirkby, 1994), although not always superior to placebo pill treatment (Corney *et al.*, 1990). See Stout (1995) for a review.

26 In the psychological and sociological literature, these barriers are usually perceived as structural, to do with poverty, housing, living conditions, the demands of small children or low-paid work, etc. From a feminist perspective, women from whatever social background will experience difficulties in taking control of their lives, because this inevitably means challenging the patriarchal structures which currently control them. It may be as unthinkable for a middle-class woman to abandon her husband for an afternoon to go to an exercise class or out jogging as it is for an impoverished woman to buy diet supplements.

27 Bancroft *et al.* (1993) found that women referred to a gynaecology out-patient clinic because of either menorrhagia, dysmenorrhea or PMS were very similar in terms of their reports of perimenstrual experiences, with over half of both the dysmenorrhea and menorrhagia groups considering themselves to be PMS sufferers. Similarly, many of the women in the PMS group also reported pain or heavy periods. The choice of treatment for PMS is likely to be influenced by any other menstrual disorders (or affective complaints) which the woman reports.

28 Withdrawal effects range from mild anxiety, dysphoria and insomnia to muscle cramps, nausea, sweating, tremor and fits (Judd, 1987, cited in Mortola, 1994).

29 A distinction can be made in sociology between the concepts of illness and disease. A disease, as defined by medicine, results from an objectively demonstrable physical change in the structure or function of the body (Helman, 1991a). Illness is a subjective state, a perception of the individual (and those around them) that there is something wrong. A person may be ill without being diseased, and vice versa (e.g. in the asymptomatic stages of cancer). While diseases are medical concepts, illnesses are social ones, with meanings attached to them (see Helman, 1991a).

30 Also known as *pasmo, jani, espanto* or *pédida de la sombra*.

31 Other conditions include anorexia nervosa (Swartz, 1985), obesity (Ritenbaugh, 1982), type A behaviour pattern, agoraphobia, parasuicide and exhibitionism (Littlewood and Lipsedge, 1987) – all cited in Helman (1991a).

32 For example, Kenya (Rupani and Lema, 1993), Hong Kong (Mao and Chang, 1985; Chang *et al.*, 1995), Italy (Monagle *et al.*, 1993), Sweden (Andersch *et al.*, 1986), Switzerland (Merikangas *et al.*, 1993), Japan, Nigeria, Turkey, Greece, Apache (Janiger *et al.*, 1972) and the 14 cultural groups in the WHO menstrual patterns study (Snowden and Christian, 1983; see chapter one), as well as studies of English-speaking women of different religious or cultural background (e.g. van den Akker *et al.*, 1995a). See Dan and Monagle (1994), Logue and Moos (1986) for reviews.

33 See Paige (1977), Paige and Paige (1981) for a discussion of menstrual taboos, and chapter one. Margaret Mead (1949) describes backache and period pain in her studies, but doesn't suggest that an illness is recognised relating to the premenstrual days.

34 The politics of health education are rarely acknowledged but nonetheless real. In Britain and North America, for instance, government-provided health education materials tend to emphasise individual responsibility for health (and therefore illness) rather than recognising structural or social influences on health. Smoking and poor diet are blamed for ill health, for example, rather than poverty or bad public housing, so health education exhorts the individual to change rather than the social structure. See Rodmell and Watt (1986) for an excellent discussion of the politics of health education.

35 The symposium was held at the British Psychological Society Annual Conference in April 1993. It was widely reported in the British press as arguing that PMS is 'all in the mind' and provoked a storm of protests that premenstrual symptoms represent a 'real medical condition'. These papers have been published in a recent issue of *Social Science and Medicine* (September 1995), edited by Precilla Choi (Choi and Salmon, 1995b; Walker, 1995a; Nicolson, 1995; Bancroft, 1995; Richardson, 1995). Interested readers should refer to these papers for what was actually said as opposed to what is reported to have been said.

36 Anna Reynolds is a well-known PMS sufferer. In 1988, she was released from a life sentence in prison on the grounds that her combined PMS and post-natal depression were severe enough to constitute a defence.

37 It is interesting to note that articles informed by feminist discussions of PMS were much more likely to appear in Scottish newspapers than in English ones, suggesting differing social constructions of PMS within Britain. This may also reflect the differing politics of the two countries in the 1990s – Scotland has a much higher proportion of Labour Members of Parliament than England, for instance.

38 See Daly (1979), Ussher (1991) for discussions of 'good' women and 'bad' women.

39 'Good' women are also heterosexual and (usually) married with children. Lesbian women are rarely if ever mentioned in the PMS self-help or medical literature. This also underlines the point that it is not women's health *per se* which is the concern here, but the behaviour of particular women.

40 Both 'transient nymphomania' and lack of interest in sex feature in descriptions of PMS.

41 These extracts were taken fairly randomly from a large filebox of letters accompanying more than 7,000 questionnaire responses to a survey in a national British magazine (*Woman*). I quoted them in my PhD thesis in 1988. Details of the survey itself can be found in Warner and Bancroft (1990), Warner *et al.* (1991).

42 The association with age is not supported in all studies (e.g. Andersch *et al.*, 1986), especially those which use medical criteria to diagnose PMS (e.g. Hallman, 1986), suggesting that the factors which encourage women to report premenstrual experiences are not necessarily the same as those which cause them.

43 Oral contraceptive use may reduce premenstrual distress for some women – see below.

44 Overall statistics do suggest that women take more time off work than men. For example, British data for the spring of 1995 shows 3.7 per cent of men taking some time off work in a given week compared to 5.3 per cent of women (Central Statistical Office, 1996). Arber (1990), in her analysis of data like this, found that the excess could be accounted for by part-time workers. Men and women working full time do not differ in their sickness absence rates. See also Blaxter (1990).

45 The 'menstrual etiquette' described by Laws would imply that only husbands or

'boyfriends' would be confided in about menstrual problems, and then in little depth.

46 These themes also emerge in press reports of PMS – see above.

47 Negative affectivity is a generalised predisposition to view events in a negative light. It was described by Watson and Pennebaker (1989). Scores on NA scales are strongly correlated with scores on the neuroticism dimension of the EPI. Watson and Pennebaker argue that NA is independent of actual health status although it may influence help seeking.

48 For example: 'cognitive style', Rapkin *et al.* (1989); 'irrational thinking', Lindner and Kirkby (1992); learning and memory tasks, Keenan *et al.* (1992a).

49 There are many feminist critiques of clinical psychology interventions as well as psychiatric ones. Fundamentally the power relationship between client and therapist is the same in CBT as it is in any biomedically oriented encounter. See Ussher (1991).

50 Effects may be task-dependent, however. For example, Tersman *et al.* (1991) found cyclical changes in physiological reactivity in response to a cold pressor test but not a mental arithmetic task. This group also found interactions between menstrual cycle phase and smoking.

51 Woods *et al.* (1994) found that only women whose experiences fit a specific PMS pattern show increased responsivity to stress. Those who experience premenstrual magnification of chronic states do not. This supports the observation of Vellacott and O'Brien (1988) of differences between women with 'primary' and 'secondary' PMS in relation to stress.

52 Burrage and Schomer (1993), more emotional expression, hostility and self-blame used premenstrually; Fontana and Palfai (1994), more 'catharsis' used premenstrually; Kuczmierczyk *et al.* (1994), more avoidant coping styles used by women with PMS and high levels of depression.

CHAPTER SEVEN

1 This distinction is also made by Parlee (1981). It is most apparent in studies of PMS (see chapter six).

2 All science is, of course, a political activity, but 'mainstream' approaches rarely acknowledge the cultural influences on the questions being asked or the possibility that research findings might be used to support particular political points of view.

3 Examples include Martin (1989), Laws (1990), Lovering (1995), Swann and Ussher (1995). Studies from this viewpoint also investigate discourses in popular media or medical literature, for example Rodin (1992), Berg and Block Coutts (1994).

4 See Smith *et al.* (1995) for an introduction to 'new paradigm' approaches in psychology. See Harding (1991) and Morawski (1994) for discussions of feminist theory and methodology in psychology.

REFERENCES

Aaron, M. (1975) 'Effect of the menstrual cycle on subjective ratings of sweetness', *Perceptual and Motor Skills* 40, 974.

Ablanalp, J., Livingston, L., Rose, R. and Sandwisch, D. (1977) 'Cortisol and growth hormone responses to psychological stress during the menstrual cycle', *Psychosomatic Medicine* 39, 158–177.

Ablanalp, J., Donnelly, R. and Rose, R. (1979a) 'Psychoendocrinology of the menstrual cycle. I: Enjoyment of daily activities and moods', *Psychosomatic Medicine* 41, 587–604.

Ablanalp, J., Donnelly, A., Rose, R. and Livingston-Vaughn, L. (1979b) 'Psychoendocrinology of the menstrual cycle. II: Relationship between enjoyment of activities, moods and reproductive hormones', *Psychosomatic Medicine* 41, 605–615.

Abraham, G. (1983) 'Nutritional factors in the aetiology of the premenstrual tension syndromes', *Journal of Reproductive Medicine* 28, 446–464.

Abraham, S. (1984) 'Premenstrual or postmenstrual syndrome?', *Medical Journal of Australia* 141, 327–328.

Abraham, S., Fraser, I., Gebski, V., Knight, C., Llewellyn-Jones, D., Mira, M. and McNeil, D. (1985a) 'Menstruation, menstrual protection and menstrual cycle problems: the knowledge, attitudes and practices of young Australian women', *Medical Journal of Australia* 142, 247–250.

Abraham, S., Mira, M., McNeil, D., Vizzard, J., Fraser, I. and Llewellyn-Jones, D. (1985b) 'Changes in mood and physical symptoms during the menstrual cycle', in M.Y. Dawood, J.L. McGuire and L.M. Demers (eds) *Premenstrual Syndrome and Dysmenorrhea*, Baltimore: Urban and Schwarzenberg.

Abramson, M. and Torghele, J. (1961) 'Weight, temperature changes and psychosomatic symptomatology in relation to the menstrual cycle', *American Journal of Obstetrics and Gynecology* 81, 223–227.

Ainscough, C. (1990) 'Premenstrual emotional changes: a prospective study of symptomatology in normal women', *Journal of Psychosomatic Research* 34, 35–45.

Aitken, R. (1969) 'Measurement of feelings using visual analogue scales', *Proceedings of the Royal Society of Medicine* 62, 989–993.

Alberts, P. and Alberts, M. (1990) 'Unvalidated treatment of premenstrual syndrome', *International Journal of Mental Health* 19, 69–80.

Alexander, G., Sherwin, B., Bancroft, J. and Davidson, D.(1990) 'Testosterone and sexual behaviour in oral contraceptive users and non-users: a prospective study', *Hormones and Behavior* 24, 388–402.

Allen, E. and Doisy, E. (1923) 'An ovarian hormone. Preliminary report on its localization, extraction and partial purification and action in test animals', *Journal of the American Medical Association* 81, 819–821.

REFERENCES

Allen, S., McBride, C. and Pirie, P. (1991) 'The shortened premenstrual assessment form', *Journal of Reproductive Medicine* 36, 769–772.

Altmann, M., Knowles, E. and Bull, H. (1941) 'A psychosomatic study of the sex cycle in women', *Psychosomatic Medicine* 3, 199–225.

American Psychiatric Association (1994) *Diagnostic and Statistical Manual of Mental Disorders*, 4th edn, Washington DC: American Psychiatric Association.

Ames, A. (1875) *Sex in Industry: A Plea for the Working Girl*, Boston: James R. Osgood and Son.

Andersch, B. (1983) 'Bromocriptine and premenstrual syndrome: a survey of double blind trials', *Obstetric and Gynecological Survey* 38, 643–666.

Andersch, B., Hahn, L., Andersson, M. and Isaakson, B. (1978) 'Body water and weight in patients with premenstrual tension', *British Journal of Obstetrics and Gynaecology* 85, 546–550.

Andersch, B., Wendestam, C., Hahn, L. and Öhman, R. (1986) 'Premenstrual complaints. I. Prevalence of premenstrual symptoms in a Swedish urban population', *Journal of Psychosomatic Obstetrics and Gynaecology* 5, 39–50.

Andersen, A. and Laake, P. (1983) 'A causal model for physician utilization: analysis of Norwegian data', *Medical Care* 21, 266–278.

Anderson, E. G. (1874) 'Sex in mind and education: a reply', *Fortnightly Review* 15, 582–594.

Arber, S. (1990) 'Revealing women's health: re-analysing the General Household Survey', in H. Roberts (ed.) *Women's Health Counts*, London: Routledge.

Arden, M., Dye, L. and Walker, A. (1996) 'Awareness and subjective experiences of menstrual synchrony', *Journal of Reproductive and Infant Psychology* 14, 300.

Asso, D. (1978) 'Levels of arousal in the premenstrual phase', *British Journal of Social and Clinical Psychology* 17, 47–55.

——(1983) *The Real Menstrual Cycle*, Chichester: John Wiley.

——(1985–86) 'Psychology degree examinations and the premenstrual phase of the menstrual cycle', *Women and Health* 10, 91–104.

——(1986) 'The relationship between menstrual cycle changes in nervous system activity and psychological, behavioural and physiological variables', *Biological Psychology* 23, 52–64.

——(1992) 'A reappraisal of the normal menstrual cycle', *Journal of Reproductive and Infant Psychology* 10, 103–110.

Asso, D. and Beech, H. (1975) 'Susceptibility to the acquisition of a conditioned response in relation to the menstrual cycle', *Journal of Psychosomatic Research* 19, 337–344.

Asso, D. and Braier, J. (1982) 'Changes with the menstrual cycle in psychophysiological and self report measures of activation', *Biological Psychology* 15, 95–107.

AuBuchon, P. and Calhoun, K. (1985) 'Menstrual cycle symptomatology: the role of social expectancy and experimental demand characteristics', *Psychosomatic Medicine* 47, 35–45.

Backstrom, T. (1992) 'Neuroendocrinology of premenstrual syndrome', *Clinical Obstetrics and Gynaecology* 35, 612–628.

Backstrom, T. and Carstensen, H. (1974) 'Estrogen and progesterone in plasma in relation to premenstrual tension', *Journal of Steroid Biochemistry* 5, 257–260.

Backstrom, T. and Hammarback, S. (1991) 'Premenstrual syndrome – psychiatric or gynaecological disorder?', *Annals of Medicine* 23, 625–633.

Backstrom, T. and Mattson, B. (1975) 'Correlation of symptoms in premenstrual tension to oestrogen and progesterone concentrations in blood plasma', *Neuropsychobiology* 1, 80–86.

REFERENCES

Backstrom. T., Wide, L., Sodergard, R. and Carstensen, H. (1976) 'FSH, LH, TBG-capacity, oestradiol and progesterone in women with PMT during the luteal phase', *Journal of Steroid Biochemistry* 7, 473–476.

Backstrom, T., Sanders, D., Leask, R., Davidson, D., Warner, P. and Bancroft, J. (1983) 'Mood, sexuality, hormones and the menstrual cycle. II: Hormone levels and their relationship to the premenstrual syndrome', *Psychosomatic Medicine* 45, 503–507.

Bancroft, J. (1989) *Human Sexuality and Its Problems*, 2nd edn, Edinburgh: Churchill Livingstone.

——(1993) 'The premenstrual syndrome – a reappraisal of the concept and the evidence', *Psychological Medicine* Suppl. 24.

——(1995) 'The menstrual cycle and the well-being of women', *Social Science and Medicine* 41, 785–791.

Bancroft, J. and Rennie, D. (1993) 'The impact of oral contraceptives on the experience of perimenstrual mood, clumsiness, food craving and other symptoms', *Journal of Psychosomatic Research* 37, 195–202.

Bancroft, J. and Sartorius, N. (1990) 'The effects of oral contraceptives on well-being and sexuality: a review', *Oxford Reviews of Reproductive Biology* 12, 57–92.

Bancroft, J., Sanders, D., Davidson, D. and Warner, P. (1983) 'Mood, sexuality, hormones and the menstrual cycle. III. Sexuality and the role of androgens', *Psychosomatic Medicine* 45, 509–516.

Bancroft, J., Boyle, H., Warner, P. and Fraser, H. (1987a) 'The use of an LH-RH agonist – buserilin – in the long-term management of premenstrual syndromes', *Clinical Endocrinology* 27, 171–182.

Bancroft, J., Sanders, D., Warner, P. and Loudon, N. (1987b) 'The effects of oral contraceptives on mood and sexuality: a comparison of triphasic and combined preparations', *Journal of Psychosomatic Obstetrics and Gynaecology* 7, 1–8.

Bancroft, J., Sherwin, B., Alexander, G., Davidson, D. and Walker, A. (1991) 'Oral contraceptives, androgens and the sexuality of young women. II. The role of androgens', *Archives of Sexual Behaviour* 20, 121–135.

Bancroft, J., Williamson, L., Warner, P., Rennie, D. and Smith, S. (1993) 'Perimenstrual complaints in women complaining of PMS, menorrhagia and dysmenorrhea: towards a dismantling of the premenstrual syndrome', *Psychosomatic Medicine* 55, 133–145.

Bardwick, J. (1971) *Psychology of Women: A Study of Bio-Cultural Conflicts*, New York: Harper and Row.

Barnes, R. (1886–87) 'On vicarious menstruation', *British Gynaecological Journal* 2, 151–177.

Barnhart, K., Furman, L. and Devoto, L. (1995) 'Attitudes and practice of couples regarding sexual relations during the menses and spotting', *Contraception* 51, 93–98.

Barris, M., Dawson, W. and Theiss, C. (1980) 'The visual sensitivity of women during the menstrual cycle', *Documenta Ophthalmologica* 49, 293–301.

Bartelmez, G. (1937) 'Menstruation', *Physiological Reviews*, 17, 28–72.

Bauer, B. (1926) *Woman: A Treatise on the Anatomy, Physiology, Psychology and Sexual Life of Woman with an Appendix on Prostitution*, London: Jonathan Cape.

Bayer, B. and Malone, K. (1996) 'Feminism, psychology and matters of the body', *Theory and Psychology*, 6, 667–693.

Bayer Products Ltd (1938) *Sex Hormone Therapy in Everyday Practice*, London: Bayer Products Ltd.

Beck, A., Ward, C., Mendelson, M., Mock, J. and Erbaugh, J. (1961) 'An inventory for measuring depression', *Archives of General Psychiatry* 4, 53–63.

Beck, L., Gevirtz, R. and Mortola, J. (1990) 'The predictive role of psychosocial stress on symptom severity in premenstrual syndrome', *Psychosomatic Medicine* 52, 536–543.

REFERENCES

Becker, D., Creutzfeldt, O., Schwibbe, M. and Wuttke, W. (1982) 'Changes in physiological, EEG and psychological parameters in women during the spontaneous menstrual cycle and following oral contraceptives', *Psychoneuroendocrinology* 7, 75–90.

Bell, B. (1976) 'Self reported activation during the premenstrual and menstrual phases of the menstrual cycle', *Journal of Interdisciplinary Cycle Research* 7, 193–201.

Belmaker, R., Murphy, D., Wyatt, R. and Loriaux, D. (1974) 'Human platelet oxidase changes during the menstrual cycle', *Archives of General Psychiatry* 31, 553–557.

Bem, S. (1974) 'The measurement of psychological androgyny', *Journal of Consulting and Clinical Psychology* 42, 155–162.

Benedek, T. (1963) 'An investigation of the sexual cycle in women: methodologic considerations', *Archives of General Psychiatry* 8, 311–322.

Benedek, T. and Rubenstein, B. (1939a) 'The correlations between ovarian activity and psychodynamic processes. I: The ovulative phase', *Psychosomatic Medicine* 1, 245–270.

——(1939b) 'The correlations between ovarian activity and psychodynamic processes. II: The menstrual phase', *Psychosomatic Medicine* 1, 461–485.

Berg, D. and Block Coutts, L. (1993) 'Virginity and tampons: the beginner myth as a case of alteration', *Health Care for Women International* 14, 27–38.

——(1994) 'The extended curse: being a woman every day', *Health Care for Women International* 15, 11–22.

Berger, C. and Presser, B. (1994) 'Alprazolam in the treatment of two subsamples of patients with late luteal phase dysphoric disorder: a double-blind, placebo-controlled crossover study', *Obstetrics and Gynecology* 84, 379–385.

Bernsted, L., Luggin, R. and Petersson, B. (1984) 'Psychosocial considerations of the premenstrual syndrome', *Acta Psychiatrica Scandinavica* 69, 455–460.

Bernstein, B. (1977) 'Effect of menstruation on academic performance among college women', *Archives of Sexual Behaviour* 6, 289–296.

Berry, C. and McGuire, F. (1972) 'Menstrual distress and acceptance of social role', *American Journal of Obstetrics and Gynecology* 114, 83–87.

Bettelheim, B. (1955) *Symbolic Wounds: Puberty Rites and the Envious Male*, London: Thames and Hudson.

Birtchnell, J. and Floyd, S. (1974) 'Attempted suicide and the menstrual cycle – a negative conclusion', *Journal of Psychosomatic Research* 18, 361–369.

Bisson, C. and Whissell, C. (1989) 'Will premenstrual syndrome produce a Ms Hyde? Evidence from daily administrations of the Emotions Profile Index', *Psychological Reports* 65, 179–184.

Blackman, J. (1977) 'Popular theories of generation: the evolution of Aristotle's works, the study of an anachronism', in J. Woodward and D. Richards (eds) *Health Care and Popular Medicine in Nineteenth-Century England*, London: Croom Helm.

Blake, C. (1990) *The Charge of the Parasols: Women's Entry to the Medical Profession*, London: The Women's Press.

Bland, L. (1995) *Banishing the Beast: English Feminism and Sexual Morality 1885–1914*, London: Penguin.

Blaxter, M. (1990) *Health and Lifestyles*, London: Tavistock.

Blehar, M. and Oren, D. (1995) 'Women's increased vulnerability to mood disorders: integrating psychobiology and epidemiology', *Depression* 3, 3–12.

Block Coutts, L. and Berg, D. (1993) 'The portrayal of menstruating women in menstrual product advertisements', *Health Care for Women International* 14, 179–192.

Blodgett, H. (1988) *Centuries of Female Days: Englishwomen's Private Diaries*, Gloucester: Alan Sutton.

REFERENCES

Blundell, J. and Dye, L. (1995) 'Syndrome premenstruel, comportement alimentaire et prise de poids' (Premenstrual syndrome and appetite control: implications for weight regulation), in J. Bringer, D. Dewailly and A. Basdevant (eds) *Prise de poids et événements hormonaux chez la femme*, France: PIL.

Bonaparte, M. (1953) *Female Sexuality*, New York: Grove Press Inc.

Boorse, C. (1987) 'Premenstrual syndrome and criminal responsibility', in B. Ginsburg and E. Carter (eds) *Premenstrual Syndrome*, New York: Plenum Press.

Borell, M.E. (1976) 'Origins of the hormone concept: internal secretions and physiological research 1889–1905', PhD thesis, Yale University. Cited in V. Medvei (1982) *A Short History of Endocrinology*, Lancaster: MTP.

Both-Orthmann, B., Rubinow, D., Hoban, C., Malley, J. and Grover, G. (1988) 'Menstrual cycle phase-related changes in appetite in patients with premenstrual syndrome and in control subjects', *American Journal of Psychiatry* 145, 628–631.

Boulding, E. (1976) *The Underside of History: A View of Women through Time*, Colorado: West View Press.

Boyle, C., Berkowitz, G. and Kelsey, J. (1987) 'Epidemiology of premenstrual symptoms', *American Journal of Public Health* 77, 349–350.

Boyle, G. (1985) 'The paramenstruum and negative moods in normal young women', *Personality and Individual Differences* 6, 49–652.

——(1991) 'Interset relationships between the eight-state questionnaire and the menstrual distress questionnaire', *Personality and Individual Differences* 12, 703–711.

Braier, J. and Asso, D. (1980) 'Two flash fusion as a measure of changes in cortical activation with the menstrual cycle', *Biological Psychology* 11, 153–156.

Brattesani, K. and Silverthorne, C. (1978) 'Social psychological factors of menstrual distress', *Journal of Social Psychology* 106, 139–140.

Briffault, R. (1952) *The Mothers: A Study of the Origin of Sentiments and Institutions*, Macmillan: New York (originally published 1927).

Brim, C. (1936) *Medicine in the Bible*, New York: Froben Press.

Briscoe, M. (1987) 'Why do people go to the doctor? Sex differences in the correlates of GP consultation', *Social Science and Medicine* 25, 507–513.

Brooks, J., Ruble, D. and Clarke, A. (1977) 'College women's attitudes and expectations concerning menstrual related changes', *Psychosomatic Medicine* 39, 288–297.

Brooks Gunn, J. (1985) 'The salience and timing of the menstrual flow', *Psychosomatic Medicine* 47, 363–371.

——(1986) 'Differentiating premenstrual symptoms and syndromes', *Psychosomatic Medicine* 48, 385–387.

Brooks Gunn, J. and Ruble, D. (1980) 'The menstrual attitude questionnaire', *Psychosomatic Medicine* 42, 503–512.

——(1982) 'The development of menstrual related beliefs and behaviours during early adolescence', *Child Development* 53, 1567–1577.

——(1986) 'Men's and women's attitudes and beliefs about the menstrual cycle', *Sex Roles* 14, 287–299.

Brown, C., Ling, F., Anderson, R., Farmer, R. and Arheart, K. (1994) 'Efficacy of depot leuprolide in premenstrual syndrome: effect of symptom severity and type in a controlled trial', *Obstetrics and Gynecology* 84, 779–786.

Brown, G. and Harris, T. (1978) *The Social Origins of Depression*, Tavistock: London.

Brown, M. and Zimmer, P. (1986) 'Help seeking for premenstrual symptomatology: a description of women's experiences', *Health Care for Women International* 7, 173–185.

Browne, S. (1995) 'Paramenstrual changes in mood and pulmonary function: a reinterpretation of the mood-peak flow relationship', unpublished M.Phil. thesis, University of Plymouth.

211

Buckley, T. and Gottlieb, A. (eds) (1988) *Blood Magic: The Anthropology of Menstruation*, Los Angeles: University of California Press.

Bucknill, J. and Tuke, D. (1874) *A Manual of Psychological Medicine*, 3rd edn, London: J. and A. Churchill.

Budieri, D., Li Wan Po, A. and Dornan, J. (1994) 'Clinical trials of premenstrual syndrome: entry criteria and scales for measuring treatment outcomes', *British Journal of Obstetrics and Gynaecology* 101, 689–695.

Budoff, P. (1980) *No More Menstrual Cramps And Other Good News*, New York: G.P. Putnam's Sons.

——(1983) 'The use of prostaglandin inhibitors for the premenstrual syndrome', *Journal of Reproductive Medicine* 28, 469–478.

Bullough, V. and Voght, M. (1973) 'Women, menstruation and nineteenth-century medicine', *Bulletin of the History of Medicine* 47, 66–82.

Burleson, M., Gregory, L. and Trevathan, W. (1995) 'Heterosexual activity: relationship with ovarian function', *Psychoneuroendocrinology* 20, 405–421.

Burnell, M. (1944) 'Gynaecological and obstetrical problems of the industrial physician', *Industrial Medicine* 13, 211–214.

Burrage, J. and Schomer, H. (1993) 'The premenstrual syndrome: perceived stress and coping efficacy', *South African Journal of Psychology* 23, 111–115.

Burrows, George Man (1828) *Commentaries on Insanity*, London: Underwood. Extract reprinted in V. Skultans (1975) *Madness and Morals: Ideas on Insanity in the Nineteenth Century*, London: Routledge and Kegan Paul.

Burton, J. (1949) *Lydia Pinkham Is Her Name*, New York: Farrar Strauss and Co.

Cadden, J. (1993) *Meanings of Sex Difference in the Middle Ages: Medicine, Science and Culture*, Cambridge: Cambridge University Press.

Cameron, A. (1984) *Daughters of Copper Woman*, London: The Women's Press.

Cameron, L., Leventhal, E. and Leventhal, H. (1993) 'Symptom representations and affect as determinants of care seeking in a community-dwelling, adult sample population', *Health Psychology* 12, 171–179.

Caplan, P., McCurdy-Myers, J. and Gans, M. (1992) 'Should "premenstrual syndrome" be called a psychiatric abnormality?', *Feminism and Psychology* 2: 27–44.

Carpenter, M. (1985) *Curing PMT: The Drug-Free Way*, London: Century.

Carr-Nangle, R., Johnson, W., Bergeron, K. and Nangle, D. (1994) 'Body image changes over the menstrual cycle in normal women', *International Journal of Eating Disorders* 16, 267–273.

Carter, J. and Verhoef, M. (1994) 'Efficacy of self-help and alternative treatments of premenstrual syndrome', *Women's Health Issues* 4, 130–137.

Casper, R. and Hearn, M. (1990) 'The effect of hysterectomy and bilateral oophorectomy in women with severe premenstrual syndrome', *American Journal of Obstetrics and Gynecology* 162, 105–109.

Casper, R. and Powell, A.-M. (1986) 'Premenstrual syndrome: documentation by a linear analogue scale compared with two descriptive scales', *American Journal of Obstetrics and Gynecology* 155, 862–867.

Cattell, R. and Scheier, I. (1961) *The Meaning and Measurement of Neuroticism and Anxiety*, New York: Ronald Press.

Cayleff, S. (1992) 'She was rendered incapacitated by menstrual difficulties: historical perspectives on perceived intellectual and physiological impairment among menstruating women', in A. Dan and L. Lewis (eds) *Menstrual Health in Women's Lives*, Urbana: University of Illinois Press.

Cekan, S., Beksac, M., Wang, E., Shi, S., Masironi, B., Landgren, B. and Diczfalusy, E. (1986) 'The prediction and/or detection of ovulation by means of urinary steroid assay', *Contraception* 33, 327–345.

REFERENCES

Central Statistical Office (1996) *Social Trends 26*, London: HMSO.

Chadwick, M. (1933) *Women's Periodicity*, London: Douglas.

Chan, W., Dawood, M. and Fuchs, F. (1979) 'Relief of dysmenorrhea with the prostaglandin synthetase inhibitor ibuprofen: effect on prostaglandin levels in menstrual fluid', *American Journal of Obstetrics and Gynecology* 135, 102–110.

Chang, A., Holroyd, E. and Chau, J. (1995) 'Premenstrual syndrome in employed Chinese women in Hong Kong', *Health Care for Women International* 16, 551–562.

Chard, T. (1987) *An Introduction to Radioimmunoassay and Related Techniques*, 3rd edn, Amsterdam: Elsevier.

Chesler, P. (1972) *Women and Madness*, New York: Doubleday.

Chesney, M. and Tasto, D. (1975) 'The development of the menstrual symptom questionnaire', *Behaviour Research and Therapy* 13, 237–244.

Choi, P. (1995) 'What is this news on the menstrual cycle and premenstrual syndrome?', *Social Science and Medicine* 41, 759–760.

Choi, P. and Salmon, P. (1995a) 'How do women cope with menstrual cycle changes?', *British Journal of Clinical Psychology* 34, 139–151.

Choi, P. and Salmon, P. (1995b) 'Stress responsivity in exercisers and non-exercisers during different phases of the menstrual cycle', *Social Science and Medicine* 41, 769–777.

Chrisler, J. and Levy, K. (1990) 'The media construct a menstrual monster: a content analysis of PMS articles in the popular press', *Women and Health* 16, 89–104.

Chrisler, J., Johnston, I., Champagne, N. and Preston, K. (1994) 'Menstrual joy: the construct and its consequences', *Psychology of Women Quarterly* 18, 375–388.

Christensen, A. and Oei, T. (1989) 'Correlates of confirmed premenstrual dysphoria', *Journal of Psychosomatic Research* 33, 307–313.

——(1995a) 'Correlates of premenstrual dysphoria in help-seeking women', *Journal of Affective Disorders* 33, 47–55.

——(1995b) 'The efficacy of cognitive behaviour therapy in treating premenstrual dysphoric changes', *Journal of Affective Disorders* 33, 57–63.

Chuong, C. and Dawson, E. (1992) 'Critical evaluation of nutritional factors in the pathophysiology and treatment of premenstrual syndrome', *Clinical Obstetrics and Gynecology* 35, 679–692.

Cibulas, B. and Howell, C. (1995) 'Ramifications of late luteal phase dysphoric disorder diagnosis', *Issues in Mental Health Nursing* 16, 79–86.

Clarke, A. and Ruble, D. (1978) 'Young adolescents' beliefs concerning menstruation', *Child Development* 49, 231–234.

Clarke, E. (1873) *Sex in Education: or a Fair Chance for the Girls*, Boston: J. R. Osgood.

Cockerill, I., Wormington, J. and Nevill, A. (1994) 'Menstrual cycle effects on mood and perceptual-motor performance', *Journal of Psychosomatic Research* 38, 763–771.

Cohen, I., Sherwin, B. and Fleming, A. (1987) 'Food cravings, mood and the menstrual cycle', *Hormones and Behaviour* 21, 457–470.

Coleman, J. and Hendry, L. (1990) *The Nature of Adolescence*, 2nd edn, London: Routledge.

Collins, A., Eneroth, P. and Landgren, B.-M. (1985) 'Psychoneuroendocrine stress responses and mood as related to the menstrual cycle', *Psychosomatic Medicine* 47, 512–527.

Collins, W., Collins, P., Kilpatrick, M., Manning, P., Pike, J. and Tyler, J. (1979) 'The concentrations of urinary oestrone-3-glucuronide, LH and pregnanediol-3α-glucuronide as indices of ovarian function', *Acta Endocrinologica* 90, 336–348.

Colverson, S., James, J. and Gregg, M. (1996) 'Changes in haemodynamic profile during phases of the menstrual cycle', *Psychology, Health and Medicine* 1, 307–314.

Condon, J. (1993) 'Investigation of the reliability and factor structure of a questionnaire for assessment of the premenstrual syndrome', *Journal of Psychosomatic Research* 37, 543–551.

213

REFERENCES

Coope, J. (1989) *Hormone Replacement Therapy*, London: Royal College of General Practitioners.

Coppen, A. and Kessel, N. (1963) 'Menstruation and personality', *British Journal of Psychiatry* 109, 711–721.

Corea, G. (1985) *The Mother Machine*, London: The Women's Press.

Corner, G. (1943) *The Hormones in Human Reproduction*, London: Oxford University Press.

Corney, R. and Stanton, R. (1991) 'A survey of 658 women who report symptoms of premenstrual syndrome', *Journal of Psychosomatic Research* 35, 471–482.

Corney, R., Stanton, R., Newell, R. and Clare, A. (1990) 'Comparison of progesterone, placebo and behavioural psychotherapy in the treatment of premenstrual syndrome', *Journal of Psychosomatic Obstetrics and Gynaecology* 11, 211–220.

Costello, A. (1982) 'Fears and phobias in women: a community study', *Journal of Abnormal Psychology* 91, 280–286.

Coughlin, P. (1990) 'Premenstrual syndrome: how marital satisfaction and role choice affect symptom severity', *Social Work* 35, 351–355.

Coulson, C. (1986) 'Premenstrual syndrome – are gonadotrophins the cause of the condition?', *Medical Hypotheses* 19, 243–255.

Cowdry, R., Gardner, D., O'Leary, K., Leibenluft, E. and Rubinow, D. (1991) 'Mood variability: a study of four groups', *American Journal of Psychiatry* 148, 1505–1511.

Crawfurd, P. (1981) 'Attitudes towards menstruation in seventeenth-century England', *Past and Present* 91, 47–73.

——(1983) *Exploring Women's Past*, London: George Allen and Unwin.

Crawfurd, R. (1915) 'Superstitions of menstruation', *The Lancet*, 18 December, 1333–1335.

Crawley, E. (1902) *The Mystic Rose: A Study of Primitive Marriage and of Primitive Thought in its Bearing on Marriage*, London: Macmillan.

Crowley, W., Filicori, M., Spratt, D. and Santorno, N. (1985) 'The physiology of gonadotrophin releasing hormone secretion in men and women', *Recent Progress in Hormone Research* 41, 473–531.

Crowther, D. (1994) 'Is there a link between the consulting patterns of premenopausal women and the menstrual cycle?', *Family Practice* 11, 402–407.

Cumming, C., Urion, C., Cumming, D. and Fox, E. (1994) ' "So mean and cranky, I could bite my mother": An ethnosemantic analysis of women's descriptions of premenstrual change', *Women and Health* 21, 21–41.

Cunnington, C.W. (1950) *Women*, London: Burke.

Curran, J. and Cattell, R. (1976) *Manual for the Eight-State Questionnaire*, Champaign: IPAT.

Currie, D. and Raoul, V. (eds) (1992) *The Anatomy of Gender: Women's Struggle for the Body*, Ottawa: Carleton University Press.

Cutler, W., Preti, G., Huggins, G., Erickson, B. and Garcia, C.(1985) 'Sexual behaviour frequency and biphasic ovulatory type menstrual cycles', *Physiology and Behaviour* 34, 805–810.

Cutler, W., Schleidt, W., Friedmann, E., Preti, G. and Sitne, R.(1987) 'Lunar influences on the reproductive cycle in women', *Human Biology* 59, 959–972.

Dalton, K. (1960) 'Effect of menstruation on schoolgirls' weekly work', *British Medical Journal* i, 326–328.

——(1961) 'Menstruation and crime', *British Medical Journal* ii, 1752–1753.

——(1968) 'Menstruation and examinations', *The Lancet* 11, 1386–1388.

——(1969) *The Menstrual Cycle*, London: Penguin.

——(1977) *The Premenstrual Syndrome and Progesterone Therapy*, London: Heinemann Medical Books.

——(1984) *Once a Month*, revised edn, Glasgow: Fontana.

Dalvit, S. (1981) 'The effect of the menstrual cycle on patterns of food intake', *American Journal of Clinical Nutrition* 34, 1811–1815.

Daly, C.D. (1935) 'The menstruation complex in literature', *Psychoanalytic Quarterly* 4, 307–340.

——(1943) 'The role of menstruation in human phylogenesis and ontogenesis', *International Journal of Psychoanalysis* 24, 151–170.

Daly, M. (1991) *Gyn/Ecology: The Metaethics of Radical Feminism*, London: The Women's Press (originally published 1979).

Dan, A.J. and Lewis, L.L. (eds) (1992) *Menstrual Health in Women's Lives*, Urbana: University of Illinois Press.

Dan, A.J. and Monagle, L. (1994) 'Sociocultural influences on women's experiences of perimenstrual symptoms', in J. Gold and S. Severino (eds) *Premenstrual Dysphorias: Myths and Realities*, Washington DC: American Psychiatric Press.

Dan, A.J., Chatterton, R., DeLeon-Jones, F. and Hudgens, G. (1992) 'Rationale and evidence for the role of circadian desynchrony in premenstrual symptoms', in A.J. Dan and L.L. Lewis (eds) *Menstrual Health in Women's Lives*, Urbana: University of Illinois Press.

Datta, N. (1960) 'Influence of seasonal variations on the reproductive cycles in women', *Population Review* 4, 46–55.

Dayus, K. (1985) *Where There's Life*, London: Virago.

de Beauvoir, S. (1963) *Memoirs of a Dutiful Daughter*, London: Penguin.

Delaney, J., Lupton, M.J. and Toth, E. (1988) *The Curse: A Cultural History of Menstruation*, revised edition, Urbana: University of Illinois Press, 1988 (originally published 1976).

De Marchi, W. (1976) 'Psychophysiological aspects of the menstrual cycle', *Journal of Psychosomatic Research* 20, 279–287.

De Marchi, W. and Tong, J. (1972) 'Menstrual, diurnal and activation effects on the resolution of temporally paired flashes', *Psychophysiology* 9, 362–367.

Dennerstein, L., Spencer-Gardner, C., Gotts, G., Brown, J., Smith, M. and Burrows, G. (1985) 'Progesterone and the premenstrual syndrome: a double-blind crossover trial', *British Medical Journal* 290, 1617–1621.

Dennerstein, L., Morse, C., Gotts, G., Brown, J., Smith, M., Oats, J. and Burrows, G. (1986) 'Treatment of premenstrual symptoms: a double-blind trial of dydrogesterone', *Journal of Affective Disorders* 11, 199–205.

Dennerstein, L., Brown, J., Gotts, G., Morse, C., Farley, T. and Pinol, A. (1993) 'Menstrual cycle hormonal profiles of women with and without premenstrual syndrome', *Journal of Psychosomatic Obstetrics and Gynaecology* 14, 259–268.

Dennis, R. (1992) 'Cultural change and the reproductive cycle', *Social Science and Medicine* 34, 485–489.

Diamond, M., Diamond, L. and Mast, M.(1972) 'Visual sensitivity and sexual arousal levels during the menstrual cycle', *Journal of Nervous and Mental Diseases* 155, 170–176.

Dinan, T. and O'Keane, V. (1991) 'The premenstrual syndrome: a psychoneuroendocrine perspective', *Ballières Clinical Endocrinology and Metabolism* 5, 143–165.

Dobbins, J. (1980) 'Implication of a time-dependent model of sexual intercourse within the menstrual cycle', *Journal of Biosocial Science* 12, 133–140.

d'Orban, P. (1983) 'Medicolegal aspects of premenstrual syndrome', *British Journal of Hospital Medicine* December, 404–409.

d'Orban, P. and Dalton, K. (1980) 'Violent crime and the menstrual cycle', *Psychological Medicine* 10, 353–359.

Doty, R., Snyder, P., Huggins, G. and Lowry, L. (1981) 'Endocrine, cardiovascular and psychological correlates of olfactory sensitivity changes during the human menstrual cycle', *Journal of Comparative and Physiological Psychology* 95, 45–60.

Doty, R., Hall, J., Flickinger, G. and Sondheimer, S. (1982) 'Cyclical changes in olfactory and auditory sensitivity during the menstrual cycle: no attenuation by oral contraceptive medication', in W. Breipohl (ed.) *Olfaction and Endocrine Regulation*, London: IRL Press.

Duncan, E., Dorwood, M. and Walker, A. (1995) 'The experience of emotion in relation to menstrual cycle phase: a prospective study using a structured diary method', *Journal of Reproductive and Infant Psychology* 13, 172.

Duncan, S., Read, C. and Brodie, M.(1993) 'How common is catamenial epilepsy?', *Epilepsia* 34, 827–831.

Dunham, F. (1970) 'Timing and sources of information about and attitudes towards menstruation among College females', *Journal of Genetic Psychology* 117, 205–217.

Dye, L. (1991) 'Attitudes to and experience of menstruation in a German university sample', paper presented at the Conference of the Society for Menstrual Cycle Research, Hamilton Cross, Seattle, June 1991.

——(1992) 'Visual information processing and the menstrual cycle', in J. Richardson (ed.) *Cognition and the Menstrual Cycle*, New York, Springer-Verlag.

——(1995) 'Menstrual cycle and appetite control', paper presented at International Federation of Fertility Societies 15th Congress, Montpelier, France, 15–16 September.

Dye, L., Warner, P. and Bancroft, J. (1995) 'Food craving during the menstrual cycle and its relationship to stress, happiness of relationship and depression: a preliminary enquiry', *Journal of Affective Disorders* 34: 157–164.

Eadie, J. (1874) *A Biblical Cyclopaedia*, London: Charles Griffin and Co.

Eagan, A. (1985) 'The selling of premenstrual syndrome: who profits from making PMS "the disease of the 1980s"?', in S. Laws, V. Hey and A. Eagan (eds) *Seeing Red: The Politics of Pre-menstrual Tension*, London: Hutchinson.

Easlea, B. (1981) *Science and Sexual Oppression: Patriarchy's Confrontation with Woman and Nature*, London: Weidenfeld and Nicolson.

Ehrenreich, B. and English, D. (1973) *Complaints and Disorders: The Sexual Politics of Sickness*, London: Writers and Readers Publishing Cooperative.

Ellis, H. (1894) *Man and Woman: A Study of Human Secondary Sexual Characteristics*, London: Walter Scott.

Elsberg, C., Brewer, E. and Levy, I. (1935) 'The sense of smell. IV. Concerning conditions which may temporarily alter normal olfactory acuity', *Bulletin of the Neurological Institute of New York* 4, 31–34.

Endicott, J. and Halbriech, U. (1982) 'Retrospective report of premenstrual depressive changes: factors affecting confirmation by daily ratings', *Psychopharmacology Bulletin* 18, 109–112.

——(1988) 'Practical problems in evaluation', in L. Gise (ed.) *The Premenstrual Syndromes*, New York: Churchill Livingstone.

Endicott, J., Nee, J., Cohen, J. and Halbriech, U. (1986) 'Premenstrual changes: patterns and correlates of daily ratings', *Journal of Affective Disorders* 10, 127–135.

Engel, G. (1967) 'Medical education and the psychosomatic approach: a report on the Rochester experience', *Journal of Psychosomatic Research* 11, 77–90.

——(1977) 'The need for a new medical model', *Science* 196, 129–136.

Engel, P. and Hildebrandt, G. (1974) 'Rhythmic variations in reaction time, heart rate and blood pressure at different durations of the menstrual cycle', in M. Fern, F. Halberg, R. Richart and R. van de Wiele (eds) *Biorhythms and Human Reproduction*, New York: Wiley.

Englander-Golden, P., Whitmore, M. and Dienstbier, R. (1978) 'Menstrual cycle as focus of study and self reports of moods and behaviours', *Motivation and Emotion* 2, 75–86.

Englander-Golden, P., Schleitner, F., Whitmore, M. and Corbley, G. (1986) 'Social and menstrual cycles: methodological and substantive findings', *Health Care for Women International* 7, 77–96.

Epps, P. (1962) 'Women shoplifters in Holloway Prison', in T. C. N. Gibbens and J. Prince (eds) *Shoplifting: A Report on Research Carried Out Under The Auspices of the ISTD*, London: Institute for the Study and Treatment of Delinquency.

Erdelyi, G. (1962) 'Gynaecological survey of female athletes', *Journal of Sports Medicine and Physical Fitness* 2, 174–179.

Eriksson, E., Sundblad, C., Lisjö, P., Modigh, K. and Andersch, B. (1992) 'Serum levels of androgens are higher in women with premenstrual irritability and dysphoria than in controls', *Psychoneuroendocrinology* 17, 195–204.

Ernster, V. (1975) 'American menstrual expressions', *Sex Roles* 1, 1–13.

Erskine, A., Morley, S. and Pearce, S. (1990) 'Memory for pain: a review', *Pain* 41, 255–265.

Eysenck, H. and Eysenck, S. (1965) *The Eysenck Personality Inventory*, London: University of London Press.

Facchinetti, G., Genazzini, A., Martignoni, E., Fiorini, L., Nappi, G. and Genazzani, R. (1993a) 'Neuroendocrine changes in luteal function in patients with premenstrual syndrome', *Journal of Clinical Endocrinology and Metabolism* 76, 1123–1127.

Facchinetti, G., Neri, I., Martignoni, E., Fiorini, L., Nappi, G. and Genazzani, A. (1993b) 'The association of menstrual migraine with the premenstrual syndrome', *Cephalalgia* 13, 422–425.

Farris, E. (1956) *Human Ovulation and Fertility*, New York: Pitman.

Fausto-Sterling, A. (1992) *Myths of Gender: Biological Theories about Women and Men*, 2nd edn, New York: Basic Books.

Feinberg, M., Carroll, B. and Smouse, P. (1981) 'The Carroll Rating Scale for depression. III. Comparison with other rating instruments', *British Journal of Psychiatry* 138, 205–209.

Feine, R., Belmaker, R., Rimon, R. and Ebstein, R. (1977) 'Platelet monoamine oxidase in women with premenstrual syndrome,' *Neuropsychobiology* 3, 105–110.

Fisher, E. (1979) *Women's Creation: Sexual Evolution and the Shaping of Society*, London: Wildwood House.

Fishman, S., Carr, D., Beckett, A. and Rosenbaum, J. (1994) 'Hypercapneic ventilatory response in patients with panic disorder before and after alprazolam treatment and in pre and postmenstrual women', *Journal of Psychiatric Research* 28, 165–170.

Fiske, S. and Taylor, S. (1991) *Social Cognition*, 2nd edn, New York: McGraw Hill.

Fluhmann, C.F. (1956) *The Management of Menstrual Disorders*, London: W.B. Saunders and Co.

Fontana, A. and Palfai, T. (1994) 'Psychosocial factors in premenstrual dysphoria: stressors, appraisal and coping processes', *Journal of Psychosomatic Research* 38, 557–567.

Frank, A. (1953) *The Diary of a Young Girl*, New York: Basic Books.

Frank, R. (1929) *The Female Sex Hormone*, Springfield Ill: Charles C. Thomas.

——(1931) 'The hormonal causes of premenstrual tension', *Archives of Neurology and Psychiatry* 26, 1053–1057.

Fraser, I., McCarron, G. and Markham, R. (1984) 'A preliminary study of factors influencing perception of menstrual blood loss volume', *American Journal of Obstetrics and Gynecology* 149: 788–793.

Frazer, J. (1922) *The Golden Bough*, abridged edn, London: Macmillan (original unabridged edition published 1890).

Freeman, E., Rickels, K., Sondheimer, S. and Polansky, M. (1995) 'A double-blind trial of oral progesterone, alprazolam and placebo in treatment of severe premenstrual syndrome', *Journal of the American Medical Association* 274, 51–57.

217

REFERENCES

Friday, N. (1979) *My Mother My Self*, Glasgow: Fontana.

Friedan, B. (1963) *The Feminine Mystique*, Gollancz: London.

Friedman, J. and Meares, R. (1978) 'Comparison of spontaneous and contraceptive menstrual cycles on a visual discrimination task', *Australian and New Zealand Journal of Psychiatry* 12, 233–239.

Gallant, S., Hamilton, J., Popiel, D., Morokoff, P. and Chakraborty, P. (1991) 'Daily moods and symptoms: effects of awareness of study focus, gender, menstrual cycle phase and day of week', *Health Psychology* 10, 180–189.

Gallant, S., Popiel, D., Hoffman, D., Chakraborty, P. and Hamilton, J. (1992a) 'Using daily ratings to confirm premenstrual syndrome/ late luteal phase dysphoric disorder. Part I: Effects of demand characteristics and expectations', *Psychosomatic Medicine* 54, 149–166.

——(1992b) 'Using daily ratings to confirm premenstrual syndrome/ late luteal phase dysphoric disorder. Part II: What makes a real difference?', *Psychosomatic Medicine* 54, 167–181.

Gamsa, A. (1994a) 'The role of psychological factors in chronic pain. I. A half century of study', *Pain* 57, 5–15.

——(1994b) 'The role of psychological factors in chronic pain. II. A critical appraisal,' *Pain* 57, 17–29.

Gannon, L. (1985) *Menstrual Disorders and Menopause: Biological, Psychological and Cultural Research*, New York: Praeger.

Gannon, L., Luchetta, T., Pardie, L. and Rhodes, K. (1989) 'Perimenstrual symptoms: relationships with chronic stress and selected lifestyle variables', *Behavioural Medicine* 15, 149–159.

Garfinkel, H. (1967) *Studies in Ethnomethodology*, Englewood Cliffs NJ: Prentice-Hall.

Garrioch, D. (1978) 'The effect of indomethacin on spontaneous activity in the isolated human myometrium and on the response to oxytocin and prostaglandins', *British Journal of Obstetrics and Gynaecology* 85, 47–52.

Gergen, K. (1985). 'The social constructionist movement in modern psychology', *American Psychologist* 40, 266–275.

Gift, A. (1989) 'Visual analogue scales: measurement of subjective phenomena', *Nursing Research* 38, 266–288.

Gilman, C. (1981) *The Yellow Wallpaper*, London: Virago (originally published 1891).

Gilmore, N., Robinson, D., Nies, A., Sylvester, D. and Ravaris, C. (1971) 'Blood monoamine oxidase levels in pregnancy and during the menstrual cycle', *Journal of Psychosomatic Research* 15, 215–220.

Gimbutas, M. (1969) *The Language of the Goddess*, London: Thames and Hudson.

Girdler, S., Pederson, C., Stern, R. and Light, K. (1993) 'Menstrual cycle and premenstrual syndrome: modifiers of cardiovascular reactivity in women', *Health Psychology* 12, 180–192.

Girdwood, G.F. (1842–43) 'Theory of menstruation', *The Lancet* 43 (1), 825–830.

Gise, L H. (ed.) (1988) *The Premenstrual Syndromes*, New York: Churchill Livingstone.

Gise, L., Lebovits, A., Paddison., P. and Strain, J. (1990) 'Issues in the identification of premenstrual syndromes', *Journal of Nervous and Mental Disease* 178, 228–234.

Gitlin, M. and Pasnau, R. (1989) 'Psychiatric syndromes linked to reproductive function in women: a review of current knowledge', *American Journal of Psychiatry* 146, 1413–1422.

Goffman, E. (1969) *The Presentation of Self in Everyday Life*, Harmondsworth: Penguin (originally published 1959).

Gold, J. (1994) 'Historical perspective of premenstrual syndrome', in J. Gold and S. Severino (eds) *Premenstrual Dysphorias: Myths and Realities*, Washington DC: American Psychiatric Press.

REFERENCES

Gold, J. and Severino, S. (eds) (1994) *Premenstrual Dysphorias: Myths and Realities*, Washington DC: American Psychiatric Press.

Golub, S. (1976) 'The magnitude of premenstrual anxiety and depression', *Psychosomatic Medicine* 38, 4–12.

——(1992) *Periods: From Menarche to Menopause*, Newbury Park, Ca: Sage.

Golub, S. and Harrington, D. (1981) 'Premenstrual and menstrual mood changes in adolescent women', *Journal of Personality and Social Psychology* 41, 961–965.

Gonzalez, E. (1981) 'Premenstrual syndrome: an ancient woe deserving of modern scrutiny', *Journal of the American Medical Association* 245, 1393–1396.

Good, P., Geary, N. and Engen, T. (1976) 'The effect of estrogen on odor detection', *Chemical Senses and Flavour* 2, 45–50.

Goodale, I., Domar, A. and Benson, H. (1990) 'Alleviation of premenstrual syndrome with the relaxation response', *Obstetrics and Gynecology* 75, 649–655.

Goolkasian, P. (1980) 'Cyclic changes in pain perception: An ROC analysis', *Perception and Psychophysics* 27, 499–504.

Gottlieb, A. (1988) 'American pre-menstrual syndrome: a mute voice', *Anthropology Today* 4, 10–13.

Gotts, G., Morse, C. and Dennerstein, L. (1995) 'Premenstrual complaints: an idiosyncratic syndrome', *Journal of Psychosomatic Obstetrics and Gynaecology* 16, 29–35.

Gouchie, C. and Kimura, D. (1991) 'The relationship between testosterone levels and cognitive ability patterns', *Psychoneuroendocrinology* 16, 323–334.

Goudsmit, E. (1983) 'Psychological aspects of premenstrual symptoms', *Journal of Psychosomatic Obstetrics and Gynaecology* 2, 20–26.

Gough, H. (1975) 'Personality factors related to the reported severity of menstrual distress', *Journal of Abnormal Psychology* 84, 59–65.

Graham, C. (1991) 'Menstrual synchrony: an update and review', *Human Nature* 2, 293–311.

Graham, C. and McGrew, W. (1980) 'Menstrual synchrony in female undergraduates living on a coeducational campus', *Psychoneuroendocrinology* 5, 245–257.

Graham, C. and Sherwin, B. (1992) 'A prospective treatment study of premenstrual symptoms using a triphasic oral contraceptive', *Journal of Psychosomatic Research* 36, 257–266.

Graham, E. and Glasser, M. (1985) 'Relationship of pregnanediol level to cognitive behaviour and mood', *Psychosomatic Medicine* 47, 26–34.

Graham, E., Stewart, M. and Ward, P. (1992) 'Seasonal cyclicity: effect of daylight/darkness on the menstrual cycle', in A. Dan and L. Lewis (eds) *Menstrual Health in Women's Lives*, Urbana: University of Illinois Press.

Grahn, J. (1993) *Blood, Bread and Roses: How Menstruation Created the World*, Boston Mass: Beacon Press.

Grant, E. and Pryse-Davis, J. (1968) 'Effect of oral contraceptives on depressive mood changes and on endometrial monoamine oxidase and phosphotases', *British Medical Journal* 3, 777.

Greenblatt, R.B., McCall, E. and Torpin, R. (1941) 'Oral progestin (anhydro-hydroxy-progesterone) in the treatment of dysmenorrhea', *American Journal of Obstetrics and Gynecology* 42, 50–53.

Greene, R. and Dalton, K. (1953) 'The premenstrual syndrome', *British Medical Journal* 1, 1007–1014.

Greenhill, J. and Freed, S. (1941) 'The electrolyte therapy of premenstrual distress', *Journal of the American Medical Association*, 117, 504–506.

Greer, G. (1971) *The Female Eunuch*, London: Paladin.

REFERENCES

Grieze-Jurgelevicius, D., Chernos, T. and Petersik, J. (1990) 'Auditory sensitivity and tone-sequence reproduction in oral contraceptive users and nonusers', *Perceptual and Motor Skills* 70, 271–278.

Griffin, C. (1995) 'Feminism, social psychology and qualitative research', *The Psychologist: The Bulletin of the British Psychological Society* 8 (3), 119–121.

Grosz, E. (1994) *Volatile Bodies: Toward a Corporeal Feminism*, Bloomington: Indiana University Press.

Gruba, G. and Rohrbaugh, M. (1975) 'MMPI correlates of menstrual distress', *Psychosomatic Medicine* 37, 265–268.

Gruhn, J. and Kazer, R. (1989) *Hormonal Regulation of the Menstrual Cycle: The Evolution of Concepts*, New York: Plenum Medical Book Co.

Gwinner, E. (1981) 'Circannual systems', in J. Aschoff (ed.) *Handbook of Behavioural Neurobiology*, vol. 4, New York: Plenum Press.

Haggard, M. and Gaston, J. (1978) 'Changes in auditory perception in the menstrual cycle', *British Journal of Audiology* 12, 105–118.

Hain, J., Linton, P., Eber, H. and Chapman, M. (1970) 'Menstrual irregularity, symptoms and personality', *Journal of Psychosomatic Research* 14, 81–87.

Halbriech, U. and Endicott, J. (1982) 'Relationship of dysphoric premenstrual changes to depressive disorders', *Acta Psychiatrica Scandinavica* 71, 331–338.

——(1985) 'Methodological issues in studies of premenstrual changes', *Psychoneuroendocrinology* 10, 15–32.

Halbriech, U., Endicott, J., Schacht, S. and Nee, J. (1982) 'The diversity of premenstrual changes as reflected in the premenstrual assessment form', *Acta Psychiatrica Scandinavica* 65, 46–65.

Halbriech, U., Endicott, J. and Lesser, J. (1985) 'The clinical diagnosis and classification of premenstrual changes', *Canadian Journal of Psychiatry* 30, 489–497.

Hall, G. S. (1908) *Adolescence*, New York: Appleton.

Hallberg, L., Hogdahl, A., Nilsson, L. and Rybo, G. (1966) 'Menstrual blood loss: a population study', *Acta Obstetrica et Gynaecologica Scandinavica* 45: 320–351.

Hallman, J. (1986) 'The premenstrual syndrome – an equivalent of depression?', *Acta Psychiatrica Scandinavica* 73, 403–411.

Halmi, K. (1982) 'The menstrual cycle in anorexia nervosa', in R.C. Friedman (ed.) *Behaviour and the Menstrual Cycle*, New York: Marcel Dekker.

Hamilton, C. (1981) *Marriage as Trade*, London: The Women's Press (original edition 1909).

Hamilton, J. and Gallant, S. (1988) 'Premenstrual symptom changes and plama beta-endorphin/beta-lipoprotein throughout the menstrual cycle', *Psychoneuroendocrinology* 13, 505–514.

——(1990) 'Problematic aspects of diagnosing premenstrual phase dysphoria: recommendations for psychological research and practice', *Professional Psychology Research and Practice* 21, 60–68.

Hamilton, J. and Halbriech, U. (1993) 'Special aspects of neuropsychiatric illness in women: with a focus on depression', *Annual Review of Medicine* 44, 355–364.

Hamilton, M. (1967) 'Development of a rating scale of primary depressive illness', *British Journal of Social and Clinical Psychology* 6, 178–196.

Hampson, E. (1990) 'Estrogen related variations in human spatial and articulatory-motor skills', *Psychoneuroendocrinology* 15, 97–111.

Hampson, E. and Kimura, D. (1988) 'Reciprocal effects of hormonal fluctuations on human motor and perceptual-spatial skills', *Behavioural Neuroscience* 102, 456–459.

——(1992) 'Sex differences and hormonal influences on cognitive function in humans', in J. Becker, S. Breedlove and D. Crews (eds) *Behavioural Endocrinology*, Cambridge Mass: MIT Press.

220

REFERENCES

Hardie, E. and McMurray, N. (1992) 'Self-stereotyping, sex role ideology, and menstrual attitudes: a social identity approach', *Sex Roles* 27, 17–37.

Harding, M.E. (1989) *Woman's Mysteries*, London: Century.

Harding, S. (1991) *Whose Science? Whose Knowledge?*, Ithaca NY: Cornell University Press.

Hare-Mustin, R. and Maracek, J. (eds) (1990) *Making a Difference: Psychology and the Construction of Gender*, New Haven: Yale University Press.

Hargrove, J., Nesbitt, D., Gaspar, M. and Ellis, L. (1976) 'Indomethacin induces rat uterine contractions in vitro and alters reactivity to calcium and acetylcholine', *American Journal of Obstetrics and Gynecology* 124, 25–29.

Harlow, S. (1986) 'Function and dysfunction: a historical critique of the literature on menstruation and work', *Health Care for Women International* 7, 39–50.

Harré, R. (1991) *Physical Being: A Theory for a Corporeal Psychology*, Oxford: Blackwell.

Harrison, M. (1987) *Self-Help with PMS*, London: Macdonald.

Hart, W. and Russell, J. (1986) 'A prospective comparison study of premenstrual symptoms', *Medical Journal of Australia* 144, 466–468.

Hart, W., Coleman, G. and Russell, J. (1987) 'Assessment of premenstrual symptomatology: a re-evaluation of the predictive validity of self report', *Journal of Psychosomatic Research* 31, 183–190.

Hastrup, J. and Light, K. (1984) 'Sex differences in cardiovascular stress responses: modulation as a function of menstrual cycle phases', *Journal of Psychosomatic Research* 28, 475–483.

Hausfater, G. and Skoblick, B. (1985) 'Perimenstrual behaviour changes among female yellow baboons: some similarities to premenstrual syndrome in women', *American Journal of Primatology* 9, 165–172.

Herberhold, C., Genkin, H., Brändle, L., Leitner, H. and Wöllmer, W. (1982) 'Olfactory threshold and hormone levels during the human menstrual cycle', in W. Breipohl (ed.) *Olfaction and Endocrine Regulation*, London: IRL Press.

Heilbrun, A. and Frank, M. (1989) 'Self-preoccupation and general stress level as sensitizing factors in premenstrual and menstrual distress', *Journal of Psychosomatic Research* 33, 571–577.

Helman, C. (1991a) *Culture, Health and Illness*, 2nd edn, London: Wright.

——(1991b) *Body Myths*, London: Chatto and Windus.

Henkin, R. (1974) ' Sensory changes during the menstrual cycle', in M. Ferin, F. Halberg, R. Richart and R. van de Wiele (eds) *Biorhythms and Human Reproduction*, New York: Wiley.

Henwood, K. and Nicolson, P. (1995) 'Qualitative research', *The Psychologist: The Bulletin of the British Psychological Society*, 8 (3), 109–111.

Henwood, K. and Pidgeon, N. (1992) 'Qualitative research and psychological theorising', *British Journal of Psychology* 83, 83–111.

Herren, R. (1933) 'The effect of high and low female sex hormone concentrations on the two-point threshold of pain and touch and upon tactile sensitivity', *Journal of Experimental Psychology* 16, 324–327.

Herrera, E., Gomez-Amor, J., Martinez-Selva, J. and Ato, M. (1990) 'Relationship between personality, psychological and somatic symptoms and the menstrual cycle', *Personality and Individual Differences* 11, 457–461.

Hesseltine, H. (1944) 'Specific problems of women in industry', *Journal of the American Medical Association* 124, 692–697.

Hewitt, J. (1994) *Self and Society: A Symbolic Interactionist Social Psychology*, 6th edn, Boston: Allyn and Bacon.

Hilgers, T., Daly, D., Prebil, A. and Hilgers, S. (1981) 'Natural family planning. III. Intermenstrual symptoms and estimated time of ovulation', *Obstetrics and Gynecology* 58, 152–155.

REFERENCES

Hill, Y., McKinlay, A. and Walker, A. (1994) 'Man, woman and premenstrual woman: stereotypes of British students', paper presented at British Psychological Society Social Psychology Section Conference, Oxford, UK, September.

Hillier, S. (1985) 'Sex steroid metabolism and follicular development in the ovary', *Oxford Reviews of Reproductive Biology* 7, 168–222.

Hirschmann-Wertheimer, I. (1927) 'Wechelseitige Bezeihungen von Menstruation und Psyche' (Reciprocal relations of menstruation and mind), *Monatsschrift für Psychiatrie und Neurologie* 66, 215–224.

Hodges, S. (1996) 'Heavy menstrual bleeding: its effect on the quality of women's lives and the language women use to describe it.' Unpublished manuscript.

Hollingworth, H.L. (1990) *Leta Stetter Hollingworth: A Biography*, Bolton MA: Anker Publishing Co. (originally published 1943).

Hollingworth, H.L. and Poffenberger, A.T. (1918) *Applied Psychology*, New York: D. Appleton and Co.

Hollingworth, L.S. (1914) 'Functional periodicity: an experimental study of the mental and motor abilities of women during menstruation', in *Contributions to Education* 69, New York: Columbia University, Teachers College.

Holtz, R. (1941) 'Should women fly during the menstrual period?', *Journal of Aviation Medicine* 12, 300–303.

Hood, K. (1992) 'Contextual determinants of menstrual cycle effects in observations of social interactions', in A. Dan and L. Lewis (eds) *Menstrual Health in Women's Lives*, Urbana, University of Illinois Press.

Horney, K. (1931a) 'Das Misstrauen zwischen den Geschlechtern' (The distrust between the sexes), *Die Ärztin* VII, 5–12. Translated and reprinted in K. Horney (1967) *Feminine Psychology*, (essays collected and edited by H. Kelman), New York: W.W. Norton and Co., pp. 107–118.

——(1931b) 'Die prämenstruellen Verstimmungen' (Premenstrual tension), *Zeitschrift für psychoanalytische Pädogogik* 5, 1–7. Translated and reprinted in K. Horney (1967) *Feminine Psychology*, (essays collected and edited by H. Kelman), New York: W.W. Norton and Co., pp. 99–106.

——(1932) 'Die Angst vor der Frau über einen spezifischen Unterscheid in der männlichen und weiblichen Angst vor dem anderen Geschlecht' (The dread of woman: observations on a specific difference in the dread felt by men and by women respectively for the opposite sex), *International Journal of Psychoanalysis* XIII, 348–360. Translated and reprinted in K. Horney (1967) *Feminine Psychology*, (essays collected and edited by H. Kelman), New York: W.W. Norton and Co., pp. 133–146.

Horrobin, D. (1983) 'The role of essential fatty acids and prostaglandins in PMS', *Journal of Reproductive Medicine* 28, 465–468.

Houlgate, C. (1987) 'PMS: mental abnormality and criminal responsibility', in B. Ginsburg and E. Carter (eds) *Premenstrual Syndrome*, New York: Plenum Press.

Hunter, M. (1996) 'Menopause', in C. A. Niven and A. Walker (eds) *The Psychology of Reproduction 1: Reproductive Potential and Fertility Control*, Oxford: Butterworth Heinemann.

Hurt, S., Schnurr, P., Severino, S., Freeman, E., Gise, L., Rivera-Tovar, A. and Steege, J. (1992) 'Late luteal phase dysphoric disorder in 670 women evaluated for premenstrual complaints', *American Journal of Psychiatry* 149, 525–530.

Iglesias, R., Terres, A. and Chavarria, A. (1980) 'Disorders of the menstrual cycle in airline stewardesses', *Aviation, Space and Environmental Medicine* 51, 518–520.

Innes, S. (1993) 'This stressful period called life', *Scotland on Sunday*, 11 April.

Israel, S. (1938) 'Premenstrual tension', *Journal of the American Medical Association* 110, 1721–1723.

——(1959) 'Premenstrual tension as an abnormal manifestation of the menstrual cycle', in C. Mazer and S. Israel (eds) *Diagnosis and Treatment of Menstrual Disorders and Sterility*, 4th edn, New York: Paul Hoeber Inc.

Ivey, M. and Bardwick, J. (1968) 'Patterns of affective fluctuation in the menstrual cycle', *Psychosomatic Medicine* 30, 336–340.

Jacobi, M. P. (1877) *The Question of Rest for Women During Menstruation*, New York: G.P. Putnam's Sons.

Jacobsen, F., Wehr, T. and Rosenthal, N. (1988) 'Pineal and seasonal reproduction in seasonal affective disorder', in P. Pancheri and L. Zichella (eds) *Biorhythms and Stress in the Physiopathology of Reproduction*, New York: Hemisphere.

Jacobus, M., Fox Keller, E. and Shuttleworth, S. (eds) (1990) *Body/ Politics: Women and the Discourses of Science*, London: Routledge.

Jalland, P. and Hooper, J. (1986) *Women from Birth to Death: The Female Life Cycle in Britain, 1830–1914*, Atlantic Highlands NJ: Humanities Press International.

Janiger, O., Riffenburgh, R. and Kersh, R. (1972) 'Cross cultural study of premenstrual symptoms', *Psychosomatics* 13, 226–235.

Janowsky, D., Gorney, R. and Kelley, B.(1966) 'The Curse – vicissitudes and variations of the female fertility cycle. Part I: psychiatric aspects', *Psychosomatics* 8, 242–246.

Jarvis, T. and McCabe, M. (1991) 'Women's experience of the menstrual cycle', *Journal of Psychosomatic Research* 35, 651–660.

Jensen, B.(1982) 'Menstrual cycle effects on task performance examined in the context of stress research', *Acta Psychologica* 50, 159–178.

Joffe, N. (1948) 'The vernacular of menstruation', *Word* 4, 181–186.

Johannes, C., Linet, M., Stewart, W., Celentano, D., Lipton, R. and Szklo, M. (1995) 'Relationship of headache to phase of the menstrual cycle among young women: a daily diary study', *Neurology* 45, 1076–1082.

Johnson, N. and Petersik, J. (1987) 'Preliminary findings suggesting cyclic changes in visual contrast sensitivity during the menstrual cycle', *Perceptual and Motor Skills* 64, 587–594.

Johnson, T. (1987) 'Premenstrual syndrome as a western culture-specific disorder', *Culture, Medicine and Psychiatry* 11, 337–356.

Jong, E.(1974) *Fear of Flying*, London: Granada.

Jorgensen, J., Rossignol, A. and Bonnlander, H. (1993) 'Evidence against multiple premenstrual syndromes: results of a multivariate profile analysis of premenstrual symptomatology', *Journal of Psychosomatic Research* 37, 257–263.

Kamm, J. (1965) *Hope Deferred: Girls' Education in English History*, London: Methuen.

Kashiwagi, T., McClure, J. and Wetzel, R. (1976) 'Premenstrual affective syndrome and psychiatric disorder', *Diseases of the Nervous System* 37, 116–119.

Keenan, P., Stern, R., Janowsky, D. and Pederson, C. (1992a) 'Psychological aspects of premenstrual syndrome. I: Cognition and memory', *Psychoneuroendocrinology* 17, 179–187.

Keenan, P., Lindamer, L. and Jong, S. (1992b) 'Psychological aspects of premenstrual syndrome. II Utility of standardized measures', *Psychoneuroendocrinology* 17, 189–194.

Keith, T. (1978) *Religion and the Decline of Magic*, London: Penguin.

Kendall, K. (1992) 'Sexual difference and the law: premenstrual syndrome as a legal defence', in D. Currie and V. Raoul (eds) *The Anatomy of Gender: Women's Struggle for the Body*, Ottawa: Carleton University Press.

Kendall, M. (1976) *Time Series*, 2nd edn, London: Charles Griffin and Co.

Kerényi, C. (1975) *Zeus and Hera*, London: Routledge.

Kesner, J., Wright, D., Schrader, S., Chin, N. and Krieg, E. (1992) 'Methods of monitoring menstrual function in field studies: efficacy of methods', *Reproductive Toxicology* 6, 385–400.

Kessel, N. and Coppen, A. (1963) 'The prevalence of common premenstrual symptoms', *The Lancet* 13 July, 61–64.

Kimura, D. and Hampson, E. (1993) 'Neural and hormonal mechanisms mediating sex differences in cognition', in P. Vernon (ed.) *Biological Approaches to the Study of Human Intelligence*, New Jersey: Ablex Publishing Corp.

——(1994) 'Cognitive pattern in men and women is influenced by fluctuations in sex hormones', *Current Directions in Psychological Science* 3, 57–61.

King, L.S. (1963) *The Growth of Medical Thought*, Chicago: University of Chicago Press.

Kirkby, R. (1994) 'Change in premenstrual symptoms and irrational thinking following cognitive-behavioural coping skills training', *Journal of Consulting and Clinical Psychology* 62, 1026–1032.

Kissling, E.A. (1996) 'Bleeding out loud: communication about menstruation', *Feminism and Psychology* 6, 481–504.

Klaiber, E., Broverman, D., Vogel, N. and Kobayashi, Y. (1974) 'Rhythms in plasma MAO activity, EEG, and behavior during the menstrual cycle', in M. Ferin, F. Halberg, R. Richart and R. van de Wiele (eds) *Biorhythms and Human Reproduction*, New York: Wiley.

Klebanov, P. and Jemmott, J. (1992) 'Effects of expectations and bodily sensations on self-reports of premenstrual symptoms', *Psychology of Women Quarterly* 16, 289–310.

Kline, P. (1993) *The Handbook of Psychological Testing*, London: Routledge.

Knight, C. (1991) *Blood Relations: Menstruation and the Origins of Culture*, New Haven: Yale University Press.

Knight, R. (1929) 'Work and rest', in C.S. Myers (ed.) *Industrial Psychology*, London: Thornton Butterworth Ltd.

Koeske, R. (1981) 'Theoretical and conceptual complexities in the design and analysis of menstrual cycle research', in P. Komnenich, M. McSweeney, J. Noack and S. Elder (eds) *The Menstrual Cycle: Vol. 2. Research and Implications for Women's Health*, New York: Springer.

Koeske, R. and Koeske, G. (1975) 'An attributional approach to moods and the menstrual cycle', *Journal of Personality and Social Psychology* 31, 473–478.

Kolodny, R. and Bauman, J. (1979) 'To the editor', *New England Journal of Medicine* 300, 626 (letter).

Kopell, B., Lunde, D., Clayton, R. and Moos, R. (1969) 'Variations in some measures of arousal during the menstrual cycle', *Journal of Nervous and Mental Diseases* 148, 180–187.

Kuczmierczyk, A. and Adams, H. (1986) 'Autonomic arousal and pain sensitivity in women with premenstrual syndrome at different phases of the menstrual cycle', *Journal of Psychosomatic Research* 30, 421–428.

Kuczmierczyk, A., Adams, H., Calhoun, K., Naor, S., Giombetti, R., Cattalani, M. and McCann, P. (1986) 'Pain responsivity in women with premenstrual syndrome across the menstrual cycle', *Perceptual and Motor Skills* 63, 387–393.

Kuczmierczyk, A., Labrum, A. and Johnson, C. (1992) 'Perception of family and work environments in women with premenstrual syndrome', *Journal of Psychosomatic Research* 36, 787–795.

Kuczmierczyk, A., Johnson, C. and Labrum, A. (1994) 'Coping styles in women with premenstrual syndrome', *Acta Psychiatrica Scandinavica* 89, 301–305.

Kuhn, T. (1962) *The Structure of Scientific Revolutions*, Chicago: Chicago University Press.

Kullander, S. and Svanberg, L. (1979) 'Bromocriptine treatment of PMS', *Acta Obstetrica and Gynecologica Scandinavica* 58, 375–379.

Kumar, S., Mansel, R., Hughes, L., Woodhead, J., Edwards, A., Scanlon, M. and Newcombe, R. (1984) 'Prolactin response to thyrotropin releasing hormone stimulation and dopaminergic inhibition in benign breast disease', *Cancer* 53, 1311–1315.

Ladisich, W. (1977) 'Influence of progesterone on serotonin metabolism: a possible causal factor for mood changes', *Psychoneuroendocrinology* 2, 257–266.

Laessle, R., Tuschl, R., Schweiger, U. and Pirke, K. (1990) 'Mood changes and physical complaints during the normal menstrual cycle in healthy young women', *Psychoneuroendocrinology* 15, 131–138.

Landgren, B., Unden, A. and Diczfalusy, E. (1980) 'Hormonal profiles in the cycle of 68 normally menstruating women', *Acta Endocrinologica* 94, 89–98.

Laqueur, T. (1990) *Making Sex: Body and Gender from the Greeks to Freud*, Cambridge Mass: Harvard University Press.

Lark, S. (1993) *Menstrual Cramps: A Self-Help Program*, Los Altos CA: Westchester Publishing Co.

Laws, S. (1985) 'Who needs PMT? A feminist approach to the politics of premenstrual tension', in S. Laws, V. Hey and A. Eagan (eds) *Seeing Red: The Politics of Pre-menstrual Tension*, London: Hutchinson.

——(1990) *Issues of Blood: The Politics of Menstruation*, Basingstoke: Macmillan Press.

Laws, S., Hey, V. and Eagan, A. (eds) (1985) *Seeing Red: The Politics of Pre-menstrual Tension*, London, Hutchinson.

Laycock, T. (1842–43) 'Evidence and arguments in proof of the existence of a general law of periodicity in the phenomena of life', *The Lancet* 43, 124–129, 160–164, 423–427, 929–932.

——(1843–44) 'Evidence and arguments in proof of the existence of a general law of periodicity in the phenomena of life', *The Lancet* 45, 85–89, 253–258, 430–432.

Lazarus, R. and Folkman, S. (1984) *Stress, Appraisal and Coping*, New York: Springer.

Lee, K. and Rittenhouse, C.A. (1992) 'Health and perimenstrual symptoms: health outcomes for employed women who experience perimenstrual symptoms', *Women and Health* 19, 65–78.

LeFevre, J., Hedricks, C., Church, R. and McClintock, M. (1992) 'Psychological and social behaviour of couples over a menstrual cycle: "on-the-spot" sampling from everyday life', in A. Dan and L. Lewis (eds) *Menstrual Health in Women's Lives*, Urbana: University of Illinois Press.

Leibenluft, E., Fiero, P. and Rubinow, D. (1994) 'Effects of the menstrual cycle on dependent variables in mood disorder research', *Archives of General Psychiatry* 51, 761–781.

Lein, A. (1979) *The Cycling Female: Her Menstrual Rhythm*, San Francisco: Freeman.

Le Magnen, J. (1948) 'Physiologie des sensations: Un cas de sensibilité olfactive se presentant comme un caractère sexual secondaire feminin', *Academie des Sciences* February, 694–695.

——(1952) 'Les phenomenones olfacto-sexuels chez l'homme', *Archives des Sciences Physiologiques* 6, 125–160.

L'Esperance, J. (1977) 'Doctors and women in nineteenth-century society: sexuality and role', in J. Woodward and D. Richards (eds) *Health Care and Popular Medicine in Nineteenth-Century England* Croom Helm.

Levitt, E. and Lubin, B. (1967) 'Some personality factors associated with menstrual complaints and menstrual attitudes', *Journal of Psychosomatic Research* 11, 267–270.

Lewis, L., Greenblatt, E., Rittenhouse, C., Veldhuis, J. and Jaffe, R. (1995) 'Pulsatile release patterns of luteinizing hormone and progesterone in relation to symptom onset in women with premenstrual syndrome', *Fertility and Sterility* 64, 288–292.

Lindner, H. and Kirkby, R. (1992) 'Premenstrual symptoms: the role of irrational thinking', *Psychological Reports* 71, 247–52.

REFERENCES

Linton, Eliza Lynn (1891) 'The wild women as politicians', *The Nineteenth Century*, 30 (July). Extract reprinted in P. Jalland and J. Hooper (1986) *Women from Birth to Death: The Female Life Cycle in Britain, 1830–1914*, Atlantic Highlands NJ: Humanities Press International, p. 25.

Little, B. and Zahn, T. (1974) 'Changes in mood and autonomic functioning during the menstrual cycle', *Psychophysiology* 11, 579–590.

Livesey, J., Wells, J., Metcalf, M., Hudson, S. and Bates, R. (1989) 'Assessment of the significance and severity of premenstrual tension. I. A model', *Journal of Psychosomatic Research* 33, 269–279.

Logue, C. and Moos, R. (1986) 'Perimenstrual symptoms: prevalence and risk factors', *Psychosomatic Medicine* 48, 388–414.

——(1988) 'Positive premenstrual changes: toward a new perspective on the menstrual cycle', *Journal of Psychosomatic Research* 32, 31–40.

Lovering, K. M. (1991) 'Young British adolescents' information and beliefs about menarche and menstruation', unpublished manuscript.

——(1995) 'The bleeding body: adolescents talk about menstruation', in S. Wilkinson and C. Kitzinger (eds) *Feminism and Discourse*, London: Sage.

Lubin, B. (1967) *Manual for the Depression Adjective Check List (DACL)*, San Diego CA: Educational and Industrial Testing Service.

Lupton, M.J. (1993) *Menstruation and Psychoanalysis*, Urbana: University of Illinois Press.

Luria, R. (1975) 'The validity and reliability of the visual analogue mood scale', *Journal of Psychiatric Research* 12, 51–57.

Lyons, P., Truswell, A., Mira, M., Oizzard, J. and Abraham, S. (1989) 'Reduction of food intake in the ovulatory phase of the menstrual cycle', *American Journal of Clinical Nutrition* 49, 1164–1168.

McCance, R., Luff, M. and Widdowson, E. (1937) 'Physical and emotional periodicity in women', *Journal of Hygiene*, 37, 571–605.

McClintock, M. (1971) 'Menstrual synchrony and suppression', *Nature* 229, 244–245.

Maccoby, E. and Jacklin, C. (1974) *The Psychology of Sex Differences*, Stanford CA: Stanford University Press.

McEwen, B. (1988) 'Basic research perspective: ovarian hormone influence on brain neurochemical functions', in L. Gise (ed.) *The Premenstrual Syndromes*, New York: Churchill Livingstone.

McFarland, C., Ross, M. and DeCourville, N. (1989) 'Women's theories of menstruation and biases in recall of menstrual symptoms', *Journal of Personality and Social Psychology* 57, 522–531.

McFarlane, J. and Williams, T. (1994) 'Placing premenstrual syndrome in perspective', *Psychology of Women Quarterly* 18, 339–374.

McFarlane, J., Martin, C. and Williams, T. (1988) 'Mood fluctuations: women versus men and menstrual versus other cycles', *Psychology of Women Quarterly* 12, 201–223.

Macht, D. (1943) 'Further historical and experimental studies on menstrual toxin', *American Journal of Medical Science* 206, 281–305.

McHugh, G. and Wasser, J. (1959) 'Application of the Thurstone-Chave attitude rating scale to attitudes towards menstruation', *Psychological Reports* 5, 677–682.

McKay, W.J.S. (1901) *The History of Ancient Gynaecology*, London: Bailliere, Tindall and Cox.

McKeever, P. (1984) 'The perpetuation of menstrual shame: implications and directions', *Women and Health* 9, 33–47.

Mackenzie, T., Wilcox, K. and Baron, H. (1986) 'Lifetime prevalence of psychiatric disorders in women with perimenstrual difficulties', *Journal of Affective Disorders* 10, 15–19.

REFERENCES

MacKinnon, I., MacKinnon, P. and Thomson, A. (1959) 'Lethal hazards of the luteal phase of the menstrual cycle', *British Medical Journal* 1 1015–1017.

McNair, D.M., Lorr, M. and Droppleman, L.F. (1971) *Profile of Mood States*, San Diego CA: Educational and Industrial Testing Service.

McNeill, E.T. (1992) *Variations in Subjective State over the Oral Contraceptive Pill Cycle: The Influence of Endogeneous Steroids and Temporal Manipulations*, University of Edinburgh, PhD thesis.

——(1994) 'Blood, sex and hormones: a theoretical review of women's sexuality over the menstrual cycle', in P.Y.L. Choi and P. Nicolson (eds) *Female Sexuality: Psychology, Biology and Social Context*, Hemel Hempstead: Harvester Wheatsheaf.

McNeilly, A. and Chard, T. (1974) 'Circulating levels of prolactin during the menstrual cycle', *Clinical Endocrinology* 3, 105–112.

Maddocks, S., Hahn, P., Moller, F. and Reid, R. (1986) 'A double-blind placebo controlled trial of progesterone vaginal suppositories in the treatment of premenstrual syndrome', *American Journal of Obstetrics and Gynecology* 154, 573–581.

Magos, A. (1988) 'Effects and analysis of the menstrual cycle', *Journal of Biomedical Engineering* 10, 105–109.

Magos, A. and Studd, J. (1985a) 'Effects of the menstrual cycle on medical disorders', *British Journal of Hospital Medicine* 33, 68–77.

——(1985b) 'Progesterone and the premenstrual syndrome: a double-blind crossover trial', *British Medical Journal* 291, 213–214, (letter).

——(1986) 'Assessment of menstrual cycle symptoms by trend analysis', *American Journal of Obstetrics and Gynecology* 155, 271–277.

——(1988) 'A simple method for the diagnosis of premenstrual syndrome by use of a self-assessment disk', *American Journal of Obstetrics and Gynecology* 158, 1024–1028.

Mair, R., Bouffard, J., Engen, T. and Morton, T. (1978) 'Olfactory sensitivity during the menstrual cycle', *Sensory Processes* 2, 90–98.

Malson, H. and Ussher, J. (1996) 'Bloody women: a discourse analysis of amenorrhea as a symptom of anorexia nervosa', *Feminism and Psychology* 6, 505–521.

Mansel, R., Preece, P. and Hughes, L. (1980) 'Treatment of cyclical breast pain with bromocriptine', *Scottish Medical Journal* 25, 565–570.

Mansfield, P., Hood, K. and Henderson, J. (1989) 'Women and their husbands: mood and arousal fluctuations across the menstrual cycle and days of the week', *Psychosomatic Medicine* 51, 66–80.

Mao, K. and Chang, A. (1985) 'The premenstrual syndrome and Chinese', *Australia and New Zealand Journal of Obstetrics and Gynaecology* 25, 118–120.

Margolis, J., Manicas, P., Harré, R. and Secord, P. (1986) *Psychology: Designing the Discipline*, Oxford: Blackwell.

Marinari, K., Leshner, A. and Doyle, M. (1976) 'Menstrual cycle status and adrenocortical reactivity to psychological stress', *Psychoneuroendocrinology* 1, 213–216.

Markum, R. (1976) 'Assessment of the reliability of and the effect of menstrual instructions on the symptom ratings on the Moos MDQ', *Psychosomatic Medicine* 38, 163–172

Marshack, A. (1972) *The Roots of Civilization*, New York: McGraw Hill.

Marshall, J. and Bundred, P. (1994) 'Menorrhagia: women's hopes, fears and expectations regarding hospital treatment', *Journal of Reproductive and Infant Psychology* 12, 205.

Martin, E. (1989) *The Woman in the Body: A Cultural Analysis of Reproduction*, Milton Keynes: Open University Press.

——(1990) ' Science and women's bodies: forms of anthropological knowledge', in M. Jacobus, E. Fox Keller and S. Shuttleworth (eds) *Body/ Politics: Women and the Discourses of Science*, New York: Routledge.

Massil, H., Thomas, M. and O'Brien, P. (1993) 'Sex hormone binding globulin concentrations in premenstrual syndrome', *British Journal of Obstetrics and Gynaecology* 100, 697–698.

Masson, J. (ed.) (1985) *The Complete Letters of Sigmund Freud to Wilhelm Fliess 1887–1904*, London: The Belknap Press.

Maudsley, H. (1873) *Body and Mind*, London: Macmillan and Co. Extract reprinted in V. Skultans (1975) *Madness and Morals: Ideas on Insanity in the Nineteenth Century*, London: Routledge and Kegan Paul.

——(1874) 'Sex in mind and education', *Fortnightly Review* 15, 466–483.

Maxson, W. (1988) 'Progesterone: biologic effects and evaluation of therapy for PMS', in L. Gise (ed.) *The Premenstrual Syndromes*, New York: Churchill Livingstone.

Mead, G. H. (1934) *Mind, Self and Society*, Chicago: Chicago University Press.

Mead , K. (1977) *A History of Women in Medicine: From the Earliest Time to the Beginning of the Nineteenth Century*, New York: AMS Press, (originally published in 1938).

Mead, M. (1949) *Male and Female*, New York: Morrow.

Meadowcroft, J. and Zillmann. D. (1987) 'Women's comedy preferences during the menstrual cycle', *Communication Research* 14, 204–218.

Medvei, V.C. (1982) *A Short History of Endocrinology*, Lancaster, MTP Press Ltd.

Mehta, Y., Mazumdar, B., Pathak, J. and Skandhan, K. (1977) 'Auditory reaction time during different phases of the menstrual cycle', *Indian Journal of Medical Sciences* 31, 107–110.

Meininger, J. (1986) 'Sex differences in factors associated with use of medical care and alternative illness behaviours', *Social Science and Medicine* 22, 285–292.

Melzack, R. and Wall, P. (1982) *The Challenge of Pain*, London: Penguin.

Merikangas, K., Foeldenyi, M. and Angst, J. (1993) 'The Zurich study. XIX. Patterns of menstrual disturbances in the community: results of the Zurich cohort study', *European Archives of Psychiatry and Clinical Neurosciences* 243, 23–32.

Metcalf, M.G. (1983) 'Incidence of ovulation from the menarche to the menopause: observations of 622 New Zealand women', *New Zealand Medical Journal* 96, 645–648.

Metcalf, M.G., Skidmore, D., Lowry, G. and Mackenzie, J. (1983) 'Incidence of ovulation in the years after the menarche', *Journal of Endocrinology* 97, 213–219.

Metcalf, M.G., Evans, J. and Mackenzie, J. (1984) 'Indices of ovulation: comparison of plasma and salivary levels of progesterone with urinary pregnanediol', *Journal of Endocrinology* 100, 75–80.

Metcalf, M.G., Livesey, J. and Wells, J. (1989a) 'Assessment of the significance and severity of premenstrual tension. II: Comparison of methods', *Journal of Psychosomatic Research* 33, 281–292.

Metcalf, M.G., Livesey, J., Wells, J and Braiden, V. (1989b) 'Mood cyclicity in women with and without the premenstrual syndrome', *Journal of Psychosomatic Research* 33, 407–418.

Metcalf, M.G., Braiden, V., Livesey, J. and Wells, J. (1992) 'The premenstrual syndrome: amelioration of symptoms after hysterectomy', *Journal of Psychosomatic Research* 36, 569–584.

Metcalf, M.G., Livesey, J. and Braiden, V. (1994) 'Assessment of the effect of ovarian suppressants on women with the premenstrual syndrome: iterative spectral analysis', *Journal of Psychosomatic Research* 38, 129–137.

Meuwissen, I. and Over, R. (1992) 'Sexual arousal across phases of the human menstrual cycle', *Archives of Sexual Behavior* 21, 101–119.

Mezrow, G., Shoupe, D., Spicer, D., Lobo, R., Leung, B. and Pike, M. (1994) 'Depot leuprolide acetate with oestrogen and progestin add-back for long term treatment of premenstrual syndrome', *Fertility and Sterility* 62, 932–937.

Millar, J. (1861) *Hints on Insanity*, London: Henry Renshaw. Extract reprinted in V. Skultans (1975) *Madness and Morals: Ideas on Insanity in the Nineteenth Century*, London: Routledge and Kegan Paul.

Millodot, M. and Lamont, A. (1974) 'Influence of menstruation on corneal sensitivity', *British Journal of Ophthalmology* 58, 752–756.

Miota, P., Yahle, M. and Bartz, C. (1991) 'Premenstrual syndrome: a bio-psycho-social approach to treatment', in D.L. Taylor and N.F. Woods (eds) *Menstruation, Health and Illness*, New York, Hemisphere.

Mira, M., Vizzard, J. and Abraham, S. (1985) 'Personality characteristics in the menstrual cycle', *Journal of Psychosomatic Obstetrics and Gynaecology* 4, 329–334.

Mitchell, E., Woods, N. and Lentz, M. (1991) 'Recognizing PMS when you see it: criteria for PMS sample selection', in D. Taylor and N. Woods (eds) *Menstruation, Health and Illness*, New York, Hemisphere.

——(1994) 'Differentiation of women with three perimenstrual symptom patterns', *Nursing Research* 43, 25–30.

Moghissi, K. (1992) 'Ovulation detection', *Endocrinology and Metabolism Clinics of North America* 21, 39–55.

Monagle, L., Dan, A., Chatterton, R. , DeLeon-Jones, F. and Hudgens, G. (1986) 'Toward delineating menstrual symptom groupings: examination of factor analytic results of menstrual symptom instruments', in V. Oleson and N. Woods (eds) *Culture, Society and Menstruation*, Cambridge Mass: Hemisphere.

Monagle, L., Dan, A., Krogh, V., Jossa, F., Farinaro, E. and Trevisan, M. (1993) 'Premenstrual symptom prevalence rates: an Italian-American comparison', *American Journal of Epidemiology* 138, 1070–1081.

Monk, T. (1989) 'A visual analogue scale technique to measure global vigour and affect', *Psychiatry Research* 27, 89–99.

Moos, R. (1968) 'The development of a menstrual distress questionnaire', *Psychosomatic Medicine* 30, 853–860.

Moos, R., Kopell, B., Melges, F., Yalom, I., Lunde, D., Clayton, R. and Hamburg, D. (1969) 'Fluctuations in symptoms and moods during the menstrual cycle', *Journal of Psychosomatic Research* 13, 37–44.

Morawski, J. (1994) *Practicing Feminisms, Reconstructing Psychology*, Ann Arbor: University of Michigan Press.

Morgan, F. (1989) *A Misogynist's Sourcebook*, London: Jonathan Cape.

Morris, N. and Udry, J. (1972) 'Contraceptive pills and day-to-day feelings of well-being', *American Journal of Obstetrics and Gynecology* 113, 763–765.

Morse, C. and Dennerstein, L. (1988) 'The factor structure of symptom reports in premenstrual syndrome', *Journal of Psychosomatic Research* 32, 93–98.

Morse, C., Bernard, M. and Dennerstein, L. (1989) 'The effects of rational-emotive therapy and relaxation training on premenstrual syndrome: a preliminary study', *Journal of Rational-Emotive and Cognitive-Behavioural Therapy* 7, 98–110.

Morse, C., Dennerstein, L. Farrell, E. and Varnavides, K. (1991) 'A comparison of hormone therapy, coping skills training, and relaxation for the relief of premenstrual syndrome', *Journal of Behavioural Medicine* 14, 469–489.

Morse, J. and Doan, H. (1987) 'Growing up at school: adolescents' response to menarche', *Journal of School Health* 57, 385–389.

Morse, J. and Kieren, D. (1993) 'The adolescent menstrual attitude questionnaire, part II: Normative scores', *Health Care for Women International* 14, 63–76.

Morse, J., Kieren, D. and Bottorff, J. (1993) 'The adolescent menstrual attitude questionnaire, part I: Scale construction', *Health Care for Women International* 14, 39–62.

Mortola, J. (1994) 'A risk-benefit appraisal of drugs used in the management of premenstrual syndrome', *Drug Safety* 10, 160–169.

229

Mortola, J., Girton, L., Beck., K. and Yen, S. (1990) 'Diagnosis of premenstrual syndrome by a simple prospective and reliable instrument: the calendar of premenstrual experiences', *Obstetrics and Gynecology* 76, 302–307.

Mortola, J., Girton, L. and Fischer, U. (1991) 'Successful treatment of severe premenstrual syndrome by combined use of gonadotrophin-releasing hormone agonist and estrogen/progestin', *Journal of Clinical Endocrinology and Metabolism* 72, 252A–252F.

Morton, J. (1950) 'Premenstrual Tension', *American Journal of Obstetrics and Gynecology* 60, 343–352.

Morton, J., Additon, H., Addison, R., Hunt, L. and Sullivan, J. (1953) 'A clinical study of premenstrual tension', *American Journal of Obstetrics and Gynecology* 65, 1182–1191.

Moscucci, O. (1993) *The Science of Woman: Gynaecology and Gender in England 1800–1929*, Cambridge: Cambridge University Press (paperback edition).

Mosher, C.D. (1916) *Health and the Woman Movement*, New York: Women's Press.

Müller, K. (1991) 'Das Erleben der Menstruation', *Gynäkologie* 24, 76–80. Cited in L. Dye (1991) 'Attitudes to and experience of menstruation in a German university sample', paper presented at the Conference of the Society for Menstrual Cycle Research, Hamilton Cross, Seattle.

Munday, M., Brush, M. and Taylor, R. (1981) 'Correlations between progesterone, oestradiol and aldosterone levels in the premenstrual syndrome', *Clinical Endocrinology* 14, 1–9.

Muse, K., Cetel, N., Futterman, L. and Yen, S. (1984) 'The premenstrual syndrome: effects of medical ovariectomy', *New England Journal of Medicine* 311, 1345–1349.

Myers, C.S. (1929) *Industrial Psychology*, London: Thornton Butterworth.

Nattero, G. (1982) 'Menstrual headache', *Advances in Neurology* 33, 215–226.

Newmark, M. and Penry, J. (1980) 'Catamenial epilepsy: a review', *Epilepsia* 21, 281–300.

Nicassio, P. (1980) 'Behaviour management of dysmenorrhea', in A. Dan, E. Graham and C. Beecher (eds) *The Menstrual Cycle*, vol. 1, New York: Springer.

Nicolson, P. (1992) 'Towards a psychology of women's health and health care', in P. Nicolson and J. Ussher (eds) *The Psychology of Women's Health and Health Care*, London: Macmillan.

——(1993) 'Deconstructing sexology: Understanding the pathologisation of female sexuality', *Journal of Reproductive and Infant Psychology* 11: 191–210.

——(1994) 'Anatomy and destiny: sexuality and the female body', in P.Y.L. Choi and P. Nicolson (eds) *Female Sexuality: Psychology, Biology and Social Context*, London: Harvester Wheatsheaf.

——(1995) 'The menstrual cycle, science and femininity: assumptions underlying menstrual cycle research', *Social Science and Medicine* 41, 779–784.

Nolen-Hoeksema, S. (1990) *Sex Differences in Depression*, Palo Alto: Stanford University Press.

Norris, R. (1987) 'Historical development of progesterone therapy', in B. Ginsburg and B. Carter (eds) *Premenstrual Syndrome*, New York: Plenum Press.

Novak, E. (ed.) (1965) *Novak's Handbook of Gynaecology*, 7th edn, Edinburgh: E. and S. Livingstone.

Novy, D., Nelson, D., Francis, D. and Turk, D. (1995) 'Perspectives of chronic pain: an evaluative comparison of restrictive and comprehensive models' *Psychological Bulletin* 118, 238–247.

Nowlis, V. (1965) 'Research with the mood adjective checklist', in S. Tomkins and C. Izard (eds) *Affect, Cognition and Personality*, New York: Springer.

Oatley, K. and Duncan, E. (1992) 'Incidents of emotion in daily life', in K.T. Strongman (ed.) *International Review of Studies on Emotion*, vol. 2, London: John Wiley.

Oatley, K. and Goodwin, B. (1971) 'The explanation and investigation of biological rhythms', in W. Colquhoun (ed.) *Biological Rhythms and Human Performance*, New York, Academic Press.

O'Brien, P. (1987) *Premenstrual Syndrome*, Oxford: Blackwell Scientific Publications.

——(1993) 'Helping women with premenstrual syndrome', *British Medical Journal* 307 1471–1475.

Odink, J., van der Ploeg, H., van den Berg, H., van Kempen, G., Bruinse, H. and Louwerse, E. (1990) 'Circadian and circatrigintan rhythms of biogenic amines in premenstrual syndrome (PMS)', *Psychosomatic Medicine* 52, 346–356.

Olasov, B. and Jackson, J. (1987) 'Effects of expectancies on women's reports of moods during the menstrual cycle', *Psychosomatic Medicine* 49, 65–78.

Olasov Rothbaum, B. and Jackson, J. (1990) 'Religious influence on menstrual symptoms and attitudes', *Women and Health* 16, 63–78.

Oleson, T. and Flocco, W. (1993) 'Randomised controlled study of premenstrual symptoms treated with ear, hand and foot reflexology', *Obstetrics and Gynaecology* 82, 906–911.

Oleson, V.L. and Woods, N.F. (eds) (1986) *Culture, Society and Menstruation*, Washington DC: Hemisphere Publishing Corp.

Öst, L.-G., Sterner, U. and Fellenius, J. (1989) 'Applied tension, applied relaxation and the combination in the treatment of blood phobia', *Behaviour Research and Therapy* 27, 109–121.

Oudshoorn, N. (1994) *Beyond the Natural Body: An Archaeology of Sex Hormones*, London: Routledge.

Owen, L. (1993) *Her Blood is Gold: Reclaiming the Power of Menstruation*, London: Aquarian/Thorsons.

Paige, K. (1971) 'Effects of oral contraceptives on affective fluctuations associated with the menstrual cycle', *Psychosomatic Medicine* 33, 515–537.

——(1977) 'Sexual pollution: reproductive sex taboos in America', *Journal of Social Issues* 33, 144–165.

Paige, K. and Paige, J.M. (1981) *The Politics of Reproductive Ritual*, Berkeley: University of California Press.

Paige Erickson, K. (1987) 'Menstrual symptoms and menstrual beliefs: national and cross-national patterns', in B. Ginsburg and B. Carter (eds) *Premenstrual Syndrome*, New York, Plenum Press.

Parker, I. (1989) *The Crisis in Modern Social Psychology – and How to End It*, London: Routledge.

Parkes, A. and Bellerby, C. (1926) 'Studies on the internal secretion of the ovary. I. The distribution in the ovary of the oestrus-producing hormone', *Journal of the Physiological Society of London* 61, 562–575.

Parlee, M. (1973) 'The premenstrual syndrome', *Psychological Bulletin* 80, 454–465.

——(1974) 'Stereotypic beliefs about menstruation. A methodological note on the Moos MDQ and some new data', *Psychosomatic Medicine* 36, 229–240.

——(1975) 'Menstruation and crime, accidents and acute psychiatric illness: a reinterpretation of Dalton's data', paper presented at American Psychological Association Conference, Chicago. Cited in S. Golub (1992) *Periods: From Menarche to Menopause*, Newbury Park CA: Sage.

——(1980) 'Positive changes in moods and activation levels during the menstrual cycle in experimentally naive subjects', in A. Dan, E. Graham and C. Beecher (eds) *The Menstrual Cycle. Volume 1: A Synthesis of Interdisciplinary Research*, New York: Springer.

——(1981) 'Gaps in behavioural research on the menstrual cycle', in P. Komnenich, M. McSweeney, J. Noack and S. Elder (eds) *The Menstrual Cycle: Volume II. Research and Implications for Women's Health*, New York, Springer.

——(1982) 'Changes in moods and activation levels during the menstrual cycle in experimentally naive subjects', *Psychology of Women Quarterly* 7, 119–131.

——(1983) 'Menstrual rhythms in sensory processes: a review of fluctuations in vision, olfaction, audition, taste and touch', *Psychological Bulletin* 93, 539–48.

——(1994) 'Commentary on the literature review', in J. Gold and S. Severino (eds) *Premenstrual Dysphorias: Myths and Realities*, Washington DC: American Psychiatric Press.

Parry, B. (1994) 'Biological correlates of premenstrual complaints', in J. Gold and S. Severino (eds) *Premenstrual Dysphorias: Myths and Realities*, Washington DC: American Psychiatric Press.

Parry, B., Rosenthal, N., Tamarkin, L. and Wehr, T. (1987) 'Treatment of a patient with seasonal premenstrual syndrome', *American Journal of Psychiatry* 144, 762–766.

——(1988) 'Reply to Severino', *American Journal of Psychiatry* 145, 133 (letter).

Parry, B., Mahan, A., Mostofi, N., Klauber, M., Lew, G. and Gillin, J. (1993) 'Light therapy of LLPDD: an extended study', *American Journal of Psychiatry* 150, 1417–1419.

Parry, B., Cover, H., Mostofi, N., Leveau, B., Sependa, P., Resnick, A. and Gillin, J. (1995) 'Early versus late partial sleep deprivation in patients with premenstrual dysphoric disorder and normal comparison subjects', *American Journal of Psychiatry* 152, 404–412.

Parry, G. (1985) 'Sensory neuropathy with low dose pyridoxine', *Neurology* 35, 1466.

Patkai, P., Johannson, G. and Post, B. (1974) 'Mood, alertness and sympathetic-adrenal medullary activity during the menstrual cycle', *Psychosomatic Medicine* 36, 503–512.

Pearlstein, T. (1995) 'Hormones and depression: what are the facts about premenstrual syndrome, menopause and hormone replacement therapy?', *American Journal of Obstetrics and Gynecology* 173, 646–653.

Pennington, V. (1957) 'Meprobamate (Miltown) in premenstrual tension', *Journal of the American Medical Association* 164, 638–641.

Perkin, J. (1993) *Victorian Women*, London: John Murray.

Pflüger, E.F.W. (1863) *Über die Eierstöcke der Säugethiere und des Menschen*, Leipzig: Englemann.

Phillips, A. and Rakusen, J. (eds) (1989) *The New Our Bodies, Ourselves*, British edition, London: Penguin.

Pickles, V., Hall, W., Best, F. and Smith, G. (1965) 'Prostaglandins in endometrium and menstrual fluid from normal and dysmenorrheic subjects', *Journal of Obstetrics and Gynaecology of the British Commonwealth* 72, 185–192.

Ploss, H., Bartels, M., and Bartels, P. (1935) *Woman: An Historical, Gynaecological and Anthropological Compendium*, ed. E.J. Dingwall, London: Heinemann (original German edition published 1885).

Plouffe, L., Stewart, K., Craft, K., Maddox, M. and Rausch, J.(1993) 'Diagnostic and treatment results from a southeastern academic center-based premenstrual syndrome clinic: the first year', *American Journal of Obstetrics and Gynecology* 169, 295–307.

Plutchik, R. and Kellerman, H. (1974) *Emotion Profile Index: Manual*, Los Angeles: Western Psychological Services. Cited in C. Bisson and C. Whissell (1989) 'Will premenstrual syndrome produce a Ms Hyde? Evidence from daily administrations of the Emotions Profile Index', *Psychological Reports* 65, 179–184.

Poovey, M. (1989) *Uneven Developments: The Ideological Work of Gender in Mid-Victorian England*, London: Virago.

Potter, J. and Wetherell, M.(1987) *Discourse and Social Psychology: Beyond Attitudes and Behaviour*, London: Sage.

Power, J. (1821) *Essays on the Female Economy*, London: Burgess and Hill.

Prior, J., Vigna, Y., Sciaretta, D., Alojado, N. and Schulzer, M.(1987) 'Conditioning exercise decreases premenstrual symptoms: a prospective controlled 6 month trial', *Fertility and Sterility* 47, 402–408.

REFERENCES

Procacci, P., Buzzelli, G., Passeri, I., Sassi, R., Voegelin, M. and Zoppi, M. (1970) 'Studies on the cutaneous pricking pain threshold in man. Circadian and circatrigintan changes', *Research and Clinical Studies in Headache* 3, 260–276.

Profet, M. (1993) 'Menstruation as a defense against pathogens transported by sperm', *Quarterly Review of Biology* 68, 335–386.

Psychological Abstracts (1928) 'Reciprocal relations of menstruation and mind', *Psychological Abstracts* 2, 705 (abstract 3120).

Pullon, S., Reinken, J. and Sparrow, M. (1989) 'Treatment of premenstrual symptoms in Wellington women', *New Zealand Medical Journal* 102: 72–74.

Quadagno, D., Shubeita, H., Deck, J. and Francoeur, D. (1981) 'Influence of male social contacts, exercise and all-female living conditions on the menstrual cycle', *Psychoneuroendocrinology* 6, 239–244.

Raciborski, A. (1842) 'Theory of menstruation', *The Lancet* 43: 644.

Ramcharan, S., Love, E., Fick, G. and Goldfien, A. (1992) 'The epidemiology of premenstrual symptoms in a population-based sample of 2650 urban women: attributable risk and risk factors', *Journal of Clinical Epidemiology* 45, 377–392.

Rapkin, A. (1992) 'The role of serotonin in premenstrual syndrome', *Clinical Obstetrics and Gynaecology* 35, 629–636.

Rapkin, A., Chang, L. and Reading, A. (1989) 'Mood and cognitive style in premenstrual syndrome', *Obstetrics and Gynecology* 74, 644–649.

Rausch, J. and Janowsky, D. (1982) 'Premenstrual tension: etiology', in R. Friedman (ed.) *Behaviour and the Menstrual Cycle*, New York: Marcel Dekker.

Reading, A. (1992) 'Cognitive model of premenstrual syndrome', *Clinical Obstetrics and Gynaecology* 35, 693–701.

Reame, N., Marshall, J. and Kelch, R. (1992) 'Pulsatile LH secretion in women with premenstrual syndrome (PMS): evidence for normal neuroregulation of the menstrual cycle', *Psychoneuroendocrinology* 17, 205–213.

Redei, E. and Freeman, E. (1995) 'Daily plasma oestradiol and progesterone levels over the menstrual cycle and their relation to premenstrual symptoms', *Psychoneuroendocrinology* 20, 259–267.

Redgrove, J. (1971) 'Menstrual cycles', in W. Colquhoun (ed.) *Biological Rhythms and Human Performance*, New York, Academic Press.

Rees, L. (1953) 'Psychosomatic aspects of the premenstrual tension syndrome', *Journal of Mental Science*, 99, 62–73.

Reid, R. (1985) 'Premenstrual syndrome', *Current Problems in Obstetrics, Gynaecology and Fertility* VIII (2), 1–57.

Reid, R. and Yen, S. (1981) 'Premenstrual Syndrome', *American Journal of Obstetrics and Gynecology* 139, 85–104.

Rice, P. (1981) 'Prehistoric Venuses: symbols of motherhood or womanhood?', *Journal of Anthropological Research* ?, 402–414.

Richardson, J.T.E. (1988) 'Student learning and the menstrual cycle. Myths and realities', *Studies in Higher Education* 13, 317–328.

——(1989) 'Student learning and the menstrual cycle: premenstrual symptoms and approaches to studying', *Educational Psychology* 9, 215–238.

——(1990) 'Questionnaire studies of paramenstrual symptoms', *Psychology of Women Quarterly* 14, 15–42.

——(ed.) (1992) *Cognition and the Menstrual Cycle*, New York: Springer-Verlag.

——(1995) 'The premenstrual syndrome: a brief history', *Social Science and Medicine* 41, 761–767.

Rierdan, J. and Koff, E. (1990) 'Premenarcheal predictors of the experience of menarche: a prospective study', *Journal of Adolescent Health Care* 11, 404 – 407.

REFERENCES

Ripper, M. (1991) 'A comparison of the effect of the menstrual cycle and the social week on mood, sexual interest and self-assessed performance', in D. Taylor and N. Woods (eds) *Menstruation, Health and Illness*, New York, Hemisphere.

Ritenbaugh, C. (1982) 'Obesity as a culture-bound syndrome', *Culture, Medicine and Psychiatry* 6, 347–361.

Rittenhouse, C.A. (1991) 'The emergence of premenstrual syndrome as a social problem', *Social Problems* 38, 412–425.

Rivera-Tovar, A., Rhodes, R. , Pearlstein, T. and Frank, E. (1994) 'Treatment efficacy', in J. Gold and S. Severino (eds) *Premenstrual Dysphorias: Myths and Realities*, Washington DC: American Psychiatric Press.

Robins, E. (1905) *A Dark Lantern*, cited in E. Showalter (1987) *The Female Malady: Women, Madness and English Culture 1830–1930*, London: Virago.

Robinson, J. and Short, R. (1977) 'Changes in breast sensitivity at puberty, during the menstrual cycle and at parturition', *British Medical Journal* 1, 1188–1191.

Rodin, J. (1976) 'Menstruation, reattribution and competence', *Journal of Personality and Social Psychology* 33, 345–353.

Rodin, J. and Ickovics, J. (1990) 'Women's health: review and research agenda as we approach the 21st century', *American Psychologist* 45, 1018–1034.

Rodin, M. (1992) 'The social construction of premenstrual syndrome', *Social Science and Medicine* 35, 49–56.

Rodmell, S. and Watt, A. (eds) (1986) *The Politics of Health Education: Raising the Issues*, London: Routledge.

Rosenblatt, P.(1983) *Bitter, Bitter Tears: Nineteenth-Century Diarists and Twentieth-Century Grief Theories*, Minneapolis: University of Minnesota Press.

Rosenthal, R. and Jacobson, L. (1968) *Pygmalion in the Classroom*, New York: Holt, Rinehart and Winston.

Rosenthal, R. and Rosnow, R. (1991) *Essentials of Behavioural Research: Methods and Data Analysis*, 2nd edn, New York: McGraw Hill.

Ross, L. (1977) 'The intuitive psychologist and his shortcomings: distortions in the attribution process', in L. Berkowitz (ed.) *Advances in Experimental Social Psychology*, New York: Academic Press.

Rossi, A. and Rossi, P. (1977) 'Body time and social time: mood patterns by menstrual cycle phase and day of the week', *Social Science Research* 6, 273–308.

Rouse, P. (1978) 'Premenstrual tension: a study using the Moos Menstrual Questionnaire', *Journal of Psychosomatic Research* 22, 215–222.

Rowland, R. (1992) *Living Laboratories: Women and Reproductive Technology*, London: Lime Tree.

Rubel, A. (1977) 'The epidemiology of folk illness: susto in hispanic America', in D. Landy (ed.) *Culture, Disease and Healing: Studies in Medical Anthropology*, New York: Macmillan.

Rubinow, D. and Roy-Byrne, P. (1984) 'Premenstrual syndromes: overview from a methodologic perspective', *American Journal of Psychiatry* 141, 163–172.

Rubinow, D. and Schmidt, P. (1995) 'The treatment of premenstrual syndrome – forward into the past', *New England Journal of Medicine* 332, 174–175.

Rubinow, D., Roy-Byrne, P., Hoban, M., Gold, P. and Post, R. (1984) 'Prospective assessment of menstrually related mood disorders', *American Journal of Psychiatry* 141, 684–686.

Rubinow, D., Roy-Byrne, P., Hoban, C., Grover, G., Stambler, N. and Post, R. (1986) 'Premenstrual mood changes: characteristic patterns in women with and without PMS', *Journal of Affective Disorders* 10, 85–90.

Ruble, D. (1977) 'Premenstrual symptoms: a reinterpretation', *Science* 197, 291–292.

Ruble, D. and Brooks Gunn, J. (1979) 'Menstrual symptoms: a social cognition analysis', *Journal of Behavioural Medicine* 2, 171–194.

Ruble, D., Boggiano, A. and Brooks Gunn, J. (1982) 'Men's and women's evaluations of menstrual-related excuses', *Sex Roles* 8, 625–638.

Rupani, N. and Lema, V. (1993) 'Premenstrual tension among nurses in Nairobi, Kenya', *East African Medical Journal* 70, 310–313.

Russell, D. (1995) *Women, Madness and Medicine*, Cambridge UK: Polity Press.

Russell, G. (1972) 'Psychological and nutritional factors in disturbances of menstrual function and ovulation', *Postgraduate Medical Journal* 48, 10–13.

Rust, J. and Golombok, S. (1989) *Modern Psychometrics: The Science of Psychological Assessment*, London: Routledge.

Ryan, M. (1841) *A Manual of Midwifery*. Extract reprinted in P. Jalland and J. Hooper (1986) *Women from Birth to Death: The Female Life Cycle in Britain, 1830–1914*, Atlantic Highlands NJ: Humanities Press International.

Salmon, W. (1973) *Logic*, 2nd edn, New Jersey: Prentice-Hall.

Sampson, E. (1996) 'Establishing embodiment in psychology', *Theory and Psychology* 6, 601–624.

Sampson, G. (1979) 'PMS: a double-blind controlled trial of progesterone and placebo', *British Journal of Psychiatry* 135, 209–215.

Sampson, G. and Jenner, F. (1977) 'Studies of daily recordings from the Moos Menstrual Distress Questionnaire', *British Journal of Psychiatry* 130, 265–271.

Sampson, G. and Prescott, P. (1981) 'The assessment of the symptoms of premenstrual syndrome and their response to therapy', *British Journal of Psychiatry* 138, 399–405.

Sanders, D. (1985) *Coping with Periods*, Edinburgh: Chambers.

Sanders, D. and Bancroft, J. (1982) 'Hormones and the sexuality of women: the menstrual cycle', *Clinics in Endocrinology and Metabolism* 11, 639–659.

Sanders, D., Warner, P., Backstrom, T. and Bancroft, J. (1983) 'Mood, sexuality, hormones and the menstrual cycle. I. Changes in mood and physical state: description of subjects and methods', *Psychosomatic Medicine* 45, 487–501.

Sarbin, T. and Kitsuse, J. (eds) (1994) *Constructing the Social*, London: Sage.

Sayers, J. (1982) *Biological Politics: Feminist and Anti-Feminist Perspectives*, London: Tavistock.

Scambler, A. and Scambler, G. (1985) 'Menstrual symptoms, attitudes and consulting behaviour', *Social Science and Medicine* 20, 1065–1068.

——(1993) *Menstrual Disorders*, London: Tavistock/ Routledge.

Scambler, A., Scambler, G. and Craig, D. (1981) 'Kinship and friendship networks and women's demand for primary care', *Journal of the Royal College of General Practitioners* 26, 746–750.

Scambler, G. and Scambler, A. (1984) 'The illness iceberg and aspects of consulting behaviour', in R. Fitzpatrick, J. Hinton, S. Newman, G. Scambler and J. Thompson (eds) *The Experience of Illness*, London: Tavistock.

Schachter, S. and Singer, J. (1962) 'Cognitive, social and psychological determinants of emotional state', *Psychological Review* 69, 379–399.

Schagen van Leeuwen, J. (1991) 'The premenstrual syndrome: some diagnostic and endocrine aspects', unpublished PhD thesis, University of Utrecht.

Schagen van Leeuwen, J., te Velde, E., Koppeschaar, H., Kop, W., Thijssen, J., van Ree, J. and Haspels, A. (1993) 'Is premenstrual syndrome an endocrine disorder?', *Journal of Psychosomatic Obstetrics and Gynaecology* 14, 91–109.

Schaumberg, H., Kaplan, J., Windebank, A., Vick, N., Rasmus, S., Pleasure, D. and Brown, M. (1983) 'Sensory neuropathy from pyridoxine abuse: a new megavitamin syndrome', *New England Journal of Medicine* 309, 445–448.

Schechter, D., Bachmann, G., Vaitukaitas, J., Phillips, D. and Saperstein, D. (1989) 'Perimenstrual symptoms: time course of symptom intensity in relation to endocrinologically defined segments of the menstrual cycle', *Psychosomatic Medicine* 51, 173–194.

Scher, D., Pionk, M. and Purcell, D. (1981) 'Visual sensitivity fluctuations during the menstrual cycle under dark and light adaptation', *Bulletin of the Psychonomic Society* 18, 159–160.

Scher, D., Purcell, D. and Caputo, S.(1985) 'Visual acuity at two phases of the menstrual cycle', *Bulletin of the Psychonomic Society* 23, 119–125.

Schering Corporation (1941) *Female Sex Hormone Therapy. Part 2: Corpus Luteum Hormone*, Bloomfield NJ: The Schering Corporation.

Schmidt, P., Nieman, L., Grover, G., Muller, K., Merriam, G. and Rubinow, D. (1991) 'Lack of effect of induced menses on symptoms in women with premenstrual syndrome', *New England Journal of Medicine* 324, 1174–1179.

Schmidt, P., Grover, G. and Rubinow, D. (1993) 'Alprazolam in the treatment of premenstrual syndrome', *Archives of General Psychiatry* 50, 467–473.

Schmidt, P., Purdy, R., Moore, P., Paul, S., and Rubinow, D. (1994) 'Circulating levels of anxiolytic steroids in the luteal phase in women with premenstrual syndrome and in control subjects', *Journal of Clinical Endocrinology and Metabolism* 79, 1256–1260.

Schneider, J. (1985) 'Social problems theory: the constructionist view', *Annual Review of Sociology* 11, 209–229.

Schneider, J. and Schneider-Düker, M. (1974) 'Conservative attitudes and reactions to menstruation', *Psychological Reports* 35, 1304.

Schnurr, P. (1988) 'Some correlates of prospectively defined premenstrual syndrome', *American Journal of Psychiatry* 145, 491–494.

——(1989) 'Measuring amount of symptom change in the diagnosis of premenstrual syndrome', *Psychological Assessment* 1, 277–283.

Schnurr, P., Hurt, S. and Stout, A. (1994) 'Consequences of methodological decisions in the diagnosis of late luteal phase dysphoric disorder', in J. Gold and S. Severino (eds) *Premenstrual Dysphorias: Myths and Realities*, Washington DC: American Psychiatric Press.

Schofield, A. (1919) *The Mind of a Woman*, London: Methuen.

Schreiner-Engel, P. (1980) 'Female sexual arousability: its relation to gonadal hormones and the menstrual cycle', *Dissertation Abstracts International* 41, 02: 527.

Schreiner-Engel, P., Schiavi, R., Smith, H. and White, D. (1981) 'Sexual arousability and the menstrual cycle', *Psychosomatic Medicine* 43, 199–214.

Schreiner-Engel, P., Schiavi, R., White, D. and Ghizzani, A. (1989) 'Low sexual desire in women: the role of reproductive hormones', *Hormones and Behaviour* 23, 221–234.

Schubert, G., Meyer, R. and Washer, S. (1975) 'Responses to short duration signals, pre and post menses, in subjects using oral contraceptive and subjects not using oral contraceptive', *Journal of the American Audiology Society* 1, 112–118.

Schuckit, M., Daly, V., Herrman, G. and Hineman, S. (1975) 'Premenstrual symptoms and depression in a university population', *Diseases of the Nervous System* 36, 516–517.

Severino, S. (1988) 'Defining late luteal phase dysphoric disorder', *American Journal of Psychiatry* 145, 132–133 (letter).

——(1993) 'Late luteal phase dysphoric disorder: a scientific puzzle', *Medical Hypotheses* 41, 229–234.

——(1994) 'A focus on 5-hydroxytryptamine (serotionin) and psychopathology', in J. Gold and S. Severino (eds) *Premenstrual Dysphorias: Myths and Realities*, Washington DC: American Psychiatric Press.

Severino, S. and Gold, J. (1994) 'Summation', in J. Gold and S. Severino (eds) *Premenstrual Dysphorias: Myths and Realities*, Washington DC: American Psychiatric Press.

Severino, S. and Moline, M. (1995) 'Premenstrual syndrome: identification and management', *Drugs* 49, 71–82.

Severino, S. and Yonkers, K. (1993) 'A literature review of psychotic symptoms associated with the premenstruum', *Psychosomatics* 34, 299–306.

Severy, L., Thapa, S., Askew, I. and Glor, J. (1993) 'Menstrual experiences and beliefs: a multicountry study of relationships with fertility and fertility regulating methods', *Women and Health* 20, 1–20.

Seward, G. (1934) 'The female sex rhythm', *Psychological Bulletin* 31, 153–192.

——(1944) 'Psychological effects of the menstrual cycle on women workers', *Psychological Bulletin* 41, 90–102.

Shainess, N. (1961) 'A re-evaluation of some aspects of femininity through a study of menstruation', *Comprehensive Psychiatry* 2, 20–26.

Shangold, M. (1985) 'Exercise and amenorrhea', *Seminars in Reproductive Endocrinology* 3, 35–43.

Shangold, M., Freeman, R., Thysen, B. and Gatz, M. (1979) 'The relationship between long distance running, plasma progesterone and luteal phase length', *Fertility and Sterility* 31, 130–133.

Sheldrake, P. and Cormack, M. (1976) 'Variations in menstrual cycle symptom reporting', *Journal of Psychosomatic Research* 20, 169–177.

Sherif, C. (1980) 'A social psychological perspective on the menstrual cycle', in J.C. Parsons (ed.) *The Psychobiology of Sex Differences and Sex Roles*, Washington: Hemisphere.

Sherman, J. (1971) *On the Psychology of Women: A Survey of Empirical Studies*, Springfield Ill: Charles C. Thomas.

Short, R.V. (1984) 'Oestrus and menstrual cycles', in C. Austin and R. Short (eds) *The Hormonal Control of Reproduction*, 2nd edn, Cambridge: Cambridge University Press.

Shorter, E. (1983) *A History of Women's Bodies*, London: Allen Lane.

Showalter, E. (1987) *The Female Malady: Women, Madness and English Culture, 1830–1980*, London: Virago.

——(1992) *Sexual Anarchy: Gender and Culture at the Fin de Siècle*, London: Virago.

Showalter, E. and Showalter, E. (1970) 'Victorian women and menstruation', *Victorian Studies* 14, 83–89.

Shuttle, P. and Redgrove, P. (1986) *The Wise Wound: Menstruation and Everywoman*, revised edition, London: Paladin Grafton Books (original edition published 1978).

Shuttleworth , S. (1990) 'Female circulation: medical discourse and popular advertising in the mid-Victorian era', in M. Jacobus, E. Fox Keller and S. Shuttleworth (eds) *Body/Politics: Women and the Discourses of Science*, London: Routledge.

Silbergeld, S., Brast, N. and Noble, E. (1971) 'The menstrual cycle: a double-blind study of symptoms, mood and behaviour and biochemical variables using Enovid and placebo', *Psychosomatic Medicine* 33, 411–428.

Silverman, L.K. (1992) 'Leta Stetter Hollingworth: champion of the psychology of women and gifted children', *Journal of Educational Psychology* 84, 20–27.

Simmer, H.H. (1977) 'Pflüger's nerve reflex theory of menstruation: the product of analogy, teleology and neurophysiology', *Clio Medica* 12, 57–90.

Singh, E., Baccarini, I. and Zuspan, F. (1975) 'Levels of prostaglandins F2α and E2 in human endometrium during the menstrual cycle', *American Journal of Obstetrics and Gynecology* 121, 1003–1006.

Skultans, V. (1970) 'The symbolic significance of menstruation and menopause', *Man* 5, 639–651.

——(1975) *Madness and Morals: Ideas on Insanity in the Nineteenth Century*, London: Routledge and Kegan Paul.

Slade, P. (1984) 'Premenstrual emotional changes in normal women: fact or fiction?', *Journal of Psychosomatic Research* 28, 1–7.

——(1988) 'Letter to the editor', *Journal of Psychosomatic Research* 32, 117–118.

——(1989) 'Psychological therapy for premenstrual syndrome', *Behavioural Psychotherapy* 17, 135–150.

Slade, P. and Jenner, F. (1979) 'Autonomic activity in subjects reporting changes in affect in the menstrual cycle', *British Journal of Social and Clinical Psychology* 18, 135–136.

——(1980) 'Attitudes to female roles, aspects of menstruation and complaining of menstrual symptoms', *British Journal of Social and Clinical Psychology* 19, 109–113.

Smith, A. (1950a) 'Menstruation and industrial efficiency. I: Absenteeism and activity level', *Journal of Applied Psychology* 34, 1–5.

——(1950b) 'Menstruation and industrial efficiency. II: Quality and quantity of production', *Journal of Applied Psychology* 34, 148–152.

Smith, J., Harré, R. and van Langenhove, L. (eds) (1995) *Rethinking Psychology*, London: Sage.

Smith, O. and Smith, G. (1950) 'Menstrual toxin', in E. Engle (ed.) *Menstruation and its Disorders*, Springfield Ill: Charles C. Thomas.

Smith, R. (1981) *Trial by Medicine: Insanity and Responsibility in Victorian Trials*, Edinburgh: Edinburgh University Press.

Smith, R., Studd, J., Zamblera, D. and Holland, E. (1995) 'A randomised comparison over 8 months of 100μg and 200μg twice weekly doses of transdermal oestradiol in the treatment of severe premenstrual syndrome', *British Journal of Obstetrics and Gynaecology* 102, 475–484.

Smith, S. and Schiff, I. (1989) 'The premenstrual syndrome – diagnosis and management', *Fertility and Sterility* 52, 527–543.

Smith, W. Tyler (1847) 'Introductory lecture to a course of lectures on obstetrics, delivered at the Hunterian School of Medicine', *The Lancet* ii, 371–544.

Smith Rosenberg, C. and Rosenberg, C. (1973) 'The female animal: medical and biological views of woman and her role in the nineteenth century', *Journal of American History* 60, 332–356.

Smolensky, M. (1980) 'Chronobiologic considerations in the investigation and interpretation of circamensual rhythms in women', in A. Dan, E. Graham and C. Beecher (eds) *The Menstrual Cycle. Volume 1: A Synthesis of Interdisciplinary Research*, New York: Springer.

Snow, L. and Johnson, S. (1977) 'Modern day menstrual folklore: some clinical implications', *Journal of the American Medical Association* 237, 2736–2739.

Snowden, R. and Christian, B. (1983) *Patterns and Perceptions of Menstruation*, Beckenham, Kent: Croom Helm Ltd.

Solbach, P. (1992) 'Menstrual migraine headache', in A. Dan and L. Lewis (eds) *Menstrual Health in Women's Lives*, Urbana, University of Illinois Press.

Solbach, P., Sargent, J., Coyne, L., Malone, L. and Simons, A. (1988) 'Tension headache: a comparison of menstrual and non-menstrual occurrences', *Headache* 28, 108–110.

Solbach, P., Coyne, L. and Sargent, J. (1991) 'A study of headache intensity and disability with the menstrual cycle', in D. Taylor and N. Woods (eds) *Menstruation, Health and Illness*, New York: Hemisphere.

Solis-Ortiz, S., Ramos, J., Arce, C. and Guevera, M. (1994) 'EEG oscillations during the menstrual cycle', *International Journal of Neuroscience* 76, 279–292.

Sollberger, A. (1965) *Biological Rhythm Research*, Amsterdam: Elsevier.

Somerville, B. (1972) 'The role of estradiol withdrawal in etiology of menstrual migraine', *Neurology* 22, 355.

——(1975) 'Estrogen-withdrawal migraine. I. Duration of exposure required and attempted prophylaxis by premenstrual estrogen administration', *Neurology* 25, 239–244.

Sommer, B.(1972) 'Menstrual cycle changes and intellectual performance', *Psychosomatic Medicine* 34, 263–269.

——(1973) 'The effect of menstruation on cognitive and perceptual-motor performance: a review', *Psychosomatic Medicine* 35, 515–534.

——(1982) 'Cognitive behaviour and the menstrual cycle', in R. Friedman (ed.) *Behaviour and the Menstrual Cycle*, New York: Marcel Dekker.

——(1983) 'How does menstruation affect cognitive competence and physiological response?', *Women and Health* 8, 53–90.

——(1992) 'Cognitive performance and the menstrual cycle', in J. Richardson (ed.) *Cognition and the Menstrual Cycle*, New York: Springer-Verlag.

Soranus of Ephesus (1956) *Soranus's Gynaecology*, translated by O. Temkin, Baltimore: Johns Hopkins Press.

Sowton, S., Myers, C. and Bedale, E. (1928) *Two contributions to the experimental study of the menstrual cycle. I. Its influence on mental and muscular efficiency. II. Its relation to general functional efficiency*, Report of the Industrial Fatigue Research Board, 45: Her Majesty's Stationery Office.

Spallone, P. (1994) 'Reproductive health and reproductive technology', in S. Wilkinson and C. Kitzinger (eds) *Women and Health: Feminist Perspectives*, London: Taylor and Francis.

Spencer-Gardner, C., Dennerstein, L. and Burrows, G. (1983) 'Premenstrual tension and female role', *Journal of Psychosomatic Obstetrics and Gynaecology* 2, 27–34.

Spender, D. (1980) *Man Made Language*, London: Routledge.

——(1982) *Women of Ideas and What Men Have Done to Them: From Aphra Behn to Adrienne Rich*, London: Routledge and Kegan Paul.

Speroff, L., Keye, W. and Steege, J. (1984) 'Helping your patients with PMS', *Contemporary Obstetrics and Gynaecology* 23, 165–192

Spielberger, C., Gorsuch, R. and Lushene, R.(1970) *Manual for the State-Trait Anxiety Inventory*, Palo Alto CA: Consulting Psychologists Press.

Stainton-Rogers, W. (1991) *Explaining Health and Illness: An Exploration of Diversity*, Hemel Hempstead: Harvester Wheatsheaf.

Stam, H. (1996) 'Introduction: the body's psychology and psychology's body', *Theory and Psychology* 6, 555–558.

Stanczyk, F., Miyakawa, I. and Goebelsmann, U. (1980) 'Direct radioimmunoassay of urinary oestrogen and pregnanediol glucuronides during the menstrual cycle', *American Journal of Obstetrics and Gynecology* 137, 443–450.

Stanley, L. and Wise, S. (1983) *Breaking Out: Feminist Consciousness and Feminist Research*, London: Routledge.

Steele, P., White, G. and Judd, S. (1985) 'Reliability of a single serum progesterone determination as an indicator of ovulation', *Clinical Reproduction and Fertility* 3, 125–130.

Steele, P., Braund, W. and Judd, S. (1986) 'Regulation of pulsatile secretion of progesterone during the human luteal phase', *Clinical Reproduction and Fertility* 4, 117–124.

Steiner, M.(1992) 'Female-specific mood disorders', *Clinical Obstetrics and Gynaecology* 35, 599–611.

Steiner, M. and Carroll, B. (1977) 'The psychobiology of premenstrual dysphoria: review of theories and treatments', *Psychoneuroendocrinology* 2, 321–335.

Steiner, M., Haskett, R. and Carroll, B. (1980) 'Premenstrual tension syndrome: the development of research diagnostic criteria and new rating scales', *Acta Psychiatrica Scandinavica* 62, 177–190.

Steiner, M., Steinburg, S., Stewart, D., Carter, D., Berger, C., Reid, R., Grover, D. and Streiner, D. (1995) 'Fluoxetine in the treatment of premenstrual dysphoria', *New England Journal of Medicine* 332, 1529–1534.

REFERENCES

Stephens, W. (1961) 'A cross-cultural study of menstrual taboos', *Genetic Psychology Monographs* 64, 385–416.

Stephenson, L., Denney, D. and Aberger, E.(1983) 'Factor structure of the menstrual symptom questionnaire: relationship to oral contraceptives, neuroticism and life stress', *Behaviour Research and Therapy* 21: 129–135.

Stewart, D. (1989) 'Positive changes in the premenstrual period', *Acta Psychiatrica Scandinavica* 79, 400–405.

Stoltzman, S. (1986) 'Menstrual attitudes, beliefs and symptom experiences of adolescent females, their peers and their mothers', *Health Care for Women International* 7, 97–114.

Stonehouse, J. (1994) *Idols to Incubators: Reproduction Theory Through the Ages*, London: Scarlet Press.

Stoney, C., Owens, J., Matthews, K., Davis, M. and Caggiula, A.(1990) 'Influences of the normal menstrual cycle on physiologic functioning during behavioural stress', *Psychophysiology* 27, 125–135.

Stopes, M. (1918) *Married Love*, London: G.P. Putnam's Sons.

——(1923) *Contraception: Theory, History and Practice*, London: G.P. Putnam's Sons.

Stoppard, J. (1992) 'A suitable case for treatment? Premenstrual syndrome and the medicalization of women's bodies', in D. Currie and V. Raoul (eds) *The Anatomy of Gender: Women's Struggle for the Body*, Ottawa: Carleton University Press.

Stotland, N. and Harwood, B. (1994) 'Social, political and legal considerations', in J. Gold and S. Severino (eds) *Premenstrual Dysphorias: Myths and Realities*, Washington DC: American Psychiatric Press.

Stout, A. (1995) 'Cognitive-behavioural treatment of premenstrual syndrome and chronic gynecologic pain', *Depression* 3, 60–65.

Strassman, B. (1996) 'The evolution of endometrial cycles and menstruation', *Quarterly Review of Biology* 71, 181–220.

Strauss, B., Appelt, H. and Lange, C. (1987) 'Deutsche Neukonstruktion und Validierung des "Menstrual Attitude Questionnaire"', *Psychotherap. med. Psychol.* 37, 175–182.

Strauss, B., Appelt, H., Daub, U. and de Vries, I.(1990) 'Generationsunterschied im Menstruationserleben und in der Einstellung zur Menstruation', *Psychother. med. Psychol.* 40, 48–56.

Stroebe, W. and Stroebe, M. (1995) *Social Psychology and Health*, Buckingham: Open University Press.

Sulloway, F. (1980) *Freud, Biologist of the Mind: Beyond the Psychoanalytic Legend*, London: Fontana.

Sussman, L. (1993) 'The PMS myth', *New Woman* June 1993, 12–14.

Sutton, I. (1989) 'Introduction', in P. Forster and I. Sutton (eds) *Daughters of de Beauvoir*, London: The Women's Press.

Sveinsdottir, H. and Reame, N. (1991) 'Symptom patterns in women with premenstrual syndrome complaints: a prospective assessment using a marker for ovulation and screening criteria for adequate ovarian function', *Journal of Advanced Nursing* 16, 689–700.

Swandby, J. (1981) 'A longitudinal study of daily mood self reports and their relationship to the menstrual cycle', in P. Komnenich, M. McSweeney, J. Noack and S. Elder (eds) *The Menstrual Cycle: Volume II. Research and Implications for Women's Health*, New York: Springer.

Swann, C. and Ussher, J. (1995) 'A discourse analytic approach to women's experience of premenstrual syndrome', *Journal of Mental Health* 4, 359–369.

Swanson, S. and Dengerink, H. (1988) 'Changes in pure-tone thresholds and temporary threshold shifts as a function of menstrual cycle and oral contraceptives', *Journal of Speech and Hearing Research* 31, 569–574.

REFERENCES

Szekely, B., Botwin, D., Eidelman, B., Becker, M., Elman, N. and Schemm, R. (1986) 'Nonpharmacological treatment of menstrual headache: relaxation-biofeedback therapy and person-centered insight therapy', *Headache* 26, 86–92.

Tauboll, E., Lundervold, A. and Gjerstad, L. (1991) 'Temporal distribution of seizures in epilepsy', *Epilepsy Research* 8, 153–165.

Tavris, C. (1992) *The Mismeasure of Woman*, New York: Touchstone.

Taylor, Dena (1988) *Red Flower: Rethinking Menstruation*, Freedom CA: The Crossing Press.

Taylor, Diana (1994) 'Evaluating therapeutic change in symptom severity at the level of the individual woman experiencing severe PMS', *IMAGE: the Journal of Nursing Scholarship* 26, 25–33.

Taylor, Diana and Woods, N.F. (eds) (1991) *Menstruation, Health and Illness*, New York: Hemisphere.

Taylor, J. (1979) 'The timing of menstruation related symptoms assessed by a daily symptom rating scale', *Acta Psychiatrica Scandinavica* 60, 87–105.

Taylor, R., Alexander, D. and Fordyce, I. (1986) 'A survey of paramenstrual complaints by overt and by covert methods', *Journal of the Royal College of General Practitioners* 36 496–499.

Taylor, R., Fordyce, I. and Alexander, D. (1991) 'Relationship between personality and premenstrual symptoms: a study in five general practices', *British Journal of General Practice* 41, 55–57.

Tersman, Z., Collins, A. and Eneroth, P. (1991) 'Cardiovascular responses to psychological and physiological stressors during the menstrual cycle', *Psychosomatic Medicine* 53, 185–190.

Than, T., Delay, E. and Maier, M. (1994) 'Sucrose threshold variation during the menstrual cycle', *Physiology and Behaviour* 56, 237–239.

Thayer, R. (1967) 'Measurement of activation through self-report', *Psychological Reports* 22, 663–678.

——(1989) *The Biopsychology of Mood and Arousal*, Oxford: Oxford University Press.

Timonen, S. and Procope, B. (1971) 'Premenstrual syndrome and exercise', *Acta Obstetrica et Gynecologica Scandinavica* 50, 331–333.

Tobias, J. (1965) 'Consistency of sex differences in binaural-beat perception', *International Audiology* 4, 179–182.

Tollan, A., Qian, P., Fadnes, H. and Maltau, J. (1993) 'Evidence for altered transcapillary fluid balance in women with premenstrual syndrome', *Acta Obstetrica et Gynecologica Scandinavica* 72, 238–242.

Tomalin, C. (1977) *The Life and Death of Mary Wollstonecraft*, London: Penguin.

Treloar, A., Boynton, R., Benn, B. and Brown, B. (1967) 'Variation of the human menstrual cycle through reproductive life', *International Journal of Fertility* 12, 77–126.

Treneman, A. (1988) 'Cashing in on the curse: advertising and the menstrual taboo', in L. Gamman and M. Marshment (eds) *The Female Gaze: Women as Viewers of Popular Culture*, London: The Women's Press.

Trunnell, E., Turner, C. and Keye, W. (1988) 'A comparison of the psychological and hormonal factors in women with and without premenstrual syndrome', *Journal of Abnormal Psychology* 97, 429–436.

Uno, T. (1972) 'GSR activity and the human menstrual cycle', *Psychophysiology* 10, 213–214.

Ussher, J. (1989) *The Psychology of the Female Body*, London: Routledge.

——(1991) *Women's Madness: Misogyny or Mental Illness?*, Hemel Hempstead: Harvester Wheatsheaf.

——(1992a) 'Research and theory related to female reproduction: implications for clinical psychology', *British Journal of Clinical Psychology* 31, 129–151.

241

——(1992b) 'The demise of dissent and the rise of cognition in menstrual cycle research', in J. Richardson (ed.) *Cognition and the Menstrual Cycle*, New York: Springer-Verlag.

——(1996) 'Female Sexuality', in C. A. Niven and A. Walker (eds) *The Psychology of Reproduction. 1: Reproductive Potential and Fertility Control*, Oxford: Butterworth-Heinemann.

Ussher, J. and Baker, C. (eds) (1993) *Psychological Perspectives on Sexual Problems*, London: Routledge.

Ussher, J. and Wilding, J. (1991) 'Performance and state changes during the menstrual cycle, conceptualised within a broad band testing framework', *Social Science and Medicine* 5, 525–534.

van den Akker, O. and Steptoe, A. (1985) 'The pattern and prevalence of symptoms during the menstrual cycle', *British Journal of Psychiatry* 147, 164–169.

van den Akker, O., Sharifian, N., Packer, A. and Eves, F. (1995a) 'Contribution of generalized negative affect to elevated menstrual cycle symptom reporting', *Health Care for Women International* 16, 263–272.

van den Akker, O., Eves, F., Service, S. and Lennon, B. (1995b) 'Menstrual cycle symptom reporting in three British ethnic groups', *Social Science and Medicine* 40, 1417–1423.

Vander, A., Sherman, J., and Luciano, D. (1980) *Human Physiology: The Mechanisms of Body Function* , 3rd edn, New York: McGraw Hill.

van der Meer, Y., Benedek-Jaszmann, L. and van Loenen, A. (1983) 'Effect of high dose progesterone on the premenstrual syndrome: a double-blind crossover trial', *Journal of Psychosomatic Obstetrics and Gynaecology* 2, 220–222.

van der Ploeg, H. (1987) 'Emotional states and the premenstrual syndrome', *Personality and Individual Differences* 8, 95–100.

van Heerington, K., Ducheyne, P., Schollaert, P., Verheyen, R., Goethals, K. and Jannes, S. (1995) 'The risk of seclusion and the menstrual cycle in female psychiatric patients', *Journal of Psychosomatic Research* 39, 629–632.

Varney, W. (1944) 'Medical management of complaints of women in the explosives industry', *Industrial Medicine* 13, 122–124.

Veeninga, A. and Westenburg, H.(1992) 'Serotonergic function and late luteal phase dysphoric disorder', *Psychopharmacology* 108, 153–158.

Veeninga, A., Westenberg, H. and Weusten, J. (1990) 'Fluvoxamine in the treatment of menstrually related mood disorders', *Psychopharmacology* 102, 414–416.

Veith, J., Buck, M., Getzlaf, S., van Dalfsen, P. and Slade, S. (1983) 'Exposure to men influences the occurrence of ovulation in women', *Physiology and Behaviour* 31, 313–331.

Veldhuis, J., Christiansen, E., Evans, W., Kolp, L., Rogol, A. and Johnson, M. (1988) 'Physiological profiles of episodic progesterone release during the midluteal phase of the human menstrual cycle: analysis of circadian and ultradian rhythms, discrete pulse properties and correlations with simultaneous luteinizing hormone release', *Journal of Clinical Endocrinology and Metabolism* 66, 414–421.

Vellacott, I. and O'Brien, P. (1988) 'Premenstrual stress', *Stress Medicine* 4, 33–40.

Vertinsky, P. (1990) *The Eternally Wounded Woman: Women, Exercise and Doctors in the Late Nineteenth Century*, Manchester: Manchester University Press.

Vicinus, M. (1972) *Suffer and Be Still: Women in the Victorian Age*, Indiana: Indiana University Press.

Vierling, J. and Rock, J. (1967) 'Variations in olfactory sensitivity to exaltolide during the menstrual cycle', *Journal of Applied Physiology* 22, 311–315.

Vila, J. and Beech, H. (1980) 'Premenstrual symptomatology: an interaction hypothesis', *British Journal of Social and Clinical Psychology* 9, 73–80.

Voda, A. (1980) 'Pattern of progesterone and aldosterone in ovulating women during the menstrual cycle', in A. Dan, E. Graham and C. Beecher (eds) *The Menstrual Cycle. Volume 1: A Synthesis of Interdisciplinary Research*, New York: Springer.

REFERENCES

Voda, A., Morgan, J., Root, J. and Smith, K. (1991) 'The Tremin Trust: An intergenerational research program on events associated with women's menstrual and reproductive lives', in D.L. Taylor and N.F. Woods (eds) *Menstruation, Health and Illness*, New York: Hemisphere.

Vollman, R. (1977) *The Menstrual Cycle*, Philadelphia PA: W.B. Saunders Co.

Walker, A. (1988) 'The relationship between premenstrual symptoms and the ovarian cycle', unpublished PhD thesis, University of Edinburgh.

——(1992a) 'Premenstrual symptoms and ovarian hormones: a review', *Journal of Reproductive and Infant Psychology* 10, 67–82.

——(1992b) 'Men's and women's beliefs about the influence of the menstrual cycle on academic performance: a preliminary study', *Journal of Applied Social Psychology* 22, 896–909.

——(1994a) 'Mood and well-being in consecutive menstrual cycles: methodological and theoretical implications', *Psychology of Women Quarterly* 18, 271–290.

——(1994b) ' "It's just the time of the month . . . ": the social acceptability of menstrual attributions and its significance for symptom reporting', *Proceedings of the British Psychological Society* 2 (2), 64.

——(1995a) 'Theory and methodology in premenstrual syndrome research', *Social Science and Medicine* 41, 793–800.

——(1995b) 'Premenstrual syndrome: mind, body or media construction?', *Proceedings of the British Psychological Society* 3, 134.

Walker, A. and Bancroft, J. (1990) 'Relationship between premenstrual symptoms and oral contraceptive use: a controlled study', *Psychosomatic Medicine* 52, 86–96.

Walker, B. (1983) *The Woman's Encyclopaedia of Myths and Secrets*, San Francisco: Harper and Row.

Walsh, R., Budtz-Olsen, I., Leader, C. and Cummins, R. (1981) 'The menstrual cycle, personality and academic performance', *Archives of General Psychiatry* 38, 219–221.

Walton, J. and Youngkin, E. (1987) 'The effect of a support group on self-esteem of women with premenstrual syndrome', *Journal of Obstetric, Gynecological and Neonatal Nursing* 16, 174–178.

Ward, M., Stone, S. and Sandman, C. (1978) 'Visual perception in women during the menstrual cycle', *Physiology and Behaviour* 20, 239–243.

Warner, P. (1994) 'Preferences regarding treatments for period problems: relationship to menstrual and demographic factors', *Journal of Psychosomatic Obstetrics and Gynaecology* 15, 93–110.

Warner, P. and Bancroft, J. (1988) 'Mood, sexuality, oral contraceptives and the menstrual cycle', *Journal of Psychosomatic Research* 32, 417–429.

——(1990) 'Factors relating to self reporting of the premenstrual syndrome', *British Journal of Psychiatry* 157, 249–260.

Warner, P., Bancroft, J., Dixson, A. and Hampson, M. (1991) 'The relationship between perimenstrual depressive mood and depressive illness', *Journal of Affective Disorders* 23, 9–23.

Warren, D., Tedford, W. and Flynn, W. (1979) 'Behavioural effects of cyclic changes in serotonin during the human menstrual cycle', *Medical Hypotheses* 5, 359–364.

Watson, D. and Pennebaker, J. (1989) 'Health complaints, stress and distress: exploring the central role of negative affectivity', *Psychological Review* 96, 234–254.

Watson, N., Savvas, M., Studd, J., Garnett, T. and Barber, R. (1989) 'Treatment of severe premenstrual syndrome with oestradiol patches and cyclical oral norethisterone', *The Lancet* 2, 730–732.

Watts, J., Butt, W. and Logan Edwards, R. (1985) 'Hormonal studies in women with premenstrual tension', *British Journal of Obstetrics and Gynaecology* 92, 247–255.

REFERENCES

Webster, S. (1980) 'Problems for diagnosis of spasmodic and congestive dysmenorrhea', in A. Dan, E. Graham and C. Beecher (eds). *The Menstrual Cycle. Volume 1: A Synthesis of Interdisciplinary Research*, New York: Springer.

Webster, S., Martin, H., Uchalik, D. and Gannon, L. (1979) 'The menstrual symptom questionnaire and spasmodic/ congestive dysmenorrhea: measurement of an invalid concept', *Journal of Behavioural Medicine* 2, 1–19.

Weideger, P. (1976) *Menstruation and Menopause: The Physiology, the Psychology, the Myth and the Reality*, New York: Alfred A. Knopf. Published in the UK in 1978 as *Female Cycles*, London: The Women's Press.

——(1985) *History's Mistress: A New Interpretation of a 19th Century Ethnographic Classic*, Harmondsworth: Penguin.

Weininger, O. (1906) *Sex and Character*, London: William Heinemann.

Weller, A. and Weller, L. (1993) 'Human menstrual synchrony: a critical assessment', *Neuroscience and Biobehavioural Reviews* 17, 427–437.

——(1995a) 'The impact of social interaction factors on menstrual synchrony in the workplace', *Psychoneuroendocrinology* 20, 21–31.

——(1995b) 'Menstrual synchrony: agenda for future research', *Psychoneuroendocrinology* 20, 377–383.

Wells, J., Metcalf, M.G. and Livesey, J. (1989) 'The use of combined scores in studying the premenstrual syndrome: does it clarify or muddy the picture?', *Journal of Psychosomatic Obstetrics and Gynaecology* 10, 129–138.

Wetzel, R. and McClure, J. (1972) 'Suicide and the menstrual cycle: a review', *Comprehensive Psychiatry* 13, 369–374.

Wetzel, R., Reich, T. and McClure, J. (1971a) 'Phase of the menstrual cycle and self referrals to a suicide prevention service', *British Journal of Psychiatry* 119, 523–524.

Wetzel, R., McClure, J. and Reich, T. (1971b) 'Premenstrual symptoms in self referrals to a suicide prevention service', *British Journal of Psychiatry* 119, 525–526.

Wetzel, R., Reich, T., McClure, J. and Wald, J. (1975) 'Premenstrual affective syndrome and affective disorder', *British Journal of Psychiatry* 127, 219–221.

Whitehead, W., Busch, C., Heller, B. and Costa, P. (1986) 'Social learning influences on menstrual symptoms and illness behaviour', *Health Psychology* 5, 13–23.

WHO (1992) *The ICD-10 Classification of Mental and Behavioural Disorders: Clinical Descriptions and Diagnostic Guidelines*, Geneva, Switzerland: WHO.

WHO Task Force (1981) 'A cross-cultural study of menstruation: implications for contraceptive development and use', *Studies in Family Planning* 12, 3–16.

Widholm, O. and Kantero, R. (1971) 'A statistical analysis of the menstrual patterns of 8,000 Finnish girls and their mothers', *Acta Obs. and Gyn. Scand.* 50, Suppl. 14.

Wilcoxon, L., Schrader, S. and Sherif, C. (1976) 'Daily self reports on activities, life events, mood and somatic changes during the menstrual cycle', *Psychosomatic Medicine* 38, 399–417.

Wilson, H. (1992) 'A critical review of menstrual synchrony research', *Psychoneuroendocrinology* 17, 565–591.

Wilson, H., Kiefphaber, S. and Gravel, V. (1991) 'Two studies of menstrual synchrony: negative results', *Psychoneuroendocrinology* 16, 353–359.

Wineman, E. (1971) 'Autonomic balance changes during the human menstrual cycle', *Psychophysiology* 8, 1–6.

Wong, S. and Tong, J. (1974) 'Menstrual cycle and contraceptive hormonal effects on temporal discrimination', *Perceptual and Motor Skills* 39, 103–108.

Wood, A. (1973–1974) 'The fashionable diseases: women's complaints and their treatment in nineteenth-century America', *Journal of Interdisciplinary History* 4, 25–52.

Wood, C. and Suitters, B. (1970) *The Fight for Acceptance: A History of Contraception*, Aylesbury: MTP.

REFERENCES

Wood, S., Mortola, J., Chan, Y.-F., Moossazadeh, F. and Yen, S. (1992) 'Treatment of premenstrual syndrome with fluoxetine: a double-blind placebo controlled crossover study', *Obstetrics and Gynecology* 80, 339–344.

Woods, N., Most, A. and Dery, G. (1982) 'Prevalence of perimenstrual symptoms', *American Journal of Public Health* 72, 1257–1264.

Woods, N., Lentz, M., Mitchell, E. and Kogan, H. (1994) 'Arousal and stress response across the menstrual cycle in women with three perimenstrual symptom patterns', *Research in Nursing and Health* 17, 99–110.

Woods, N., Mitchell, E. and Lentz, M. (1995) 'Social pathways to premenstrual symptoms', *Research in Nursing and Health* 18, 225–237.

Woollett, A. and Marshall, H. (1996) 'Reading the body: young women's accounts of the meanings of the body in relation to independence, responsibility and maturity', *European Journal of Women's Studies* 3, 199–214.

Wright, P. and Crow, R. (1973) 'Menstrual cycle: Effects on sweetness preferences in women', *Hormones and Behaviour* 4, 387–391.

Wuttke, W., Arnold, P., Becker, D., Creuzfeldt, O., Langenstein, S. and Tirsch, W. (1975) 'Circulating hormones, EEG and performance in psychological tests of women, with and without oral contraceptives', *Psychoneuroendocrinology* 1, 141–152.

Youdale, J. and Freeman, R. (1987) 'Premenstrual Assessment Form typological categories: classification of self defined premenstrually symptomatic and asymptomatic women', *Journal of Consulting and Clinical Psychology* 55, 418–422.

Younglai, E., Smith, S., Cleghorn, J. and Streiner, D. (1975) 'Variations in ovarian steroid levels during the luteal phase of the menstrual cycle', *Clinical Biochemistry* 8, 234–238.

Yuk, V., Jugdutt, A., Cumming, C., Fox, E. and Cumming, D. (1990) 'Towards a definition of PMS: a factor analytic evaluation of premenstrual change in non-complaining women', *Journal of Psychosomatic Research* 34, 439–446.

Zaharieva, E. (1965) 'Survey of sportswomen at the Tokyo Olympics', *Journal of Sports Medicine and Physical Fitness* 5, 215–219.

Zborowski, M. (1952) 'Cultural components in responses to pain', *Journal of Social Issues* 8, 16–30.

Zealley, A. and Aitken, R. (1969) 'Measurement of mood', *Proceedings of the Royal Society of Medicine* 62, 993–996.

Zimmerman, E. and Parlee, M. (1973) 'Behavioural changes associated with the menstrual cycle: an experimental investigation', *Journal of Applied Social Psychology* 3, 335–344.

Zondek, B. (1953) 'Does menstrual blood contain a specific toxin?', *American Journal of Obstetrics and Gynecology* 65, 1065.

Zuckerman, M. and Lubin, B. (1965) *Manual for the Multiple Affect Adjective Check List*, San Diego CA: Education and Industrial Testing Services.

INDEX

menstruation 191–5; assumptions in
research 182–3; attitudes towards
menstruation 106–13; behavioural
studies 125–31; biological rhythm
theory 184–5; biosocial models 187–8;
cognition 113–14; concentration on
uterus and ovaries 33–5; cyclical
fluctuation in cognition 89–91;
disordered menstruation and madness
30, 35–7; empirical research 40–2;
feminist approaches 192, 193–4; first
ideas about PMT 50; humans as
passive or active agents 84–5;
interactional models 186–7; nervous
system studies 98–100; postmodern
approach 194; psychosocial treatment
for PMS 156–7; the question of
women's character 30–3; sensory
processes 94–8; social cognitions 100–1;
trait theories 183–4; wartimes and post-
war research 45–51; *see also*
methodology
puberty rites 22

*The Question of Rest for Women During
Menstruation* (Jacobi) 43–4

Raciborski, A. 17
radioimmunoassay (RIA) 79
Rakusen, J. *Our Bodies, Ourselves* (with
Phillips) 52
Ramcharan, S. 130–1
Reading, A. 186
Red Flower: Rethinking Menstruation (Taylor) 5
Redgrove, J. 93
Redgrove, Peter 14, 21, 22
religion: attitudes 107–8; introduction of
calendar 14; taboos and fear of
menstruation 19–20, 27
remedies and treatments 26; hormones 49;
for irregularity 36–7; leeches, injections
and cauterisation 33–4
research: challenging negative views 57;
feminist standpoint 85–6; nineteenth
century 'science of woman' 42–3; types
of 40–2; wartimes and post-war 45–51
Reynolds, Anna 165, 171–2
rhythm and time 12–15; biological rhythm
theory 52–3, 184–5; cycles in health 50;
link with moon 13–14; oestrus 17;
synchrony of women 12
Richardson, John T. E. 65, 92, 93

Ripper, M. 124
Rittenhouse, C. A. 164–5, 187
Rivera-Tovar, A. 156
Robinson, J. 97
Rodin, Mari 161, 162–3, 170
Royal College of Obstetricians and
Gynaecologists 149
Rubenstein, B. 61
Rubinow, D. 159
Ruble, Diane 62, 100, 161; behavioural
studies 128, 129; dysmenorrhea 138;
Menstrual Attitudes Questionnaire 69,
107, 108–9; social cognition 185
Rupani, N. 161
Ryan, Michael *A Manual of Midwifery* 24

Sagan, Miriam 5–6
Salmon, Peter 127–8, 133
Sampson, G. 119
Sanders, D. 136
Scambler, Annette and Graham 86,
111–12, 174, 177–8, 180–1
Schachter, S. 128–9
Schick, Prof. Bella 48
Schmidt, P. 159
Schnurr, Paula 149, 150
Schofield, Alfred 31
sensory processes 94–8
Severino, S. 147–8, 150, 154–5, 156
Severy, L. 103
Seward, Georgene 46, 92, 99–100
Sex in Education: or, a Fair Chance for the Girls
(Clarke) 39–40, 58
Sex in Industry: A Plea for the Working Girl
(Ames) 43
Sex in Mind and Education (Maudsley) 39–40
sexuality: abstinence during menstruation
102, 135; behavioural studies 133–6;
defining activity 134; and desire to
conceive 135; masturbation and
testosterone 136; matchmaking instinct
versus desire for sex 32; measuring
reports 76; menstruation as heat 16–18
Sheldrake, P. 119
Sherwin, B. 131
Short, R. V. 12, 97
Shuttle, Penelope 14, 21, 22
Silverman, Linda Kreger 45
Singer, J. 128–9
Skultans, Vieda 86, 111, 112
Slade, Pauline 119
sleep and relaxation 156–7